June 2013

North American T-6

Other titles in the Crowood Aviation Series

Aichi D3A1/2 Val	Peter C. Smith
Aeroplanes of the Royal Aircraft Factory	Paul Hare
Avro Lancaster	Ken Delve
BAC One-Eleven	Malcolm L. Hill
Bell P-39 Airacobra	Robert F. Dorr with Jerry C. Scutts
Boeing 747	Martin W. Bowman
Boeing 757 and 767	Thomas Becher
Boeing B-17 Flying Fortress	Martin W. Bowman
Boeing B-52 Stratofortress	Peter E. Davies and Tony Thornborough
Consolidated B-24 Liberator	Martin W. Bowman
Curtiss SB2C Helldiver	Peter C. Smith
De Havilland Mosquito	Martin W. Bowman
McDonnell Douglas A-4 Skyhawk	Brad Elward
Douglas AD Skyraider	Peter C. Smith
English Electric Canberra	Barry Jones
English Electric Lightning	Martin W. Bowman
Fairchild Republic A-10 Thunderbolt II	Peter C. Smith
Gloster Meteor	Barry Jones
Hawker Hunter	Barry Jones
Hawker Hurricane	Peter Jacobs
Junkers Ju 87 Stuka	Peter C. Smith
Lockheed C-130 Hercules	Martin W. Bowman
Lockheed F-104 Starfighter	Martin W. Bowman
Luftwaffe – A Pictorial History	Eric Mombeek
Messerschmitt Bf 110	Ron Mackay
Messerschmitt Me 262	David Baker
Nachtjagd	Theo Boiten
Night Airwar	Theo Boiten
North American F-86 Sabre	Duncan Curtis
Panavia Tornado	Andy Evans
Short Sunderland	Ken Delve
Sopwith Aircraft	Mick Davis
V-Bombers	Barry Jones
Vickers VC10	Lance Cole
Vickers-Armstrongs Wellington	Ken Delve
World War One in the Air – A Pictorial History	Ken Delve

NORTH AMERICAN T-6

SNJ, Harvard and Wirraway

Peter C. Smith

The Crowood Press

First published in 2000 by
The Crowood Press Ltd
Ramsbury, Marlborough
Wiltshire SN8 2HR

British Library Cataloguing-in-Publication Data
A catalogue record for this book is available from the British Library.

ISBN 1 86126 382 1

Typefaces used: Goudy (*text*),
Cheltenham (*headings*).

Typeset and designed by
D & N Publishing
Baydon, Marlborough, Wiltshire.

Printed and bound in Great Britain by Bookcraft.

Dedication

To Simon Watson, for all your help and advice down the years.

Contents

Wing-tip to wing-tip as the RCAF Aerobatic Team roar over another of the team during rehearsals in 1961. CFPU

Introduction

This is the story of one of the most successful and best-loved aircraft of all time. Born on the eve of war, when the need to train unprecedented numbers of young men to become pilots was first being realized, so outstanding was the design, and so great the demand that the North American Advanced Trainer 6 (AT-6) went on to be built in ever greater numbers to serve the mushrooming of Allied military aviation. If you became an Allied pilot during World War Two, the chances are that you learned your skills in the AT-6, the SNJ (as the US Navy termed it) or, if you were British, Australian, Canadian, Rhodesian, South African or any other flyer from the Empire, the Harvard.

Names abounded. In an effort to make her more media-friendly the Americans christened later Dallas-built versions the 'Texan', to equate with the British naming their versions the 'Harvard'. It never caught on, and 'T-6' or just 'The Six' was how the bulk of her USAAF pilots always called her; to the US Navy and Marine Corps flyers she was known as the 'SNJ', or sometimes the 'J-Bird'. In Korea she became the 'Mosquito' after her call-sign, and air forces the world over came up with their own names for North American Aviation's most famous product.

Brought about by the needs of World War Two, the T-6's story did not end in 1945; indeed, it had hardly begun! Far from ending her days with the end of the war, the T-6 continued to form a basic part of most Western air forces' training systems. Many former T-6 pilots, now civilians once again, seized the opportunity to renew their love affair with this unique flying machine; whether as stunt plane, aerobatics mount, crop sprayer, mail-plane, pylon racer or just plain fun machine, ex-military T-6s were snapped up in ever increasing numbers by flyers from Los Angeles to Lahore, from London to Lima, and so the T-6 began her second career.

Not that her fighting days were over; whether it be as a ground strafer in India, hunting down terrorists in Algeria, overthrowing dictators in Portugal or holding the line against communist aggression in Korea, this 'training' aircraft showed she could use her teeth as well.

And so for six decades the distinctive growl[1] of this unique aircraft has shaken and broken the peace of the skies all over the globe. Her popularity shows no sign of decline in her dotage. The story of the noisy North American is by no means over, and recording it is therefore a unique and special privilege.

Acknowledgements

The author would particularly like to thank the following for their unstinting aid, advice and help in compiling the chequered history of the AT-6 in all her many guises, and acknowledges his deep debt to their contributions to this continuing story.

First and foremost to Andrew and Karen Edie, Mike Chapman, Rod Dean, and all at Transport Command, Shoreham-by-Sea, for their kindness and hospitality; Squadron Leader Norman E. Rose, that outstanding and exceptional RAF pilot and instructor whose knowledge of the Harvard in all her moods is unrivalled; my good friend Group Captain Arthur Murland Gill, RAF, who commanded the Ferry Training Unit at Abingdon post-war and had previously flown twenty assorted Harvards at different points in his distinguished career; Flight Lieutenant Harry Knight, MBE, RAFVR, an outstanding instructor and pilot whose memoirs and photographs of training in Canada are invaluable; Robert S. Mullaney of Bellport, who was equally at home in the SNJ; George J. Walsh who also shared memories of her with me; Dan Hagerdorn of the Smithsonian NASM, Washington DC, whose own contribution to the whole T-6 family story in his book *WarBird Tech* is outstanding and whose knowledge of Latin American T-6s is second to none; Captain Donald Wesley Monson of Palm Desert, California, for permission to quote from his book *Autobiography of a Tailhooker*[2]; Charles Shuford; Chuck Downey of Poplar Grove, Illinois; John Hamlin, whose outstanding volume, *The Harvard File*[3], is the essential starting point for anyone who wishes to know anything at all about the Harvard; Doug MacPhail of Dundas, Ontario, Canada, who produced the essential book on *Harvard! The North American Trainers in Canada*[4] and was very helpful to me; Neville M. Parnell who provided much help and photos on the Wirraway and Ceres for me, and whose book, *Australian Air Force since 1911*[5], is the standard source; Kirsten Tedesco and Stephanie Mitchell of the Arizona Aerospace Foundation, Pima Air & Space Museum, Tucson; Kate Igoe of the Smithsonian NASM, Washington DC; George J. Walsh of Darien, Connecticut; William J. Armstrong, Department of the Navy, Washington DC; Colonel Sabri Aydogan, Ministry of Defence, Ankara, Turkey; D.S. Baker, Hawker de Havilland Victoria Ltd, Melbourne; Dr Fred Beck, Office of Air Force History, Bolling AFB; Giancarlo Garello from Italy for his kindness in providing photos and details of Italian T-6s; Major-General Ahmed I. Behery, Commander Royal Saudi Air Force, Riyad; Mrs Anne Bell, Fleet Air Arm Museum, Yeovilton; M. Benoits, SIRPA, Paris; David V.S. Berrington, Ohai; Warrant Officer P.L. Boulton, Air Staff Defence HQ, Wellington, New Zealand; Chaz Bowyer, Mulbarton, Norfolk; Commander B.J. Bromfield, Royal Australian Navy, RAN Air Station Nowara; Jack Bryant, TAGS, Langley; Meg Campbell, Palmerston North; Herr Cimander, Armando da Silva Coelho, Forca Aerea Portuguesa, Lisbon; Der Bundersminster der Verteidigung, Bonn; Group Captain B. Cole, Ghanian Air Force HQ, Accra; Dr Ira Chart, Northrop Corporation, Hawthorne, California; M.B. Chenel, Musée de l'Air et de l'Espace, Le Bourget; John A. Collver, Lomita, California; Terry Dowman, RNZAF Museum, Christchurch; Group Captain Theo J. MacLean de

Lange, Rotorua; Chas Dellow, Mermaid Beach; Steven D. Eisner, Van Nuys, California; Major K.W. Farrell, Canadian Forces Photographic Unit, Ottawa; Colonel Francesco Fino, Stato Maggiorer dell Aeronautica, Rome; James L.R. Flynn, Ringwood, Victoria; Warrant Officer D.W. Gardner, RAAF Museum, Point Cook; Group Captain John E. Gerber, RAAF, Turner, ACT; Wing Commander Arthur Murland Gill, Llanwarne; Colonel H.R. Haberli, Berne; Brian Hall, Myrtle Bank, SA; Anthony E. Hutton, The Squadron, North Weald; Dr J.A.M.M. Janssen, Royal Netherlands Air Force, Soesterberg; Colonel Eduardo Jimenez-Carles, Madrid; Lieutenant-Colonel Sidney F. Johnson Jr, Albuquerque; Lieutenant-Colonel Zeev Lachish, IDF, Tel Aviv; J. Laneiro, Loures; Reine Maily, Canadian Government Expositions and AV Centre, Ottawa; Cyril R.B. MacPherson, East Ringwood, Victoria; Tenente QFO Solandge Teixeria de Menezes, Ministerio de Aeronautica, Brasilia-DF; Paul L. Muir, Condell Park, New South Wales; Brigadier-General Najjar, Royal Jordanian Air Force, Amman; William C. Northrop Jr, RCMB Inc, Newport Beach; the late Arthur Pearcy, Sharnbrook, Bedford; Bob Piper, Royal Australian Air Force Historical Office, Canberra ACT; Flight Lieutenant P.B. Ratnayake, Sri Lanka AF HQ, Colombo; Air Commodore S. Sahay, Air HQ, IAF, New Delhi; Sadao Seno, Aichi, Japan; Hanfried Schliephake, Kónigsbrunn; F.D. Sheppard, RAF Museum, Hendon, London; Ray C. Sturtivent, St Albans, who over the years has been a great boon to me with the sharing of his unrivalled knowledge of Fleet Air Arm history; Martin Pengelly at Landrake, Saltash, Cornwall for much information and advice; Group Captain Bhisit Sukhum, Royal Thai Air Force, Bangkok; Dr G.A. 'Doc' Swayze, Phoenix, Arizona; Anna C. Urband, Dept of the Navy, Washington DC; Bill C. Walmsley, Rockwell International, Los Angeles; Nicholas M. Williams, American Aviation Historical Society, Waverly, Iowa; Helen Vaughan-Dawkes, National Archives, Wellington, New Zealand; Nick Veronico, *In Flight*, Woodside, California; Louis J. Vosloo, Fish Hoek, South Africa; David Wilson, Department of Defence, Canberra, ACT.

The North American Charge Number System

Much confusion has arisen over the various model numbers of North American aircraft of this period. These were account numbers of orders to which all the costs of tooling, materials, labour and manufacture were set, or 'charged' against. These charge numbers were how the company themselves tended to identify each individual contract and these are chronologically more accurate than the various confusing model numbers given by the various air forces. Occasionally the charge number and the model number were identical; more often than not they were different.

Peter C. Smith, Riseley, Bedford,
October 2000

Canadian Harvard 4, RCAF 20450, pictured here in 1953 with Maple Leaf insignia. CFPU

CHAPTER ONE

Building on Success

The lineage of the North American AT-6, an aircraft of its time but destined to outlive almost all of her contemporaries, was a long and distinguished one. The direct line of descent can be traced back through a whole series of training aircraft designs that sprang from the fertile and inventive minds of two of the giants of the American aviation industry of the 1930s, James H. ('Dutch') Kindleberger and John Lelan ('Lee') Atwood, a formidable team who, under the presidency of the former, brought the relatively new aircraft manufacturing company of North American Aviation to the forefront of aircraft design just prior to the Second World War. Not only was this duo responsible for the design of the AT-6, herself to be the forerunner of more than 17,000 of her type, with numerous additional and world-wide spin-offs, but they were the team that brought the immortal P-51 Mustang to fruition, via the A-36 dive bomber, in what proved to be one of the most outstanding fighter aircraft types of the period.

There was no lack of talent at North American in the late 1930s, but the story of the company itself pre-dates that period and underwent a number of convoluted changes, as various small concerns metamorphosed into a winning and innovative major company.

North American Aviation Inc. was initially incorporated in the State of Delaware on 6 December 1928, and for some six years it remained a holding company for a number of well-known and lesser known air transportation and manufacturing firms.[1] Included in its original charter was the directive to acquire and hold stocks and securities in other corporations. As such, the company acted to provide the funding for these companies and aircraft designs, and nothing more than that. However, the company brief also included the manufacture of all types of aircraft, as well as managing air navigation facilities through either direct operations or as an agency.[2] Thus it remained until 1 January 1935. It was on this date that North American became associated with the actual design and manufacture of its own products, when it took under its own name the General Aviation Manufacturing Corporation.

The history of North American then also became the history of General Aviation, and for that we must go back in time still further, to 1923 and the incorporation of the Fokker Aircraft Corporation of America. Famous for his contributions to Imperial Germany's wartime air fleet, the Dutch aeronautical engineer Antony Fokker had a reputation for successful design and immigrated to the United States in that year. Here he founded the Atlantic Aircraft Corporation, which later became the Fokker Aircraft Manufacturing Corporation. This famous name had been associated with many notable pioneering aviation feats in the 1920s and 1930s, notably providing the aircraft that made the first North Pole flight, under Commander Richard E. Byrd, US Navy, in 1926. That aircraft had been the Fokker tri-motor monoplane. Two years later another Fokker product, the *Southern Cross*, piloted by Squadron Leader Charles E. Kingford-Smith, made the 7,400 mile flight from Southern California to Australia, another 'first', and the same year saw the company's Fokker Friendship aircraft carry the famous woman pilot Amelia Earhart across the Atlantic. In 1929 Captain Ira C. Eaker, piloting the Fokker aircraft *Question Mark*, set the refueling-in-air endurance record.

It was in 1930 that Antony Fokker returned home to the Netherlands and the General Aviation Manufacturing Corporation acquired the Fokker Company. Another famous aviation name that was also acquired by General Aviation that same year was the Berliner–Joyce Aircraft Corporation, and three years later, in 1933, these companies were merged. Berliner–Joyce had produced some notable aircraft of its own in the previous decade but, although rich in ideas and innovative personnel, it was cash-strapped. The following year, General Aviation was reorganized and a new management team was established under Kindleberger and Atwood as president and vice president, respectively.

Both men had moved over from the Douglas Aircraft Company, where they had already established a reputation for themselves when, as vice president in charge of engineering and chief structural engineer, respectively, they had helped design and develop the outstanding Douglas DC-1 transport. This famous aircraft, notable for its original features, had come to General Aviation's attention when it had beaten their own tri-motor design to a vital Transcontinental and West Air Competition. In 1934, unable to compete, General Aviation poached this winning team!

In its new guise, General Aviation produced two outstanding designs: the GA-15 (GA = General Aviation), which later became the O-47 Observation aircraft; and the GA-16, which first as the NA-16 and then as the BT-9 (BT= Basic Trainer) for the United States Army Air Corps (USAAC), was to lead, ultimately, via the BT-10, BT-14 and BC-1, to the AT-6, the SNJ and Harvard family of advanced air trainers.

When, in its turn, General Aviation was absorbed into North American, manufacture gradually assumed the dominant role and between 1934 and 1938, the majority of the other concerns, including Curtiss Aircraft, Sperry and Trans World Airlines (TWA) airline holdings, were disposed of; but some plant and facilities were retained, in particular the former Curtiss–Caproni plant located at Dundalk, Maryland, and it was here that General Aviation, as the manufacturing division of North American, first set up shop for the production of their own designs.

GA-16 (NA-16, BT-9)

As the grandfather of the T-6, the GA-16 is worthy of detailed study. The Army requirements for their basic trainer (BT) type, which again came up for competition in January 1935, were for an aircraft that would closely simulate the modern single-seater monoplane pursuit and attack aircraft then entering service to replace the old biplane types, in both their layouts (open cockpits and fabric-covered wings and airframes) and general layout, while at the same time providing separate cockpits for the instructor and pupil to be seated in tandem. The BT type would also have to be tough enough to withstand the probable hard handling of the novice pilot, and, for the same reason, be easy to repair and maintain in the face of such usage. But she also had to be simple enough to fly and safe enough to ensure that the trainees progressed through to the next stage of their training, the advanced trainer (AT).

Kindleberger and Atwood approached this perennial dilemma with their usual expertise and flair. The GA-16 was built with traditional materials; the fuselage was of fabric-covered steel-tubed framing; the two cockpits, in tandem, were open to the elements, save for a small frontal windshield. The original design sketches show that Kindleberger *always* had a fully enclosed cockpit in mind for his project ultimately[3] and, in truth, the aircraft did not long exist in its original form. The design also incorporated a cantilever, all-metal, flush riveted, stressed-skin wing based on the DC-1 type, and also incorporated several novel and notable features not seen before but which were destined to become standard features on such aircraft for the next decade. Four of the main innovations introduced by the GA-16 were as follows.[4]

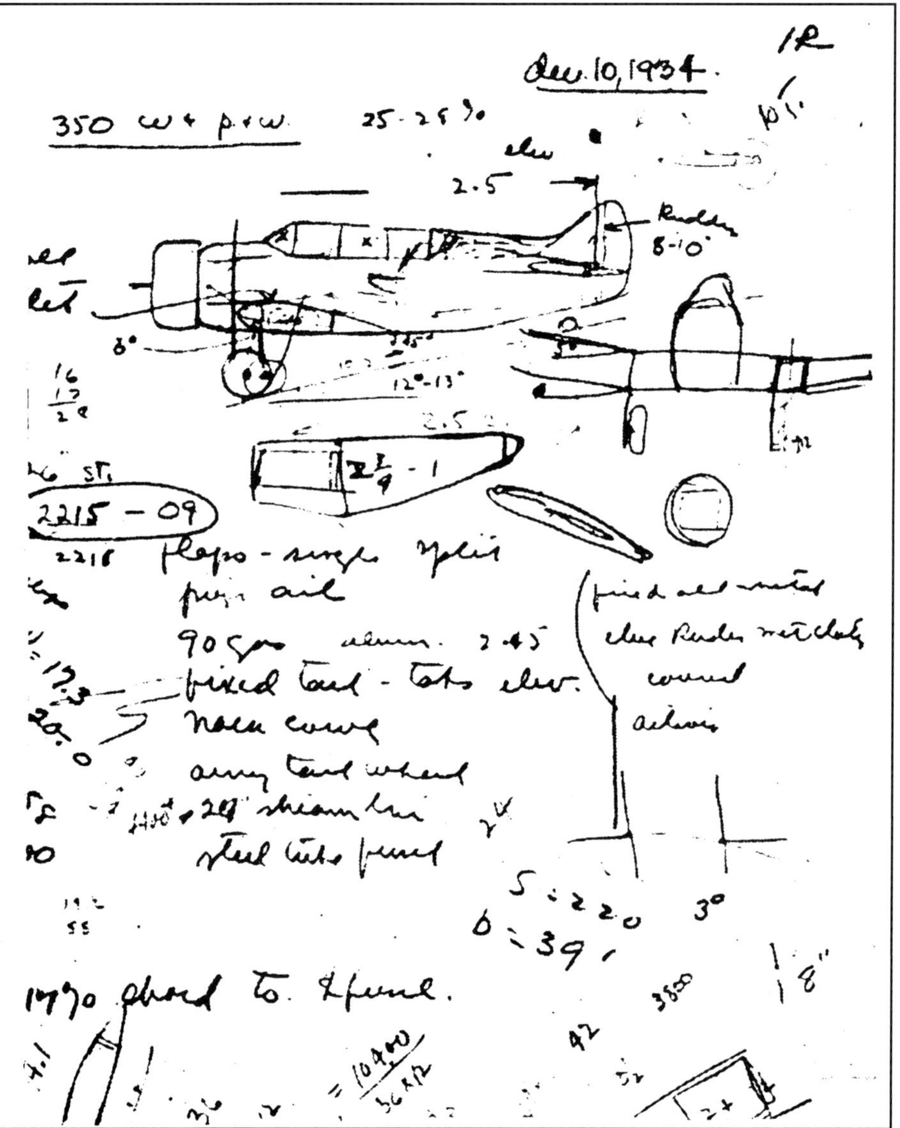

The NAA design teams original sketches of the GA-16, dated 10 December 1934. Even at this stage a Pratt & Whitney engine is mentioned and although the undercarriage is of the fixed type, an elongated and fully enclosed cockpit canopy features and is faired into the after fuselage. Rockwell International

1. *Accessibility of internal mechanisms.* The introduction, to a larger extent than hitherto, of fabric-covered removable side panels, which allowed ground mechanics quick and simple access to most areas of the fuselage and engine cowlings, in order to get at the working parts of the 400hp Wright R-975-E7 Whirlwind nine cylinder, air-cooled radial that powered the aircraft. The panels could be quickly detached to allow instant and rapid ingress to all the internal mechanisms and structures, which could then be easily inspected, and parts repaired or replaced with the minimum of 'down' time on the aircraft itself. With restricted defence budgets in the 1930s, the need to keep the maximum number of aircraft flying with the minimum delay was paramount; this feature greatly assisted the North American design in comparison to rivals. Of course, once the war had commenced, a similar requirement to optimize battle availability obviously meant that such features were required on combat aircraft as well.

2. *Interchangeable parts and components.* Equally lending itself to the same maximizing of the aircraft's active flying time was the interchangeability of parts, which gave for speedy turn-rounds of faulty equipment. By making as many parts as possible quickly detachable and attachable, and by assembling those components in steel jigs, which ensured universal fitting, the GA-16 presented a new standard. The entire powerplant installation was designed as a single unit, which could be unbolted and a new one bolted on within the time-span of eight man-hours. The whole wing followed the design of the DC-2, being of three basic components, with the two outer panels bolted to the constant-chord centre section of the fuselage by simple bolts through the flange angles that could be removed with ease and rapidity. Even the wing-tips were designed as detachable assemblies, so that they could be replaced quickly in response to that most common

T-6 MEN – James Howard 'Dutch' Kindleberger

The man who brought the T-6 into being, in addition to a host of other great airplanes of the 1930s and 1940s, was a legend in the aviation industry of that period. He combined innovative and fresh thinking with practical qualities that resulted in that happy combination of atheistic functionality. Of his aircraft, it could usually be said, 'If it looks right, it is right'.

Dutch first saw the light of a spring West Virginian day on 8 May 1895, the son of Charles Frederick and Rose Ann (née Riddle) Kindleberger. In 1911, at the age of sixteen, he left college and commenced work at the National Tube Company, Wheeling. Two years later he joined the Army Engineering Corps as a draughtsman and inspector. An outstanding talent, by the time he had come of age in 1916 he was studying at the Carnegie Institute of Technology and laying the ground for a lifetime of highly successful contributions to the American aviation industry.

He qualified in 1917, just as the Great War began to enmesh the United States in its bloody grip. Already the aeroplane, still a novel thing of struts and wire, had made its influence felt worldwide and Howard knew what his future was to be. He entered the Air Corps in 1917 and served as a second lieutenant. The dashing young pilot courted and married his first wife, Thelma Beatrice Knarr, in April 1919 and together they had three children, daughters Ruth, Joan and son, Howard Byron.

That same year he took the great step into aviation by joining the famous seaplane building company of Glenn L. Martin, based at Cleveland, Ohio. Dutch rapidly rose through the Martin company's hierarchy between 1919 and 1925. He left to join the up and coming Douglas Aircraft Company, then headquartered at Santa Monica, California, where he remained until 1934, rising to become their vice president and chief engineer. The switch to General Aviation's president, at first in Baltimore, and then to North American Aviation at El Segundo, followed. With that company he achieved the acme of his fame.

Kindleberger proved himself to be a shrewd businessman as well as an outstanding designer, as witnessed by his clever adaptation of the Mustang fighter to the A-36 dive bomber just in time to keep production going and despite his own doubts about whether such a conversion would work. It did, and worked outstandingly well,[5] but the main effect was to keep the line intact, which reaped dividends with the P-51 Mustang later in the war, one of the premier fighter aircraft types of World War II. Producing the first Mustang in record time (100 days!) produced a different reaction from British designer Sidney Cam, whose Hawker Hurricane fighter the Mustang outclassed totally. He accused Dutch of being a liar! Kindleberger certainly knew how to play his cards to the best effect publicity-wise.

With North American, Dutch rose to become chairman of the board and chief executive officer. He had another, largely hidden, side to him, however. He made his home in California and devoted much time to the Good Samaritan Hospice and the St John's Hospice there. He divorced his first wife in 1945 and married Helen Louise Allen the following year. This marriage also ended in divorce, however, in 1960.

For his war work and contribution to aviation, further honours were heaped upon him; the French awarded him Chevalier Legion of Honour in 1951; the Italians the Order Al Merito Della Republica Italiana three years later. Even more exotic was Thailand's award, made in 1956, as a Companion of the Exalted Order of the White Elephant! Dutch would have seen the humorous side of that. His fellow countrymen were no less grateful, and among the many such honours Kindleberger received were the Alumni Merit Award from the Carnagie Institute of Technology, the Presidential Certificate of Merit for War Production in 1948, the Exceptional Civil Service Award from the United States Air Force in 1953 and the General William E. Mitchell Award in 1959.

Dutch was also deeply involved with the various American aviation bodies. He was a fellow of the Aeronautical Sciences Foundation, and became their president in 1950. He also became vice president of the Manufacturing Aircraft Association, governor of the Aerospace Industries Association of America, as well as being director of the California Chamber of Commerce.

Honoured and revered in the aviation world, at sixty-seven years of age Dutch Kindleberger died on 27 July 1962. Despite the plethora of his great aircraft designs his name will always be associated with the Mustang and the Texan/Harvard.

'Dutch' Kindleberger shaking hands with Jimmy Doolittle after the famous raid on Tokyo in 1942.

of training aircraft accidents, ground looping! The outer-wing panels' leading and trailing edges' sweep and the wing dihedral angle exactly matched the DC-2, as did the flaps, with a single full span slat on the centre section and split flaps on the outer panels, although of course the wing area was much smaller. All control surfaces, however, were fabric-covered, except for the vertical and horizontal stabilizers, which were of stressed skin aluminum composition.

3. *Duplication of handling characteristics of combat aircraft.* Great care and attention was paid by the design team to ensure that the GA-16, as near as possible, duplicated the handling, performance and take-off/landing characteristics of the single-engined combat aircraft that the young pilots would eventually have to fly. This made transition from student pilot to qualified pursuit or attack pilot easier and more rapid, a major plus in what was soon to become a massively expanding pilot training programme, as events in Europe and the Far East led, with increasingly inevitability, to the onset of war.

4. *Fixed landing gear.* At a time when thoughts in design were increasingly turning to fully or partially retractable landing gear, to provide for smoother air flow and greater speed in both fighter and bomber aircraft, the GA-16 design retained the fixed landing gear with a single oleo leg mounted close to the centre-wing section leading edge. This was a deliberate choice for strength, in much the same way that the German Junkers Ju 87 *Stuka*[6] and Japanese Aichi D3A1[7] dive-bombers were to be designed and for similar reasons. They were meant to operate in rough, tough conditions: the German aircraft from forward airstrips close to the front line in fast-moving land warfare scenarios; the Japanese from the decks of carriers. In both cases, hard landings and wear-and-tear were expected to be minimized by holding out for a fixed undercarriage. In the same way, the expected treatment of any basic training aircraft (BT) was less than gentle landings, and so the same policy was adopted, at least for the time being. The landing gear leg itself was not shielded in any way.

According to the policy of the time, BTs did not carry any type of defensive or offensive armaments, either fixed or flexible machine guns, as training in air-to-air combat did not come into the syllabus until AT, the next stage. The prototype was duly completed at a cost of US$36,000.

The GA-16 design, carrying the civilian registration X-2080, had her maiden flight from Dundalk on 1 April 1935, piloted by Eddie Allen, after a mere nine weeks gestation period. She was also flown and tested by both North American Company and USAAC military test pilots out of Logan Field, Baltimore, Maryland, which had just been made operational. Subsequently submitted to the USAAC in February 1935, she was enthusiastically received by them.[8] However, a delay ensued, which was caused by the re-organization under the aegis of North American and the subsequent intended move to California. Thus it was as the NA-16 that the prototype was next displayed. Approval had been given to go ahead with this prototype and within the incredible space of time of a mere six weeks, the first NA-16 was piloted by test pilot Eddie Allen on 1 April, carrying the standard blue fuselage and yellow wings training colours. She was pronounced ready to compete in the USAAC Basic Trainer Competition later that same month at Wright Field, Ohio, where she duly arrived on the 22nd of the month. Before the trials she was fitted with a fully enclosed cockpit.[9] The other contestants provided stiff opposition. One was the Seversky SEV-3XAR, which performed well enough to be rewarded with a contract for

Carrying the civilian registration X-2080 is the first of the line, the original configuration of what was now the NA-16, seen here at Dundalk, Maryland, in April 1935. Note the open cockpit layout and overall blue paint scheme of the USAAC even though still a works speculative machine. Rockwell International

The same aircraft seen on 26 August 1935, but now known as the NA-18 with an enclosed cockpit as tested by the Air Corps at Wright Field in June and accepted. She also sports the larger engine, twin 0.30-calibre nose guns, wheel fairings and other modifications as well as a new paint job. Rockwell International

thirty aircraft, and became the BT-8. The other contender was the Curtiss-Wright 19R, which had many advanced features also. The Army finally opted for the North American product, probably influenced by the special ease of maintenance features Kindleberger had built in.[10] Whatever the truth of the matter she proved a great success and was declared the winner of the competition.

Pleased as they were with North American's contribution (the NA-16 being the first aircraft to carry the corporation's name into production), the Army was not entirely uncritical. They insisted on a number of alterations to the basic design before allowing full-scale production to proceed. A general 'clean-up' of the aircraft was called for, which included adding fairings to streamline the landing gear legs and the fitting of small, detachable 'spats' to the inside of the wheels. The cockpit ceased to be two separate and wider compartments, each open to the elements, and became a fully enclosed 'greenhouse', with sliding canopies for access. To improve engine performance, the original small air intake atop the forward fuselage abaft the NACA engine cowling was much enlarged. The wingspan of 42ft (13m) inner to outer wing flange was fitted with a half-round cover to improve airflow.

In addition to the Army's alterations to the NA-16, North American put forward their own modifications and improvements. The main powerplant was to be replaced by a more powerful Pratt and Whitney R-1340 Wasp radial developing 600hp. They also proposed that machine guns be fitted for both offence and defence, with two fixed forward-firing 0.30 calibre from the cowling, with a single 0.30-calibre machine gun on a flexible mounting carried in the after cockpit. This latter arming was not acceptable to the US Army at this period, but was probably brought on by the need for North American to sell the type to foreign purchasers, whose air arms' limited resources might require the aircraft to perform other duties in addition to basic training. As such, the selling line was that the aircraft was not just a BT but in fact a general purpose (GP) design, which might better fit their various requirements. The ability to mount such armaments on the basic BT design was a good selling point, especially south of the border.

As the AT-18-1, initiated on 13 May 1935, this concept was drawn up with Argentina as the principal potential customer. Basically this was the original NA-16-1 re-worked at Dundalk in the GP mould for demonstration purposes, designed to be customized into a two-placed pursuit, a two-place light bomber or a single-place fighter. Options were also available to fit retractable landing gear. As C/NC-2080 this aircraft continued to undergo transformations as it was paraded before potential customers, until it was finally sold to Argentina two years later.[11]

The modifications, both Army (accepted) and North American (rejected), changed the company designation to the NA-19[12] and the first contract was awarded by the USAAC on 3 October 1935, for forty-two of the new trainers, at a total cost of $560,000. These received the Army designation BT-9. A later alteration was the fitting of a higher cockpit canopy than that featured on the prototype, which gave improved crew headroom. The first production BT-9 was flown by test pilot Paul Balfour on 15 April 1936.

The BT-9 as she appeared in 1936 with full 'greenhouse' canopy and enormous D/F loop below the forward fuselage. Rockwell International

Transfer of North American to California

The decision to up-sticks and move the entire North American Corporation from the restricted facilities at Dundalk to the wider open spaces of California was influenced by the placing of the BT-9 orders, which at that time had been one of the largest orders placed by the USAAC. The first move came with the transfer of seventy-five key employees from the company headquarters at Dundalk to Inglewood, California, on November 1935.

The brand-new, custom-built factory adjoined the runways of Mines Field, which later became Los Angeles Airport (LAX); this meant that flight testing and the flying away of production aircraft was much simplified. The more clement climate also helped, enabling all-year round flying and the area had a large, skilled, labour force from which to recruit. The new factory officially opened on that site in January 1936, which initially totalled some 158,678ft^2 (14,741m^2) of factory floor area. State-of-the-art features included maximum use of this area by alternating high bay sections with two-story sections. The mezzanine and sub-mezzanine floors in the two-storey sections were utilized for the fabrication and assembly of parts and subassemblies, which were then led into the final assembly areas located in the high bay sections. Again, larger assemblies from these subassembly areas were transported by overhead monorails to the main assembly areas, the first use of this method of conveyor systems in the aircraft industry.[13]

At the time of the opening of the new plant, just 150 men were ready to move in, and both the first tooling and machinery had been transported west and was being installed. By 1 September 1939, this tiny force had expanded to 3,400 – a remarkable growth record even for the period. To cope with such an expansion, the original thinking applied to the aircraft designs was also given over to the smooth running and organization of the plant. Kindleberger established an apprentice training department but, more than this, the whole basic concept was redesigned around the breaking down of job structuring into simple segments, in the same way as the BT-19 parts were broken down to facilitate fast production. In the design stage, large assemblies were systematically broken down into smaller parts to aid this process. Initially the jigs and tools for the 161 sets of SOC-1 metal floats were utilized to formulate this revolutionary policy, '...these large metal floats, or pontoons often stood side-by-side on the assembly floor with the first units of the BT-9...'.[14] This enabled the company to build up its work force in preparation for the trainer and observation work that followed, and ensured a smooth transition.

The company set new standards in customer care, and by producing its aircraft on time, or even early, gained a high reputation very quickly in the aviation industry – a stark contrast to then (*and now!*) current practice. Lee Atwood was quoted as putting this down to the result of, 'intelligent application of all forms of mass production aids to the problems at hand, plus a high spirit of teamwork throughout the organisation'.[15]

BT-9

Despite the upheaval of the move west, this first batch of trainers, order number AC-7881, were produced and the initial aircraft first took to the air on 15 April 1936, with production deliveries, still painted in blue and yellow at this period, following very quickly. The engine remained the 400hp Wright R-975-7 Whirlwind that drove a two-bladed propeller. The gross weight of the early BT-9 came out at 3,860lb (1,750kg) and performance was unexceptional. The maximum speed was 175mph (280km/h), with a cruise speed 20mph (32km/h) below this figure. The range was an acceptable 810 miles (1,300km), with a service ceiling of 19,000ft (5,800m) and a rate of climb of 1,051ft/min (320m/min).

They proved popular and welcome additions to the Army's training aircraft fleet and the bulk were assigned to Randolph Field, Texas, the USAAC flight school, and known as the West Point of the Air. In view of the future nomenclature and progression of the AT-6 as the Texan, this proved to be an auspicious choice! After some weeks in service, yet another modification was called for by the Army, and this was the retrospective fitting of leading-edge slats to the outer-wing leading edges to minimize or negate the potentially lethal wing-tip stall tendency that the early production aircraft were found to have.

This was another first for the Air Corps. They failed to fully solve the problem and some aircraft had stall-control strips fitted from 1941 onward.

Also in the spring of 1941, surviving aircraft had the fabric areas of their fuselages stripped away. These sections were replaced with spare metal-covered side-panels from the current production line. Further developments of this successful type followed thick-and-fast from 1936 onward. Developments included major orders for the USAAC and Army Reserve, with many modifications; the beginning of US Navy interest (and the adoption of a different powerplant); the sale of the design rights to Australia, thus initiating that country's production of the Commonwealth Wirraway and Boomerang types; and numerous one-offs and small batches as foreign buyers, from all parts of the globe, took an increasingly keen interest in North American's new product. These many variants are summarized below.

NA-19A

This model was ordered by the USAAC to equip their organized reserve units, forty being produced in the serial ranges NA-19-4, NA-19-12/19, NA-19-34/49 and NA-19-68/83. They became the BT-9A.

BT-9A

The main differences that the -A had over the basic BT-9 were both stability driven. The overall length of the fuselage was increased by 5 inches, and the leading-edge slats introduced to obviate the wing-tip stall problem were replaced by a complete re-design of the outer-wing leading edge. This incorporated a 2° washout, which helped considerably. This meant shifting the pitot tube, located on the extreme starboard-wing leading edge, to a position further inboard closer to the in-built landing light.

Equally radical was the gun mounting: for the first time in USAAC trainers, of the two 0.30-calibre Browning M-1 machine guns, one, with 200 rounds per gun, was forward-firing and mounted inside the starboard engine cowling, while the other, with 500 rounds per gun, was defensive, on a flexible mounting located in the rear cockpit. Type K-3B cameras could replace both these guns if required. The rear section of the forward cockpit was mobile and could be slid backward to provide a windshield for the rear-seat instructor. Some carried the type R-16 inter-telephone set, but the radio compass and marker beacon of the BT-9 was omitted from the rear cockpit.

NA-20

This design was an adaptation of the GP-type and a single demonstration machine was produced (NA-16-2). With the civilian registration NR-16025 she was used to show off the GP potential to the Chinese Government and featured a Wright Whirlwind radial engine and carried two 0.30-calibre machine guns. Orders for similar aircraft (*see* NA-41) resulted.

Subsequently refitted with the Pratt and Whitney 550hp Wasp radial, and with two 0.30-calibre machine guns and light bomb racks below the centre section of the fuselage, according to the specification of the Government of Honduras, on 9 December 1937 she became the NA-16-2H (H = Honduras) carrying civilian registration NC-16025.

NA-16-2H

The resultant machine was one of many one-offs designed with specific Latin American conditions and requirements in mind, and was delivered to Tegucigalpa airfield by company pilot Harold White on 4 March 1938, where she was evaluated by the Cuerpo de Aviacion Militar Hondurena (the Honduran Military Aviation Corps).

NA-22

This was a further modification of the GP concept, fitted with a 225hp Wright R-760ET (J-6-7) Whirlwind engine. She was flown as No. 36-28 (PT Demonstrator) at

Wright Field, both with and without a NACA cowl, in June and July 1937. She was proposed for USAAC use, as the NA-16-1, but her lack of power found no enthusiasm in the United States.

NA-23

On 1 December 1936, order AC-9345 for 117 of this model was placed for the USAAC, and they entered service as the BT-9B.

problems. She became the solitary BT-9D and led to the BT-14.

NA-26

A new prototype was produced on 20 October 1936, in response to the USAAC Basic Combat Trainer Competition, proposal 37-220. She featured the basic NA-18 configuration, but kept the fabric-covered fuselage panels. Wingspan was increased by one foot and the wing area

contract AC-9345, Navy requisition 327-37, for forty specially modified machines for Navy use. These became the NJ-1.

NJ-1

The Navy had long lacked a high-performance instrument training aircraft with a closed cockpit, and with the development of its new dive and torpedo bombing monoplanes, to equip the new *Essex* class aircraft carriers being built for the fleet,

The solitary NA-22 (NA-19-11, AC 36-36) which was the NAA entry for the Air Corps Circular Proposal No. 36-288 (PT Demonstration) held on 7 July 1936. She was powered by a Wright R-760ET (J-6-7) Whirlwind engine which developed 225hp. Notice she reverted to the open cockpit configuration.
Rockwell International

BT-9B

The -B reverted to the pure training role and carried no armament whatsoever. The lack of a machine gun in the rear cockpit enabled a section of the rear canopy to be fixed and therefore made stronger. Most were initially assigned to Randolph Field, Texas.

BT-9D

One BT-9B aircraft was altered with panels, as in the BC-1A, and new tail surfaces in another effort to overcome the stall

went up by seven square feet. The powerplant was the Pratt and Whitney R-1304-40 Wasp radial. This aircraft became the BC-1. In Doug MacPhail's words, 'this was the aircraft which unleashed the unearthly howl of the Harvard on the world'.[16]

NA-28

The United States Navy was very keen to adopt the new North American trainer for their own needs, but they lacked sufficient funds to place any contracts at this time. Instead, orders were placed through the USAAC on 14 December 1936, under

the need was more acute than ever. However, among the many changes required for carrier usage, an additional factor complicated matters. The Wright R-975 was exclusively an Army engine, the Navy had none in its inventory and they required the more tried-and-trusted Pratt and Whitney R-1340-6 Wasp engine, which developed 550hp, for the job. The Army had meanwhile moved on to the NA-29 and this was taken as the base for the modified naval aircraft to be built upon.

After experiments with the YIBT-10 (*see* below), the Navy was convinced this combination fitted their bill and the first order for forty machines was placed on 14 December 1936. They received the designation of NJ-1 (Navy category identifier, N = trainer; Navy company identifier, J = North American; and mark number = 1). The different engine necessitated cosmetic changes to the engine cowling: the single exhaust stack of the Wright, which protruded from the starboard edge of the front cowl, was replaced by twin exhaust stacks positioned beneath the rear cowl section. The two vents either side of the rear cowl section from the Wright's engine were done away with completely. Finally, the small air intake mounted atop the rear of the cowl for the BT-9 was relocated with a much larger fitting at the front ventral position of the cowling.

Delivery of the first aircraft was on 3 July 1937. After service at Pensacola, one aircraft (BuNo 0949) was fitted with a Wright R-1340-18 radial engine in March 1940 and survived thus until 31 July 1944. The bulk of these aircraft were assigned to VN5D8 at Corry Field, Florida, serving as instrument trainers. Three (serials 0927, 0931 and 0947) were sent out to the West Coast at NAS San Diego, and then two were later re-assigned back to Anacostia, Maryland, while one, (0931) was retained with VB-3 from the carrier *Saratoga*. Many ended up as instructional airframes from 1943 onward.

NA-29

Further modifications brought forth the NA-29, which the USAAC was enthusiastic enough about to place two new orders for, on 22 December 1936. They showed only a slight cleaning up of the -B design. These two batches became the BT-9C.

BT-9C

A batch of thirty-two of these machines was ordered for the USAAC on 22 December 1936, and received serial numbers 29-353/384. A second batch of thirty-four more was simultaneously ordered for the reserve units, and these had the serial numbers 29-505/538. They were basically the same as the -B but the lines were smoothed up, some with canvas-covered walkways for access on the wings' centre section. Steps were also fitted on the port side of the cockpit. They featured the wing leading-edge slats, and carried a single forward-firing 0.30-calibre machine gun in the engine cowling, as well as an after-firing gun on a flexible mounting. They also featured a Navy-type fixed telescopic gunsight mounted forward of the pilot's windshield, with the radio mast offset to port to accommodate it. A type T-3A camera could be carried but the marker beacon and radio compass were omitted.

The night shift at Inglewood with T-6s for a whole range of customers stacking up in the yard outside. Two CITU aircraft can be seen far left, with both USAAC and RAF marked aircraft in the foreground and background. Rockwell International

YIBT-10

A modification from the first BT-9C (NA-29) production order for the USAAC was built (s/n 29-385) and received the designation YIBT-10. She carried the Army experimental designation of YIBT-10, later modified to BT-10. She was fitted with a 600hp Wright R-1340-41 engine on arrival at Wright Field on 18 November 1936.

BT-10

Wright Field's exhaustive testing was impressive enough for the USAAC to consider a production run as the NA-30/BT-10, but nothing finally came of this idea. In November 1941, this solitary aircraft was flown to Mines Field, Los Angeles and was later purchased by the Reconstruction Finance Corporation, finally ending her life at the University of Santa Barbara Airfield (now Santa Barbara Municipal Airport).

NA-30

The YIBT-10 concept was taken further in this design but never got beyond the drawing board. The US Army was already convinced that the combination of the BT-9C and the Pratt and Whitney engine would suit their purposes admirably, while the USN placed orders for the first batch of what was to become the NJ-1.

On the line at Inglewood. Working on the engine fitting section with an excellent view of the big radial. Aircraft in the foreground carries the number 165 on her striped tail. Rockwell International

NA-31

European interest had been aroused and Fokker in Holland was not the only company in that part of the world to want to evaluate the North American's merits. A general order was issued on 8 February 1937 and the machine was delivered on 2 August 1937. This single prototype was delivered as the NA-16-4M.

NA16-4M

As a result of a hard sales pitch, the Swedish Air Force took delivery of a single aircraft (s/n 31-386) built with their special needs in mind. This aircraft was delivered to Sweden on 15 November 1937 and was used as a prototype for a licence-built version by A. B. Svenska Jarnvagsverkstaderna (ASJA) and later by SAAB.

ASJA licence-built fifty-three aircraft for the Royal Swedish Air Force (Flygvapnet) based on this design. They also obtained the licence for the Wright R-975-ES engine, which developed 455hp. These aircraft received the Swedish designation Sk-14 and were produced in three batches, (6-3/609; 672/699; and 5810/5827) from May 1939 onward. A further batch of twenty-three more were constructed and fitted with the Piaggio P VIIc RC-35 radial engine, which developed 525hp, as the Sk14a. Yet a third batch was constructed by SAAB in May 1942. Some of these aircraft were used as test beds for various concepts, one having a ski undercarriage instead of wheels; four others were fitted with tricycle undercarriages to trial the system for the SAAB T-21A fighter programme.

NA-32

The Australians had for long seen the need to produce their own aircraft and become semi-independent of the British motherland, whom, as the clouds of war fast approached, they knew would be increasingly hard-pressed to meet their own needs, let alone supply Australia. She faced her own threats from a militant Japan, a threat which London viewed with less concern than events closer to them in Germany, Italy and Spain. There was a need to establish an exclusively Australian production industry and the Commonwealth Aircraft Corporation Pty Ltd (CAC) was set up on 17 October 1936.

After much hard pressure from British, European and American companies, an evaluation mission deliberated and decided that the North American trainer, with GP adaptation and other modifications to suit their own particular operational and construction needs, would be the answer. A pattern aircraft was built for the CAC to evaluate and base their planes on, and this aircraft took the designation of NA-16-1-A (A = Australia).

The licence fee demanded (and received) by North American was considerable, being US$100,000 as the fee itself, with royalties of US$30,00 for the specifications and manufacturing data, plus a further royalty of US$1,000 for each of the first twenty-five aircraft built by CAC. This latter figure reduced to US$600 per aircraft on the subsequent seventy-five Wirraways (as they became) and thereafter lapsed.

NA-16-1-A

On 10 March 1937, North American built the first pattern aircraft (32-387) especially for the CAC. She featured the fixed undercarriage and a two-bladed propeller of what was later to be named the Yale by the RAF.

NA-33

A second pattern or template aircraft also was built by North American for the CAC, incorporating more changes in the basic specification – this was designated as the NA-16-2K. She had the retractable landing gear and three-bladed propeller of what was to later become the Harvard. Both the NA-16-1-A and the NA-33 arrived in Australia and were transferred to the Royal Australian Air Force (RAAF) on 2 February 1938. Both these machines were the templates for the licence building of what was to become the Wirraway.

NA-16-2K

Produced for the CAC on the same order as the NA-32, this machine (33-388) was also delivered to Australia for evaluation.

NA-34

The earlier interest of the Argentinean Air Force, for a GP aircraft based on the basic trainer design, resulted in the first substantial foreign order on 19 March 1937. This received the designation NA-16-4P.

NA-16-4P

Some thirty of these GP aircraft were built for Argentina under order AE-39 and received the North American serial numbers 34-389/418. They were engined with the 420hp Wright R-975-E3 Whirlwind radial. They were armed with two fixed forward-firing 0.30-calibre machine guns and a third on a flexible mount aft. They also had enhanced radio equipment. Such orders helped keep the production line ticking over between United States funded requirements.

These aircraft, plus the solitary NA-18 sold at the same time and intended as the prototype for a licence-built version that never happened, joined the Argentine Army Air Force and served not only as advanced trainers but with the observation group and were remarkably long-lived, half of them still being in service as late as 1955.

NA-36

With this aircraft, the Texan/SNJ/Harvard was born on 16 June 1937, and although the fixed undercarriage of the BT-14 continued into production after this date, the future development lay irresistibly with the BC-1 and her descendants. Long before the BT-14 took to the air, the team at North American was hard at work designing the next stage of development. As was obvious from the fighting types on drawing boards all over the world, the day of the fixed rigid undercarriage, except for some very specialized types of war plane, were rapidly passing away. With the new generation of fighter aircraft, all featuring fully retractable undercarriages, trainee pilots would have to learn how to handle this gear. The same trend was obvious in the switching away from old fuselage and wing construction methods, with the all-metal fuselage becoming more and more a standard feature for strength and speed. The signs were obvious to Dutch Kindleberger and his team and so the NA-36 came about to forestall these needs; although, as always, procession to the ultimate came in a series of steady changes and not all at once.

It was here that Dutch showed his negotiating and sales skills to considerable effect. Although the Latin American nations had been keen to accept his GP concept, a hostile congress strictly limited the USAAC to any increase in defence spending above a certain limit. Any monies from the tight budgets that could be spared from the development of strictly combat aircraft, fighters like the P-40 or bombers like the A-20, trickled reluctantly into genuine training aircraft, while the GP type was considered neither fish nor fowl. Here was a problem, but Kindleberger had the ear of the man who mattered. He buttonholed the commander of the newly designated Army Air Force, the famous General Harry H. 'Hap' Arnold and, not for the last time,[17] sold the general on a new concept, which enhanced the North American design in his, and therefore the Army's, eyes.

Kindleberger persuaded Arnold that, equipped with 0.30-calibre machine guns, his new retractable-undercarriage training aircraft would become a new combat type for the Army Air Force, an aircraft that would be suitable for the training of all types of aircrew – in his own words, a basic combat (BC) aircraft. He outlined North American's detailed proposal for the new type, which was in fact the NA-36. Whether Arnold was convinced by Kindleberger's arguments alone (as the latter's biographers would have it), or whether Arnold was shrewd enough to know a sales-pitch when he saw it but even more shrewd to recognize it as a way of getting more aircraft, he went along with it (my own view); the concept of the BC was actively promoted.

In line with the common practice of the period, an Army Air Force competition was duly announced for the design of such a BC machine. The competition was really rigged for it was based almost entirely on the NA-16 and thus North American was hardly surprised to be declared the outright winner! Thus, almost by the back door but thankfully, wholeheartedly, the BC-1 was born.

BT-9D

A solitary aircraft of this variant was converted from one of the standard BT-9Bs, serial number 37-208, with modified retractable landing gear and redesigned tail surfaces and wing panels. Impressed by the increased power of the Pratt and Whitney on the naval versions, the BT-9D featured an improved R-1340-S3H1 air-cooled radial which developed 600hp. This first retractable-undercarriage trainer was soon re-designated as the BC-1 once Arnold had got his way, and she was used as an experimental test bed at Chanite Field from October 1937 onward.

CHAPTER TWO

The Genus of the AT-6

Although there was still a complicated story to weave and many differing modifications and variants to follow before the classic AT-6 design became relatively firm and fixed, the arrival of the basic combat (BC) concept laid the final cornerstone of our story and set North American's trainer firmly on the path to immortality.

Origins of the BC-1

The BC-1 was ordered on 16 June 1937 for the USAAC and a total of eighty-five was built in two batches. They received the company numbers 36-420/504 and 36-596/687, respectively (USAAC serial numbers 37-372/456 and 38-356/447, respectively). Changes were many, the most obvious were the spat main landing-gear legs and the inboard 'pants' of the BT-14 being replaced by the retractable landing gear, with the wheels folding upward and inward into wheel wells in the wings' centre section, which left the wheel and tyre fully exposed. These wells necessitated the addition of a leading edge fairing to cope with them and the wing centre section increased by 12in (30cm) for the same purpose.

The fuselage construction was unchanged at this stage of development, and the final powerplant fitted in these two batches was the Pratt and Whitney R-1340-47 Wasp, developing some 550hp. This drove a two-bladed, controllable pitch wooden propeller. Major modifications of styling were otherwise restricted, after the initial trials of the first BC-1, in order to improve directional control. This led to an alteration, *after* the first aircraft (c/n 36-420) of the vertical tail profile, with the rounded bottom of the rudder on the BT-9 being made straight at the rear, vertical edge, and with a straight, slight angle to the flat bottom, while the rudder trim tab was elongated. The fuselage still remained of composite form, with fabric covering as before. To justify Kindleberger's and

The NA-26 (BC-1, serial 26-202) as she first appeared in 1937. She was initially assigned the civilian registration X-18990, and later N-18990, but never carried either painted up! She was the real final prototype for all the thousands of T-6's which followed for she featured retractable landing gear, and the Pratt & Whitney R-1304-49 Wasp engine. There was provision made for two 0.30-calibre machine guns, one mounted in the after cockpit and one either firing through the nose or from the starboard wing. The wingspan was 1ft (30cm) greater than the NA-18, which increased wing area by 7sq ft (0.64m²). She was entered in the Air Corps design competition for the new Basic Combat specification at Wright airbase in March 1937. She was sold to the Canadian Government on 23 July 1940 and, on being brought up to Harvard II specification, received their serial number RCAF 3345, surviving until 20 May 1942. Rockwell International

Arnold's *raison d'être*, the prototype had been fitted with 0.30-calibre machine guns, which were again mounted to fire fore and aft, fixed and flexible, respectively. The BC-1s that followed, however, did not mount any armaments, although these could have been fitted if required. A good recognition feature was the fitting of a large direction finding (DF) loop below the forward fuselage.

The first flight of a BC-1 took place on 11 February 1938, with test pilot Paul Balfour at the controls. Thus the fixed undercarriage BT-14 actually preceded the retractable undercarriage BC-1 by just one day!

The USAAC called for the conversion of three dozen of these aircraft as instrument trainers, with the new designation of BC-1-I, but, in practice, it would seem that only thirty were finally converted and re-designated, in January 1940.[1]

Foreign Interest Continues

Before going on to describe the BC-1 and her metamorphosis into the AT-6, we will follow, chronologically, the various developments of the North American trainer that followed between 1937 and 1939. Two main strands emerge: the continued wide interest evoked by the new trainer all over the world; and the mounting crisis in Europe, which triggered the frantic (and almost too late) re-armament of the two principal democracies, Great Britain and France, in face of the mounting threat from Nazi Germany and Fascist Italy.

Again, the various nations' requirements resulted in a number of single aircraft for evaluation, which sometimes resulted in small orders, and more often did not. This interest led to a widening still further of the basic trainer's capabilities, with not just GP and/or bomber versions appearing, but fighter adaptations also.

NA-37

Japan had for long been seen as a potential rival to both the British Empire and the United States, and, under an increasingly militaristic leadership, was busy expanding her conquests in Manchuria and China, with an ongoing war that saw her conquering ever increasing swathes of territory. It was a war in which she used her air power to good effect to offset the numerically superior but technically inferior Chinese. Public sentiment in the United States was pro-China and increasingly anti-Japanese, but even stronger was the isolationism, which no American president dared to challenge yet.

This explains how the Japanese came to be involved in the T-6 story at such a critical juncture, for all nations had to be treated equally at this period. The importation of important new types into Japan, whether from the United States, Germany or elsewhere, was common practice and enabled the home-grown industries to benefit from new technology without having to go through long stages of development. Thus it was that the Mitsubishi Jukogyo K. K. placed orders with North American for two of the new training aircraft, the first of these on 19 March 1937. This machine was designated the NA-16-4R and carried the serial number 37-539.

NA-16-4R (KXA-1)

This export version had the Navy type 450hp Pratt and Whitney R-985-9CG radial engine, which drove a three-bladed propeller and was shipped to Japan in September 1937, being handed over to the Imperial Japanese Navy for evaluation on 15 November. She received the Japanese designation KXA-1 and the Navy title Navy Experimental Type A Intermediate Trainer. She was later joined by a second evaluation machine.

NA-38

Sweden's Royal Air Force, the Flygvapnet, ordered a second trial trainer from North American on 28 September 1937. This was the NA-16-4M with the serial number 38-540.

NA-16-4M

This aircraft was merely a repeat of the NA-31 design. It was shipped from the States crated and on arrival in Sweden this solitary example was re-designated as the Sk-16 and was to have been utilized with the NA-16-4M in extensive trials pending the licence agreement as already described. However, this proved superfluous and she was not assembled until 1938 and was assigned to the Flygvapnet the year after. By this sleight-of-hand, she appeared in their listing as the fifth production aircraft and was assigned the serial number 676. She served for a decade, initially with the F5 Flying School Wing and later with the F20 Cadet School Wing, before being burnt out on 26 January 1949.

NA-41

Fighting desperately against further Japanese incursions, the Chinese were badly outclassed in both aircraft and pilot skills. Their need for a modern training aircraft was obvious and they turned to North American to help fill the gap. On 23 February 1938, the Chinese Kuomintang Government placed an order for thirty-five aircraft and these were given the designation NA-16-4. They were armed with two synchronized 0.30-calibre machine guns firing forward and a flexible-mounted 0.30-calibre machine gun mounted aft.

NA-16-4

These trainers-come-light-attack aircraft received the serial numbers 41-697/731, inclusively, and were sent to China during 1938/39 where they were quickly employed in putting fledgling Chinese aviators through their hasty training in time to man the many foreign types of fighter aircraft being imported from all over the world. Some fell to Japanese attacks, others were quickly written off in accidents or abandoned during the many Chinese routs and retreats. None survive today.

NA-42

The Honduras Government placed an order for two GP types on 9 December 1937. They were built as the NA-16-2A and followed the general practice for the variant.

NA-16-2A

These two 'two-placed fighters', with North American serial numbers, 42-691 and 42-692, were repeats of the NA-20 and were powered by the same 520hp Wright Wasp radial as that machine. They both served with the Cuerpo de Aviacion Militar Hondurena until as late as June, 1957. One still exists as a static display at Tegucigalpa airfield, having been restored as part of the Cuerpo's 50th anniversary celebrations in 1979. She carries the serial FAH 20 and was given various replacements for the missing parts but is a most presentable exhibit.

The NA-44 (44-747) was another one-off in the evolution of the T-6. She received (and wore!) the civilian registration NX-18981 and was described as a light attack bomber/dive bomber, although the latter claim is dubious as she was not fitted with dive brakes! She would have made a good ground strafer for there was provision for four forward-firing 0.30-calibre machine guns, two in the nose and one in each wing, and light bomb racks could be fitted on the outer wing panels capable of carrying a total of four 100lb weapons. The power plant was the Wright SG-1820-F52 Cyclone which developed 890hp and gave her the fastest speed yet attained in the series, 250mph. Her smooth appearance was due to her semi-monocoque aluminium after-fuselage which replaced the fabric-covered area to good effect and was painted silver overall at first. Later she was used as a demonstration aircraft re-painted in USAAC colours, blue fuselage and yellow wings.

Like the NA-26, after she finished her sales tours, she was sold to the Canadian Government on 6 August 1940 and received the serial RCAF 3344. Painted yellow overall, and nicknamed the 'Super Harvard' (which indeed she was) she served in 2 SFTS and was not finally deleted until as late as 20 February 1947.

Rockwell International

NA-43

Brazil, always wary of the intentions of her Argentinean neighbour, expressed an interest in the type, and on 9 December 1937 was ready to place an order. The order was, basically, for BT-9Cs with slight modifications, and negotiations had got far enough for North American to allocate the designation of NA-16-1Q in anticipation of the signature. Before any could be built, however, the Brazilian Army cancelled the order.

NA-44

On 9 December 1937, North American produced what they termed a 'light attack/dive bomber' under this designation. The powerplant was the Wright SG-1820-F52 (R-1820-F52) Cyclone radial developing some 890hp at 2,200rpm, far more potent than any preceding engine, which gave her a reputed top speed of 250mph (400km/h). To aid speed, both the after fuselage was of semi-monocoque aluminium, instead of the fabric covering hitherto employed, and the vertical fin was streamlined.

The company history recalled how:

> Principal significance of this design is that it incorporated a number of new and desirable features which were later adapted to the trainer series. Among these were a fuel tank built integrally with the wing centre section instead of as a removable unit, resulting in 50 per cent increase in fuel capacity in the same size centre section; an aluminium alloy monocoque rear fuselage section instead of the conventional tubular steel framework with attaching panels; and metal side panels replacing the conventional fabric side panels on the front fuselage section. The latter two items resulted in the all-metal fuselage exterior which subsequently became standard on all North American basic and advanced trainers.[2]

As befitting her more aggressive role, the NA-44 was well armed with no less than four forward-firing 0.30-calibre Colt machine guns, two in the nose and one in either wing, as well as the usual rearward-firing machine gun on a flexible mounting. Ground strafing was obviously one of the main features of the design, but she also carried light bomb racks under the central fuselage and on the outer wing panels, which could take two pairs of 100lb bombs or ten smaller weapons.

She was allocated the civilian registration NX-18981 and conducted a series of whistle-stop demonstrations dressed up (unofficially) in the USAAC training colour scheme of the day: blue fuselage and yellow wings. She should have caught the eye, but failed to do so until late in the day.

It was not until 6 August 1940, by which time every plane had enormous value to the war effort, that the Canadian Government purchased her for evaluation purposes along with the NA-26, as mentioned earlier. This aircraft, s/n 44-747, joined the earlier BC-1 for a feasibility study into the prospect of Canadian licence-built examples. She was stripped down to bare metal and received the RCAF serial 3344 and roundels. She served in the 2nd SFTS at Uplands (allegedly dubbed the 'Super Harvard' due to her engine power and speed), but soon went to RCAF Station Trenton and was used as the personal 'hack', during which time she was again painted blue and yellow with red flashes. She also carried a cartoon of a Willys Jeep and 'Jeep' quickly became her enduring nickname. She had the DF casing removed and had a spinner fitted, and was later painted the usual yellow. She survived until 20 February 1947, by which time she had logged 739 hours, and was sold (buyer unknown) at Trenton. Regrettably, it seems that all that now remains of this special aircraft is her three-bladed Hamilton-Standard propeller.

NA-45

Three of these GP variants ('basic combat, general purpose planes') were ordered by Venezuela on 14 December 1937 under this charge number and were given the designation NA-16-1GV (V = Venezuela). In addition to the usual 0.30-calibre machine guns, two forward-firing and one rear, they were fitted with A-3 bomb racks under the fuselage centre section.

NA-16-1GV

These three aircraft, carrying the North American serial numbers 45-693, 45-694

(*Above*) Described by the NAA sales team as a Basic Combat General Purpose aircraft, a term which covered a wide enough spectrum to ensure some foreign interest, the NA-45 (NA-16-1GV) was the result of a 14 December 1937 contract and first appeared the following year. They carried the A-3 light bomb racks under each wing centre-section and had two fixed forward-firing 0.30-calibre machine guns firing over the nose and one firing aft. Three were built (45-693 to 45-695 inclusive) and sold to Venezuela where they received the serials 1–3. Rockwell International

The NA-45 (NA-16-1GV) as they first appeared in 1937. The bomb racks under the central section of the wing can clearly be seen as can the two large landing lights mounted in the leading edge of both. One of these three aircraft was still in service in Venezuela as late as June 1954, after a career of sixteen years. Rockwell International

and 45-695, served in the Servicio Aereo Militar Venezolana (Venezuelan Military Air Service). On delivery they were given the serial numbers 1–3 respectively. They were the first retractable undercarriage aircraft to serve with the force. They had mixed fortunes, one lasted only a short time, crashing with no survivors on 9 June 1938; a second was scrapped while the third was still serving as late as June 1954.

NA-46

The Brazilian Naval Aviation Corps placed an order for a dozen of the general-purpose type on 2 December 1938, and they were designated as the NA-16-4. Although described as advanced trainers and used as such, they were capable of carrying the same armament and had the same bombing facilities as the NA-45. They were also fitted with the fixed wing-tip slots for stall minimization as with the BT-9Cs.

NA-16-4

These twelve aircraft were delivered in two batches of six, carrying the North American serial numbers 46-972/977 and 46-1991/1996. The first batch of six, which arrived in October 1939, served with the Naval Air Arm's 1a Esquadrilha de Adestramento Militar based at Galeao as the D1Na, where they were nicknamed Stiff Legs ('*Perna Duras*') by the navy pilots and trainees. They took Navy serials 192/203. The second half-dozen arrived at the same base in April 1940, but a year later the Naval Air Arm was incorporated into the Forca Aerea Brasileira. They, in turn, re-designated the surviving eleven aircraft as the BT-9 and assigned serials 1037/1047 to them. They soldiered on for a considerable time, the last one being struck off charge on 7 March 1958.

NA-47

A second order for a trial aircraft was received from Mitsubishi Jukogyo K. K. Japan on 16 December 1937. This aircraft was designated as the NA-16-4RW.

NA-16-4RW

This aircraft, serial number 47-699, was fitted with the Wright R-975-E3 radial engine, which drove a two-bladed propeller. She arrived in Japan and the Imperial Japanese Navy flew comparison trials with her against the NA-16-4R. She received the Navy designation KXA2, again as a Navy Experimental Type A intermediate Trainer.

Trials with both types were carried out and the Imperial Navy decided that the NA-16-4R was the most suitable for use as a template for home production. The rights to so manufacture were negotiated through an intermediary company to avoid bad publicity back in the States. In order to fulfil the requirements of the 14-Shi specification, the Navy ordered a much-modified version to be built by the K. K. Watanabe Tekkosho, at Kyushu, designated as the K10W1. The main modification was the substitution of a Nakajima Kotobuki 2 Kai air-cooled radial, developing 600hp. Appearance-wise the vertical tail surface was changed considerably for improved stability.

The K10W1 prototype first appeared on the eve of the Pacific War in 1941, and the Navy placed orders for them as their Type 2 Intermediate Trainer. They were to replace the Navy's existing K5Y1 trainer. K. K. Watanabe built the first twenty-six aircraft of this order, but, because of limited capacity, were ordered by the Navy to hand over production to the Nippon Hikoki K. K. The transfer of both blueprints and considerable tooling followed, and subsequently the latter concern built 150 Kyushu K10W1 trainers between February 1943 and March 1944. Like all wartime Japanese aircraft, the K10W1 was assigned an Allied code name, becoming the *Oak* for easy identification.[3]

NA-48

The Chinese Government placed a second order for the North American trainer on 23 February 1938, and these two-place light bomber variants were designated as the NA-16-3C (C = China).

NA-16-3C

Fifteen of these trainers were delivered to the Chinese Government. They carried the North American factory serial numbers 48-732/74-746, inclusively. They carried the 0.30-calibre machine guns and light bomb racks under the fuselage common to this variant. They arrived in China in May and June 1938 and were almost immediately thrown into the fierce fighting then raging, where they were soon decimated.

The NA-49 (NA-16-1E) was ordered by the RAF on 7 February 1938, and became the Harvard I. The first aircraft arrived in England in December of that year, and orders rapidly built up with the outbreak of World War II. The original RAF two-tone paint scheme for UK usage is shown here on N7033, one of the first batch of 200 machines. She served with 2 FTS, 2 SFTS, 15 SFTS and 71 OUT before being struck off charge on 1 December 1943. Ray C. Sturtivent

NA-49

Great Britain at the time of Munich had given in to Hitler's demands yet again. There were not many outcries at this by the British public, who desperately yearned for peace, almost at any price. However, Prime Minister Neville Chamberlain was playing for time as Britain had disarmed almost totally in the 1920s and her neglected defence industry was not up to the job of creating new forces very quickly. What aircraft manufacturing capacity there was would be needed to produce mainly fighting aircraft, and so it made sense to order trainer aircraft from other sources, principally the United States.

Accordingly, a British purchasing commission was established with the specific aim of touring the USA aircraft factories and purchasing three types of essential aircraft. They had a $25 million wallet for what caught their eye. They arrived in Washington DC in 1937 and began to cast their eye over any companies that they decided could fill their shopping list.

The first aircraft they purchased, on 7 February 1938, under contract no. 791588/38, were 200 NA-49s. These aircraft were to be built at Inglewood and transferred to the United Kingdom, where British-type equipment would then be fitted in place of the standard USAAC fittings. These 200 aircraft were designated as the NA-16-1E (E = England). Following normal RAF practice at the time, they were allocated names and, being trainers built in the USA, followed the trend of naming them after US universities: the retractable trainer became Harvard I and the fixed undercarriage trainer taken over after the crash of France became the Yale.

Harvard I

The placing of the British Purchasing Commission's order in the summer of 1938 put intense pressure on the NAA to meet the commitments they had entered into.

> ...the company's engineering department shattered all design records in revising the basic airplane to meet British requirements and accommodate British equipment. Although 990 of the original 2,000 design drawings required changes for this rush export project, the engineers performed their work so rapidly that the first completed airplane was test flown in England only 120 days after design work had started...[4]

The 22 June 1938 contract between the British Air Ministry and the company provided for the manufacture of 200 Harvard I aeroplanes, plus twenty-five equivalent airframes in spare parts, at a total money value of US$6,500,000. The first resident British representatives arrived at the Inglewood plant in July: H. Luttman, of the Aeronautical Inspection Directorate, who was assigned to the North American company full time; H. Thomas, Directorate of Technical Development; and the RAF representative, Squadron Leader James J. Addams. They divided their time between NAA and Lockheed, and oversaw the work and witnessed the first Harvard test flight, made from the adjoining airfield on 28 September 1938 by test pilot Louis S. Wait.

The main complaint, voiced by Addams, was lack of cockpit heating and one of the completed aircraft was assigned by the RAF to the company for modification to overcome this. The solution was found by extending the exhaust shroud over the right wing and allowing the heat, through filters, into the cockpit. This became an identification feature of British Harvards and one that was adopted by the Canadians as well.

Once the initial test flight programme had been completed, the British formally accepted the first production aircraft in the middle of October and this machine was shipped from Los Angeles harbour aboard the MS *Lochatrine* (Furness Line) sailing on 24 October via the Panama Canal, and disembarking the Harvard at Liverpool. This first Harvard was test flown in England on 26 November by an NAA company pilot, and he was soon joined by a staff of mechanics whose job was to help the British uncrate, assemble and test the rest of the order as they arrived. Follow-up deliveries were impressive, on 31 March 1939, twenty crated Harvard Is were shipped to Liverpool.

> This shipment then constituted the largest quantity of airplanes of a single type ever to leave the United States on one vessel. The last airplane of the initial RAF contract for 200 airplanes was shipped from Los Angels Harbor on 20 May 1939, less than eleven months after the company had received the contract from the British Air Ministry.[5]

According to the *New York Sun* newspaper, some RAF officers were very pleased with their new trainer. This eulogy was delivered by one chief flying instructor on the Harvard:

> What I think so good is their marvellous cockpit layout. It's like a car. In some airplanes the controls seem to be put anywhere there is space. The result is knobs, buttons and levers everywhere; under the seat, behind your back, over your head, under your arms. The Harvard trainer gives the impression that the designer sat down and made a plan of his controls before he began to build his machine. It was decided that one place was just right for every instrument and gadget and there it went.[6]

Others were more caustic in their comments, the editor of the British magazine *The Aeroplane*, C. G. Grey, giving voice to the general consensus that the mere sound of a Harvard with her propeller at low pitch and her engine at maximum revs over Berlin would have forced the Nazi's to surrender immediately! Forever, the British knew the Harvard as 'The Noisy North American'.

NA-16-1E

The two trainers of the first British order received the North American factory serials 49-748/947, inclusive. They were quickly followed by a second batch ordered at the same time, for a further 200, and these received the North American factory serials 49-1053/1252, inclusive. The full story of these and subsequent Harvards, is contained in Chapter 5.

The second batch of a further 200 NA-16-1Es quickly followed the initial RAF order and this Harvard I (serial P5823, 'K') is one of the first of that delivery and is shown in the RAF two-tone UK trainer paint scheme. She saw service with 14 SFTS, 15 SFTS and then went out to Southern Rhodesia to join 20 SFTS, surviving to be deleted on 31 October 1944. Ray C. Sturtivent

NA-50

The Government of Peru placed an order for seven NA-50s on 1 August 1938, under contract FO 53169. These aircraft were allocated the North American factory serial numbers 50-948/954 inclusive. They were of the single-seater fighter design variant, which the company had been hawking around for a considerable time, and they proved the first actual sale of this type. The company history recorded that:

> Another project of this prewar period which, although it was military, still represented a divergence from the company's concentration on trainers and observation planes, was a single-engined fighter called the NA-50, of which seven units were built for the Peruvian Air Force. Although smaller and more powerful than the trainer series, this airplane incorporated many of the features of the trainer series. Delivery of these airplanes was made in May, 1939.[7]

The power-plant adopted was the 840hp Wright R-1820-G3 Cyclone radial, which delivered a top speed of just under 300mph (480km/h) at 9,500ft (2,750m) altitude. However, the actual armament for a fighter was derisory, merely the usual two 0.30-calibre machine guns synchronized to fire through the propeller arc. Despite being rated as a fighter aircraft, light bomb racks were mounted on the wings capable of carrying four 100lb bombs in total for ground-attack work. These, plus the sparse offensive armament, put the NA-50 more in the GP mode, but there were other differences that countered these.

The cockpit was redesigned as a single-seater and was both roomy and afforded excellent visibility. Pilot protection, however, was nil! Novel features for the Peruvians were internal fuel tanks protected with Neobest and Neoseal against leakage, the forerunners of self-sealing tanks.

The NAA grand design not only allowed for trainers and light attack aircraft, but was designed to produce fighter aircraft as well. One of the earliest examples of this configuration was the NA-50. Seven of these little single-seater pursuit aircraft (50-948 to 50-954) were built to the Peruvian Contract FO 53169 of 1 August 1938 and delivered from March 1939 onward. Powered by a Wright R-1829-G3 Cyclone developing 840hp they had a top speed of 295mph but were poorly armed with just two 0.30-calibre machine guns firing over the nose, but had bomb racks fitted. They were the first NAA product to go into actual combat, during the July 1941 clash with Ecuador, one being destroyed in that conflict. Another remains preserved at Lima. Rockwell International

A potent little fighter plane was the NA-68 which was built for Thailand. With that country's flirtation with Japan and the humiliation of the Vichy-French in 1941, these aircraft were seized by the US Government and handed over to the USAAC, who dubbed them P-64s and took them on charge with new serials. They were used for fighter training only. Rockwell International

The first aircraft underwent her flight testing at Inglewood in February 1939 and the first batch arrived in Peru the following month. They duly served with the Cuerpo de Aeronautica del Peru (the Corps of Aeronautics of Peru). While the French and Dutch aircraft had become the first combat victims in May 1940 in Europe, the Peruvian fighters were the first to go into battle on the offensive during the clash with neighbouring Ecuador, which took place in July 1941, when one was shot down. They had remarkably long careers: five of them lasting in active service until June 1950. There is one survivor, an exhibition aircraft mounted on a plinth at the Lima air force base.

NA-52

The need to train pilots for the new generation of dive bombers (like the Vought SB2U Vindicator and the Douglas SBD Dauntless) and torpedo bombers (like the Grumman TBF Avenger), which were on the drawing boards for the expanding fleet of aircraft carriers then under construction, made the US Navy eager to purchase as many of the new trainers as they could afford. A special requirement was established for a scout trainer (ST), and evaluation trials were conducted with the BC-1.

Navy requirements were more stringent, of course, their pilots had to cope with deck landings, which are notoriously more difficult and dangerous than conventional airfield operations; consequently a general toughening-up of the design was called for in the US Navy specification that was issued. The first details were given to North American on 23 September 1938, and they called for a batch of sixteen to start with under contract no. 62916. These aircraft received the Navy designator SNJ-1 and were allocated North American factory serials 52-956/971, inclusive.

SNJ-1

To meet the Navy's requirements for the ST, the all-metal fuselage of the BT-14 was re-introduced. Modifications to the wing, with reduced length outer panels and squared-off tips, resulted in a shorter overall wingspan. The rudder was squared off at the bottom, rather than being round. The powerplant was finally settled as the Pratt and Whitney R-1340-6 radial developing 550hp, which drove a two-blade, controllable-pitch propeller.

This first aircraft of the batch (Bu 1552) was delivered to the Navy on 29 May 1939, after testing at Inglewood by the Inspector of Naval Aircraft. She was then flown into Naval Air Station (NAS) Anacostia for further intensive testing. No major faults were found other than the engine cutting on right-hand spins and this involved a lengthy period of problem-solving that lasted from the end of May right through to 4 December. Despite this the first aircraft was officially 'accepted' into the service on 22 August, even though several Navy requirements, CO_2 system, blind flying hood, and pilots chart board, had not been fitted when delivered.

Under the command of the head of the Anacostia test centre, Lieutenant Commander M. E. A. Gouin, and later Commander George Henderson, the team,

(Above) **The first NA-52 (SNJ-1) was accepted into the US Navy on 22 August 1939, and went to NAS Anacostia for extensive trials. This machine (52-956, BuNo 1552) was a combination of the best features of the BC-1 and the NA-44 and was designated as a Scout Trainer. She also incorporated the squared wing-tips of the NA-50 and was powered by a R-1340-6 engine which developed 500hp. Sixteen were built and many were later re-engined with the R-1340-18 from April 1940 onward.** Rockwell International

Aerial view of the first SNJ-1 airborne over NAS Anacostia during extensive trials. US National Archives

Ground view of the first of the US Navy's SNJ-1s (NA-52). Note the squared off wing-tips on this model, and they carried no armament. Rockwell International

comprising Captain William Saunders, Lieutenant W. K. Goodney, Lieutenant S. A. Johnson, Lieutenant C. E. Giese and Mr E. W. Rounds, extensively trialed the SNJ-1 to solve this problem. The original NAY8C6M carburettor was deemed to be at the root of the trouble and, between 3 and 22 June, various alternatives were tried out on the aircraft, which had been fitted with a spin chute. The most satisfactory carburettor was found to be the NAY8J. The aircraft was then test flown at Dahlgren, Virginia, for a further period, and finally accepted back to flight status on 22 July.

Even then the teething problems were not done with. The engine was changed and the propeller re-indexed to spice up performance a little, but most serious was the appearance of braking faults, high oil consumption and lack of cockpit water tightness integrity, considered vital for Navy planes. By August the Navy insisted on rectification of these faults, and others, which led to the return of the aircraft to Inglewood for improvements to cockpit integrity and the fitting of a larger rudder tab, replacement of Army-type fuses by Navy ones, a vent for the CO_2 system, a spring-loaded slip joint control rod for the emergency extension of the landing gear and a globe valve for the hydraulic system. These modifications jacked up the unit cost, of course, but were considered vital. On 7 November the aircraft was returned to Anacostia for yet further trials.

Between 8 November and 4 December flights were conducted by Captain Saunders, Lieutenant Robert E. Dixon and others. Again the oil consumption was found to be unacceptably high (on one occasion 2½ gallons or 11l in 1½ hours) and various remedies had to be resorted to in order to complete the tests. In other respects the aircraft came up to expectations, with a top speed of 205mph (330km/h), a climb rate of 1,200ft/min (365m/min) and a service ceiling of 24,000ft (7,300m). Finally, after seventy-nine flights totalling 104.1 flying hours, the SNJ-1 was passed as satisfactory on 4 December, 1939.

This aircraft proved to be a crucial stage of development before the design finally gelled into the AT-6, as we know her. After initial service, the Navy took the opportunity to upgrade the powerplant to the Wright R-1340-18 radial engine from April 1940 onward. However, by November 1943, they had had their day and were deemed unworthy of modernization. All were discarded, the majority being flown to NATT Jacksonville, Florida, where they were struck off charge on 7 January 1944 and subsequently scrapped. A few lingered on a little longer, BuNo 1556 being stricken at NAS Glenview on 31 July 1944. Two aircraft served with US Marine Corps and these, BuNo1559 and BuNo 1561, were not scrapped until 20 and 30 November 1944, respectively.

NA-54

The combining of the all-metal fuselage with a retractable undercarriage was the most obvious improvement that the Navy's SNJ-1 had shown over its Army counterparts and this was acknowledged by the USAAC. They decided to adopt this measure and, on 3 October 1938, ordered the last three BC-1s (NA-36), under contract no. AC9964, to be completed to a new specification, which they designated as the BC-2.

BC-2

These three aircraft were therefore completed to the new standard, with the all-metal, semi-monocoque fuselage and fully retractable undercarriage. They also adopted a new, broader chord wing profile, and the rounded wing-tips were squared off. The rudder ceased to have a rounded profile and became straight and raked, and was also all metal (all these features were also adopted by the near contemporary BT-14). A single Pratt and Whitney R-1340-45 radial, developing 600hp, which drove a three-bladed propeller, powered them. The new engine resulted in the fitting of a second intake at the rear of the port cowling, midway up, while the main air intake in the ventral position was located further back in the form of a large scoop.

The first trio received the North American serial numbers 54-688, 54-689 and 54-690, respectively. One was very briefly used in evaluation trials and tests at Wright Field, Ohio. The principal finding here was that the three-bladed propeller made no difference to the aircraft's performance and thus production models reverted to the two-bladed, constant-speed type once more. All three were then transferred to the United States Air Mission were their function was really in an export demonstration role, even if it was no so termed. Their presence laid the foundation for Latin American interest in the type.[8] Their final assignment was with the 6th Air Force.

NA-55-1

After placing a production order for eighty-three aircraft, the USAAC changed the designation from BC-2 to BC-1A. Their role was more than just as a BC trainer, however, and had a wider remit. North American described their scope as including tactical missions, reconnaissance and liaison for ground forces, thus including the observer training in the range of their responsibilities.

As a reflection perhaps of their expanded expectations, there was provision for two M-2 0.30-calibre machine guns, forward and rearward firing and a Type N-2A optical gunsight could be shipped forward. There was, however, no provision for bombing. For navigation training a large DF loop was mounted under the forward fuselage. The initial five aircraft from the first batch were powered by the Wright R-1340-47 radial, all subsequent models adopted the slightly improved R-1340-49 but with no increase in horsepower.

They received the North American charge number NA-55-1.

BC-1A

Of the eighty-three trainers of this type ordered, fifty-four were allocated to the Army Reserve with the remaining twenty-nine going to the National Guard. They received the North American serials 55-1548/1630, inclusive. Subsequent to intensive war training service the survivors were trashed post-war, save one aircraft that was purchased by Sweden and a second bought by Peru.

Continued Development of the NA-16 type

Although all-metal, semi-monocoque construction and retractable landing gear pointed the way ahead for the major development of the North American trainer, the contemporary BT-14 continued to attract overseas interest and did not immediately disappear from the Inglewood production line.

The Chinese Government placed a large order with NAA on 18 April 1939, and these aircraft were NA-55s in effect, but reverted to the fixed landing gear. These fifty aircraft were the NA-56s (NA-16-4) and were described as General Purpose aircraft. A repeat order for a further five was received on 15 April 1940. They were completed with a drab olive finish overall and no national markings. Rockwell International

NA-56

On 18 April 1939, the Chinese Government placed a third order with North American for fifty more NA-16-4 (BC-1A, NA-55) trainers and these received the North American charge number NA-56. They took the North American serial numbers 57-1453/1502, inclusive. The first five were ready in April 1940 and were delivered the following August. Like all such deliveries to the Kuomintang Government, they were shipped out without any national markings or other indicators, and were painted dark brown. Their subsequent fate is apparently unknown.

NA-57

France, like Britain, was facing the unpalatable fact that war with Nazi Germany was just around the corner, and, in the same manner as the British, the French despatched a purchasing mission, under M. Monnet, to the United States to obtain the necessary aircraft her own small aviation industry just could not supply in time or in quantity. During 1939, the French actively sought to purchase the latest American bombers and pursuit types, some of which had not yet entered service with the USAAC. This angered their chief General Arnold considerably.[9]

However, the French need for training aircraft caused less controversy and, on 16 January 1939, Monnet recommended the purchase of 200 North American trainers for L'Armée de L'Air.[10] The French Government were not tardy and, indeed, went better than this by ordering 230 of the NA-57s on 21 February 1939. The US Government granted official approval for this order to proceed on 14 February 1939 and the actual order was placed a week later, on 21 February. The contract also provided for twenty-seven equivalent airframes and spare parts, for a total cost in excess of $7 million and was the largest order NAA had received up to that time.

Like the British, the French naturally required the fitting of their own equipment, metric instrumentation and the like, including reverse throttles. Their preferred powerplant was the Wright R-975-E3 radial engine, which developed 420hp. These differences apart, they were basically modified NA-23s.

These aircraft received the North American serials 57-1253/1452, inclusive.

The first production aircraft was accepted at Inglewood by a French Government representative as early as April. The routine was established whereby the airframes were crated up at Inglewood, taken by low-loaders to the Los Angeles docks and shipped on French vessels. One of North American's test pilots was sent to England and then to France, and he made the first NA-57 test flight from Chateaudun on 29 June 1939. They received the French designation of NAA 57 et 2. A few were intended for a photographic reconnaissance role, being camouflaged for operational duties and designated as the NAA 57 P 2.

Subsequent batches of NA-57s were re-routed via the port of New Orleans for faster transit, the largest shipment being made on 31 July 1939, when the French liner *Louisiane* embarked no less than forty machines. A staff of North American factory workers joined the French at Chateaudun and helped uncrate and assemble these airframes, ready for fitting out with French equipment.[11] The initial thirty aircraft were assigned to the Aéronavale, the French Navy Air Arm, and carried the Navy serials U-416/445, inclusive. In November 1939, a report from New York confirmed that 54 NA-57s were crated and ready for shipment, and that five more would be ready by the end of that month. In fact, forty of the trainers arrived on Christmas Day. However, the joy at receiving them was tempered by the problems encountered by Colonel Stéphane Thouvenot, in getting them operational in time.[12]

Fast and speedy though the aid was, however, events proved they were not fast enough. On 15 June 1940, with France almost totally defeated, of the remainder of the first batch of forty machines just eight had been transferred to L'Armée de L'Air and the remaining two were still being assembled. A further forty had arrived at Casablanca, in French Morocco, this port being selected as making the transporting vessels less vulnerable to German U-boat attack but extending the time taken to get them to France herself.

All 230 were eventually delivered, of which approximately 50 were used by the Germans. They equipped A/B 116 training school at Goeppingen, while others went to 2.Versuchsverband OKL to teach German pilots how to fly captured Allied aircraft. The remainder stayed under Vichy French control until November 1942.

NA-64

On 25 May 1939, the French placed a second order for a further 199 BT-14 trainers, equipped with reverse throttles and the Pratt and Whitney R-985-25 engine. They resembled more the NA-58 (BT-14) with all-metal fuselage. They were intended for an additional role as a tactical reconnaissance aircraft and carried the French designation NAA 64 P2. The order was soon afterwards increased by another thirty-one machines to match the previous order (NA-56) and were again divided between L'Armée de L'Air and the Aéronavale. These aircraft were produced in two batches under the charge number NA-64 and received the North American serials 64-2033/2232 and 64-3018/3047, respectively. The first aircraft test flew from Inglewood on 12 February 1940 but France was not to be granted enough respite for more than 111 to reach her shores.

A few were transferred to the Vichy Government after the armistice, the bulk of which also fell into the hands of the Luftwaffe in November 1942, save for those captured by the British and Americans in North Africa at this time.

Again, some 119 remained undelivered at the armistice in June 1940, and again these were taken into Canada and re-designated by the RCAF in August and September 1940 as the Yale 1. They were assigned the RCAF serial numbers 3346/3464, inclusive.

A total of 119 aircraft, sixteen of which remained in the United States awaiting shipment, were immediately taken over by the Canadians, who allocated them to the Royal Canadian Air Force (RCAF), who named them the Yale 1. The bulk (103) were actually in transit at the time and their transporting ships were diverted to the islands of St Pierre and Miquelon off the Newfoundland coast, where they were off-loaded. The RCAF allocated them serials in the range 3346 to 3463, inclusive.

The RCAF used them, even though all the lettering inside was in French, by painting English and imperial translations around the dials. They also had their reverse throttle units replaced by Harvard ones at the National Steel Car Plant. As an intermediate trainer, prior to the trainee moving on to the Harvard or AT-6 itself, Yales served with No. 1 Service Flying Training School (SFTS) at Camp Borden, the first entering service in August 1940, and also at No. 2 SFTS, Uplands, Ottawa, No. 6 SFTS at Dunnville and No. 14 SFTS at Aylmer, Ontario, until May 1943. Eight (RCAFs 3347, 3373, 3379, 3381, 3383, 3401, 3420 and 3422) were later transferred to the Royal Navy Fleet Air Arm School, No. 31 SFTS at Kingston. None were retained post-war.

The NA-64 resulted from a repeat French order for the NA-57 but with some of the upgraded all-metal fuselage and re-designed wings and empennage of the NA-58. The first aircraft carried the US Civil registration NX-13397. They were powered by the Pratt & Whitney R-985-25 engine and first flew on 12 February 1940. Of the 130 completed, in two batches, just 111 actually managed to reach France before she surrendered. The remaining 119 were delivered to the Royal Canadian Air Force between 23 August and 27 September 1940, who lumped them all together with the 16 NA-57s they also received and named them all as the Yale I. They were allocated RCAF serials and some survived through the war until 1 October 1946. This is RCAF 3451 seen serving with 6 SFTS, RCAF in 1942. Ray C. Sturtivent

Exports Spur Production Development at Inglewood

The Inglewood plant was having to work flat out to meet the increased demands of the success of their trainer series abroad and this led to new thinking about how to cope with expected future orders. The company history recorded how:

> Further refinements of the company's quality production techniques were made possible when the factory received its first large orders from the British in 1938 and from the French in 1939. When war broke out in Europe, the factory had almost completed its first two contracts for the British, totalling 230 airplanes. The main assembly floor was crowded with straight lines of trainer fuselages in progressive stages of assembly. Production procedures and processes were being constantly studied and improved with an eye to the accelerated schedules looming ahead.[13]

By 1 September 1939, North American Aviation had delivered a total of 1,075 trainer series aircraft and was producing further trainers at the rate of sixty per month.

NA-58

Following trials with the NJ-1, the best features of previous fixed-undercarriage marks were incorporated into this charge number. The aircraft was largely redesigned, in fact, and differed considerably, becoming the BT-9D.

(Top) **The production lines at North American Aviation in full swing. The various stages of manufacture are very clearly seen in this photograph taken at Inglewood, with aircraft number 54 having wings fitted and undercarriage in the process of being adjusted. She also carries the large D/F loop under her chin.** Smithsonian Institute, Washington DC

(Bottom) **Main fuselage assembly lines at Inglewood leading to wing assembly and, just seen in the left background, a completed aircraft is wheeled out of the hangar doors.** Rockwell International

BT-9D

Chief features that were altered in this machine were the adoption of the Pratt and Whitney R-985-25 Wasp Junior engine, a radial that developed 450hp. This engine necessitated a larger (and much smoother) engine cowling and a relocation of the exhaust pipe to a central position on the starboard side.

The fuselage was lengthened by 14in (35cm) and an all-aluminium semi-monocoque construction replaced the old stretch skin and stringers composition of the BT-9C.

The wing profile was totally changed, with the introduction of a broad chord, coupled with the squaring off of the formerly rounded wing-tips. These changes reduced the overall wingspan to 41ft (12.5m). The vertical tail surfaces followed the Navy practice, the rounded rudder becoming straight and angular, with the leading edge also becoming more acutely angled to meet it and also being all-metal instead of fabric covered.

YBT-14

One prototype was produced introducing all these radical changes, and she was designated as the YBT-14. The USAAC carried out a very detailed inspection of this machine and, convinced of her merits, placed orders for another 251 to be built to the same specification. These received the designation BT-14.

BT-14

An order was placed by the USAAC on 23 April 1939 for 251 of this mark. They received the North American serial numbers 58-1655/1905, inclusive. The first machine was delivered to Wright Field on 9 September 1939. Some twenty-seven of these were subsequently modified, *circa* 1941, by the substitution of the Pratt and Whitney R-985-11A engine, which developed 400hp, then being fitted to the BT-14A. They were the last fixed-undercarriage trainers built by North American for the USAAC. The first flight of the BT-14 took place on 3 January 1940, Louis S. Wait again being the test pilot concerned.

CHAPTER THREE

The Design Comes of Age

NA-59

Although the ninety-four aircraft ordered by the USAAC on 28 April 1939 were identical to the BC-1A, and were ordered under contract AC-12969, they were given a new designation as the NA-59. Because the Air Corps had reservations about the BC description as applying to advanced training (AT) aircraft for active duty units rather than as issues to the Reserve and National Guard, they received the old designation of AT, which was resurrected, thus finally becoming the immortal AT-6.

AT-6

The changes in configuration hardly warranted all this hassle, the principal external one being the highly prominent DF loop mounted vertically to the underside of the fuselage just abaft the engine cowl. The 600hp Wright R-1340-47 radial remained the powerplant. Despite the re-designation, they remained adaptable for carrying armaments with a single synchronized 0.30-calibre fixed forward-fire machine gun mounted in the nose on the starboard side and the usual flexible mounted rearward-firing gun of the same calibre in the rear cockpit position. Because of this, the bulk of this batch were principally employed as air gunnery training aircraft.

They were built in two blocks, of which the first, nine aircraft with the North American serial numbers 56-1631/59-1639, inclusive, were actually NA-55s modified and included in the AT-6 designation. Test pilot Louis S. Wait made the first flight of the type on 6 February1940. The second batch of eighty-five was a new order and had North American serials 59-1906/1990, inclusive. USAAC serials allocated to these two batches were 40-717/725 and 40-2080/2164 inclusive. Of these the very first AT-6 (serial number 40-717) was accepted into the Air Corps on 24 June 1939 and served briefly at Bolling AFB before being assigned to the US Military Mission and based at Ottawa, Canada, until 8 April 1944. The other aircraft followed in short order.

NA-61

An order for thirty aircraft was placed by the Royal Canadian Air Force, quite independently of the British purchasing commission orders, on 25 May 1939. Although they were similar in almost every respect to the Harvard Is ordered for the RAF a few months earlier, they did not receive this name until later on when all British Empire Air Training Scheme aircraft were standardized to give simpler conformity. These thirty aircraft were given the North American designation of NA-16-1E.

NA-16-1E

Deliveries of this batch commenced on 20 July 1939 and two are known to have survived the war, being stricken from charge on 9 May 1946. Although almost identical to the British Harvard I they did feature some distinctive Canadian features, mainly reflections of that country's particular climate and environmental problems.

To help keep these aircraft operational in temperatures that frequently fall below zero, one plane from this batch was fitted as a trial aircraft to test a 'heat muff' exhaust shroud. This proved quite successful and a modified version went into production for subsequent RCAF Harvards. In order to operate above the snowline, plans were put in train to equip all these aircraft with skis in place of wheels. The Canadian firm of Noorduyn manufactured a set of skis for each aircraft, plus four spare sets.

In Canada, cadets trained initially on the Tiger Moth or the Fleet Finch for 65h at the St. Kitts, Ontario, flying school, and then reported to the No. 14 Service Flying Training School at Aylmer, Ontario, for Harvard training. The RCAF did not fly the last Harvard mission until as late as 19 May 1956, when Flight Lieutenant J. A. Cratchley and his student O/C J. W. Lussier, flew Harvard 20384 from Penhold, Alberta RCAF base on the very last Canadian training mission.

NA-65

On 24 June 1940, the US Navy, faced with massive expansion of its Air Arm, placed another order with North American for thirty-six trainers. They were to be used as instrument and scout trainers by the Navy Reserve squadrons. They were assigned the North American serial numbers 65-1997/2032, inclusive, and became the SNJ-2.

SNJ-2

The powerplant adopted was the Navy's preferred Pratt and Whitney radial, being the R-1340-36, which developed 600hp and drove a two-bladed wooden propeller. Maximum speed went up to 213mph (343km/h) at 6,000ft (1,830m) altitude, a climb rate of 1,200ft/min (365m/min) and a ceiling of 24,000ft (7,315m). The wingspan was increased to 42ft 7in (12.97m) giving an enlarged wing area of 258.6ft^2 (23.96m^2). Although no armament was carried, the weight increased to 4,954lb (2,247kg) as a result.

Visible differences over the SNJ-1 included a larger cowl ring, and a vent scoop on the port-side forward just abaft it, necessitated by the moving of the oil cooler to the port side of the engine. The carburettor air intake scoop was also moved to the port side of the forward fuselage, while a streamlined fairing covered the fuel transfer equipment on the underside of the forward fuselage. Internally, special Navy requirements included a leather headrest for the pilot and his cabin was fitted out with a hinged, folding chart board on the starboard side of the cockpit, which doubled as an anti-glare shield when in the upright position. The instrument panel

The NA-65 was the first batch of trainers ordered for the US Navy, which received the designation SNJ-2. These three dozen machines had a greater wing span and therefore wing area than the NA-52, were powered by the R-1340-36 engine which increased their best speed to 213mph (342km/h) at 6,000ft (1,800m), and they carried no armament. The hump under the forward fuselage abaft the wheel wells can just be made out. This contained the fuel transfer gear and was a ready identification feature. This aircraft is seen working at NAS Pensacola, Florida, in May 1942. Pima Air & Space Museum, Tucson

Also classified as the SNJ-2 were twenty-five NA-79s ordered via a USAAC contract on 24 June 1940. They were similar to the NA-66 and were powered by the Pratt and Whitney R-1340-6. They received the NAA serials 78-3983 to 79-4007 inclusive (BuNo 2548 to BuNo 2572). National Archives

was also upgraded. This first batch of SNJ-2s received the Bureau of Aeronautics (BuAer) serials 2008/2043, inclusive.

The first aircraft, BU 2008, made her debut flight at Inglewood on 29 March1940 and, after contractor demonstrations that continued until 5 April, was flown to Anacostia on 11 April. Led by Commander George Henderson, the same test team as on the SNJ-1 carried out the usual trials over the following month. Exactly the same braking problems were encountered and, additionally, problems were encountered with the integral fuel tanks, which developed leaks and necessitated the removal of the wings for an inspection and fix. Top speed was logged at 214mph (344km/h) at 6,000ft (1,830m), and a service ceiling of 24,600ft (7,500m) was exceeded. Only twenty-six test flights were made, totalling 38.6 flying hours before the aircraft was passed as a scout trainer.

However, as usual, the Bureau of Aeronautics insisted on some modifications and improvements before passing her into service; these included changes to both fuel tanks and brakes, as recommended. Once more the watertight integrity of the cockpit was criticized and improvements demanded, while an instrument flying hood was to be installed in the rear cockpit. The prop governor control mechanism also needed a redesign to bring it up to the required standard. Again these modifications were costly, increasing the unit price of each of the thirty-six machines by $16,034.

On completion in 1940, the majority of the SNJ-2s went, as planned, to reserve units, while others were assigned to NA Stations as far apart as New York, Long Beach and Pearl Harbor. One machine, BuNo 2018, was assigned to the Naval Attaché in Buenos Aires, no doubt doubling as a sales vehicle, and remained in Argentina for her whole life, until stricken on 31 December1945.

Of those still flyable at the end of the war many were sold out of service to foreign buyers, notably the Flygvapnet who purchased two in 1953, and civilian clubs, company's and individuals.

NA-66

On 17 November 1939, and now at war and urgently requiring large numbers of young pilots, Great Britain ordered another 600 trainers from North American, and they were assigned the charge number NA-66. These aircraft were just about identical to the BC-1A, but carried British radio equipment, instrumentation and armaments. The powerplant was the Pratt and Whitney R-1340-53H1 Wasp. They became the Harvard II in Commonwealth service. They received the North American serials 66-2234/2833, inclusive.

Cross-Border Transfers

Coincidental with the placing of this order, the British had decided to concentrate training activities in Canada and to have the Harvards flown directly to training centres there. The stumbling block to this neat plan was initially the American Neutrality Act, which debarred such activity to combatants. President Franklin D. Roosevelt finally had this embargo revised, but this did not take effect until September1940. Prior to that date it was necessary to evade the Act by the farce of having the Harvards physically pulled across the International boundary by Canadian nationals, before they could then be turned over to Canadian pilots to fly away.

The first Harvard to be hauled across the frontier, from the small township of Pembina, North Dakota close to the Canadian border, was in the summer of 1940. Some twenty-five Harvards followed this route before direct flight delivery was approved.

Once authorization was cleared, a much more efficient system of transport was agreed between North American and Canadian authorities. This involved American pilots flying the aircraft direct from Inglewood to the Canadian training bases, the pilot returning to Los Angeles by scheduled airlines ready for their next delivery.

By the end of 1940 North American had delivered more than 800 Harvard advance trainers to various parts of the British Empire. In January 1941 Kindleberger received a personal cablegram from Lord Beaverbrook, British Minister of Aircraft Production, congratulating the company on its achievement in bettering the production schedule set for 1940 on the Harvard II type.[1]

The NA-66 (known as the 'Modified Harvard') was part of a bulk order by the British Government and became the Harvard Mk II in service. They received the NAA serials 66-2234 to 66-2833 and were divided up between the RCAF, the RNZAF and the RAF. This is RCAF 2501, one of thirteen allocated to Canada. They could be distinguished from the Mark I by the squared off wing-tips and the angled rather than rounded, trailing edge rudder as well as the smoother metal after-fuselage structure. Rockwell International

Harvard II

The order of 600 was originally subdivided into allocations as follows:

- Royal Canadian Air Force (RCAF): 513 (serials 2501–3013)
- Royal New Zealand Air Force (RNZAF): 66 (serials NZ901–967)
- Royal Air Force (RAF): 21 (serials AH185–205).

However, actual deliveries varied quite a lot from this 'intentions' list as will be explained later.

The most obvious external difference was the moving of the radio mast from its most inconvenient place smack in front of the pilot's windshield, as was American practice. This took place on later production models. Internally the colder climates of Great Britain and Canada had led to complaints that the California-built aircraft had inadequate cockpit heating. This was rectified to some degree by the fitting of an exhaust shroud to the starboard side of the forward fuselage. This funnelled warm air from the engine, through filters, over the top of the wing's leading edge and back into the cockpit. Both these British modifications made good identification points. The most obvious difference between the Harvard I and Harvard II was squared-off wing-tips on the latter, with the rounded rudder trailing edge giving way to the straight-angled version on the Harvard II. A semi-monocoque aluminium alloy section formed the rear fuselage on the latter, with the front fuselage sections being of metal panels.

The armament consisted of only two 0.303 Vickers machine guns, one fixed firing forward, the other on a flexible mount in the after cockpit. British training aircraft were painted bright yellow and the aircraft were delivered direct from the Inglewood plant in this colour.

Exotic Foreign Orders

While the standard trainer was settling down to some degree of standardization with the placing of large orders by the US Army, US Navy, Great Britain, France and Canada, North American was still kept busy turning out small batches of more specialized variants for various clients around the world. Their original concept of single place fighters and light attack bombers had finally paid off and chronologically the following aircraft were ordered.

NA-68

On 30 November 1939 the Government of Thailand (formerly Siam) placed an order for six modified NA-50s, which were basically the same as the early Peruvian order. There were some differences of course, the shorter cockpit canopy was altered to give a smoother line blending into the turtleback of the rear fuselage, and the tail and rudder were as the AT-6 configuration. These became the NA-50A.

NA-50A

These were powered by a 870hp Wright R-1820-77 Cyclone 9 radial piston engine, driving a three-bladed propeller. They had a maximum speed of 270mph (435km/h) at 8,700ft (2,650m) and a service ceiling of 27,500ft (8,380m) with a range of 635

Some Harvard IIs had extended lives. This is AJ 561, which was an RAF allocation. Very few actually served in the UK and most went to RAF training units in Canada, Southern Rhodesia and South Africa. This aircraft served with 31 SFTS between October 1941 and November 1943 and was then handed over to the RCAF when British training units were withdrawn. Post-war she was renovated and modified and became part of the French Navy (Aéronavale) training units first in Morocco and then back in France where this photograph was taken. Ray C. Sturtivent

miles (1,022km). Wingspan was 37ft 3in (11.35m), overall length 27ft (8.23m), height 9ft 4in (2.84m) and the wing area was a modest 227.5ft^2 (21.13m^2) All-up weight was 6,800lb (3,084kg).

The principal change over the NA-50 was greatly enhanced fire-power, which showed a better appreciation of the way things were to develop than hitherto. The forward fire was massive for its size and its time, with four fixed 0.30-calibre Colt Browning machine guns, two nose-mounted and two wing-mounted, plus two 20mm cannon carried in under-slung pods under either wing. They were also built to accommodate much heavier bombs than earlier types, with an under-fuselage rack capable of carrying a single 550lb bomb and light racks for 110lb bombs under the wings. A formidable little aircraft indeed! The maiden flight took place on 1 September 1940.

P-64

The Thai Government, following the Japanese occupation of Vichy French Indo-Chinese air bases, closely associated itself with Nippon. This led to fighting with the Vichy French as they, emboldened, re-took some provinces that, in 1893, France had forced them to cede to Laos. The six aircraft had actually been completed, with full camouflage paintwork, and were sitting in crates on the dockside at Los Angeles awaiting shipment[2] when the United States Arm Embargo was put into force with the issuing of AEC 140 on 4 March1941, which saved both North American and the Government some embarrassment.

The six crated aircraft were appropriated by the US Authorities and taken to McClellan Field near Sacramento. Here they were uncrated once more and assembled, being taken in charge by the USAAC as the P-64 fighter (presumably because they were single-seaters). Other than painting, the American national insignia over the Thai roundels, and changing the instrument labelling from Siamese to English, they remained as built. A plan to convert the machine guns to M-2s was put forward but not immediately carried out.

However, despite the designation, the USAAC only finally used these aircraft as fighter trainers and the armament was later removed. They were assigned the US serials 41-18890/18895, inclusive. They never did fit in and most ended their days as hacks.

NA-69

On the same date as they ordered the NA-68, the Thai Government also ordered from North American ten modified NA-16 types for the Royal Thai Air Force. These were termed 'attack bombers' and were two-seaters. They received the North American designation NA-44 and formed the basis for several other orders. They were assigned the NAA serial numbers 69-3064/3073, inclusive.

NA-44

The power-plant for this (and subsequent NA-44s) was the 745hp Pratt and Whitney R-1820-F52 Cyclone radial, which drove a three-bladed propeller. Provision was made to mount an armament of four fixed forward-firing 7.7mm-calibre machine guns, two mounted in the nose and one in each wing, with the usual rear-firing weapon of the same calibre on a flexible mounting in the after cabin. Due to a manufacturing mistake at the Wright plant, however, incorrect plungers meant that the nose guns could not be fitted and the correct parts had to follow on later for local fitting. A bomb rack could be fitted under the centre fuselage section and this could supplemented by fixing points for four 110lb bombs under the wings. The first aircraft of this batch made her maiden flight from Inglewood in June 1940. Procurement for the Royal Thai Air Force was conducted by Aerial Transport Company and, at first, it seemed as if they would fare better than the NA-68s in that they would actually *reach* their destination.

The first four aircraft completed were crated up and shipped from California via the Philippines and were actually in dock at Manila when hasty moves were made to block their further progress. The export licence was revoked by the US State Department and on 28 February AEC 138 was issued requisitioning them, along with the six remaining aircraft still at Inglewood. After much diplomatic to-ing and fro-ing the ten aircraft were taken in charge of the USAAC, and re-designated as the A-27 'Two Place Light Attack-Dive Bomber, Thai'.

A-27

The four crated aircraft were unshipped and stored at the Philippine Air Depot while the remainder were similarly assembled at the Sacramento Air Depot. Here they received the US serial numbers 41-18890/18899, inclusive. One aircraft was flown to Wright Field for evaluation and the issuing of a suitable manual for American aircrews to fly these hybrids.

All ten A-27s were assigned to the 4th Composite Group, based in the Philippines. Here they received rough service and no less than half had been written off in accidents before the Japanese attack on those islands in December 1941.[3] The surviving five (41-18894, 41-18895, 41-18897, 41-18898 and 41-18899) were based at Clarke Field but did not survive the first Japanese air attack. As Walter D. Edmonds described it, 'When after 45 minutes the Japanese at last withdrew, they had done a thorough job. Clarke Field as a tactical base was virtually destroyed. There was not a single flyable plane on the base'. He added, '... most of these were observation types or outdated or obsolete bombers like the B-18s, B-10s and A-27s'.[4]

However, not all the A-27s were written off and, contrary to some accounts, two of them *did* take part in limited combat operations, flying reconnaissance and bombing missions, before the end. On 24 December, for example, a single A-27 piloted by Lieutenant McAfee took off from Nielson Field near Manila as the Japanese approached and he attempted to fly her into Kindley Field, Corregidor.

When the Japanese occupied Clarke Field the remaining three, in varying states of damage or disrepair were captured, but they were not written of by the Americans as 'condemned' until almost a year later on 8 November1942.

NA-71

Following her good experience with the NA-45, the Government of Venezuela placed a second order with North American on 18 January 1940 for three more aircraft of the 'ground co-operation' type. They received the NAA charge number of NA-44 and the designation of NA-16-3.

NA-16-3

The powerplant for this trio was the Pratt and Whitney R-1340-S3H1 Wasp radial, which developed 550hp. Only a light armament was carried, just two forward-firing 0.30-calibre machine guns with the synchronized firing through the propeller arc, and a single flexible mounting aft.

Light bomb racks were capable of being mounted under each wing.

In May 1940 the first aircraft of the three to be completed was assigned the US registration of X19973 to cover the flight trials. Following this all three were crated and shipped out to Caracas in July 1940. They were assigned the Servicio Aereo Militar Venezolana serials FAZ 1/3, inclusive, and served throughout the war before being pensioned off.

NA-72

Charge number NA-72 was given to an order placed with NAA on 7 August 1939 by the Brazilian Government for twenty 'light attack bombers'. Partly influenced by the original NA-44, they were also designated as the NA-44 (BC-1A) and took the NAA serial numbers 72-3077/3096, inclusive. They could be distinguished by the mounting of the ADF fairing under the fuselage at the wing centre section. The order was increased on 7 August 1939 for an additional ten machines. These received the NAA serials 72-4757/74-4766, inclusive.

On completion in October 1940, rather than face the long and hazardous sea journey, the Brazilians elected the, at that time, daring idea of flying these aircraft down to Rio de Janeiro in groups of six to eight aircraft between October 1940 and February 1941. They undertook this 10,000 mile (16,000km) journey by stages, following the west coast south from California to Santiago before crossing the Andes mountains to Buenos Aires, and back up the east coast of Argentina and Brazil. The first group arrived at Rio on 13 October 1940, accompanied by Louis B. Bouchelle, North American Aviation's general representative in Latin America. These aircraft were taken on charge by the Aviacao Exercito do Brasil and assigned the serial numbers 01/30, inclusive.

NA-74

The Latin American preferences that made these North American products so popular with the smaller air forces (sophisticated, easily maintained and versatile, but not too complex), resulted in yet a further export order, this time from Chile. On 7 August 1940 the Chilean Government ordered twelve light attack bombers, under charge number NA-74. They were designated as NA-44s and received the NAA serial numbers 74-4745/4756, inclusive.

They were almost identical to the Brazilian aircraft but mounted three forward-firing fixed 0.30-calibre machine guns, one in the nose and one in either wing. They were fitted with A-3 light bomb racks under each wing outer panel and had a slightly smaller ADF profile. All were delivered safely in two batches, in May and June 1941.

More Harvard Orders Placed

The growing role of Canada as a place in which Commonwealth pilots could be safely trained up away from the restricted (and increasingly dangerous) British skies, led to a running down of UK-based training and its spread across the globe. Canada was in the forefront of this, being adjacent to the principal supplier nation. Further orders followed the disastrous Dunkirk evacuation, when Britain and her Empire were forced to realize that they would have to stand up to the victorious Axis alone.

NA-75

The Canadian Government placed an order (CAN-15) with North American on 3 June 1940, for an additional 100 trainers. These received the NAA Charge number NA-75 and were in all respects repeat NA-66s.

Harvard II

This repeat order for the RCAF was completed in two batches of ten and ninety, and they received the NAA serial allocations of 75-3048/3057 and 75-3418/3507, respectively.

NA-76

In a last desperate attempt to rectify years of neglect, the French Government was still placing orders for further training aircraft after the onset of the German blitzkrieg and just two weeks before the French were forced to sue for unilateral peace. To speed matters up, the planes in this order, for no less than 450 aircraft, which was placed on 5 June 1940, were to be repeats of the Harvard II but were to have been equipped with French radios, extended antenna and internal equipment. With the final debacle on the continent, the British lost no time in taking over the French order and they were completed as Harvard IIs.

Harvard II

The bulk of this order ended up in the Canadian Air Training Squadrons (CATS), but a few reached other destinations with the RAF, including two to the Royal New Zealand Air Force, two to India, forty-two to the Middle East and 100 to Southern Rhodesia (now Zimbabwe). One aircraft crashed in the United States and one was a write off prior to delivery. The aircraft in the order received the RAF serial numbers AJ538/987, inclusive. Some were transferred to the French Navy (Aéronavale), one of which, serial number 3820, RCAF serial 3829, 81-4087, ended up in the Musée des Traditions de l'Aéronautique Navale, at Rochefort Naval Air Base, France. Another, ex-RCAF serial 2784, 66-2517, was sold out to civilian usage and flew for a while as civil registration N88P.

NA-77

Ordered on 28 June 1940 were some 517 aircraft for the USAAC (Contract AC-15977) and 120 aircraft for the USN (BuAer Req. 1255). Another major first for the United States aviation industry was achieved with this model. As the company history recorded:

> For what is believed to have been the first instance in the history of Army and Navy aviation of a single type being ordered by both services, the order placed with North American Aviation in the summer of 1940 for AT-6A combat trainers for the Air Corps and SNJ-3 scout trainers for the Navy provided for airplanes identical in all respects except external markings.[5]

It was not quite like that but certainly, although totally interchangeable aircraft, the airframe, wing and vertical fin and rudder of the empennage were the same. Where the Army and Navy still parted company was in the official designation of the powerplant, but here again the differences had been narrowed down until they were marginal, between the former's Pratt and Whitney R-1340-49 radial and the Navy's tweaked R-1340-38 from the same company, which both developed 600hp.

They were designated by NAA as the AT-6A-NA and the SNJ-3, respectively. Both could accommodate a single fixed forward-firing, synchronized 0.30-calibre machine gun mounted in the starboard upper cowl and a flexible mounted rear-firing machine gun of the same calibre in the rear cockpit. Many of these were used for air-to-air gunnery training and for this a special 360 degree rotating seat was fitted. The NAA and service serials were as shown in the table below.

NA-77: Manufacturers and service serials

Batch qty	*NAA serial*	*Service serial*
175	77-4107 to 77-4282	AC 41-149 to AC 41-323
10	77-4283 to 77-4292	BuNo 6755 to BuNo 6764
20	77-4293 to 77-4312	AC 41-324 to AC 41-343
10	77-4313 to 77-4322	BuNo 6765 to BuNo 6774
30	77-4323 to 77-4352	AC 41-344 to AC 41-373
10	77-4353 to 43-4362	BuNo 6775 to BuNo 6784
20	77-4363 to 77-4382	AC 41-374 to AC 41-393
10	77-4383 to 77-4392	BuNo 6785 to BuNo 6794
30	77-4393 to 77-4422	AC 41-394 to AC 41-423
10	77-4423 to 77-4432	BuNo 6795 to BuNo 6804
20	77-4433 to 77-4452	AC 41-424 to AC 41-443
10	77-4453 to 77-4462	BuNo 6805 to BuNo 6814
30	77-4463 to 77-4492	AC 41-444 to AC 41-473
10	77-4493 to 77-4502	BuNo 6815 to BuNo 6824
30	77-4503 to 77-4532	AC 41-474 to AC 41-503
10	77-4533 to 77-4542	BuNo 6825 to BuNo 6834
40	77-4543 to 77-4582	AC 41-504 to AC 41-543
10	77-4583 to 77-4592	BuNo 6835 to BuNo 6844
40	77-4593 to 77-4632	AC 41-544 to AC 41-583
10	77-4633 to 77-4642	BuNo 6845 to BuNo 6854
40	77-4643 to 77-4682	AC 41-584 to AC 41-623
10	77-4683 to 77-4692	BuNo 6855 to BuNo 6864
30	77-4693 to 77-4722	AC 41-624 to AC 41-653
10	77-4723 to 77-4732	BuNo 6865 to BuNo 6874
12	77-4733 to 77-4744	AC 41-654 to AC 41-665

The NA-77 was a great advance in integration between the USAAC as the AT-6A, and USN as the SNJ-3. Here, USAAC AT-6A No 1568 and a sister are seen over Napier Field, Alabama in March 1942. Ray C. Sturtivent

A close formation of NA-77s is pictured here over Napier Field, Alabama in March 1942, with a wide range of serial identifications. Ray C. Sturtivent

Coping with the New Order

This 'large and vital trainer program' which followed the President's National Defence message to Congress in May 1940, saw Kindleberger taking a risk, albeit with almost all the odds on his side. The company history put it this way:

> On the strength of verbal indications from Air Corps officers that a quantity of AT-6 combat trainers would be required when and if appropriations became available, the management issued a general order for the manufacture of the first group of these planes on June 28 1940, and work proceeded immediately. The board of directors of the corporation formally supported this action by the management in a resolution adopted at its meeting on July 12 1940. The supporting contract was executed by the Government on August 13 1940, calling for 637 planes of the AT-6A (later changed to 517 AT-6A type for the Air Corps and 120 SNJ-3 type for the US Navy). Thanks to the head start gained by the company by going ahead with production work on its own risk, the first airplane under this contract was delivered to the Air Corps on September 27 1940, just 45 days after the contract was signed.[6]

Consequent to the fact that the Navy aircraft were effectively being procured under an Army contract, all these aircraft were collected, initially flown and inspected by the Air Corps *before* being handed over to the Navy.

AT-6A

The NA suffix came about at this time to distinguish between those aircraft built at Inglewood in California and the new company plant opened in Texas. The Army took delivery of the first of the line, AC 41-149, on 27 September 1940. Tests revealed a continuing tendency to spin and yet another 'solution' was introduced by the strengthening of the vertical stabilizer.

(Above) **This is the very first AT-6A (NA-77, c/n 77-3958), serial number 41-149, which is carrying the logo of Wright Field during the extensive testing she undertook there after delivery on 27 September 1940. A total of 637 of this type were built and were capable of mounting one 0.30-calibre machine gun in the nose, one in the starboard and a third could be carried on a flexible mount to fire aft if required. The first of the series to be built at Dallas, they were christened the 'Texan' but the name never really caught on among service personnel.** National Archives, Washington DC

The US Navy's version of the NA-77 became the SNJ-3 but was in most respects identical to the AT-6A, save for engine designation and essential anti-corrosion treatments against salt-laden air conditions. This is BuNo 6799 (s/n 77-4427) as first delivered. Ray C. Sturtivent

SNJ-3

The USAAC accepted the first of the batch, BuNo 6755, at Inglewood on 7 March 1941 and flew her to NAS Anacostia for the usual trials. The shorter centre wing section reduced the overall span to 42ft 2in (12.85m). The two extra 55.2 US-gallon removable fuel tanks increased endurance, and provision was made for a single fixed forward-firing 0.30-calibre machine gun and a flexible mounted rearward-firing 0.30-calibre machine gun. The rear cockpit canopy hood was re-designed to fold forward automatically when the rear sliding hatch was opened and an instrument hood could be fitted over the rear seat. The fuel selector was internally mounted on the SNJ-3 and some revision of the instrument panel followed. A retrograde step was the fitting of a steerable tailwheel. Provision was also made for the carrying of an aerial camera in the after fuselage behind the rear cockpit seat with camera-bay doors and a viewfinder.

Trials at Anacostia revealed a slight fall in performance from the SNJ-1 and SNJ-2, with a top speed of only 206.5mph (332.3km/h) being attained at 6,000ft (1,830m) and a lower service ceiling. The changes in the rudder, and influence on the wing and tail incidence angles, produced problems not encountered in the earlier models, with complaints about the poor lateral stability and directional stability, while the flight testers strongly recommended replacing the tailwheel with a lockable one. They also requested that the aileron trim tabs be controllable from the pilot's position. This latter came under the desirable-contractor's responsibility (DC) heading and, like the watertight integrity, this was never done by NAA who just ignored it, as the production lines at Inglewood and Dallas were turning out identical machines for both Navy and Air Force and this would have complicated matters and slowed things down.

Many were allocated as instrument trainers in Florida on completion. Some fifty-seven of these aircraft were modified at NAS Pensacola, Florida, by fitting standard tail-hooks for carrier deck landings or simulations and they were given the suffix '-C'. The first SNJ from the line, BuNo 6775, was actually accepted by the Air Corps on behalf of the Navy and made her debut flight in March 1942.

CHAPTER FOUR

Enter the Texan

North American Aviation was now faced with the dramatic fact that in a few short years they had completely outgrown the 'new' Inglewood plant. There was no choice but to open a completely new plant elsewhere in order to cope with the every increasing order book. Yet more orders flooded in during the autumn of 1940 after the dramatic events in Europe brought home to more and more Americans the fact that peril was looming.

By March 1941, the Inglewood plant has exceeded the 1,000 quantity mark for Harvards for the British and Commonwealth forces, and this in itself was a tribute to the workers there, for it was an all-time record for a single model. But, as the company history recorded:

> Although identified as a single model, these were not 1,000 identical planes, however. Actually there were 2,500 drawing changes made after the first Harvard was produced, and among the 1,000 combat trainers there were actually more than 25 different models, each varying from the other in some major or minor detail of construction.[1]

Selection of Dallas for New Plant

By the summer of 1940 it was clearly evident that even a planned expansion of Inglewood to a million square feet of floor area would not be sufficient to meet the future requirements of both domestic and overseas needs for advanced trainers. There was no more room at Los Angeles and, with so many other aviation companies in the region, the beginnings of a man-power shortage. North American were therefore forced to look much further afield, and finally their eyes rested on a very desirable site in a hitherto untapped human resource area. The site selected was adjacent to an Army Reserve strip, Hensley Field close to the city of Dallas in Texas.

That the choice was a prime one was not in doubt, for rival manufacturer Consolidated Aircraft Corporation was hot for the same location to build the B-24 Liberator heavy bomber. The Air Corps had to decide on which contender would be awarded the prize and they chose North American, mainly because the need for training aircraft was pressing and immediate, while the B-24 programme was, at that stage, still a long-term one.

The plant itself was to be built with Defense Plant Corporation money, and the decision was duly announced on 17 August 1940. It was an appropriate choice for there were a number of major Air Corps training bases in Texas from which the bulk of the trainers had already been operating for some time. New training airfields were also under construction there.

Little time was wasted in getting things underway. Following the awarding of the general contract for construction on 13 November, the first steel uprights were erected on 2 December, nine days after the concrete was poured into the forms. By 20 January 1941, North American was beginning to move key personnel into the still incomplete factory and actually commenced limited operations as early as 8 March.

> The record accomplishment was dramatically climaxed on April 7 1941, when the first three AT-6A advanced trainers were turned over to the Air Corps on the occasion of the plant dedication ceremony. This was just 120 days after construction had begun.

Aircraft built at Dallas carried the suffix -NT and, from its opening, advance trainer production was concentrated there. Following a decision by the Air Corps to allocate names to its new warplanes (in the British fashion), rather than just numbers, so that the men of the vastly expanded service could more easily familiarize themselves with their aircraft, a competition was held among the workers at the plant for a name for the AT-6. The name they came up with was destined to be as apt as it was immortal, the Texan!

NA-78

These aircraft were from the enormous batches ordered on 1 October 1940 for the USAAC and the USN under contract AC-15977. Under the original provisions, some 1,330 AT-6As were to be built for the Air Corps along with 150 additional SNJ-3s for the Navy. They were exactly identical to the AC-12969 contract machines but some 400 of them were later altered and were produced under the NA-84 charge number instead.

Both could carry the sparse two machine-gun armament, as before; there was no provision for any bomb racks.

AT-6A

The original order was reduced by reallocations to the Navy or by redesign to the AT-6B until only 1,032 were built as AT-6As. In early lend-lease days there was a need to equip Latin American nations with modern aircraft, for both political and good sound business reasons. Such supplies of modern aircraft emphasized the Monroe Doctrine feeling of the Western Hemisphere standing together, untainted by the catastrophe in Europe or the carnage in China. Moreover, opportunism beckoned, for with their British and German aircraft suppliers fully extended in their war efforts the field was largely left open for further United States dominance. Thus, by Presidential decree, three AT-6A-NTs were delivered to Bolivia in 1941,[2] where they served with the Cuerpo de Avidores Boliviano.

SNJ-3

The original order was increased by reallocations from the Army batch, and no less than 448 were finally produced. The fifty-five utilized in carrier deck-landing training and toting a tail-hook carried the suffix -C. Like all SNJs, these aircraft had their wing interiors coated with hot linseed oil and their airframes, nuts, bolts,

NA-78: Manufacturer's and service serials

Batch qty	NAA serial	Service serial
70	78-5932 to 78-6001	AC 41-666 to AC 41-735
10	78-6002 to 78-6011	BuNo 6875 to BuNo 6884
20	78-6012 to 78-6031	AC 41-736 to AC 41-755
10	78-6032 to 78-6041	BuNo 6885 to BuNo 6894
20	78-6042 to 78-6061	AC 41-756 to AC 41-775
10	78-6062 to 78-6071	BuNo 6895 to BuNo 6904
10	78-6072 to 78-6081	AC 41-776 to AC 41-785
10	78-6082 to 78-6091	AC 41-15824 to AC 41-15833
10	78-6092 to 78-6101	BuNo 6905 to BuNo 6914
20	78-6102 to 78-6121	AC 41-15834 to AC 41-15853
10	78-6122 to 78-6131	BuNo 6915 to BuNo 6924
30	78-6132 to 78-6161	AC 41-15854 to AC 41-15883
10	78-6162 to 78-6171	BuNo 6925 to BuNo 6934
30	78-6172 to 78-6201	AC 41-15884 to AC 41-15913
10	78-6202 to 78-6211	BuNo 6935 to BuNo 6944
40	78-6212 to 78-6251	AC 41-15914 to AC 41-15953
10	78-6252 to 78-6261	BuNo 6945 to BuNo 6954
40	78-6262 to 78-6301	AC 41-15954 to AC 41-15993
10	78-6302 to 78-6311	BuNo 6955 to BuNo 6964
50	78-6312 to 78-6361	AC 41-15994 to AC 41-16043
10	78-6362 to 78-6371	BuNo 6965 to BuNo 6974
50	78-6372 to 78-6421	AC 41-16044 to AC 41-16093
10	78-6422 to 78-6431	BuNo 6975 to BuNo 6984
25	78-6432 to 78-6456	AC 41-16094 to AC 41-16118
40	78-6457 to 78-6496	BuNo 6985 to BuNo 7024
110	78-6497 to 78-6606	AC 41-16119 to AC 41-16228
30	78-6607 to 78-6636	BuNo 01771 to BuNo 01800
145	78-6637 to 78-6781	AC 41-16259 to AC 41-16403
35	78-6782 to 78-6816	BuNo 01801 to BuNo 01835
19	78-6817 to 78-6835	AC 41-16439 to AC 41-16457
16	78-6836 to 78-6851	BuNo 01836 to BuNo 01851
105	78-6852 to 78-6956	AC 41-16474 to AC 41-16578
37	78-6957 to 78-6993	BuNo 01852 to BuNo 01888
38	78-6994 to 78-7031	AC 41-16616 to AC 41-16653
39	78-7032 to 78-7070	BuNo 01889 to BuNo 01927
86	78-7071 to 78-7156	AC 41-16693 to AC 41-16778
42	78-7157 to 78-7198	BuNo 01928 to BuNo 01969
58	78-7199 to 78-7256	AC 41-16821 to AC 41-16878
7	78-7257 to 78-7263	BuNo 10970 to BuNo 10976
38	78-7264 to 78-7301	BuNo 05435 to BuNo 05472
56	78-7302 to 78-7357	AC 41-16924 to AC 41-16979
54	78-7358 to 78-7411	BuNo 05473 to BuNo 05526

washers and rivets zinc chromated, to keep out the salt. Manufacturers and service serial allocations are given in the table above.

Three of these aircraft were assigned to Bolivia under lend-lease during the war. Some of those that survived the wholesale sell-offs at knock-down prices post-war were later re-designated as T-6A-NTs.

NA-79

Twenty-five machines were ordered for the US Navy on 2 June 1940, but under Army contract AC-12969, change number 7. Consequently they received the NAA charge number NA-79 out of chronological sequence. They were NA-66s more-or-less with the Wright R-1340-56 engine. They were designated repeat SNJ-2s.

SNJ-2

These twenty-five 'extras' had an increased wingspan of 42ft 7in (13m) compared to the SNJ-1 and were powered by the 600hp Pratt and Whitney R-1340-36 with a two-bladed propeller.

The first machine, BuNo 2548, was accepted by the Navy at Inglewood on 20 December 1940, and flight-tested at Anacostia from 5 January 1941, onward. As this aircraft was identical to the previous test machine from the first batch, the tests were brief and similar results were obtained. On this occasion, happily, the brakes worked satisfactorily.

NA-81

Ordered on 11 July 1940 for the RAF, these 125 aircraft were again repeats of the NA-66 type. They received the charge number NA-81 and the NAA serials 81-4008/4132, and went into service with both the RAF and the RCAF as Harvard IIs.

Harvard II

These 125 aircraft were produced in three batches as shown in the table below.

NA-84

Ordered on 6 December 1940 for the USAAC, the last 400 aircraft under the NA-78 order were completed instead as bombing and gunnery trainers and thus were assigned a new charge number, NA-84. They became the AT-6B. They were the first to receive the name 'Texan' but this never stuck and was hardly, if ever, used by those who flew the aircraft, who simply referred to her as 'The Six'.

AT-6B

Even the engine choice that had distinguished the AT-6A from the SNJ-3 went by the board with the AT-6B, for the Army adopted the Navy-preferred 600hp R-1340-AN-1 radial engine for these 400 machines.

The chief difference over the AT-6A, due to its intended role, was the mounting of additional armament: a single forward-firing 0.30-calibre machine gun was

NA-81: Service serials

Batch qty	NAA serial	Assigned	Service serial
20	81-4008 to 81-4027	RCAF	3014 to 3033
81	81-4028 to 81-4108	RCAF	3761 to 3841
24	81-4109 to 81-4132	RAF	BW 184 to BW 207

mounted in the starboard wing, while the forward-firing machine gun, of the same calibre, mounted in the starboard nose and synchronized to fire through the propeller arc, remained – as did the flexible-mounted 0.30-calibre machine gun in the after cabin. Further, there was provision for light under-wing bomb racks, which could carry a total of four 100lb (45kg) bombs, two under either wing. For gunnery training, the swivel seat of the AT-6A was made permanently rearward-facing and the rear canopy section could be moved to enable firing port or starboard, as well as astern. No dive brakes were fitted, which made them of less value to the Navy who much preferred this more accurate delivery of ordnance, while the Army, in the main, remained wedded to the low-level strafing type of attack, which was to prove so vulnerable.

The initial production NA-84 (41-17034) arrived at Wright Field for tests on 12 January 1942. Not all the aircraft ended up on the USAAF inventory, however, for, with their built-in capacity to act as light bombers, the AT-6B proved an attractive proposition to many nations below the Panama Canal. Thus, four early batch -Bs were assigned, by special decree, to Uruguay, while others were acquired by Brazil, Chile, Colombia, Ecuador, Peru and Venezuela – a total of fifty in all, as shown in the table.

AT-6B-NTs assigned to Latin American air forces

No.	Nation	Chief user
14	Brazil	Aviacao Exercito do Brasil/Forca Aerea Brasileira
15	Chile	Fuerza Aerea Nacional de Chile
4	Colombia	Fuerza Aerea Colombiana
4	Ecuador	Fuerza Aerea Ecuatoriana
9	Peru	Cuerpo de Aeronautica del Peru
4	Venezuela	Servicio Aereo Militar Venezolana

At least two of these aircraft were used as test-beds at Wright Field, serial number 41-17136 being converted to assess a mock-up of a retractable armoured pilot's hood, while serial number 41-17034 was assigned to the testing of laminated wood propeller blades. During the great disposals of the post-war years, the Swedish Flygvapnet acquired nine AT-6Bs from 1951 onward.

In 1979, at the end of their service, the Fuerza Aerea Ecuatoriana preserved three of their AT-6s, serials 20310, 43233 and 53233, as exhibits in the Museo Aereo de FA Ecuatoriana, Quito Air Base.

Similarly, the Fuerza Aerea Colombiana sold off her lend-lease AT-6s in 1990, but four were retained as museum exhibits and gate guards at that time (*see* table below).

Fuerza Aerea Colombiana preserved AT-6s

FAC No.	Location
FAC 720	Gate guard at Madrid-Barroblanca Air Base
FAC 772	Museo Aeronautico, Bogata, El Dorado
FAC 791	Gate guard Luis F. Pinto Air Base
FAC 798	Gate guard at Cali Air Base

One Aeronautica Militar Uruguaya machine, an AT-6D, serial number 366, 88-18228, 42-86447, was transferred from Peru, survived and is currently under restoration.

Although not usually credited with receiving any of the type, two AT-6As (76-6661, 41-16283 and serial number 797, 78-7228, 41-16850) turned up with a Fuerza Aerea Mexicana sale in 1963 and were bought for civilian usage, flying for a while as N65512 and N7055D.

NA-85

Ordered on 6 December 1940 for the USN, these 150 gunnery and bombing trainers, requisitioned for the US Navy by the Army, formed part of the total of 400 machines and were originally allocated a fresh charge number of NA-85. Because they were identical to the Army equivalent (AT-6B), NAA reverted them to the same charge number of NA-84. They were listed as SNJ-3 under NA-78.

NA-88

Four separate orders were placed with the Dallas plant on 10 April 1941 for the USAAF and USN as the American war expansion finally really got underway, big time. These orders were for 2,970 (AC-19192) and 2,604 (AC-29317), both for the US Army Air Force (USAAF) as it had now become, and these became the AT-6C. Of these totals, some 747 were assigned to the RAF and they became the Harvard II. They also ordered a further 2,400 (DA-8) and 1,357 (DA-2799) for the US Navy (USN), and these became the SNJ-4 and SNJ-5, respectively. Later, 630 offsets from the T-6Ds total were added to the SNJ-5 total. The serial allocations are given in the table below.

NA-88/AT-6D: Manufacturers and service serials

NAA serials	Batch allocation	Service serials
5371 to 5372	RAF	EX 847 to EX 848
5373 to 5412	USAAF	AC 42-44412 to AC 42-44451
5413 to 5462	US Navy	BuNos 51677 to 51726
5463 to 5482	RAF	EX 849 to EX 868
5483 to 5502	USAAF	AC 42-44452 to AC 42-44471
5503 to 5527	US Navy	BuNos 51727 to 51751
5528 to 5547	RAF	EX 869 to EX 888
5548 to 5593	USAAF	AC 42-44472 to AC 42-44517
5594 to 5643	US Navy	BuNos 51752 to 51801
5644 to 5663	RAF	EX 889 to EX 908
5664 to 5683	USAAF	AC 42-44518 to AC 42-44537
5684 to 5703	US Navy	BuNos 51802 to 51821
5704 to 5719	RAF	EX 900 to EX 924
5720 to 5787	USAAF	AC 42-44538 to AC 42-44605
5788 to 5812	US Navy	BuNos 51822 to 51846
5813 to 5832	USAAF	AC 42-44606 to AC 42-44625
5833 to 5857	US Navy	BuNos 51847 to 51871
5858 to 5877	RAF	EX 925 to EX 944
5878 to 5897	USAAF	AC 42-44626 to AC 42-44645
5898 to 5922	US Navy	BuNos 51872 to 51896
5923 to 5947	RAF	EX 945 to EX 969
5948 to 5987	USAAF	AC 42-44646 to AC 42-44685
5988 to 6037	US Navy	BuNos 51897 to 51946
6038 to 6057	RAF	EX 970 to EX 989
6058 to 6077	USAAF	AC 42-44686 to AC 42-44705
6078 to 6102	US Navy	BuNos 51947 to 51971
6103 to 6112	RAF	EX 990 to EX 999
6113 to 6127	RAF	EZ 100 to EZ 114
6128 to 6147	USAAF	AC 42-44706 to AC 42-44725
6148 to 6197	US Navy	BuNos 51972 to 52021
6198 to 6218	USAAF	AC 42-44726 to 42-44746
6219 to 6222	USAAF	AC 41-34123 to 41-34126
6223 to 6247	US Navy	BuNos 52022 to 52046
6248 to 6267	RAF	EZ 115 to EZ 134
6268 to 6287	USAAF	AC 41-34127 to 41-34146
6288 to 6290	US Navy	BuNos 52047 to 52049

(Top) **The NA-88 became the largest block of wartime Texans and resulted from four separate contracts, which included in the 9,331 total numbers for both the USAAF and the USN. The AT-6D (SNJ-5) had the 24-volt electrical system which replaced the earlier blocks AT-6C's (SNJ-4) 12-volt and some were constructed with wooden parts to avert an aluminium shortage that never, in fact, occurred. They were otherwise similar to the AT-6B. Provision was made to mount two forward-firing 0.30-calibre machine guns, one in the nose and one in the starboard wing, but few actually did so. This is 41-32505, one of the first block (AT-6C-NT) produced.**
National Archives, Washington DC

(Bottom) **Many NA-88s went via lend-lease straight to the RAF in South Africa or the Middle East. This machine is one of the few to carry the two forward-firing 0.30-calibre machine guns, one in the nose and one in the starboard wing. The nose-gun fairing, on the starboard side in front of the cockpit, can be clearly seen as can the trough through which it fired. This meant the radio antenna had to be offset to port.** National Archives, Washington DC

AT-6C

There were practically no alterations to the basic design in these aircraft from their immediate forebears. The initial aircraft (serial number 41-32073) was taken on charge on 12 February 1942, surviving to be among those sold to Turkey as late as March 1948. There was always the provision for them to be equipped as the AT-6B for gunnery and bombing trainers, but this was rarely applied in practice and they remained mainly in the AT mode for most of their lives. Where they were so converted, they shipped the usual rearward mounting 0.30-calibre machine gun, removeable cockpit canopy and a slot was cut in the upper rear fuselage to house the gun when not in use. After some 964 had been produced, the Army introduced some very minor alterations and modifications, allocating dash numbers -1, -5, -10 and so on, to signify these, but the Navy and the RAF did not bother with it.

There was, however, one significant change that affected many of these batches. In 1941, a serious shortage of aluminium was expected due to the huge mushrooming of demand brought on by the war; this worry was reinforced by the sinking of ships transporting it off the American coast by U-boats early in 1942. Consequently, the Army decided that some aircraft parts could revert back to wood (of which North America at that time had an abundant and totally secure source of supply), in order to eke out what aluminium there was and concentrate it in combat aircraft. As the company history recorded:

> Early in 1942 the company redesigned its AT-6 combat trainer to utilise plywood and low carbon steel in most structural assemblies in order to conserve on critical supplies of aluminium alloy. It was estimated that this program would save 623 tons of aluminium in each 1,000 North American trainers built. This was based on a saving of 1,246 pounds of aluminium alloy per plane.[3]

In the event the scare came to nothing but, nonetheless, this modification took place, thus forming distinct sub-types visually and structurally, as follows:

- 181 AT-6C-5s and 270 SNJ-4s, which were built with wooden horizontal stabilizers, control columns and floor panels (serials 41-33068/33072, 42-3884/4063 and BuNo 26869–27138, respectively).
- 443 AT-6C-10s, 640 AT-6D-15s and 1,040 SNJ-4s (serial numbers 42-4064/4243, 42-48772/49069, 42-43847/44411, BuNo 27139/27851 and BuNo 51350/51676), all of which were built with tails and entire rear fuselage sections, skins and bulkheads constructed of moulded three-ply mahogany plywood. Externally, aluminium dope was applied but the stringers still showed through, of course. Internally, solid spruce was used for all stringers, stiffeners, bulkhead flanges and longerons. In places where extra strength was desirable, Maple Compreswood was spliced to the spruce members. This wood substitution, it was estimated, saved about 200lb (90kg) of aluminium per aircraft, but it increased the total weight of each aircraft and accordingly reduced performance marginally.

Other experiments were carried out in conjunction with this aluminium saving exercise with other materials, including laminated plastic rear sections, which were manufactured by the Virginia Lincoln Corporation for the AMC and trialled on three aircraft: serial number 40-2080 (an AT-6), serial number 41-149 (AT-6A) and serial number 41-32113 (an AT-6C)

In later years, when the crisis did not materialize, many of the above aircraft were upgraded and aluminium replaced the wood, but this was not universal.

AT-6C: Dash numbers and service serials

Batch qty	*Dash number*	*Service serial*
963	AT-6C-NT	AC 41-32073 to AC 41-33035
759	AT-6C-1-NT	AC 41-33036 to AC 41-33794
25	AT-6C-5-NT	AC 41-33795 to AC 41-33819
160	AT-6C-5-NT	AC 42-3884 to AC 42-4043
200	AT-6C-10-NT	AC 42-4044 to AC 42-4243
223	AT-6C-10-NT	AC 42-43847 to AC 42-44069
342	AT-6C-15-NT	AC 42-44070 to AC 42-44411
298	AT-6C-15-NT	AC 42-48772 to AC 42-49069

In addition to wooden after-fuselage sections this particular AT-6C (serial 40-2080) was one of three experimentally fitted with plastic rear section panels (the darker shaded panels aft the cockpit) by the Virginia Lincoln Corporation in January 1943. National Archives, Washington, DC

This AT-6C-1-NT (Serial 41-32357, coded B237), part of the second block, is seen toting an interesting paint job while serving with the 6 BFTS at Ponca City in 1943. Ray C. Sturtivent

Lend-Lease to Latin America

As with the earlier -B, the AT-6C proved a popular aircraft south of the border, where they were known as T-*seis* in Bolivia, Brazil, Chile, Colombia, Cuba, Dominican Republic, Ecuador, Guatemala, Haiti, Mexico, Nicaragua, Paraguay, El Salvador, Venezuela, and under lend-lease even in pro-German countries like Chile.

AT-6Cs assigned to Latin American air forces

No.	*Dash number*	*Chief user*
9	AT-6C-NT	Cuerpo de Avidores Boliviano
20	AT-6C-NT	Aviacao Exercito do Brasil/ Forca Aerea Brasileira
5	AT-6C-5-NT	Aviacao Exercito do Brasil/ Forca Aerea Brasileira
10	AT-6C-10-NT	Aviacao Exercito do Brasil/ Forca Aerea Brasileira
36	AT-6C-15-NT	Aviacao Exercito do Brasil/ Forca Aerea Brasileira
5	AT-6C-10-NT	Fuerza Aerea Nacional de Chile
10	AT-6C-15-NT	Fuerza Aerea Nacional de Chile
2	AT-6C-NT	Fuerza Aerea Colombiana
2	AT-6C-10-NT	Fuerza Aerea Colombiana
4	AT-6C-15-NT	Fuerza Aerea Colombiana
6	AT-6C-NT	Cuerpo Aerea Ejercito de Cuba
3	AT-6C-10-NT	Cuerpo Aerea Ejercito de Cuba
3	AT-6C-15-NT	Cuerpo de Aviacion Dominican Republic
3	AT-6C-NT	Fuerza Aerea Ecuatoriana
3	AT-6C-15-NT	Fuerza Aerea Ecuatoriana
3	AT-6C-15-NT	Cuerpo de Aeronautica Militar Guatemalteca
2	AT-6C-15-NT	Corps D'Aviation D'Haiti
31	AT-6C-NT	Fuerza Aerea Mexicana
6	AT-6C-5-NT	Fuerza Aerea Mexicana
12	AT-6C-15	Fuerza Aerea Mexicana
3	AT-6C-15-NT	Fuerza Aerea de la Guardia Nacional de Nicaragua
3	AT-6C-NT	Fuerza Aerea Nacional del Paraguay
3	AT6C-NT	Aviacion Militar Salvadorena
5	AT-6C-NT	Servicio Aereo Militar Venezolana
5	AT-6C-15-NT	Servicio Aereo Militar Venezolana

Post-war the AT-6C became the T-6C, and this interesting duo, seen in 1952, show some of the differences, with the USAF aircraft (which was on loan to the Canadian Air Force) coded TA-613, mounting the new smaller antenna aft the cockpit but with the extended exhaust muffler of the British/Canada Harvard, while her sister in RCAF markings (DA-J) carries the radio compass loop in the 'football' in the same position. Ray C. Sturtivent

Two former Fuerza Aerea Mexicana machines, FAM serial 791, 88-12150, 42-4071 and FAM serial number 709, 88-12151, 42-4072 were sold out to the civil register and flew for a while as N7055H and N7054X, respectively.

SNJ-4

These 2,400 aircraft became the first US Navy trainers to have provision for the 0.30-calibre machine gun as built, and also under-wing bomb racks, although these had limited value to the Navy for the reasons already pointed out. Aside from an extra forward-firing, starboard wing-mounted 0.30-calibre machine gun, port wing-mounted camera gun and light bomb racks the -4 was virtually a repeat. Nonetheless, the usual trials were required at NAS Anacostia and the first of the batch, BuNo 05527, arrived there on 7 June 1942. Trials were completed by 20 July, and were generally satisfactory; requirements were for an automatic carburettor, strengthening of the wooden footrests and another plea for the cockpit control of the aileron trim, which NAA once more turned a blind eye to.

Most of the -4s went to the rapidly-expanding Navy schools at Corpus Christi, Texas, which included Beeville, Cabiness, Cuddihy, Kingsville (fighter and dive bomber training), Rodd and Waldron (torpedo bomber training) fields. Some eighty-five were subsequently modified to carry tail-hooks for carrier deck landings and these the Navy designated as the SNJ-4C.

SNJ-4: Dash numbers and service serials

Qty	*Service serial*	*Composition*
148	BuNo 05527 to BuNo 05674	All-metal
500	BuNo 09817 to BuNo 10316	All-metal
442	BuNo 26427 to BuNo 26868	All-metal
270	BuNo 26869 to BuNo 27138	Wood stabilizers
713	BuNo 27139 to BuNo 27851	Wood rear sections
327	BuNo 51350 to BuNo 51676	Wood stabilizers and rear sections

US Marine Corps SNJs

It must always be remembered that Navy SNJs were also allocated to the US Marine Corps, whose aviators were in the front line all through the Pacific War flying from island air strips at Wake, Midway and in the Solomon's, up through the Philippines and onward. They flew every type and variety of SNJ and often their J-birds were utilized close to the action, where they carried out a wide variety of secondary duties, much like the RAAF Wirraways in the same area, working as artillery spotters, message droppers, liaison aircraft, aerial photographers, passenger aircraft and wireless trainer planes.

The First Marine Air Wing at Noumea, New Caledonia, fed men and machines into the murderous Guadalcanal and Solomon Islands' campaigns from 1942 onward. Their VMD-154 had six SNJ-4s on establishment (BuNo 05668, BuNo 09863, BuNo 09865, BuNo 09866, BuNo 09873 and BuNo 26507) working out of the Magenta airstrip. They conducted aerial photographic surveys of all the islands in the group vertically from 10,000ft (3,000m) and obliquely at 2,000ft (610m) using a 12in (9.5cm) K-17 camera. This included several islands held by the pro-Axis Vichy-French forces, which were considered potentially dangerous. This unit later transferred to Espirito Santo in the New Hebrides group and worked out of Turtle Bay airstrip in the same role.

Disposals

A former Fuerza Aerea Nacional del Paraguay aircraft (88-13067, BuNo 27611), was sold out to the civil register and flew as N7437C.

Harvard II

Those 747 AT-6Cs and AT-6C-5s allocated to the RAF under lend-lease became Harvard IIA (and later, when the RAF changed its designations from Roman to Arabic as Harvard 2A) and were still allocated USAAF serials, although, naturally, the RAF allocated its own serials. A total of 284 had the wooden fuselages and stabilizers fitted. The change over to the new style of designations also incorporated the new mission identity lettering before the Mark, i.e. those converted as Target Tugs were prefixed TT, those that remained as Trainers were prefixed T and so on.

The SNJ-4 (coded J4N) was the US Navy equivalent to the AT-6C from the earlier NA-88 blocks.
Pima Air & Space Museum, Tucson

US Navy allocation included the US Marine Corps aircraft, like this lovingly restored specimen, the 'War Dog'. John A. Collvers

AT-6D

Although still produced under the North American charge number NA-88, this aircraft was designated AT-6D because it switched from the long-established 12-volt electrical system to the 24-volt system. Deliveries of this variant commenced during the summer of 1943. Of a grand total of 3,958 AT-6Ds built at Dallas, some 440 had the wooden rear assemblies, but the rest reverted to all aluminium. The -Ds did not replace the -Cs but continued in production side-by-side at the Dallas plant.

AT-6D: Dash numbers and service serials

Batch qty	Dash number	Service serial
553	AT-6D-NT	AC41-33820 to AC 41-34372
335	AT-6D-1-NT	AC 42-44412 to AC 44-44746
2,400	AT-6D-NT	AC 42-84163 to AC 42-86562

Lend-lease saw deliveries to Great Britain while, as before, many Latin American nations received batches of the AT-6D: Bolivia, Chile, Colombia, Dominican Republic, Ecuador, Mexico, Peru, El Salvador, Uruguay and Venezuela, with deliveries made up as shown in the table.

AT-6Ds assigned to Latin American air forces

No.	Dash number	Chief user
15	AT-6D-NT	Cuerpo de Avidores Boliviano
25	AT-6D-NT	Aviacao Exercito do Brasil/ Forca Aerea Brasileira
20	AT-6D-1-NT	Aviacao Exercito do Brasil/ Forca Aerea Brasileira
32	AT-6D-NT	Fuerza Aerea Nacional de Chile
38	AT-6D-NT	Fuerza Aerea Colombiana
6	AT-6D-1-NT	Fuerza Aerea Colombiana
3	AT-6D-1-NT	Cuerpo de Aviacion Dominican Republic
3	AT-6D-NT	Fuerza Aerea Ecuatoriana
6	AT-6D-1-NT	Fuerza Aerea Ecuatoriana
10	AT-6D-NT	Fuerza Aerea Mexicana
20	AT-6D-1-NT	Fuerza Aerea Mexicana
25	AT-6D-NT	Cuerpo de Aeronautica del Peru
3	AT-6D-1-NT	Aviacion Militar Salvadorena
6	AT-6D-1-NT	Aeronautica Militar Uruguaya
5	AT-6D-NT	Servicio Aereo Militar Venezolana

One former Fuerza Aerea Mexicana aircraft (FAM serial 812, 88-15212, 42-44728), later flew with civilian register N7054R for a time; a second (serial number 781, 88-17575, 42-856794), flew as N991GM; while yet another is reportedly under restoration in Texas. An AT-6 of the Aeronautica Militar Uruguaya (serial number 336) also later flew as civilian register N8160Y.

American claims that, in July 1942, a Mexican-based unit of T-6s, 'scored two direct hits on a German submarine off the coast of Tampico', and that, 'the sub is believed to have sunk'[4], are continually repeated. The only U-boat sinking that might qualify for this claim is the *U-166* sunk on 1 August 1942 by aircraft of USAAC Squadron 212 in the Gulf of Mexico.

SNJ-5

These followed the same route as the AT-6D, but with a 24-volt electrical system replacing the 12-volt system. Of a total of 1,987 built, 276 had the wooden rear assemblies before reverting to all-aluminium construction. They mounted two fixed forward-firing 0.30-calibre machine guns, one over the starboard cowl and one dorsal, and a single rear-firing 0.30-calibre machine gun firing aft on a flexible mounting.

The trial aircraft, BuNo 51847, arrived at the new Navy test centre of Patuxent River, Maryland, on 5 October 1943 and testing continued until 20 November 1943. Radio, electrical and armament testing followed, the latter being delayed five weeks as the Browning machine guns had not been installed by NAA when the aircraft left their plant! The guns were finally installed as late as 27 March 1944, and trials started three days later. Apart from some stoppages during prolonged firings, these weapons passed muster, but problems were found when it came to the simulated dive bombing trials.

The Navy relied heavily on the dive bomber, it was its main war-winning asset and destroyed more enemy shipping than any other arm. It was hoped that the new J-Bird would prove suitable for training young pilots in this important arm. Experienced SNJ men might have told them differently. Even before the aircraft got off the ground events proved ominous. The SNJ-5 was fitted with an R-1502 bomb rack under each wing, with five stations on each. This gave a total capacity of either ten M-41 20lb bombs or ten M-5 50lb bombs. Stations two and four could be over-fitted with shackles capable of carrying six fragmentation and two 100lb bombs, or ten 20lb or 30lb fragmentation bombs, or two fragmentation and four 100lb bombs or four 100lb bombs. The two-man bombing team found it took some sixty man-hours to install the various bomb racks, cables and release handles on the -5, which was far too long. More importantly, the 100lb bombs tended to hang up.

The first dive bombing of the bomb rack took place on 6 April 1944, and it proved to be the last! The 'red-line' for the -5 was 250mph (400km/h) but, not being equipped with drive brakes of any kind at all, when the pilot went into what was considered a 'modest' 60-degree dive (and combat pilots usually went in at 70 degrees or more) from a height of 4,000ft (1,200m) the plane took over! Speed rapidly built up to 280mph (450km/h) and the result was conclusive. The pull out was made without the aircraft disintegrating, but the test team declined to carry out the experiment a second time – SNJ was never going to be a dive bomber, not even a *pretend* dive bomber. (Strangely enough, at the very same time, the Wirraway was being produced, with dive-brakes, to perform exactly that task, without any adverse effects being recorded by the RAAF, and the Fleet Air Arm Training School at Kingston Ontario was carrying out dive bombing as a regular part of their itinerary.)

Apart from this hair-raising episode, for which the -5 could hardly be blamed, no major problems were encountered and tests were completed on 26 May. There were no major Bureau demands – only the forlorn plea for the aileron tab controls to be cockpit-controlled went out, yet again in vain. NAA continued to deliver them with steerable tailwheel too and it was not until after the war that the Navy got their way and they were changed to the lockable type.

Again the SNJ-5 did not *replace* the SNJ-4 but continued in simultaneous construction with it. Some 276 SNJ-5s were subject to the wooden weight-saving exercise (serials BuNo 43638/43850, BuNo 34031/44037, BuNo 52047/52049 and BuNo 84819/81871). Eight received tail-hooks for carrier deck trials and became SNJ-5Cs. They were popular in the service. The US Navy's most decorated flyer, Lieutenant E. C. Dickinson, stated that the SNJ was, '...the best scout trainer in the world'.

SNJ-5: Original service serials

Batch qty	*Service serial*
400	BuNo 43638 to BuNo 44037
373	BuNo 51677 to BuNo 52049
905	BuNo 84189 to BuNo 85093
309	BuNo 90582 to BuNo 90890

One of these aircraft, which later saw service with the Fuerza Aerea Mexicana (serial number 718, 88-16756, BuNo 84895), flew at various periods under civilian registers, N3189G and N75055C, and was restored once more in 1993.

SNJ-5B

This designation appears in some accounts as a modified Navy requirement, but remains (at the time of writing) a bit of a mystery. No such designating suffix appears in the official serial number lists. Previously the 'B' suffix had been applied by the US Navy to three different modifications:

- special armament;
- special modification (seaplane, target tug, courier); and
- modified to British standards (and this remains the most likely as Britain *did* receive some as Harvard IIIs).

Otherwise none of these applications would seem to obviously apply in this case, and the armament remained the same as for the earlier NA-88s.

Harvard III

Those 529 AT-6Ds allocated to the RAF under lend-lease were similarly allocated USAAF serial blocks and kept on the books as -Ds despite subsequent RAF dispersals.

NA-119

An order placed on 10 January 1944 called for eighty-one Brazilian equivalents to the USAAF aircraft as AT-6Ds; these received the distinguishing charge number NA-110 and were produced as AT-6Ds, and they were allocated the NAA serial numbers 119-40086/40166, inclusive. Under a licence agreement with the Construcoes Aeronauticas SA, eighty-one[5] were shipped out as kits of subassemblies. Another ten aircraft were dispatched from Dallas as partly-assembled airframes, while yet a third batch was shipped as completed airframes partially subassembled. This was the first instance of NAA being given Army Air Force contracts for the fabrication and partial assembly of T-aircraft parts. Whatever form the crated aircraft took, they somehow had to be painstakingly assembled by the Brazilians, a process that took a long time and most were not ready for use until post-war.

AT-6D

The Forca Aerea Brasileira actually took delivery of only forty-five aircraft, these being twenty-five AT-6D-NTs and twenty

AT-6D-1-NTs. They were allocated military serial numbers in two batches, FAB 1387/1394, inclusive, and in the range FAB 1531/1592. Many had extremely long careers, thirty years, and when the survivors later were concentrated at Lagoa Santa base they were re-designated as T-6 1LSs, although their serials remained the same.

NA-121

The final wartime orders were placed on 11 February 1944 and were originally for 2,175 AT-6Ds for the USAAF. They received the charge number NA-121. Yet a further order for 1,200 AT-6Ds under charge number NA-128, placed on 1 June 1944, was subsequently cancelled. They were identical to the earlier models at this stage. With the end of hostilities in sight, 417 NA-121s were cancelled outright, only 589 being completed as AT-6Ds. A further 211 were completed for the US Navy as the SNJ-5, while yet another 545 were re-designated to the Army as AT-6F and 411 as the Navy SNJ-6.

NAA serial number allocations were 121-41567/42366 for the AT-6Ds, and 121-42367/43322 for the AT-6Fs.

AT-6F

Ultimately, 545 were completed under the NA-121 charge number. There were several changes over the previous mark – there being no question of using any of these aircraft as gunnery or bomber trainers, the rear-firing flexible-mounted 0.30-calibre machine gun was abolished and the rear seat was fixed facing forward under a redesigned clear bubble, non-movable canopy. No bomb rack provision was made at all and even the two fixed, forward-firing 0.30-calibre machine guns were omitted.

Visually they were the first of the series to be fitted with large propeller spinners. In place of under-wing bomb racks the -6F had a single 20 US gallon finned drop tank, which was carried on sway braces under the main fuselage centre-line with twin fuel lines leading up to the forward edge of the wheel wells. Wright Field had 44-81661 on its charge to experiment with various designs of such tanks for a while. Lend-lease supplies included to the Soviet Union, with the 7th Ferry Squadron flying numbers up via Ladd Field, Alaska for hand-over to Soviet pilots for transfer to Siberia. At the other end of the scale, Cuba received three AT-6F-NTs, also under lend-lease.

The NA-121s received Army serial numbers 44-80845/81644 for the AT-6D-NTs and 44-81645/82600 for the AT-6F-NTs, 411 of which were finally completed as SNJ-6s.

ET-6F

This was a unique aircraft, the only one to be so designated. She was the former serial number 44-81661 and was converted to the specialist role of cross-wind landing-gear installation tests on 1 December 1950.

SNJ-6s

Altogether, 411 were completed under the NA-121 charge number. None, or very few, were ever fitted with tail-hooks. They were not fitted with bomb racks (probably due to the experience at Anacostia with the SNJ-5), nor did they have the wing gun, rear gun or wing or vertical camera guns fitted. The redundant tail gunner's hood was replaced with a full-vision rear hood and a baggage compartment fitted in the after fuselage, while a centreline 20 US gallon drop tank could be fitted. The outer-wing panel was strengthened. They received the BuNos 111949/112359. Some 164 extra of this type were allocated BuNos 112360/112523 but were subsequently cancelled at the end of the war.

Harvard IIB

The licence arrangements with Australia and Brazil were extended with excellent results across the border to Canada. Not only was the RAF establishing many of their Harvard training schools under the Commonwealth Air Training Scheme (CATS) there but the RCAF was itself mushrooming. It was a logical arrangement then, and one that saw a large number of aircraft built to RAF requirements from scratch in brand-new plants.

The chosen power-plant was the Pratt and Whitney R-1340-AN-1 Wasp radial. Armament comprised just one fixed forward-firing 0.303 Browning machine gun carried in the starboard wing. Light E. M. bomb carriers could be emplaced underneath either wing for 110lb bombs.

In fact the Canadian company of Noorduyn Aviation Ltd, which was based in Montreal, Quebec, had purchased a licence for the BC-1 as long ago as 1938, but it was to take the impetus of the defeats of 1940 and the dynamic thrust of the new Minister for Aircraft Production, Lord Beaverbrook, himself a Canadian with great faith in his country's ability, to provide such GP training aircraft, that brought about the main orders.

Three large orders followed each other in quick succession:

- 210 Harvard IIBs for the RCAF in January 1940;
- 1,800 Harvard IIBs ordered by the US Government under lend-lease, 300 of which (serials 43-34615/34914) were later cancelled; of these, 157 (serials 43-34615/34771) were later re-instated and received RAF serials FX 198/354, inclusive;
- 900 Harvard IIBs for the RAF ordered by the US Government under lend-lease.

For a potential total of 2,910 aircraft, of which 2,757 were eventually delivered to the RCAF, RAF and the USAAF, the US Government orders were given the purely paperwork designation of AT-16. Such a vast total requirement swamped Noorduyn's existing facilities and, like North American Aviation south of the border, they had to both extend it and open up a whole new custom-built plant at Longue Pointe, also in Quebec.

The RAF specifications followed the normal practice, with a shorter radio mast, extended exhaust shrouds for cockpit heating, British instrumentation and armaments, and other modifications, like the circular grip of the control column rather than the US-type pistol grips. They were finished in bright yellow paint overall. Otherwise they equated to the NAA BC-1A/AT-6 design. They received the Noorduyn serials 14-1/800, inclusive and 14A-801/1800, inclusive, respectively.

Although similar experiments were conducted by the Canadian company with regard to substitution of aluminium, none of their production aircraft featured any such materials. A solitary experimental prototype was built as a bombing and aerial gunnery trainer type, with a belly-blister for a prone bomb aimer, but nothing came of this initiative.

Noorduyn-produced Harvard IIB serials

Batch qty	USAAF serials	Operator	Serials
100	–	RCAF	3034 to 3133
110	–	RCAF	3234 to 3343
300	43-34615 to 43-34914	RAF	FX 198 to FX 497
658	–	RAF	KF 100 to KF 757
142	Cancelled	RAF	KF 758 to KF 900
99	–	RAF	KF 901 to KF 999
210	Cancelled	RAF	KG 100 to KG 309
500	42-464 to 42-963	RAF	FE 267 to FE 766
233	42-12254 to 42-12486	RAF	FE 767 to FE 999
67	42-12487 to 42-12553	RAF	FH 100 to FH 166
339	43-12502 to 43-12840	RAF	FS 661 to FS 999
361	43-12841 to 43-13201	RAF	FT 100 to FT 460

Ex-RCN Harvard II and IIB survivors

Type	RCAF serial	C/n	Civil registration
Harvard IIB	3039	07 6	C-FNDS
Harvard IIB	3096	07 62	C-FMGO
Harvard II	3134	75-3048	N9893Z
Harvard II	3165	75-3439	N3231H
Harvard II	3167	75-3441	N999NS
Harvard II	3188	75-3465	CF-MWJ
Harvard II	3191	75-3465	N3191G
Harvard IIB	3275	07 144	C-FGME
Harvard IIB	3276	07 145	–
Harvard IIB	3297	07 166	–
Harvard IIB	3318	07 184	N92019
Harvard IIB	3324	07 191	N3653G

The first aircraft arrived at Wright Field, Ohio from the Montreal plant on 11 May 1942, where she remained until scrapped in 1946. The rest followed to both Canadian and British Training units in Canada itself, until the end of the Empire Air Training Scheme at the end of 1943. Others were shipped direct to RAF training squadrons in both the United Kingdom and India (500 plus), seventeen being lost at sea *en route*. More than 100 reverted to the USAAF and were scrapped post-war but the majority of RAF survivors were sold to a huge variety of customers world-wide by diverse means. Dealers like the Charles Babb Company made wholesale purchases from the Canadian War Assets Corporation of 478 Harvards in September 1947. Of these, 415 had been refurbished and re-sold within the year, at a considerable profit, to states like Nationalist China (200), Sweden (139), Holland (75), Switzerland (40), and the Dutch East Indies (20), as well as civilian operators.

Two went into museums: RCAF serial 3096 to the Reynold Aviation Museum, Wetaskiwin, Alberta, Canada; and RCAF serial 3191 to the Seminole Air Center, Seminole, Oklahoma, USA.

A number of both the Harvard II and the Harvard IIB were transferred from the RCAF to the Royal Canadian Navy (RCN). Several of these survived the war and were sold out to civil registry later. A few still fly today (*see* table above right).

Ranger-Engined Texan: XAT-6E

Before the war, the Fairchild Company had promoted the merits of the in-line engine to the US services, both of them long and addictively wedded to the radial. European manufacturers had largely gone this route for the new generation of monoplane fighter aircraft for a variety of

The famous experimental Ranger-engined aircraft, the only official in-line engine 'Six' (although there was also a post-war civilian copy produced which puzzled many!). Converted to mount the Ranger air-cooled inverted V, 12-cylinder SGV-770-D4 engine which developed 575hp, this machine was a standard AT-6D (serial 42-84241) which became the XAT-6E. She actually had a best speed of 231mph (372km/h) at 22,000ft (6,700m) but such a requirement was hardly a necessity nor did it justify the disruption to the existing NAA production lines which were churning out thousand upon thousand of quite adequate -Cs and -Ds at this stage of the war. And so the concept died, although the aircraft did enjoy a second fleeting moment of fame in the post-war air races. National Archives, Washington DC

reasons. The in-line engine with its balanced crankshaft–connection rod configuration offered smoother running with resulting diminished vibration, which reduced wear-and-tear on both airframe and aircrew alike. An added factor was that, as the propshaft for the in-line was the highest physical point of the engine, a bigger diameter propeller could be carried, which theoretically could provide better pulling power. If the same diameter propeller was fitted, then the advantage was that the aircraft would require a shorter undercarriage with its equivalent simplicity and weight reduction. From the pilot's point of view, and this applied in particular to the tyro learning the trade, the view ahead over the T-6s great radial would be done away with and much better visibility for landings and take-offs presented.

With the vast expansion of the military air arms there were fears that the supply of the Pratt and Whitney radial might not be able to keep up with demand. Also, with the success of such aircraft as the British Supermarine Spitfire and Hawker Hurricane on the one hand and the German Messerschmitt Bf 109 on the other, and with the similar adoption in the US of the Curtiss P-39, Curtiss P-40 and North American P-51 fighter aircraft, the USAAC finally agreed to have a provisional look at such an arrangement and commissioned Fairchild to produce a prototype. They took a standard AT-6D (serial number 42-84241) and fitted her with an in-line engine. The nose was extended by 2ft (0.6m) to give an overall length of 31ft (9m), and the aircraft was completely rebuilt forward of the fire wall; this modification required compensatory balancing aft. This machine was to present a unique profile and became the XAT-6E.[6]

The conversion was done at the Fairchild Hagerstown plant in Maryland and the selected power-plant for the experiment was the Ranger air-cooled inverted V 12-cylinder SGV-770-D4 in-line engine, which developed 575hp. The two rows of cylinders were in a 60-degree inverted V. The engine had a 770in^3 (12,620cm^3) displacement. This engine was supercharged for high-altitude flying and drove a two-bladed propeller, which had a prominent spinner fitted. However, the Ranger only rated 520hp for take-off, which was 80hp less than the Pratt and Whitney R-1340.

The transformation was completed at Hagerstown in 1944 and, after initial flights from the Fairchild Company airfield, was transferred to Elgin Army Air Force Base in Florida. Here she underwent a series of comparative tests against a conventionally-powered AT-6D fitted with the 600hp radial. Superficial comparisons of the 1,340in^3 (21,962cm^3) radial against a 770in^3 (12,620cm^3) in-line do not tell the whole of the story. The lower profile presented by the Ranger with its much smaller frontal area of 5.16ft^2 (1.46m^2), against the radials 13ft^2 (1.2m^2), achieved a calculated reduction of drag coefficient of 15%. At the same time propeller efficiency increased by 5 per cent.[7]

The results of the tests were revealing. At sea level, the margin of performance improvement shown by the XAT-6E was a mere 3mph (4.8km/h) over the AT-6D, being 196mph (313km/h) against 193mph (308km/h). However, as height increased the ratio got better being 19mph (30km/h) faster at 10,000ft (3,048m) with 220mph (352km/h) against 201mph (321km/h), and 59mph (94km/h) at 20,000ft (6,096m) as the Ranger gave 231mph (370km/h), while the Radial fell away sharply to 172mph (275km/h). These figures were achieved despite the fact that the in-line was forced to work harder to produce the same bhp per cubic inch displacement. The supercharged in-line pushed the Fairchild up to 236mph (377km/h) at 22,000ft (6,705m). Finally, the XAT-6E reached a service ceiling of 30,000ft (9,144m) at which altitude she was clocking 244mph (390km/h).

Impressive as these figures were, and the air-cooled Ranger in-line certainly turned in some of the best speeds for any Texan of that period, the Army showed no interest in developing the type for further production. First and foremost the Ranger engine gave endless trouble and required continued mechanical attention. This despite the fact that Fairchild had boasted years before that their radials have 'a record of low maintenance which is not equalled by any other engine'.[8] The other most probable reason for the rejection of the concept was that the AT-6 production-line was flowing at full-tilt by this time, and the introduction of the radial would have complicated and slowed it down. Furthermore, by the time the trials were completed, the end of the war was clearly, if distantly, in sight with more than sufficient Texans in stock to complete the expected further training requirements. So XAT-6E remained in solitary splendour, save for one interesting fact.

A private owner who had purchased a surplus T-6 airframe similarly converted it to an in-line engine. With civil registration NX 7410 he then took part in several air races in the late 1940s. The most spectacular of these events pitched the XAT-6E against this young pretender, a unique event!

In front of makeshift hangars Chinese groundcrew work on the prop of one of their NA-56s. On the steadily losing side of that sprawling conflict, heavily outclassed by the Japanese air force and constantly harried and on the move, maintaining their air fleet with primitive equipment was just another tough assignment for these few skilled men. Author's collection

CHAPTER FIVE

Britain Takes the Harvard

The placing of Air Ministry contract No. 791588/38 for the first North American NA-49 in the summer of 1938 was the start of a long, and still continuing, love affair between the British and what they came to know as the Harvard. While Spitfire and Hurricane earned immortality in 1940, and Halifax and Lancaster won fame (and later notoriety) in 1943–44, while the Gloster Meteor, English Electric Lightning and Hawker Harrier all earned similar acclaim in the succeeding post-war years, the Harvard, the 'Noisy North American' as she was dubbed, saw them all come and go and is still flying with both state and civilian owners.

In total, the British took delivery of 400 Mark I, 519 Mark II, 747 Mark IIA, 2,557 Mark IIB and 537 Mark III Harvards for a grand total of 4,760 aircraft. In addition, orders for a further 594 machines (EZ 458/699; KF 758/900 and KG 100/309) were cancelled. Conversely, the total is made up by the inclusion of five aircraft (EZ 305/309) received via the US Navy for the Royal Navy.[1]

The first Harvard I to grace the UK skies was serial number N 7000, which arrived at the Martlesham Heath Aeroplane and Armament Experimental Establishment (A&AEE) near Ipswich, Suffolk, on 3 December 1938. Here she undertook an intensive series of test flights, which were followed by flights in all conditions in order to prepare the standard RAF pilot's notes and handbooks on the type.[2] By January 1939, the second Harvard I, serial number N 7001, joined her sister at Martlesham. That this radial-engined 'monster' was to be no walkover for trainer or trainee was very quickly established and, in February, N 7000 spun-in near the village of Eyke, near Woodbridge killing the pilot, Squadron Leader Bob Cazalet.

The initial allocation of the first 400 planes saw one Harvard I (serial number N 7020) retained in the United States, where she was utilized by the British purchasing commission. Another (serial number N 7002) was sent direct to the RAF Central Flying School for the senior instructors to get the measure of the type. Three other Harvard Is (serial numbers P 5921, P 5928 and P 5931) were shipped to the South African Air Force: one in February 1940 and two in December of the same year. A total of 332 Harvard Is reached the UK in three main batches thus:

A trio of early Mark I Harvards in the original RAF paint scheme, these are N7140 (later to be written off in a crash near Taynton, Oxfordshire on 20 May 1940), N7018 (which survived until November 1945) and P5894 (which went out to Southern Rhodesia and survived until 1947). They are pictured here flying with 2 SFTS early in 1940.
Ray C. Sturtivent

- N7000/7019 arrived between December 1938 and February 1939. These equipped No. 12 Flying Training School (FTS) at Spitalgate near Grantham, Lincs, in January, but they only remained on their books until that autumn. Next to be supplied was 2 FTS at Brize Norton, Oxon and 10 FTS at Ternhill, near Market Drayton, Shropshire, in March; 1 FTS at Netheravon, on Salisbury Plain, in April and 6 FTS at Little Rissington, Gloucestershire in May of that year.
- N7021/7199 arrived between February 1939 and August 1939. Two fighter operational training units, 11 Group at Sutton Bridge and 12 Group Pool at Aston Down took delivery of Harvard Is late in 1939 and, in March of the following year, these units were re-designated as 6 Operational Training Unit (OTU) and

5 OTU, respectively. Service Flying Training Schools (SFTS) were also established and Harvard Is from 12 FTS were assigned to 14 SFTS at Kinloss along with some newly arrived aircraft.

- P5783/5915 arrived between August 1939 and July 1940: some went to 1 and 6 FTS, and then on to 1, 6, 14 and 15 SFTS at Lossiemouth, Scotland, which had 139 Harvard Is on its books at one time or another until April 1941.

The establishment of the Empire Air Training Scheme (EATS) and the Commonwealth Air Training Scheme (CATS) saw later batches of Harvard Is head for more distant climes, with training schools in Canada and Southern Rhodesia. Here the skies were not so dangerous and, in the case of the latter, weather conditions were uniformly perfect. The establishment of the Empire Air Training Scheme thus saw the diversion of later batches of Harvard Is, and 64 aircraft (serial numbers P5916/5920, P5922/5927, P5929 and P5930, and P5932/5982) went to Southern Rhodesia in March 1940. Here, in this most pleasant environment, many survived right through until November 1945.

After July 1940 there was a dramatic change of policy with regard to pilot training. Existing training units were run down and the bulk of the training was transferred overseas – Canada and Southern Rhodesia being the main sites selected. Closure of UK SFTS was swift with no less than 216 surviving aircraft being crated up, initially at 52 Maintenance Unit (MU) at Cardington, near Bedford, and thereafter by a private firm, Crosby and Co. Ltd, at a purpose-made depot established at Odiham, Hants. A further eight were transferred to the RAF in the Middle East, once Italy had joined the war and the Mediterranean theatre had become crucial. Some of these had extremely long service lives, two not being struck off charge until January 1947.

This is an early Mark II Harvard, AJ 614, which served initially with 33 Flying Instructors School but is seen here flying with the Central Flying School over Southern Rhodesia and carrying the code 614. She survived until November 1945. Ray C. Sturtivent

By August 1941, just thirty-eight Harvard Is remained at home, mainly with units like 41 OTU based at Old Sarum, Hampshire; 52 OTU at Debden, Essex; 53 and 61 OTUs both based at Heston, Middlesex. Other users in the UK were the Air Transport Auxiliary, whose Flying School, 1, 2 and 3 Ferry Pilots Pools were so equipped, and some lingered until March 1946. Others became squadron 'hacks' all over the country.

With EATS and CATS in full swing, the arrival of the first six Harvard IIs (serials BD 131/135 and BJ 413), in October and November 1940, was a more muted affair as they were no longer required. Other deliveries followed in the spring of 1941, before the bulk were shipped straight to Canada under CATS and Southern Rhodesia under EATS. Two UK arrivals (BD 136 and BD 137) were transferred to the USAAF for use by the 8th Air Force's forward echelons. Six Harvard IIs (serials DG 432 and DG 435/439) were lost when their transport was sunk by a U-boat. The bulk of the other Harvard IIs that reached England were sent to the Southern Rhodesian Air Force with some Mark Is.

They were joined by 103 Harvard IIs, which were transported by sea to South Africa and then up-country to Rhodesia from April 1941 onward. Here they joined earlier arrivals serving with 20 and 22 SFTS. Sixty-two survived the war, of which thirty-one were written off in November 1945. Of these survivors, twelve were sold to the Southern Rhodesian Air Force (SRAF) in February 1949, while the rest had been struck off charge by the RAF by end of that same year.

By far the greater deliveries were across the border to Canada, 305 taking this route between July 1941 and May 1942 and receiving Canadian serials RCAF 2501/3013, inclusive. Fifteen RCAF Harvards were, conversely, transferred to RAF units and had their serials changed (RCAF 2529 to BJ 410, RCAF 2530 to BJ 411, RCAF 2534/2537, inclusive, to BJ 412/415, inclusive, RCAF 2538 to BS 808, and RCAF 2539/2546, inclusive, to DG 432/439). Those RAF Harvard IIs that served in the SFTS of the CATS (serials AH 185/205) operated alongside Canadian Harvards until they closed down in October 1944. When this happened, the surviving Harvard IIs were absorbed into the RCAF. After the war, during the mass sell-offs, some Canadian Harvard IIs came into the possession of the Flygvapnet.

A further forty-seven Harvard IIs were shipped out to the RAF in the Middle East Theatre of Operations, and the few survivors from the war were finally struck off charge in January 1947. Four more found their way to India but by November 1943, all had gone. Finally, sixty-seven more Harvard IIs were assigned to the Royal New Zealand Air Force and shipped directly to that country. They were assigned RNZAF serials NZ 901/967, inclusive.

Similar dispositions affected the Harvard IIBs when they began to arrived in the autumn of 1942. Not a single aircraft of this Mark is thought to have reached the UK, but both South Africa and Middle East Command took delivery of the first batches of these aircraft, while New Zealand and Southern Rhodesia followed suit in December 1942 and January 1943, respectively. South Africa (SAAF, 436 aircraft), Southern Rhodesia (SR, 149 aircraft) and New Zealand (RNZAF, fifty-three aircraft) allocated their own serial numbers to these aircraft, while the Middle East (100 aircraft) naturally retained their RAF serials. A few went to West Africa and to the Royal Navy.

Post-war disposals were, in the main, swift and ruthless: from those that survived from Middle East Command (forty-seven), only one was left at Deversoir in November 1950. The Royal New Zealand Air Force officially took over the survivors on her shores in September 1946 but the majority were gradually struck off by them in the same period of time. The final Harvards were retired at a special ceremony on 24 June 1977 at the RNZAF base of Wigram. Here eighteen aircraft belonging to the Flying Training Wing were lined up before taking their final flights.

The Southern Rhodesian complement that remained were mostly absorbed into the Rhodesian Air Training Group from 1947: eleven of them being bought by the SRAF in November 1953, when the remaining surplus forty-five were sold off charge. Many of these did survive, however, turning up in the Belgian Congo flown by the Belgian Air Force.

The greatest operator of the type, South Africa, managed to make her Harvard IIBs soldier on well past the ages when other nations were scrapping them wholesale. Many of them survived in flying condition until the 1990s, when batches were sold off and ended their days in Angola and other former Portuguese African colonies. Some went to Gabon and served with the Fuerza Aerea Gabonais. One of the latter later survived to fly as civilian ZS-WLV for a time. Several, including SAAF serials 7040, 7083, 7229, 7320, 7324, 7500, 7694, 7695, 7690 and 7699, were sold to Paraguay who listed them as T-6s. A bulk lot of 147 aircraft were re-assigned their old RAF serial numbers and shipped to the UK, being the first Harvard IIBs to reach those shores. However, they were really surplus to any requirement of the much-reduced RAF and most went straight into storage with 15 MU at Wroughton, Wiltshire, until scrapped *circa* 1950. Twelve other South African Harvard IIBs were sold to the Royal Netherlands Air Force in 1947 and cannibalized.

It was much the same story with the Harvard IIIs, which arrived on the scene around the same time, 1943–44. They too were shipped in bulk to South Africa (197), to EATS in Southern Rhodesia (seventy), to the RAF Middle East Command (eighty-one) and to New Zealand (forty-one). One of the Middle East allocation was later returned back to the USAAF; the rest served briefly between 1944 and 1945. However, a new customer for the Mark was the Royal Navy's Fleet Air Arm, which was undergoing expansion and conversion, and flying mainly American-built radial-engined Grumman Avenger bombers and Chance–Vought Corsair fighter-bombers from its carriers in battle in both the Indian Ocean and the Pacific at this time.[3] The need for radial-engined trainers was obvious and no less than 143 aircraft initially, with others later, transferred to them from RAF stocks.

With the end of the war, the Harvard IIIs were treated as ruthlessly as the other Marks and struck off wholesale, many never ever seeing service. In contrast, the bulk of these aircraft – many belonging to the Royal Navy – continued to give good service, with both front-line and reserve squadrons, some

This Mark IIa Harvard, EX 163, started her flying career with the Rhodesian Air Training Group HQ Communications Flight as pictured here. She later went on to fly with 28 Elementary Flying Training School (EFTS) and 20 SFTS before being involved in a flying accident on 2 July 1943. RAF Museum

This Harvard Mark IIB was one of 507 which went out to the British India (present-day India, Pakistan and Sri Lanka). She arrived at the beginning of 1944 and served with 5 Squadron, and is seen here with No 2 (India) Group's Communications Flight (CF) at Yelahanka airfield, near Bangalore on 5 August 1946. She was one of many RAF Harvards handed over to the Indian Air Force in September 1947. Ray C. Sturtivent

lasting until 1956. The last 'Naval' Harvards ended their service with Royal Navy reserve units. With the closure of EATS at the end of war, of those that survived in Southern Rhodesia, sixty-four went into mothballs, emerging only to be sold in 1952–53. A few saw some service with 4 FTS of the Rhodesian Air Force for a while between 1948 and 1952, then shared the general fate of the rest. RAF Middle East Command's aircraft had only short service careers before they, also, were sold off charge, two lonely Harvard Mark IIIs managing to survive until 1950. Another was crated and shipped back to England only to

This Harvard IIB (FE 992) served with the RAF in both 31 and 14 SFTSs in Canada, but was handed over to the RCAF when all RAF training units were pulled out in 1944. She survived post-war and became civilian registered G-BDAM. She is seen here taxying at West Malling airfield on 26 August 1985. RAF Museum

(Below) **This RAF Harvard II, AJ 930 (coded 39), served with the 39, 34 and 13 SFTS in Canada for four years before being handed over to the RCAF on the withdrawal of British training units. She is pictured here in this beautiful in-flight study, flying with her sisters from 34 SFTS over Medicine Hat.** Ray C. Sturtivent

be scrapped in 1947, hardly worth all the effort.

Again it was South Africa who got the most out of the Mark III, for although most of them (100) were shipped back to the UK in 1946–47 and placed directly in storage until scrapped in 1950, one exception saw some service, while another twenty-six were sold off and eleven remained in South Africa and saw extended service there before being 'acquired' by various other nations like Mozambique for their own civil wars.

Noorduyn Aviation's contribution to the Harvard story, the Mark II, dominated the RAF's CATS and EATs from the time the first aircraft arrived in May 1942 and continued to do so long after the war was a memory. Initially it was Canada herself that received the bulk of these aircraft (639 up to December 1943) and they served in both RAF and RCAF SFTSs from then on until the RAF schools were closed down. Many IIBs were then transferred to the Canadian schools but retained their RAF serials, and, to further muddy the waters, a block of seventy-two was taken out of storage and shipped to the UK in March 1944.

A new destination for another huge batch of Harvard IIBs was the Indian subcontinent, and between February 1943 and July 1944 a total of 525 of this mark was shipped to the RAF and Royal Indian Air Force (RIAF) units there, seventeen of these being lost at sea in transit. Here they joined 1 (India) FTS, as well as many OTUs. Eleven were turned over to USAAF units based in India at that time and reverted to the White Star but kept their RAF serials! Others were widespread and turned up all over India. At the end of the war and disposal was, to say the least, haphazard. Officially many of these were US property, supplied under lend-lease, and, strictly-speaking all should have been handed back to the USAAF. In fact, the only ones that appear to have been so dealt with were fifteen handed back ('recaptured' in the rather offensive USAAF parlance) in June 1946; another eighty-seven were handed over and scrapped *in situ*, and a further fourteen in November 1947. Those retained by the RAF post-war during the finals days of Empire, were all scrapped on the British withdrawal in 1947. The two newly formed states from the former British India, India (eighty-two) and Pakistan (twenty-nine), both received allocations of Harvard IIBs to their respective air arms on partition.

This beautiful early air-to-air photo is of RCAF Harvard IIB FE 827, one of 639 allocated to Canada. She is seen flying with 34 SFTS over Medicine Hat. Ray C. Sturtivent

This RAF Harvard IIB was shipped directly to Southern Rhodesia when the bulk of RAF training was moved out of England's hazardous skies. She flew with 20 SFTS right through the war, and continued to serve (coded H-46) with 4 FTS for many years afterwards. She finally came to grief, as seen here, in a belly landing on 25 September 1952. Ray C. Sturtivent

This Harvard Mark IIB (FX 479) went out to India and post-war served with Far East Command from March 1947 onwards, and is seen here at Kallang in that year. She later flew with No 84 Squadron in 1948 and then with Far East Communications Squadron (FECS), Examining Squadron (FEAFxS) and Training Squadron (FEAFTrS) until 1952. She ended her days with SF Seletar in October 1952 and was badly damaged in a take-off accident there on 8 February 1956. Ray C. Sturtivent

Shipments of the Harvard IIB direct to the UK commenced on 9 April 1943, when the first pair (serials numbers FE 787 and FE 788) arrived at Liverpool docks aboard the transport *Kaipaki*. This first batch was followed by another eight aircraft but that was it until September when regular shipments started to arrive from Canada. A handling procedure was set up to deal with these large numbers of aircraft. On off-loading from the ships, the IIBs went to the Lockheed facility at Speke for initial checking and were then taken to one of two nearby plants[4] set up to convert them to RAF requirements. This process, which was not regarded as a priority at this period of the war, was followed by transit to an MU for storage and allocation.

With so few Mark IIBs, initially only a few units got to know the type. The Empire Central Flying School did not receive a solitary example to look at until as late as January 1944, some time after two others (FH 107 and FH 115) went to the Air Transport Auxiliary in October 1943. In July, 2 and 3 Flying Instructor Schools (FIS) started to receive their allocations. But after this came the deluge! Between July 1944 and the following March, Harvard IIBs flooded into 5 and 9 (Pilots) Advanced Flying Units (AFUs), 16 and 17 SFTS as well as 7 FIS and elsewhere. Others found more exotic homes: eight machines were handed over to the USAAF in England; yet a further seven reached the Free French Air Force in North Africa via the USAAF and shipment to Algiers.

Finally, in August 1944, two were initially assigned to Middle East Command, but only one of these (serial number KF 222) arrived in fit enough condition to be used. She was later joined by forty-two others that had been converted to target tugs.[5] Of these later post-war disposals, seven were sold to Greece and used by the Royal Hellenic Air Force from February 1947; twenty-nine were struck off charge out there and four survived to be shipped back to the UK in June 1947, whereupon they were put into storage and then also struck off charge three years later!

British Wartime Harvard allocations 1938–44

Mark	No.	USAAF serials	RCAF serials	RAF serials
I	200	–	–	N 7000 to N 7199
I	200	–	–	P 5783 to P 5982
II	20	–	–	AH 185 to AH 204
II	450*	–	–	AJ 538 to AJ 987
II	8	–	2521 to 2528	BD 130 to BD 137
II	2	–	2529 to 2530	BJ 410 to BJ 411
II	4	–	2534 to 2537	BJ 412 to BJ 415
II	1	–	3538	BS 808
II	24	–	–	BW 184 to BW 207
II	2	–	–	DG 430 to DG 431
II	8	–	2539 to 2546	DG 432 to DG 439
IIA	747	41-33073 to 41-33819	–	EX 100 to EX 846
III	153	41-33820 to 41-33972	–	EX 847 to EX 999
III	150	41-33973 to 41-34122	–	EZ 100 to EZ 249
III	9	42-84163 to 42-84171	–	EZ 250 to EZ 258
III	20	42-84182 to 42-84201	–	EZ 259 to EZ 278
III	20	42-84282 to 42-84301	–	EZ 279 to EZ 298
III	10	42-84362 to 42-84371	–	EZ 299 to EZ 308
III	20	42-84453 to 42-84472	–	EZ 309 to EZ 328
III	20	42-84543 to 42-84562	–	EZ 329 to EZ 348
III	10	42-84633 to 42-84642	–	EZ 349 to EZ 358
III	20	42-84723 to 42-84742	–	EZ 359 to EZ 378
III	20	42-84803 to 42-84822	–	EZ 379 to EZ 398
III	10	42-84923 to 42-84932	–	EZ 399 to EZ 408
III	20	42-85013 to 42-85032	–	EZ 409 to EZ 428
III	20	42-85103 to 42-85122	–	EZ 429 to EZ 448
III	10	42-85223 to 42-85232	–	EZ 449 to EZ 458
III	–	Cancelled	–	EZ 459 to EZ 799
IIB	500	42-464 to 42-963	–	FE 267 to FE 766
IIB	233	42-12254 to 42-12486	–	FE 767 to FE 999
IIB	67	42-12487 to 42-12553	–	FH 100 to FH 166
IIB	339	43-12502 to 43-12840	–	FS 661 to FS 999
IIB	361	43-12841 to 43-13201	–	FT 100 to FT 460
III	20	42-44539 to 42-44558	–	FT 955 to FT 974
IIB	300	43-34615 to 43-34914	–	FX 198 to FX 497
III	1	BuNo 26800	–	KE 305
III	1	BuNo 26812	–	KE 306
III	3	BuNo 26816 to BuNo 26818	–	KE 307 to KE 309
IIB	658	–	–	KF 100 to KF 757
IIB	–	Cancelled	–	KF 758 to KF 900
IIB	99	–	–	KF 901 to KF 999
IIB	–	Cancelled	–	KG 100 to KG 309

* Ex-French order.

Those that had remained 'mothballed' in MU units in the UK since their arrival were clearly equally surplus to requirements in the post-war RAF. Wholesale selling off therefore took place as early as 1946. The Royal Dutch Air Force took delivery of no less than 116 up to October 1948 from this source of supply. The Royal Danish air force received eight of them between April and June 1947; the Belgian Air Force took seven via Rollason's, who had bought them cheap; the French Air Force took a further eighteen in April and May 1949, while the Royal Norwegian Air Force acquired twenty-three more for their Winkleigh training facility in October of the same year. The RAF itself found use for small numbers of Harvard IIBs in both the Middle East and Far East in the immediate post-war period. Some of these remained in service with the Hong Kong and Malayan Auxiliary Air Forces until May 1947. The Rhodesian Air Training Group was the grateful recipient of sixty-four of the type between November 1950 and December 1951. These machines were passed via 394 MU to 4 FTS. When the Mau-Mau terrorist attacks began in

Kenya in 1953, fourteen of these aircraft, reinforced by four others flown in from the UK, were sent north as 1340 Flight. They were used in combat action against these elusive murder groups carrying 20lb bombs on makeshift under-wing racks – a role they performed quite well for a couple of years during which four were written-off in accidents. Finally, and incredibly, no less than 151 pristine and unused Harvard IIBs were summarily struck off charge by the RAF without ever being flown, between April 1950 and May 1951.

Despite these figures, demand for the Harvard IIB in RAF service continued in

***(Top)* A few Mark IIB and many Mark III Harvards were allocated to the Royal Navy's Fleet Air Arm training squadrons during the war, at least 214 in total. None is thought to have made a carrier deck landing but this unknown machine was photographed at Gatwick airfield sporting a tail-hook.** Ray C. Sturtivent

***(Above)* Many Harvards continued to serve in the Royal Navy post-war, working from Naval Air Stations from Lee-on-Solent and Yeovilton at home, to bases all over the world. This Mark IIA (EZ 348) is seen over Hal Far airfield, Malta, were she served with the Station Flight between March 1947 and February 1952.** FAA Museum, Yeovilton

One of the first Harvard Mark Is (N7060) started flying with the RAF as early as April 1939 with 1 FTS wearing code 20, as pictured here, and then 1 SFTS. She joined 10 SFTS in March 1940, but she was almost immediately written off in a collision with an Anson on 21 March. FAA Museum, Yeovilton

A bit of a mystery: this is Royal Navy Fleet Air Arm Mark III Harvard, EZ 244, which is normally listed as being allocated to the RNZAF.
FAA Museum, Yeovilton

(Below) **This is a Harvard II (BD 136) which served with SF Squadron from July 1941 to June 1942, and then briefly with 2 FF. She was one of the few RAF Harvards actually handed back to the USAAF 8th Air Force in England, at Bovingdon airfield in August 1942.** FAA Museum, Yeovilton

limited form and the aircraft remained a prominent sight at various training bases up and down the UK. The Korean War saw a brief resurgence of usage, and between 1945 and 1953, when they began to be phased out in favour of the Hunting Provost trainer, they served with no less than six FTS, three Flying Refresher Schools (FRS), the Central Flying School and the RAF College, Cranwell, as well as with university air squadrons of Home Command until May 1957.

A fresh orgy of RAF disposals took place from 1953 onward, and by April 1955 the very last FTS-employed Harvard was pensioned off from 3 FTS at Feltwell. The RATG itself was finally shut down in December 1953 and the surviving twenty-nine Harvard IIBs were sold out for scrap.

Back home, three Harvard IIBs (FT 375, KF 183 and KF 314) were maintained on the strength of the Ministry of Defence (Procurement Executive) at the A&AEE at Boscombe Down. Here they were employed for air-to-air photography and other duties, not least in piston-engined training for jet pilots who fly the RAFs Memorial Flight of Spitfire, Hurricane and Lancaster. Sadly one of these veterans (KF 314) was lost in an accident on 22 February 1982 but the other two still survive at the time of writing (July 2000).

Finally, mention should be made of twenty-seven Harvards of all types that were allocated as instructional airframes between July 1940 and January 1958. These performed a very useful function, even though their flying days were over, and were allocated their own maintenance (M) serials.

NB: One aircraft, KF 331, served as 6316M from January 1947 for a period but later reverted to a fully airworthy condition. Another, FE 866, was allocated as 6534M at Moreton-in-the-Marsh but this was later cancelled.

British instructional (M) airframes

Original serial	*M serial*	*Date allocated*	*User*
N 7092	2056M	July 1940	2 SoTT
N 7070	2123M	July 1940	RCAF as A 100
N 7096	2124M	July 1940	RCAF as A 102
N 7129	2203M	August 1940	15 SFTS
FH 107	4913M	October 1944	16 SFTS
FH 115	4927M	November 1944	16 SFTS
FS 832	5015M	January 1945	17 SFTS/22 FTS
FS 814	5208M	April 1945	17 SFTS
FX 241	5250M	May 1945	Church Lawford
FX 306	5568M	August 1945	11 (P) AFU
KF 155	5569M	August 1945	Spitalgate
FT 356	5768M	December 1945	Little Rissington
KF 351	5769M	January 1946	South Cerney
FX 293	5770M	January 1946	1 SoTT
FX 321	5771M	January 1946	1 SoTT
KF 219	6161M	October 1946	8 SoTT
FS 906	6276M	February 1947	2 SoTT
FX 244	6312M	April 1947	Little Rissington
FE 866	6314M	April 1947	Moreton-in-Marsh
EX 684	6521M	February 1948	4 FTS
EX 697	6522M	February 1948	4 FTS
FT 429	6530M	April 1948	Finningley/Syerston
FT 303	7107M	September 1953	2 FTS
KF 513	7113M	October 1953	3 FTS
KF 209	7116M	December 1953	3 FTS
KF 126	7229M	July 1955	Malaya
FS 890	7554M	January 1958	Little Rissington

CHAPTER SIX

'The Six' Described

Whatever the mark or constructor, the basic details of the Harvard/SNJ/Texan, known in USAF pilots parlance merely as 'The Six', remained basically the same. She was a single-engined, low-wing monoplane, of either all-metal stressed skin construction or with composite construction aft and fabric-covered control surfaces. It was a two-seater advanced trainer (AT) built either by North American Aviation Inc. at Inglewood, California or Dallas, Texas, or sub-contracted to Noorduyn of Canada.

Taking a typical example, which equated with the BC-1/AT-6/SNJ-5/Harvard in most, but not all, respects, the following general profile applies.

The T-6D figures came out as an empty weight of 4,250lb (1,928kg) and she could tote a useful load of 905lb (410kg) giving a gross weight of 5,155lb (2,338kg). Her top speed was 210mph (336km/h), with a cruising speed of 146mph (233km/h) and a landing speed of 67mph (107km/h). Range at 70 per cent power was given as a modest 629 miles (1,006km). Wing area, including ailerons, was 253.73ft^2 (23.57m^2) and wing loading came out at 22.2lb/ft^2. Power loading was 9.37lb/ ft^2. Service ceiling was 24,700ft (7,528m). Fuel capacity was given as 110 US gallons (500l) in the two wing tanks, with oil capacity as 12.2 US gallons (55l) including a 2-gallon (9l) expansion space.

Based on the Harvard IIB[1] (roughly equivalent to the BC-1A/AT-6A/SNJ-3) the follow description applied (with obvious variations according to nation and role).

Specification	
Powerplant:	A single Pratt and Whitney 550hp Wasp R-1340-AN-1 (AN = Army/Navy) radial piston engine directly driving a two-bladed Hamilton counter-weight, constant-speed propeller. The Wasp ran on 91 octane fuel
Weights:	Empty 4,158lb (1,886kg); maximum take-off weight 5,300lb (2,404kg)
Dimensions:	Wingspan 42ft ¼in (12.8m); length 28ft 6in (8.99m); height 11ft 9in (3.58m); wing area 253.7ft^2 (23.57m^2).
Performance:	Maximum speed 205mph (330km/h) at 5,000ft (1,525m) Cruising speed 170mph (274km/h) at 5,000ft (1,525m) Service ceiling 21,500ft (6,555m) Range 750 miles (1,207km)
Armament:	*Harvards* One fixed forward-firing gun, or sometimes nil *Texan/SNJ* Varied according to role. Usually one fixed forward-firing 0.30-calibre machine gun and one flexible-mounted (scarf ring) 0.30-calibre machine gun aft. Light bomb racks or shackles could be carried under the wings or fuselage

The Fuel and Oil System

Fuel Tanks and Gauges

There was a total fuel capacity in this mark of 92 imperial gallons (417l) in two 46-gallon (208l) wing tanks. The maximum was rarely carried in practice as the tanks could only be completely filled with the aircraft in a tail-up position. When in the normal tail-down position on the mat, only 40 gallons (181l) could be put into each tank. There was a stand-pipe in the port tank which held 16 gallons (73l) reserve fuel. Only the pilot was in a position to keep on eye on the direct reading fuel gauges, which were badly positioned on the front cockpit floor on either side of the pilot's seat, where they attracted dirt, oil and grime which tended to obscure them.

Fuel Cocks

There was a four-position cock on the port-hand side of each cockpit. The positions were marked in block capitals as: Off; Reserve; On; Left On and Right On.

Fuel Pumps and Pressure Gauge

There was a hand-pump lever located on the port side of each cockpit; the levers being interconnected. The hand-pump was used when starting the engine and as an alternative to, or in support of, the engine-driven pump.

There was a priming pump fitted at the top starboard side of the instrument panel in the front cockpit only. Those with a Ki-gas pump fitted had the handle locked by pushing it in and screwing it to the right to lock, and pushed in before turning to unlock.

There was a fuel pressure gauge at the top starboard side of the instrument panel and some aircraft were fitted with a separate warning light on the instrument panel, which indicated when the pressure fell appreciably below normal (3–5lb/in^2).

Oil System

The oil tank held 8½ imperial gallons (38.5l) of oil with 1½ gallons (6.8l) air space. Below the instrument panel (in the front cockpit only) was mounted an oil cooler shutter control. There was an oil dilution switch fitted among a bank of switches to the port of that panel.

(Above) **The bare bones of 'The Six'. Clearly illustrating the basic structure this photo shows one of the restoration projects of the Western Museum of Flight at the Hawthorne Municipal Airport. The float, seen here at the Armed Forces Day Parade at Torrance, California, portrayed the wartime days of 'Rosie the Riveter', when women replaced male factory workers entering military services of the United States. The ladies on the float are Ruby Lee, Patty Fritschi, Manon Amrhein, Gloria Schable and Rachael Garrison, who were all members of the Southern California Historical Aviation Foundation.**

This particular aeroplane, an SNJ-5, Navy Trainer for advanced student pilots, was built by North American Aviation on Aviation Boulevard. It was used in the movie Swing Shift **starring Goldie Horne and Kurt Russell.** Dr Ira Chart, Western Museum of Flight, Hawthorne

(Left) **Although obviously 'posed', like so much wartime British propaganda, this photo of RAF 'erks' working on a Harvard does give a good view of how easy it was to get at the big radial engine in the field.** RAF Museum, Hendon, London

Hydraulic System

The undercarriage and flaps were operated by the main power-driven hydraulic system, with its alternative hand-pump if required. The tail-wheel was not retractable. A secondary, master-unit type, hydraulic system was used for brake operation. In the main system, a lever on the port side of each cockpit (marked Power Control Push) cut in the engine-driven pump; these levers were interconnected. It was more convenient to operate this before moving the flaps or undercarriage selector. The power control returned to the idle position of its own accord after 1 or 2min. A pressure gauge on the port side of the front cockpit only showed the output pressure of the engine-driven pump or the hand-pump. After pushing the power control, the gauge would read 900–1,000lb/in^2, but returned to zero when the power control returned to idle position. If it failed to do so the system was defective and continued operations under pressure might then well damage the pump.

Suction System

There was an engine-driven pump, which operated the gyro instruments and a suction gauge on the lower left-hand side of the instrument panel. The normal suction was 3½–4½in of Hg.

Pneumatic System

Compressed air, stored in a cylinder behind the rear seat, was used only to operate the camera and the single gun (if fitted). No engine driven compressor was fitted and the available pressure was shown by a gauge on the lower right-hand side of the front instrument panel.

Electrical System

A 750W generator charged a 12V battery, which supplied the usual lighting and other services. Should either a gyro gun-sight or tuneable beam approach equipment be fitted, two 12V batteries were used in parallel. An external supply socket was fitted on the port side of the fuselage above the wing leading edge.

An electrical panel on the left-hand side of the instrument panel included an ammeter, a battery switch and a generator main line switch, which was normally wired On. The ammeter showed the generator output and the reading could vary according to the services used. It could read as low as 5A, if the batteries were fully charged and no services were switched on, or as high as 50A, with the services on. If 50A was exceeded and could not be reduced by switching the services off, the generator main line switch had to be turned off. The batteries could be isolated when the engine was running, by means of the battery switch. A panel in the rear cockpit carried only rear cockpit lighting and fuel gauge light switches.

Spare bulbs were stowed on the rear cockpit floor. The fuses were not accessible in flight. If a short-circuit was suspected, the battery and generator main line switches were turned off.

The Aircraft Controls

Flying Controls

The rear control column was detachable and could be stowed in a socket on the starboard side of the cockpit. The controls were locked by first placing the control column in the fully forward and central position, centralizing the rudder bar, and then pulling up the handle in the front cockpit to the left of the control column. The rudder pedals were adjustable by foot-operated release levers on the inboard side of each pedal. Care had to be taken to ensure that the pedals were in corresponding holes after any adjustment.

Brakes

Each main wheel brake could be independently operated by pressure on its respective toe pedal in either cockpit. Movement of the rudder pedals alone did not affect the brakes. The brakes were applied for parking by depressing the pedals, pulling out the Park Brake knob on the right-hand side of the instrument panel in the front cockpit only, releasing the pedals, and then releasing the knob, which had

The engine being fitted on the SNJ restoration project of the Western Museum of Flight at the Hawthorne Municipal Airport. Dr Ira Chart, Western Museum of Flight, Hawthorne

very little movement. The brakes were disengaged by depressing the pedals in either cockpit. Single-cylinder type brakes were fitted, which could not be relied on to hold the aircraft when parked facing uphill.

Steerable Tailwheel

The tailwheel was steerable over the full range of rudder movement, and was held in the steerable position by a spring-loaded cam. In order to assist manoeuvring in a confined space, the tailwheel and the fore and aft axis of the aircraft exceeded approximately 25 degrees, which thus allowed the wheel to caster freely. Normally a sharp application of the brake, as well as rudder, would be required to unlock the cam, but sudden application of opposite rudder when turning could also cause unlocking.

Trimming Tab Controls

The elevator hand-wheel was on the port side and operated in the natural sense. The rudder hand-wheel was on the same axis and was turned forward to apply right trim. There was a notch on each hand-wheel, and the neutral positions were with both notches vertical. The controls were fitted in both cockpits.

Undercarriage Control

The undercarriage lever was located on the port side of each cockpit and had two normal positions only, Up and Down! In the Down position a stud on the lever (in the front cockpit only) engaged in a notch on the quadrant. This lever had to be lifted to disengage the stud and then moved smartly back to raise the undercarriage. If the lever was moved slowly it tended to stick due to the hydraulic pressure reaching the jacks before the locks were disengaged. When this occurred, the lever had to be returned to the Down position for a few seconds and then moved quickly back again.

The fully forward position of the undercarriage lever was marked Emergency Push Handle Down To Engage Pin and was for use only if the wheels were down, but the lights indicated the locks were not engaged. The lever then engaged the locking pins manually. Great care had to be taken to ensure that it was not inadvertently moved into this position when lowering the undercarriage normally. If this was done it had to be immediately returned to the normal Down position, or the locking pins could be damaged by the legs when lowering was nearly completed. The undercarriage could be raised, and the emergency fully forward position operated, only from the front cockpit. The undercarriage could be lowered from either cockpit. This was not always a good idea in practice!

Undercarriage Position Indicator and Warning Light

A standard electrical indicator was fitted in the front cockpit to the left of the electrical panel and in the rear cockpit on top of the instrument panel. Indications were:

- two green lights – both wheels locked down;
- two red lights – both wheels unlocked;
- no lights – both wheels locked up.

In addition, both cockpits had a red warning light on the top left-hand side of the instrument panel, which came on whenever the undercarriage was not locked down, and the throttle was less than one-third open.

Flap Control and Indicator

The flap lever was adjacent to the undercarriage lever in both cockpits and had three positions, Up, Lock and Down. The levers were interconnected. In order to obtain an intermediate position of the flaps, the lever was moved Up or Down as required, and was then moved to the Lock position when the flaps had reached their desired setting. A mechanical indicator reading in degrees was fitted on the port side of each cockpit. Unlike the undercarriage lever, the flap lever was designed to be moved to the Up position without first being lifted.

Engine Controls

Throttle

The throttle lever moved in a quadrant on the port side of each cockpit wall. The quadrant was gated at the take-off position and had a friction nut at the side. There was no automatic boost control.

Mixture Control

The mixture control was adjacent to the throttle and was manually operated and served by the same friction nut. It was moved over a range from Rich (fully back) through increasingly weak mixtures to the cut-out position (fully forward). In the front cockpit only, a catch on the throttle drew the mixture lever back to the Rich position as the throttle was closed. This catch could be released and the mixture control lever moved fully forward to stop the engine.

Propeller Control

The rpm control lever was adjacent to the mixture control and was again served by the throttle friction nut. The fully aft position gave Positive Coarse Pitch: in all other positions of the lever, the propeller was under constant speed control, the range being from about 1,400 to 2,250rpm. Positive Coarse Pitch would give lower rpm than 1,400 at low airspeeds.

Air Intake Heat Control

This control was located below the electrical panel in the front cockpit only and could be set to any desired position.

Engine Instruments

Both instrument panels mounted a boost gauge, an rpm indicator, and a combined oil pressure, oil temperature and fuel pressure gauge and a cylinder head temperature gauge. A carburettor mixture thermometer was fitted on the front instrument panel only, while in the rear cockpit this was replaced by a clock.

Ignition Switch

This switch was mounted on the left-hand side of both instrument panels and had four positions, Off, L, R, Both. The two switches were mechanically interconnected.

Starting Equipment

An inertia starter was fitted. A three-position switch mounted at the bottom of the instrument panel in the front cockpit only was held down to Energize the starter, and up to Engage the flywheel and energize the booster coil; before engaging, a pause was made in the general (Off) position.

Cockpit Equipment

Sliding Hoods

From outside, the cockpit hoods could be moved after their respective catches on the port side; these catches had release handles inside the cockpits. If they failed to open in emergencies, it was sometimes possible to escape through the side panels of the sliding portions, which were jettisoned by pulling down the handle at the centre of the appropriate panel and pushing outwards.

Seat and Harness

The seats were adjustable for height by levers on the right of each seat. On some aircraft, a lean-forward release lever was fitted on the left of the seat.

Cockpit Heating

The heating for both cockpits, the windscreen and the gun (when fitted) was controlled by a single lever, mounted on the starboard side of the front cockpit. There was also a foot-operated cooling ventilator on the front cockpit floor.

Instrument Lighting

In the front cockpit were three red lights controlled by two dimmer switches, and two ultra-violet lights controlled by a second dimmer switch. Red and white compass lights were also fitted with their adjacent switches; the white light was only used when the two-stage screens were in place.

In the rear cockpit there were two red lights (one for the instrument panel, and one over the compass) and two ultra-violet lights, all controlled by dimmer switches.

Each cockpit had a red emergency light (located at the top left of each instrument panel) operated from a pair of dry cells stowed in a canvas pocket to the left of the front seat. Each light had a separate switch to the left of the instrument panel.

External Lights

The navigation lights were operated by a switch on the left of the row in the front cockpit only. When this switch was On, a separate tail-light switch operated the tail lights.

(Top) **Preparing for that crucial first flight. Pre-flight checking on 'The Six' prior to take-off, which shows cockpit hood and internal detail.** Smithsonian Institution, Washington DC

(Bottom) **The controls of Harvard AJ 662 of the Fleet Air Arm Flying School at Kingston, Ontario, 1942.** Harry Knight

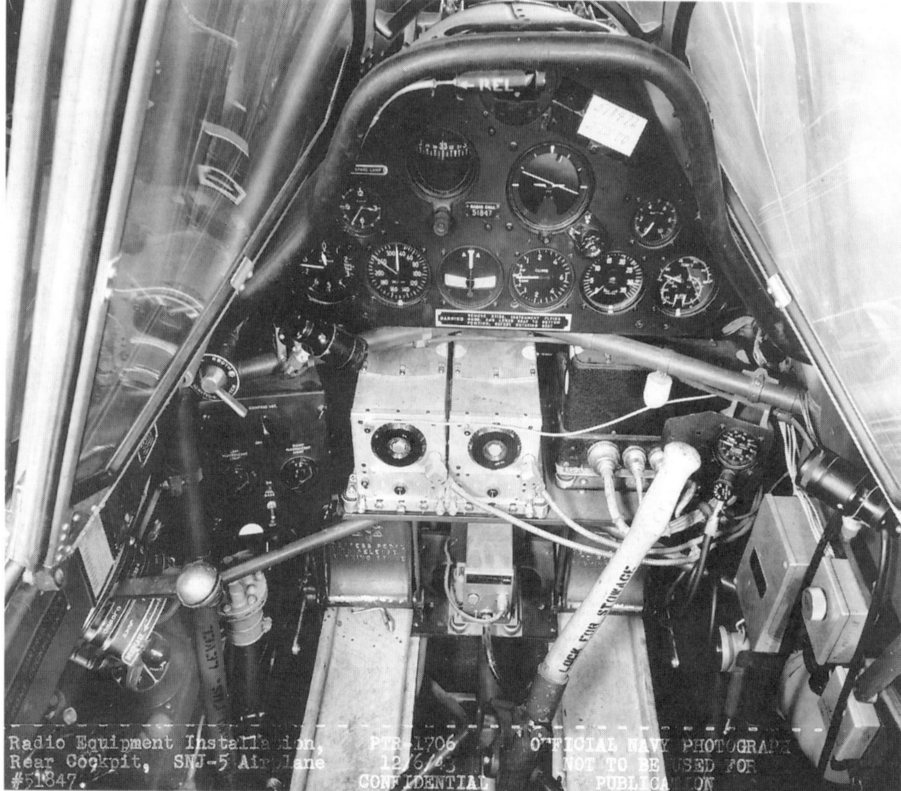

***(Top)* The 'front office' of an AT-6, a familiar sight to tens of thousand of 'rookie' and 'wanna-be' pilots the world over from 1939 onward.** Smithsonian Institution, Washington DC

***(Bottom)* The radio equipment installation, rear cockpit on SNJ-5, No. 51847, 12 June 1943.** Smithsonian Institution, Washington DC

The next two switches on that row separately controlled the landing lamps mounted in the port and starboard leading edges.

A switch box was located on the right of the front cockpit and controlled the white signalling lamp, and the red, green and amber identification lamps mounted beneath the rear fuselage. The switches were placed in the Down position to emit a steady light; in the Up position, morse code could be transmitted when the key on top of the box was operated.

Radio Controls

British Harvard's, of course, had totally different radio systems to the American Marks. In the Harvard, a four-channel VHF transmitter–receiver, incorporating intercom, was used, with its press-button type control unit fitted on the port side of the front cockpit.

On RAF IIBs, a press-to-transmit switch was fitted inside the spade grip of the front control column. In the rear cockpit, it was located at the top of the control column and a press-to-mute switch was fitted below.

On Royal Navy IIBs, however, these switches were re-positioned. In the front cockpit the press-to-transmit and the bomb-firing controls were reversed. The transmit button was on the throttle and the bomb-firing switch on the stick, while in the rear cockpit the transmit button was above the throttle on the port coaming. Two press-to-mute switches were fitted, one in each cockpit above the throttle.

The control unit for the tuneable beam approach equipment was fitted on the starboard side of the front cockpit, with its tuning control mounted above.

Armament Equipment

Optional fittings applied to these according to the training role assigned.

A G.45 cine camera could be fitted in the port wing of the Harvard IIB, which could be operated in one of two ways:

- by pressing the gun firing push button, provided that the camera master switch was On and the selector was set to either Gun and Camera Cine, or Camera Cine; or
- by pressing the camera pushbutton with the G.45 camera master switch

On, irrespective of the setting of the selector.

The camera footage indicator was fitted below the camera master switch.

The gyro gunsight (GGS) could be fitted in the front cockpit, with its range control on the throttle lever, and a selector dimmer switch at the rear of the left-hand control shelf. The GGS master switch was on the right-hand side of the instrument panel.

A GGS camera recorder could be fitted above the gunsight and was operated by the pushbutton on the front control column, provided that the GGS master switch was on.

In the rear cockpit a ring and bead sight was fitted.

The bomb release button was mounted in the end of the throttle lever in the front cockpit on RAF IIBs and the bomb selector switches and the bomb jettison switch on the right of the instrument panel. The bomb master switch had to be On before the bombs could be either released normally or jettisoned.

Static Pressure Selector Switch

This was an optional fitting and, when fitted, was locked in the Pressure Head position.

Two-Stage Screening

The 'fixed' screens were fitted on the ground to the top and sides of the front cockpit and a folding front screen (which could be fitted in the air) was carried in a stowage to the right of the front seat. The map case was then re-positioned behind this stowage. In order to eliminate misting-up of the two-stage goggles, the extractor tube of the goggles in use was plugged into one of the two vent holes in the fuselage wall on the port side of the front seat. Stowage for these goggles was provided on the starboard side of the front cockpit.

Miscellaneous Equipment

- De-icing equipment. The only de-icing equipment fitted was a pipe for de-frosting the front windscreen with an internal warm air stream, controlled by the cockpit heating lever, and the pressure-head heater controlled by a switch at the electrical panel.

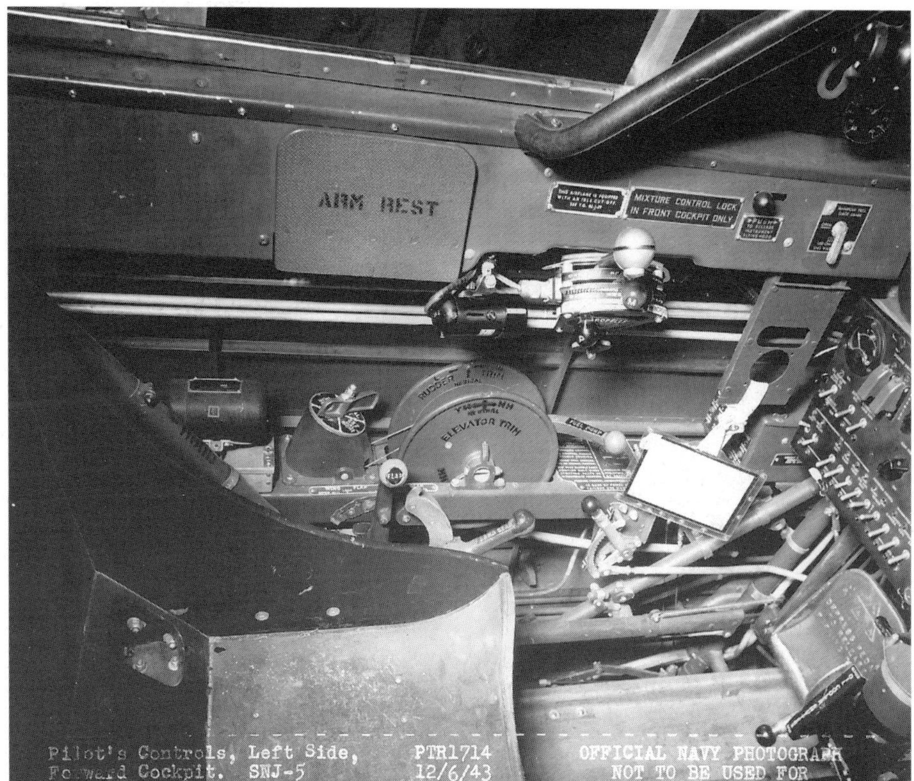

(Top) **The pilot controls, port side, forward cockpit on SNJ-5, No. 51847, 12 June 1943.**
Smithsonian Institution, Washington DC

(Bottom) **The pilot controls, port side, rear cockpit on SNJ-5, No. 51847, 12 June, 1943.**
Smithsonian Institution, Washington DC

- Two P.11 magnetic compasses were fitted: one to the right of and below the front instrument panel; and the second below the centre of the rear instrument panel.

- Outside air thermometer. The gauge for this was fitted at the top of the front instrument panel.

External Fitments

If we take for our example the AT-6D (SNJ-5), the following are the usual accruements and fittings as standard, but which again could vary from mark to mark, and operator to operator.

Propeller

The Hamilton–Standard, two-bladed, wooden, constant-speed propeller had a low pitch of 11½ degrees and a high pitch of 27 degrees. It had a diameter of 9ft (2.7m), which gave a ground clearance of 12.75in (32.38cm), although on some SNJ-5s this was reduced to 8ft 4in (2.54m) in order to clear the carrier deck landing wires. No propeller bosses were fitted as a rule, where they were on the re-built T-6Gs, an 18in (45cm) diameter spinner was utilized. In practice, they were most often quickly discarded, as they hindered maintenance.

Undercarriage and Tyres

Main wheel tyres had a diameter of 27in (68.5cm), with an oleo travel of 8.8in (22cm). Distance between undercarriage centres was 8ft 6½in (260cm). They retracted inwards into doorless wells that left the tyres exposed. The steerable rear wheel had a diameter of 12½in (31.75cm) and protruded aft from a small fairing. They were fitted with Bendix shock struts and Hayes hydraulic brakes.

(Left) **Port midships fuselage detail with fire extinguisher compartment, pilot's step and access-port flaps lowered on a Harvard 2B.** Peter C. Smith

(Above) **Starboard centre section with walkway (left), fuel filling points and centre-section, wing fairing and rivet detail, Harvard 2B.** Peter C. Smith

(Left) **The lead into the cockpit from the engine exhaust led over the starboard wing centre section, with walkway (left), fuel filling points and centre-section, wing fairing and rivet detail, Harvard 2B.** Peter C. Smith

***(Above)* Close-up of the prop boss and the Pratt & Whitney radial engine configuration on the T-6G.** Peter C. Smith

***(Right)* Cowling, air scoop and nose detail on the T-6G.** Peter C. Smith

***(Above)* Starboard undercarriage detail on the T-6G.** Peter C. Smith

Starboard wheel and housing and leading edge fairing on Harvard 2B. Peter C. Smith

Radio Mast and Antenna

The US positioning was for a large wooden mast slightly offset to starboard, mounted smack-dab before the cockpit. An ADF sensing antenna ran back to the tip of the tail-plane. A retro-fit in later years was a Lear ADF loop antenna on a fairing mounted abaft the rear cockpit.

Rear Fuselage

On the starboard side, abreast of the rear cockpit, were located, front to rear, the air intake door for the rear cockpit, the red fire extinguisher panel, the fixed access step and the baggage compartment. Atop the fuselage there was a scarf mount for the 0.30-calibre M-2 Browning flexible machine gun, when fitted, and to the rear, the access hatch for the dynamotor compartment.

Wings

The outer sections had a NACA 2215 profile with a maximum breadth of 7ft 6in (22.28m), which merged to a NACA 4412 profile at the tips with a breadth of 4ft (1.2m). The other wing section had a 5 degree 11 minute dihedral. The pitot tube was mounted on the extreme outer leading edge of the starboard wing, just inside the tips. The fabric-covered ailerons were 7ft 11½in (2.42m) wide with 18in (45.7cm) metal trim tabs. Non-slip walkways

Close-up of wheel recesses, actuators and underwing riveting, Harvard 2B. Peter C. Smith

(Below) **Leading edge of wing, landing light, lowered flaps, and undercarriage detail, port side, Harvard 2B.** Peter C. Smith

featured on both sides of the cockpit on the inner-wing section. Outboard of these, on the forward edge of the wing, were the two fuel fill points and the lock pins strut oleo filler points. When a fixed forward-firing machine gun was fitted, it protruded from the leading edge of the outer wing panel just outboard on the centre section.

On the under-surfaces, the ground adjustable trim tabs had locking arms. Just inboard of the wing-tips, tie-down rings were mounted for mooring the aircraft to the deck. 0.30-calibre free-firing Browning M-2 fixed machine guns could be mounted on the starboard side with a gun camera sight in the equivalent port-side location. The gun eject chute was mounted to the rear of this gun.

Close-up of tail and port rear horizontal tail surfaces of the repainted T-6G (G-BKRA) of Andrew and Karen Edie's Transport Command, seen at Shoreham-on-Sea, 8 April 2000. Peter C. Smith

Empennage

Overall height of the vertical fabric-covered rudder was 11ft 8½in (3.56m), and the rudder had an elongated metal trim tab. Width of the rudder was 29⅜in. The fabric covered elevators had a length of 5ft 9 21/32in and the overall width of the horizontal tail surfaces was 12ft 11 5/16in.

Lights

There were two rectangular light wells, painted matt black in both wings' leading edges in mid-chord. The starboard well held a clear 450W landing light inboard and a 50W red passing light outboard, while the port well had just a 50W red passing light. The lenses conformed to the wings' leading edge contours. In the ventral position of the fuselage, abaft the camera doors, were three recognition lights mounted in tandem with, from front to rear, red, green and amber lights.

Paint Scheme

USAAF The brilliant blues and yellows with their red 'meat-balled' white stars, had given way to a more simplified scheme by mid-war. The Texan for the most part now appeared in natural aluminium (or aluminium dope on fabric-covered surface when of composite construction, but this tended to fade rapidly). The forward upper nose and cockpit area was painted with anti-glare flat bronze-green, which later gave way to matt black, and the seating followed this exactly. The cockpit interiors were zinc-chromate with yellow-green primer with black crinkle finish for instrument panels.

USN[2] The colour schemes were subjected to several dramatic changes of style between 1942 and 1944. On 6 February 1942, the US Navy issued a nine-page directive, which laid down the basic camouflage scheme as overall blue-grey from above and light grey from below. Although this applied to front-line units, the SNJs normally followed suit. On 5 January 1943, an exterior colour change took effect, which changed things. All airfoil surfaces viewed from above became semi-gloss sea blue, those from below were to be finished in NS insignia white. The leading edge of the wing was to be counter-shaded between the two, with NS insignia white and NS sea blue, the latter extending back to the top of the wing surface approximately 5 per cent of the wing chord. Upper fuselage surfaces extending down to a line approximately 60 degrees from horizontal were to be painted NS sea blue, lower surface NS insignia white. The national insignia was removed from the top of the starboard wing and the bottom of the port wing. Finally, on 13 March 1944, another directive changed things once more and all Navy aircraft became overall glossy sea blue, a colour scheme that survived until June 1947.

RAF and RCAF. An overall bright yellow finish was the standard painting during the war years and immediately thereafter, although to individual units and aircraft there came a myriad of unique alternatives. Many wartime aircraft in the UK carried the standard drab olive-green/brown camouflage. Similarly, the post-war finish was primarily overall silver.

North American's Contribution to the War Effort

By the end of World War II, North American training aircraft dominated the scene. Of the 54,642 total US deliveries of the trainer type from all manufacturers, NAA had produced no less than 12,968, or 23.7 per cent. The table below provides a breakdown of that impressive output.

NAA training production 1942–46[3]

Types	*Year*	*Quantity*	*Contract unit price*	*Average actual unit price*
AT-6A, -B, SNJ-3	1942	1,880	$18,311	$17,076*
AT-6C, -D	1943–44	5,506	$17,668	$13,333
SNJ-4, -5	1943–44	3,825	$12,989	$13,311
AT-6D, -F	1945	2,185	$13,100	$11,762
AT-6F	1946	1,200	$12,780	$11,350

** This average unit price had not been adjusted to give effect to a blanket voluntary refund amounting to $3,000,000 which was made under this contract.*

CHAPTER SEVEN

Flying 'The Six'

A crowded sky somewhere in the western USA. Massed formation flying in 'The Six' was a feature of the vast American training schools that sprang up in the aftermath of Pearl Harbor. Huge sprawling complexes were established in Texas especially, hence the name 'Texan', and when massed formations of students met in mid-air there was mayhem. Some bases earned formidable reputations as the fatal casualties piled up, 'Bloody' Barrin being one of them, but tens of thousands of young men survived the embrace of 'The Six' and went on to win the air war against the Axis. National Archives, Washington DC

Final checks for take-off and landing

TAKE-OFF		LANDING	
Trim	Elevator: slight back (11 o'clock) Rudder: full right	*Fuel*	Check contents Correct tank selected
Mixture	Full rich	*Mixture*	Full rich
Propeller	Maximum rpm	*Wheels*	Down and locked Green lights on
Fuel	Check contents Correct tank selected	*Brakes*	Park brake off Test
Flaps	Up or 15 degrees down.	*Propeller*	2,000rpm
		Flaps	As required

And so to the crux, what was the T-6 like to fly? As with most famous aircraft, legends abound and this aircraft, like every other, quickly earned itself a reputation for spinning, for ground-looping and for being a pig to land. How true were these statements? Like any generalizations, each can be taken with a pinch of salt, but one thing those that flew 'The Six' seem to agree on: she was one unforgiving mother! For many a young rookie pilot (and almost as many long-suffering instructors), the T-6 was a plane with lots of character, but once you had tamed her, you loved her for evermore!

In this chapter, we examine the basic routines involved in flying the T-6, but then hand over to the men who did the job, and from them we learn the true facts.

Flying 'The Six' Part One: Theory

The laid-down procedure for the Harvard IIB was as described below. Once again the routines varied from Mark to Mark, and as to whether the trainee or pilot was British, American or French, and indeed Air Force or Navy, because the instruments differed. We will examine these differences later in the chapter.

The RAF, as with all users, laid down a basic set of survival rules for both take-offs and landings, which, if adhered to, ensured the best opportunity of a second chance and these are listed in the box (*left*).

The Management of the Fuel System

The tanks could be selected in any convenient order, but if all of them were full, the recommended order was: right, left, reserve. When flying at low altitude and the right gauge showed 10 gallons, the tanks were changed from right to left, and when the left gauge got down to 25 gallons, the tanks were changed from left to reserve.

At a safe height, the left and right tanks could remain selected until the fuel pressure dropped. If the engine cut out, the throttle was closed before another cock setting was selected, in order to avoid over-speeding of the propeller, and the hand-pump was used to assist in the engine pick-up.

The hand-pump could also be used in flight, as above, for priming the fuel system before starting and at any time should the fuel pressure drop appreciably below normal.

Starting and Warming Up the Engine

After carrying out the external, internal and cockpit checks the pilot made the checks, as listed in the box.

Fuel cock	Reserve tank
Throttle	Open ½in
Mixture control	Rich (fully back)
Rpm control lever	Maximum rpm position
Carburettor heat control	Cold
Oil cooler shutter	As required
Ignition switch	Off
Battery switch	On

Once these checks were completed, procedures were as follows:

1. The propeller was hand turned by the mechanics through two revolutions to check for hydraulic locking.
2. If the engine was to be started from an external source, the ground starter battery was plugged in and switched on.
3. The hand-pump was worked to fill the fuel lines and carburettor.
4. The engine was primed. If it was cold and a Parker-type pump was fitted, four to six strokes were required; if a Ki-gas pump was fitted, three to four strokes were required. A hot engine did not require priming or, if it did, only one or two strokes at the most with the Parker pump or one stroke with the Ki-gas pump.
5. The ignition was switched on, and the starter energized electrically for 12–15s or until the hum became constant. Never was 20s to be exceeded. If the starter was hand-cranked the brushes had to be lifted first.
6. The starter switch was returned to the central position and, after a second's pause, the starter engaged. The starter engaging switch was kept on until the engine ran evenly, as it also operated the booster coil. The starter switch had to be returned positively to the Off position immediately the engine began running.
7. It was sometimes necessary to continue gently priming and to operate the hand pump to maintain the pressure in the carburettor until the engine picked up.
8. In the event of the engine still failing to start, the sequence was:

   (a) Wait until the propeller stops rotating, keep the engaging switch On to ensure that the flywheel stops. Immediately the propeller stopped rotating, ensure that the starter switch was returned to the Off position.
   (b) Switch off the ignition.
   (c) If the engine had been over-primed, the throttle was fully opened, the mixture control was moved forward to the Cut-off position and the propeller was then turned through several revolutions by hand. In any case, it should have been turned half a revolution to ensure that the flywheel was not engaging with the engine. The engine could be damaged if the starter switch was set to Energize, either with the flywheel running or with it meshed with the engine.

9. Once the engine was firing evenly, the priming pump was screwed down or locked, the throttle was slowly opened and the warm up at 1,000rpm followed.
10. While warming up at 1,000rpm, the checks listed in the box below were carried out.

Fuel cock	Left-hand tank
Flaps	Lower Indicator reading Hydraulic pressure reading Raise Selector up
Direction indicator	Set with magnetic compass Uncage
Radio	Test VHF and other radio aids Check altimeter setting with control
Fuel pressure warning light	Out

Exercising and Testing

After warming up to 40°C and 120°C cylinder-head temperatures, the oil cooler shutter was adjusted as necessary and then the following procedures were carried out.

1. Each magneto was tested as a precaution before increasing power.
2. Open up to 2½lb/in² and the constant-speed unit was checked by moving the rpm control lever over the full governing

Whether you taught or whether you learnt, whether you were a pupil in an AT-6, an SNJ, a Harvard or a Wirraway, that first flight is usually etched in your memory. Who was the most apprehensive, trainer or trainee? Here that moment is captured as another pair board a Harvard on a snow-bound field in England in readiness for another flight. Author's collection

range at least twice. The lever was returned fully forward and the operation of the vacuum pump was checked as well as the charging of the generator.

3. The static boost reading was opened up and the rpm checked to see that they were within fifty of the reference figure quoted in Form 700.
4. During the same boost, each magneto was tested by switching from Both to R, back to Both, Both to L and again back to Both. The single ignition drop was not to exceed 100rpm. If this occurred, and there had been no undue vibration, the ignition was checked at higher power. If there was a marked vibration, the engine was shut down and the cause investigated.
5. The gate was opened up and the boost briefly checked (+3lb/in² and about 2,200rpm to a maximum of 2,250rpm).
6. Throttle back until the rpm fell, thus ensuring that the propeller is not constant-speeding, steadily moving the throttle to the fully closed position, and checking the minimum idling rpm, before opening to 1,000rpm.

Taxying

Before taxying, the checks given in the box below had to be carried out.

Fuel cock	Right-hand tank
Chocks	Clear
Taxying	As soon as possible test brakes Check direction indicator for accuracy Check artificial horizon for accuracy Check temperatures and pressures Check that pressure head heater is on, if required

NB: If the brakes proved fierce, then harsh use while taxying could cause the steerable tailwheel to unlock.

Take-off

After completing the final checks (as given in the table 'Final checks for take-off and landing' on page 70) the aircraft was aligned with the runway, and the tailwheel was checked as being straight. The throttle was opened smoothly to the gate (there was a slight tendency to swing to port). The aircraft was then flown off at an approximate speed of 70 knots. If the flaps were used, they were raised at a safe height and before a speed of 110 knots was reached.

Climbing

The speed for a maximum rate of climb was 100 knots to 5,000ft (1,525m). Above that height speed was reduced by 5 knots per 5,000ft, and the mixture control was moved forward to prevent rough running due to over-richness. As height was gained, so the throttle was progressively opened to maintain +1½lb/in² boost at 2,200rpm.

(Top) **While the American cadets enjoyed the all-round good weather conditions of the mid-West, it was a welcome relief for British trainees and instructors alike when many advanced training units moved out of snowbound England early in 1940 and set up in the perfect climate of Southern Rhodesia (now known as Zimbabwe). Here Mark IIA Harvards, EX 523 nearest camera (coded 'P'), are practising formation training with 20 SFTS. This particular aircraft later flew with 5 and 4 FTS post-war but crashed near Meilloo on 16 July 1948.** RAF Museum, Hendon, London

(Bottom) **Mark IIA Harvards EX 523 (coded 'P') and EX 754 (coded '18') seen flying formation practice with 20 FTS over Southern Rhodesia.** RAF Museum, Hendon, London

For maximum range on the climb, the flying speed was 110 knots, using –2lb/in² boost and 1,850rpm with the mixture control up to the throttle.

If the cylinder head pressure proved excessive, speed was increased and the mixture control was kept in the fully rich position.

General Flying

Changes of Trim

These are given in the box below.

Wheels down	Slightly nose down
Wheels up	Slightly nose up
Flaps down	Nose down
Flaps up	Nose up

Flying at Reduced Airspeeds

At reduced airspeeds of 110 knots, lower 15 degrees of flap and select 2,000rpm. Speed could then be reduced to not less than 75 knots. The stalling speed under these conditions was 55 knots.

Mixture Control

In general, mixture control should have been operated as follows (according to RAF practice of the day).

1. For flying at power in excess of that permitted for a weak mixture (–2lb/in² and 1,850rpm), the control was only advanced from the fully rich position as necessary, to avoid rough running and loss of power due to over-richness.
2. For flying at power below that permitted for a weak mixture, the control was advanced up to, but not beyond, the throttle. Care had to be taken, however, not to render the mixture over-weak, which would show up as a drop in rpm and/or a rise in the cylinder head temperature.
3. For cruising at moderate and high altitudes, it was found that beyond a certain throttle opening, no further increase in boost or power was obtained. To simplify the operation of mixture control, the throttle was not advanced beyond that point. Economical mixture strength was still obtained under those conditions by operating the mixture control, as above.

Use of Hot Air

On the ground and in the air, hot air was used when airframe icing conditions existed or when humidity was such that, when combined with the temperature drop through the induction system, it was liable to cause carburettor icing. The hot-air intake was then adjusted to give a reading of 0–10+°C on the carburettor temperature gauge.

Normally, take-off was made with the intake control fully cold, but under icing conditions it was advisable to set the control before take-off to give 5+°C carburettor temperature at about –2lb/in² boost and set it in the same way for the approach.

A change from cold to hot, or vice versa, was not to be made at full power.

Flying for Range and Endurance

- *Flying for maximum range.* For maximum range, both on the climb and in level flight, the recommended speed was 110 knots at –2lb/in² boost. The recommended rpm was 1,850 on the climb, adjusted to give 110 knots in level flight. As the rpm was varied, it was necessary to readjust the boost setting. The rpm could be as low as 1,400, but below that figure the generator output was considered inadequate. If at low altitude the recommended speed was exceeded at minimum rpm, the boost was reduced accordingly. The use of hot involved very little loss of range if the mixture control was kept up to the throttle.

- *Flying for endurance.* The lowest practical altitude was flown. The minimum rpm required to keep the generator charging, a weak mixture and the smallest throttle opening at which height could be maintained at 90 knots were selected.

Fuel Consumption

Consumption at high power was as shown in the table below left.

Consumption under weak mixture conditions (imperial gallons) was as shown in the table below.

A trio of early Harvard Mark IIs of the RAF, which operated in Canada during the war under the Commonwealth Air Training Scheme, first with 39 and then 13 SFTS, prior to being handed over to the RCAF on the conclusion of British flight training in that country. RAF Museum, Hendon, London

Harvard IIB: Fuel consumption at high power

Mixture control	*rpm*	*Boost lb/in²*	*Gallons/h*
Rich	2,250	+3	56
Rich	2,200	+11/2	48
Rich	1,925	0	30

Harvard IIB: Fuel consumption (gallons per hour) under weak mixture conditions

rpm	*Boost lb/in²*				
	–2	–3	–4	–5	–6
1,800	26	23½	22	20	17½
1,700	24	22	20½	19	17
1,600	22	21	19	17	16
1,500	20	19	17	16	14
1,400	18	17	15	14	13

In addition to Canada and Southern Rhodesia, the Empire Air Training Scheme also saw the Harvard working hard in South Africa, New Zealand and the Indian Empire. Here an impeccable quartet of Harvard IIBs are seen wheels down at an Indian air base in 1944. Ray C. Sturtivent

The RAF continued to train in Southern Rhodesia during the immediate post-war years. Here a trio of Harvards (coded SE = Single-Engined) fly over the base at Heany. RAF Museum, Hendon, London

Position error correction was as shown in the table below.

Harvard IIB: Position error correction

	Knots			
From	85	105	120	140
To	105	120	140	160
Add	2	3	4	5

Stalling

The approximate stalling speeds in knots were as shown in the box below.

POWER OFF	
Undercarriage and flaps up	60 knots
Undercarriage and flaps down	55 knots
POWER ON	
Under typical landing conditions	50 knots

Indicated stalling speeds (mph)

Gross wt (lb)	*Gear and flaps up*				*Gear and flaps down*			
	Power on (Max. continuous power)		Power off (Windmilling propeller)		Power on (Approach power)*		Power off (Windmilling propeller)	
	Level	*30-degree bank*	*Level*	*30-degree bank*	*Level*	*30-degree bank*	*Level*	*30-degree bank*
6,000	72	78	78	84	63	70	67	72
5,500	67	74	75	80	60	66	63	69
5,000	61	70	71	76	55	62	59	65
4,500	54	64	66	72	51	57	55	61

** Approximately 2,000rpm, 18in Hg*

There was slight elevator buffeting just before a stall, but this could not be relied upon to give adequate warning. At the stall, with flaps up or down, the nose and either wing might drop. With flaps down, the wing dropped more quickly than with flaps up. In both cases, if the stick was held hard back, the aircraft would spin.

If the aircraft was stalled in a steep turn, buffeting would occur and the aircraft would flick. Recovery was normal and immediate if pressure on the control column was relaxed. The aircraft would spin if the control column was held hard back.

Items affecting stalling speed and characteristics

Item	*Stall characteristics*	*Stall speeds*
Abrupt control movement	✓	✓
Altitude		
Cg location	✓	
Co-ordination	✓	✓
Gross weight		✓
Landing gear		
Power	✓	✓
Turns	✓	✓
Wing flaps	✓	✓
Attitude	✓	✓

Spinning

Both hoods had to be closed to avoid panels blowing out of the canopy.

In either direction, the aircraft readily entered the spin. Considerable shuddering occurred for approximately two turns and then the spin became smoother. Normal recovery action was effective; the aircraft took 1½–2 turns to recover, during which time the rate of rotation increased and then abruptly stopped. The rudder was then centralized and the speed allowed to build up to 120 knots before easing out of the dive. In order to avoid over-speeding the propeller, the throttle was opened slowly during the recovery.

Owing to the strain on the undercarriage and flaps, spinning was not recommended to be carried out with them down. In the case of an unintentional spin, normal recovery action was effective if applied immediately.

Diving

The rpm control lever was left at a moderate cruising position and the throttle kept open to give –7 to –5lb/in^2 boost. With the throttle so set, 2,250rpm could be exceeded for 20s to a maximum of 2,650rpm. The boost rose as height was lost.

For a dive with the throttle closed, the rpm control lever had to be set to the minimum rpm position before the throttle was closed and 2,250rpm could not be exceeded.

Aerobatics

The recommended speeds in knots were as shown in the box below.

Roll	130–140 knots
Loop	170–180 knots
Half roll off the loop	190–200 knots

Confidence grows, and here several RCAF Harvard Mark IIs fly inverted to prove they have 'made it'. Canadian Government Official, Ottawa

***(Below)* A gaggle of Harvards flying in close formation.** FAA Museum, Yeovilton

An rpm of 1,850 and a boost of –2lb/in² was sufficient for all the above manoeuvres, and the mixture control could be kept up to the throttle.

If the engine cut while in inverted flight, or through negative 'g', the throttle was closed to prevent subsequent over-speeding. During prolonged flight in cold temperatures, the oil in the propeller cylinder could congeal sufficiently to make pitch changing sluggish. In those circumstances over-speeding could occur in a dive, due to the reluctance of the propeller to change quickly into a coarser pitch. This could be prevented by moving the rpm control lever over its full range slowly before commencing aerobatics manoeuvres.

Approach and Landing

The pilot's checks that were carried out prior to landing are given in the box below.

Harness	Tight and locked
Fuel	Contents and cock setting
Carburettor air intake	As required
Mixture	Fully rich
Undercarriage	Down and locked
	Green lights on
Brakes	Tested by depressing the pedals
rpm control lever	Set at the 2,000rpm position
Flaps	As required

The recommended speeds in knots at which the airfield boundary was to be crossed were as shown in the box below.

	Flaps down	*Flaps up*
Engine assisted	70–75	75–80
Glide	75–80	80–85

In a strong crosswind or in rough weather it was preferable to make a wheel landing. In the three-point attitude, particularly with full flap, there was a tendency in those conditions to balloon either before or after touch down, and control could then be found to be insufficient.

After touchdown, when the tail was on the ground, the control column was held hard back; this helped to keep the tailwheel in the steerable position. The application of rudder alone was not always sufficient to maintain directional control and brake could then be used as necessary. When a swing occurred, the rudder was only to be used consistent with the effective use of the brake.

Mislanding and Going Round Again

Open up to 0lb/in² boost. If more power was required, the rpm control lever was moved fully forward before opening up to +3lb/in².

The undercarriage was raised and the aircraft re-trimmed.

The climb away was made at 80–85 knots. Once at a safe height, the flaps were raised in stages and re-trimmed. The flaps would start to come up when the flap lever was moved, even if the power control had not been pressed.

After Landing

Before taxying the following checks had to be carried out, as shown in the box below.

Brakes	Test
Flaps	Up Selector up
Pressure head heater	As required

On reaching the dispersal area, the engine was idled at about 800rpm for about a minute, or until the cylinder head temperature fell below 205°C, whichever was the longer. Each magneto was tested and the mixture control moved fully forward past the throttle catch.

The RAF Ferry Training Unit, at RAF Abingdon, 30 August 1951, commanded by Squadron Leader Arthur M. Gill, RAF. No 1 Hangar with two Harvards, three Mosquito T3s, three Meteor T7s and two Vampire Mark Vs. Arthur M. Gill

Flying 'The Six' Part Two: Fact

So much for theory, now how did 'The Six' actually fly? Several veteran pilots and instructors have described what it was like and these give excellent insights to the true idiosyncrasies of the type.[1] For the sake of convenience I have grouped these accounts under the following headings: Start, Take-Off and Climb; Formation-Flying and Aerobatics; Night and Instrument Flying; Endurance and Fuel System; Stalling and Spinning; Landing and Ground-Looping.

Start, Take-Off and Climb

After the student had climbed into the cockpit and carried out the pre-flight checks, the engine had to be started according to the book. The propeller attached to the Pratt and Whitney radial had to be pulled through seven blades in order to move the oil out of the lower cylinders and thus avoid hydraulic action that could cause damage. Jeff Ethell described the procedure thus:

> As the engine is primed three or four strokes, one must pump up fuel pressure manually with the left hand while priming with the right. Battery on, throttle cranked half an inch, foot pedal forward to build up inertia on the flywheel, then heel down to engage the starter – after four prop blades pass in front, magnetos to both. When the engine fires, continue priming until it smoothes out. Under no circumstances should the throttle be pumped since that much raw fuel being dumped in the cylinders can start a raging fire.
>
> A few cylinders catch and pop, blue smoke swirls everywhere around the cockpit, then the engine settles into a rich rumble.[2]

Squadron Leader Norman E. Rose accrued 779.10h flying the Harvard and although he modestly told me, 'I would not consider myself to be any sort of an expert on it', I feel he should know a *little* about the type. He told me of his first impressions as a very junior student in 1943:

> The Mark I had a partly canvas fuselage whereas the later Marks were all metal and the tail fin was more pointed. The cockpit was spacious and well appointed. The instrumentation was typically American with 'inches' of mercury (I think) instead of our British 'pounds' of boost. One thing I remember well was the beautiful green glow of the instruments at night (ours were normally white). It took a while to become accustomed to the runway disappearing beneath the bulbous nose when holding off in the three-point attitude prior to touch-down, which probably accounted for so many wing-tips!

Colonel John DeVries, USAF, has similar memories:

> Someone 'on high' decided that landing a Texan from the back seat was just like landing a P-40 or P-51. It wasn't! Even disregarding the 1000hp difference in the aircraft, the student couldn't see beyond the overturn structure between the cockpits, no matter how many cushions he used. It was an experiment in sheer terror! Transition instructors, who regularly flew from the rear seat, always skidded the AT-6 on final approach so that they could see the field, to say nothing about seeing the runway.[3]

Early T-6 instrumentation was somewhat basic to say the least. The original high frequency (HF) radio equipment had to be tuned in by means of a hand-cranked piece of kit known to the students as 'the coffee grinder'. It took for ever to wind this round until the base tower frequency of 4,495 kilocycles (kHz) was tuned in. Similarly, the notorious Detrola radio range received was similarly churned in order to tune it into 200–400 kHz to home on the four-legged aural radio ranges. Even if it could find the right frequency, it invariably cut out at the crucial moment. The microphones were hand-held at this stage, adding yet one more instrument that the pilot had to cope with while flying the aircraft.

With the AT-6D things got better. This Mark was built with the four-button VHF radio, which had three channels and a 'guard' emergency frequency. They also had the automatic direction-find (DF) loop antenna, which allowed radio-range flying and ADF approach patterns. As well as being a much better instrument, it had one DF band of 550–1,600kHz, which in the USA was the commercial radio station band, so long flights *could* be accompanied by Tommy Dorsey, Frank Sinatra and Glen Miller, if conditions permitted!

Formation-Flying and Aerobatics

One thing that 'The Six' excelled at was formation-flying due to her inherent responsiveness. The controls were light and responsive and the aircraft was stressed to take 5.67 positive and 2.33 negative g forces. As Jeff Ethell described it:

> 'The Six' has wonderfully harmonized controls and this is where the real love affair starts – no stiffness at all, just put the stick and rudder where you want to go and it goes there. The ailerons are boosted with servo tabs so I couldn't wait to get up to our manoeuvring altitude to do a roll. Unbelievable – nothing should handle this well. The entire aerobatic spectrum was available...[4]

Colonel DeVries described this major attribute graphically as a 'right now! reaction'.[5] Either by increasing the prop pitch or lowering the big flaps speed could be quickly decreased and she also responded to putting the 'pedal to the metal'. Side-slipping was definitely a 'no-no' of course. The reliable R-1340-AN burnt up about half a gallon of fuel per minute but could achieve the red-line of 250mph (400km/h) via an extended dive flat out.

All this made for ease of station-keeping during daylight flying, and led to the enormous popularity of the T-6 post-war with civilian flyers, pylon racers, aerobatic teams and sky-typers. Inverted flight, however, was limited to a mere 10s because the Pratt and Whitney engine had the dry-sump oil system, which meant that upside-down the fuel ran out, much of it on the windshield!

Night and Instrument Flying

Although not famed for her nocturnal activities 'The Six's' night-flying capabilities were limited and, some felt, unnecessarily hazardous. Colonel John A. DeVries was among the latter:

> Night-flying, solo, in a Texan was a semi-harrowing experience, particularly in the earlier models. Not that the airplane flew any differently after dark, but the night-lighting system in the cockpit was marginal. The system consisted of two ultra-violet lamps, mounted one on each side of the cockpit. They had ball-swivel holders and activated the phosphorescent markings on the instruments. There was never enough light to see all of the instruments at any one time. The ultra-violet light was produced by a removable filter fitted over the end of a white-light fixture. If your arm hit the lights, the cockpit would suddenly be filled with white light, thus killing any night-adaptation your eyes may have attained. Incidentally, the sudden appearance of white light would scare the hell of out you as well! An arm between light and instruments would black-out half the panel. Late aircraft had individually red-lit instruments and the swivel lights received red filters that would permit a map to be read or a radio-facility chart to be consulted. Early AT-6 pilots had specially printed night-flying maps that reacted to ultra-violet light.[6]

Veteran US Navy flyer George J. Walsh recalled that he, at least, enjoyed night flights in the 'J-Bird':

> In 1945, after my second tour of fleet duty, I was assigned to Carrier Air Acceptance Test Center

George J. Walsh, USN. George J. Walsh

at Mustin Field in Philadelphia. It was a pilot's dream billet, because we had little to do. It was more of a utility squadron than a test center. We had a great variety of aircraft to play with, including Cubs, a Stearman, Widgeon, twin-engined Cessna's, a stripped down SB2C, Beechcraft, Lodestar, and a tired old SNJ!

When I went through Pensacola we had our advanced training in the SNCs so this was my first introduction to the SNJ. It was a lively and beautiful plane to fly and I fell in love with it. So much so that I would volunteer to take the night flying duties for the married officers. For some reason the squadron had to log night flying hours and I enjoyed tooling around at night over Philadelphia and the surrounding countryside.

Night flying in formation was something else again. Colonel DeVries stated that it was never popular because the right wingman stared into the blinding flame of the leader's right-mounted exhaust, which blinded him. The fitting of blue, lighted discs as formation lights on some T-6s enabled night-formation to be conducted with some degree of safety, but the basic problems still remained. The later fitting of red, green and amber flush-mounted recognition lights was equally unhelpful for this type of flying, as these were meant to aid identity from the ground, rather than as night navigation aids.

The AT-6D was employed as an instrument flying training aircraft, principally at the Instrument Instructor's School at Bryan, Texas, with radar-directed landings (ground-controlled approach or GCA) and the instrument landing system (ILS). Training and practice of instrument flying was learned by the student from the back seat, which had an aluminium and canvas hood covering it for realism. The suction-powered gyro system was employed, with air sucked by an engine-driven vacuum pump through the instrument cases, which turned the air-driven gyro-wheels. With 3.5–4.8in of mercury, sufficient vacuum was obtained to work the turn and bank, directional and artificial horizon gyros. To make them safe, these instruments each had an immobilizer knob and operating this was called 'caging'.

Endurance and Fuel System

The fuel system caused its own problems. The two wing tanks located in either centre-wing section of the AT-6 each held 55+ US gallons, but the port tank was fitted with a standpipe that controlled the 'reserve' and effectively locked it off, giving the ratio of 55 Starboard/35 Port. The red warning light indicated when either tank reached 10 gallons (45l), when the 20 gallons (90l) reserve held in the port tank could be kicked in, which was just as well, for any hungry engine that gulped down extra 91 octane would result in an emergency landing at best and sometimes worse. This was accentuated by the floor-mounted fuel gauges, which, even if in pristine condition (which they seldom were) could only be read by the pilot swivelling around in his seat, and were not readable at all from the rear cockpit. Perhaps this was not considered important for a training aircraft that would always remain close to base, but during ferry trips across the United States, Canada or the Indian subcontinent, this could cause embarrassment. Arthur Gill described for me one such incident:

When I commanded No. 84 Dive-Bomber Squadron in India, I decided to visit Doris Hammond (a captain in the WAC(I) – Women's Auxiliary Corps (India), part of the Indian Army) whom I had first met in Quetta and who was then stationed at Ranchi in the State of Bihar in Northern India. Instead of flying one of our new Vultee Vengeance dive-bombers, with which the squadron was equipped, I used the squadron's Harvard II (serial number FE 413), which I normally used for dual-instruction, to check the flying of all my pilots. I took with me one of my flight commanders, Flight Lieutenant Dick Johns, RNZAF, as my navigator.

(*Above*) Squadron Leader Arthur Murland Gill flying Harvard FE 413 across India. Arthur M. Gill

(*Right*) The backseat driver who fell asleep! Flight Lieutenant Dick Johns, RNZAF. Arthur M. Gill

Swamped at Ramgah! When Mark II Harvard FE 413, the No 84 Squadron RAF 'Hack', was forced to put down at Ramgah in the State of Bihar, India, on 5 February 1943, the locals, who had never seen an aircraft before, quickly congregated in their hundreds. Arthur M. Gill

We took off from Cholavaram on the east coast of South India, where the squadron was training with its new American aircraft, and flew to Gonnavaram on 5 February 1943, to refuel. We flew on to Vizagapatam, to refuel again, before setting course for Ranchi. The visibility deteriorated as the heat haze increased and, to make matters worse, a dust storm blew up at ground level as the wind increased. I asked Dick Johns over the intercom how much further he thought we had to go before we reached our destination. There was no reply: he was sound asleep! I too was becoming drowsy. We had been in the air for a total of 7.20 hours.

There was no radio or navigational aids in that vast, featureless area. No rivers or railway lines to follow; and no means of telling from which direction the wind was blowing – unless one spotted the smoke from a fire on the ground – or the speed of the wind at the height we were flying. We were lost! Before the tanks ran dry, I decided to find a flat area in that dry, dusty 'desert' on which to land; if possible, near a village or habitation. I chose what looked like a reasonably flat area, but I was horrified to discover, as I was landing, that the whole area was covered with rocks and small boulders! Fortunately, I missed every one and the aircraft came to a standstill undamaged.

After I had stopped the engine, and before I had time to climb out of the cockpit, the aircraft was surrounded by a large crowd of Indians – men, women and children of all ages. I discovered that none of them had ever seen an aircraft on the ground and very few in the sky above. The head man told me that there was no telephone in the village. So, whilst I left Dick to clear the rocks and prepare a 'runway' with the help of all the villagers, I borrowed a bicycle and rode several miles in the heat to find the nearest police post, which I hoped had a serviceable telephone, and phoned the RAF maintenance party at the staging post at Ranchi to send a truck with petrol in four-gallon cans.

The fuel arrived, eventually, and after I had refuelled the Harvard, I decided to take off on my own, because of the short, rough runway and the risk involved. Dick travelled over two hours by truck over bumpy roads, while I flew the 40 miles to Ranchi.[7]

Stalling and Spinning

Squadron Leader Norman Rose gave me this account of his introduction to these special qualities of the Harvard:

I first flew one on 25 October 1943 – a Mark I, N 7017, at 22 SFTS Thornhill, Southern Rhodesia. After the Tiger Moth it seemed enormous, but its roomy and comfortable cockpit was a vast improvement, not least a canopy that closed away from the slipstream. The Mark I had rounded wing-tips and round tail fin and could be a really vicious beast at the stall (good for pilot training!) but an embarrassment on landing as I soon found out.

Testing of the new Harvard Marks as they appeared took place at the Aeroplane & Armament Experimental Establishment (A&AEE) during the war. This Mark II is seen under test there on 6 November 1941. Ray C. Sturtivent

Later in the course I graduated to the Mark II, IIA and IIB. They were slightly less vicious and a little nicer to fly. I was very apprehensive of spinning in the Tiger Moth, but I felt much more confident in the Harvard, maybe because of the enclosed cockpit. It always responded immediately to spin corrective action. It was also much more satisfying and fun to do aerobatics. And, of course, it was that much faster – or, at least, it seemed to so in those days for an eighteen year old![8]

Norman also recalled his time with 5 METS at Shallufa in the Canal Zone for rocket-firing training prior to joining No. 6 Squadron in Italy:

Here the Harvard came into its own with its 'flicking' characteristic. By whipping into a steep turn and pulling back hard on the stick, the aircraft would high speed stall but it was very sudden and could flick either way leading to complete loss of control even to the extent of flipping onto its back. Recovery was instantaneous as soon as the backward pressure on the stick was released. Obviously if you were near the ground it could be fatal if the flick was into the inside of the steep turn. The Hurricane had very similar 'flick' characteristics and the method of delivery rockets in those early days was to fire at 200 or 400 yards at about 50ft straight and level at 225 knots and then involved a very sharp hard turn to avoid the debris from the target. The combination of a 90 degree banked turn and a hard pull back resulted in many pilots' deaths, quite apart from being clobbered by the 60lb rocket explosion! Thus the Harvard demonstration and training was a vital life-saving exercise for us young inexperienced pilots.[9]

Later, while serving as an instructor at the Central Flying School, Ternhill in 1949, Norman had a close shave due to the natural inclination of the T-6 to spin at the slightest opportunity:

Teaching flying was not without its moments of terror! I had one cadet who became absolutely petrified at his first attempt at spinning – he entered the spin as usual by reducing speed to the stall, applying full rudder while holding the central control column fully back, but when told to 'recover' nothing happened. I repeated my instruction several times with increasing intensity and loudness but still no reaction. I called 'I have control' and tried to take corrective action of full opposite rudder and stick firmly forward but I found that I could not move the controls! He had frozen solid with fright and his foot was locked in the 'in-spin' position. Try as I might I could not unjar his locked leg. I shouted and banged on the combing behind his head but we continued down turn after turn. Fortunately, we commenced the spin at a good height and eventually he released and I was able to recover but I was a bit shaken and breathless and he was as white as a sheet and trembling. It was necessary to debrief him both on the way back to the airfield and on the ground, then take him up again almost straight away and coax him slowly into spinning again. The experience did not help my phobia about spinning either I can tell you! I am quite happy with spinning if I am handling the controls but if someone else is flying the aircraft, especially a student, I am a little apprehensive and ever after I always carried the memory of that occasion, which made me a bit paranoid at the point of entry of a spin, especially in the Harvard![10]

Landing and Ground-Looping

One account describes a ground-loop as a spiral with ever-decreasing circles.[11] 'The Six' was prone to this unfortunate trait, so hazardous to trainee and even veteran pilots if they relaxed their guard, and this was especially the case if landing cross-wind. The reasons for this were as follows:

- The landing wheels were placed close together. Their location was dictated by the fact that all of the retraction mechanism, the struts and the wheels themselves, were located in the straight centre-section wing.
- The relationship of the wing to the tail surfaces. In a three-point landing attitude, the wing partially blanketed the tail surfaces, rendering them slightly less effective. The widest, and therefore the most effective, part of the rudder was in the area of disturbed air, so directional control was reduced.
- The relative shortness of the landing gear struts, which meant that when a ground-loop developed, there was little space between the wing-tip and ground to play with.

Squadron Leader Norman Rose confessed that, in his early days on the type, he also, 'scraped two wing-tips by holding off too high in the three-point attitude before I learned to land it properly'.[12]

A good description of what occurred in these conditions was given by DeVries:

> The plane began to turn soon after touch-down. A slight turn, uncorrected with the rudder, increased rapidly. Assuming that the cross-wind was from the left, and the 6 was weather-vaning into it, the right wing-tip dropped as the left tip was raised. At this point in the ground-loop the pilot began to hear awful scraping sounds as the right tip met the runway. Attempts at control, too late, had little or no effect on the ground-loop process. In fact, violent efforts at controlling a ground-loop aggravated the situation because full rudder plus brake (in early AT-6s) kicked the steerable tail wheel into full-swivel position! This, of course, deprived the pilot of any control over the back end of his bird! Many AT-6 pilots adopted the wheel-landing technique in an attempt to avoid ground-loops (rather than three-pointing) but a flicker as the tail dropped produced almost as many ground-off or bent-up wing-tips.[13]

Norman Rose recalls a more terrifying experience while he was with the Central Flying School at Little Rissington in 1948. He recalled that operating and landing from the back seat successfully:

> ...wasn't the easiest of manoeuvres! You had to stick your head out into the slipstream with the hood open to see the runway at all – it was easiest if there was a cross-wind from the right so that the aircraft had its nose pointing into the cross-wind crabbing down the runway centre-line. It was not so easy the opposite way because the throttle was positioned on the left wall of the rear cockpit making reaching it a problem.
>
> One day I was safety pilot to a co-student practising landings from the back seat at the satellite field of Moreton-in-the-Marsh. He was an ex-Lancaster pilot, a Flight Lieutenant with a DSO and DFC (I was a lowly P2, a rank called Pilot Two, a weird and short-lasting rank system introduced for NCO aircrew after the war), who had never flown single-engined aircraft before and he was having severe difficulties landing the Harvard from the back seat. On one landing he held off high, stalled and scraped the wing-tip, which pulled us about 40 degrees from the runway heading whereupon

The switch to semi-tropical climes meant all-year-round and round-the-clock flying conditions for the RAF and Commonwealth trainee pilots from 1940 onward, which greatly facilitated the CATS scheme. RAF Museum, Hendon, London

he opened the throttle taking us, in a parlous state, directly towards the Control Tower! It was the policy to let student instructors extricate themselves from their own mistakes as part of the learning process so that when an *ab-initio* student pilot made similar mistakes he could be rescued at the very last minute through experience. In this case I felt forced to take over and close the throttle, straighten up and apply the brakes to prevent a disaster! Here I must again mention the size of the American cockpit – the rudder pedals were designed for 6ft long-legged Americans with the brake pedals attached immediately above them so that a shorty like me of 5ft 6in had great difficulty stretching leg and foot to apply full rudder AND brakes at the same time even with the rudder pedals adjusted fully rearwards![14]

George J. Walsh gave me this memory of a similar experience, which he remembers as 'First Flight of the Captain's Nurse':

> It happened that the Captain had some minor surgery at the hospital where the attending nurse told him she had never been up in an airplane. He gallantly offered her the services of his personal pilot to fly her home on her next leave. When the day came we loaded the somewhat hesitant nurse with a parachute and stuffed her in the back seat of our tired old SNJ and filled her in on emergency procedures for her first flight. Not exactly like a stewardess's care on American Airlines but we were casual about flying.
>
> We took off in clear weather and headed for Pittsburgh. As we approached Allentown the Air Force Weather Station advised us of severe thunderstorms in our path and advised us to land.
>
> The landing was smooth but on the run out the storm hit. The SNJ flipped around like a leaf in the wind. The right wheel collapsed and the wing dragged us around in a ground loop that left us facing back the way we came.
>
> I switched everything off and took inventory, then turned to look at my passenger. She was gone! The last I saw of her was a panicky figure racing up the steps of the administration building with her parachute flapping madly against her backside. I wondered where she was going in such a hurry but never did find out what happened to her or the parachute. For that matter it was also my last flight in an SNJ. The Captain never once mentioned the incident in our later flights!

The J-Bird was equally prone to ground-loop, although one Navy flyer, Robert S. Mullaney, told me that he *never* had that experience:

> The SNJ (and I don't remember anyone calling it anything else!) was a fairly agile machine with only one delicate characteristic. It would ground-loop easily. While I never did do it, my wingman landing in formation with me at Pensacola Naval Air Station during training 'spun' on two consecutive occasions! However, for me it was the right airplane – at the right time – while on my way to combat with the SB2C Helldiver and the F6F Hellcat.[15]

Even when safely down there were other hazards that inexperienced students could bring out of the Harvard. Squadron Leader Norman Rose recalled one incident while he was detached to No. 2 FTS at South Cerney in 1949:

> 2 Flying Training School was at that time equipped with Harvard IIBs and here my memory seems to falter, as I am unsure of the location of the undercarriage lever in the rear

SNJ MEN: Robert S. Mullaney, US Navy

One of many great Navy flyers who has fond memories of his brief association with the SNJ was Robert Mullaney. He was born in Chicago on 10 September 1920 and always wanted to be an aviator. The Navy flyers were the most skilled and he set his heart on that career early on. The first major step was attaining an aeronautical degree (BS) at the University of Notre Dame in May 1942. A month later, Robert was old enough to enlist in the USN V-5 Flight Training programme and he was called to active duty that same August.

The first three months Robert spent at the pre-flight training unit at the University of North Carolina, and his first flight followed on 23 November when he went aloft in a Naval Aircraft factory N3N from Grosse Isle, Michigan. During his training period, and on his way to his commission, Robert flew a variety of aircraft, N3N, N25, NP (Spartan), the Vultee SNV and finally majored on the SNJ on which he clocked up 100h of flying time.

Robert was commissioned as an Ensign on 16 July 1943, at Pensacola NAS and then proceeded back home to Illinois where carrier deck-landing training was conducted on the training carrier USS *Sable*, which ploughed up and down Lake Michigan for just that purpose. This done, it was operational training, which was carried on the SBC, the BT and the OS2V aircraft at Miami, Florida. Robert became a dive-bomber pilot and joined VB-80 training, first on the docile Douglas SBD Dauntless and then on the meaner and more powerful Curtiss SB2C Helldiver types. This completed, his squadron joined Carrier Air Group (CAG) at Oceana, Virginia. Working up the group continued until they were pronounced combat fit and joined the new aircraft carrier *Ticonderoga* (CV-14) one of the new *Essex* class ships scheduled for the Pacific Theatre and taking the war on to Japan in the fall of 1944.

Robert did not long have to wait to see action, both on the giving and the receiving end. His Helldivers blasted a path through the Philippines via Iwo Jima to the home Japanese islands, leaving a trail of wrecked hangars and sunken vessels in their wake. In turn, the *Ticonderoga* was attacked several times by a new type of enemy, the Kamikaze suicide bombers. She was eventually hit and badly damaged on 21 January 1945 and Robert was wounded. He was forced to spend the next six months in hospital and did not return to active duty until VJ Day itself. For his actions that day Robert was the worthy recipient of the Purple Heart.

Post-war, Robert was assigned to the Bureau of Aeronautics at Washington DC but served for only a short period there before he was discharged in September 1945. He was not idle for long, the next month saw him hired as a flight test engineer for the Grumman Corporation, where he remained for the next forty years. During that time Robert did a variety of jobs: flight test; jet propulsion engineer; XF10F test group at Edwards AFB; F11F Tiger Project engineer; and became a fellow of the MIT with MS in Management. For four memorable years Robert was Manager of the Lunar Excursion Module Programme and later Manager for Operations on the F-14 programme. He crowned his career as vice president, Grumman International and retired in November 1985. He logged some 813h flying time in those years, but now lives at Bellport, New York and has 80 per cent completed an RV-4, two-place, tail dragger experimental airplane of his own.

cockpit, but I remember I used to keep my left hand firmly on it after landing to prevent the student from inadvertently raising the undercarriage instead of the flaps – a not uncommon occurrence from time to time! After landing one day, my P2 rank student did just that but because my hand was stopping him he obviously thought his front cockpit lever for the flaps (so he wrongly thought) was stiff so he exerted more pressure, which I was unable to completely override. I pushed as hard as I could but the two undercarriage red lights illuminated indicating an unlocked undercarriage situation. I shouted at him immediately and he released his handle realising what he had done but although my handle was now back in the fully down position, the red lights were still on. I stopped the aircraft and switched off the engine to eliminate any hydraulic pressure and hoped for the best. I called for the ground crew to bring out the undercarriage ground locks and the aircraft was towed back to the hangar with the red lights still on! My student was suitably shame-faced and it cost him an evening of free beer for me! It could have been very embarrassing if the undercarriage locks had fully disengaged![16]

Not every experience could be blamed on 'The Six', however. Designed for training pilots at established training bases, the expediency of a world-wide war led to them being placed in quite unexpected situations. Arthur Gill recalled one such incident:

> After I left No. 84 Squadron in September 1944, after commanding the squadron for three years, I was posted back to Burma as the 'Air Plans' staff officer on the joint 14th Army/221 Group RAF Headquarters. In October 1944, I had to attend an urgent meeting at HQ 3rd Tactical Air Force at Comilla in Assam and then fly on to Alipore in India. The Beechcraft Expediter I normally flew was unserviceable, so I asked the Air Officer Commanding, Air Vice Marshal Stanley Vincent, if I could borrow his personal Harvard II (FE 773) to which he agreed.
>
> So, with my 'Admin Planner', Squadron Leader John Curd in the rear seat, we had an uneventful flight to India on 28 October 1944. However, when I tried to restart the engine for the return flight, the starter-motor failed. No spare motor was available at Alipore and it was not possible to start the engine with the starting-handle. The AOC was not very pleased when I hitched a ride back to Burma, during the height of the war against the Japanese, in a C-47 Dakota of No. 52 Squadron RAF, and without his precious aeroplane! He eventually forgave me when his Harvard returned safely a week later, after he thought he had lost it forever![17]

HARVARD MEN: Group Captain Arthur Murland Gill, RAF

Arthur Murland Gill was a flyer's flyer! He achieved an incredible amount of skilled and outstanding achievements during a long RAF career during which he flew long-nosed Bristol Blenheim bombers with No. 84 Squadron over Greece and the Middle East during 1941, and then again in a hopeless effort to smash the Japanese invasion of Sumatra in 1942. He survived that debacle by the skin of his teeth after many adventures and got the last convoy out, arriving in India to find the squadron decimated and the Air Ministry indifferent to its fate. By sheer force of will, Arthur held the cadre No. 84 Squadron together, kept its best surviving aircrews and had it re-equipped with the new Vultee A-36 Vengeance dive bomber. The RAF had little or no experience of dive bombers or dive bombing, other than being on the receiving end of the Stukas, and so Arthur and No. 84 had to build up their own expertise virtually on their own, as they went along. He told me:

> We had no experience with the plane, and knew nothing of dive-bombing techniques. Another concern was that there were no dual aircraft. On very few of the aircraft that I have ever flown – Javelins, Spitfires, etc. – were there no dual aircraft to train on. With the Vengeance you just climbed in, looked at the pilot's notes, and you were off. I also had a lot of pilots who were comparatively fresh from training, who had flown only Tiger Moths and Harvards, so the first thing I asked for was a Harvard. When one was allotted to us, I took up all the pilots in the front seat to check out what I'd got. Once in the air, I'd tell the pilot that it was all his and see what happened! Some were a bit slow and converted to navigation, but some went on.

It is one of Arthur's many great achievements that he did this, and in the subsequent operations at Kohima and Imphal, in supporting Orde Wingate's Chindit forces and in the final attacks that drove the Japanese out of Burma, No. 84 Squadron played both a leading and a crucial role.

His subsequent meetings and adventures with the Harvard are recorded in these pages. After a long and extremely exciting RAF career he later took on a second career working for a famous brewery chain and criss-crossing the UK for suitable new sites for them. This also came to an end finally and Arthur, and his wife Doris, live in retirement in the hamlet of Llanwarne close to Hereford with magnificent views of the Black Hills. He still travels widely and maintains strong and close links with No. 84 Squadron and their reunions. Their great spirit of comradeship owes much to his drive and dedication. As Norman Rose, who also served with him in No. 1 Overseas Ferry Unit from 1951 to 1954, told me: 'Arthur was the epitome of one of life's real gentlemen – kind, sensitive, very tolerant and always helpful', words which this author can only endorse with sincerity and gratitude.

CHAPTER EIGHT

The Global Pilot Trainer

The spread of 'The Six' was world-wide during the war. The British and Commonwealth forces utilized it in the United Kingdom, Canada, Southern Rhodesia, South Africa and in a myriad of bases around the Empire. It should also be remembered that, under the Arnold scheme, about 8,000 RAF cadets were trained by the USAAC to become pilots, between June 1941 and June 1943. Advanced training was done by them on USAAC AT-6s. To preserved the façade of American neutrality, the legal fiction of 'contract instructors' was created and, although the USAAC took over after 8 December, these aviation instruction contractors continued to teach.[1] The United States had training centres all over North America, including Alaska and Hawaii. As we have seen, Southern American states had been in the forefront of buyers

Excellent air-to-air view of a Canadian Harvard II, RCAF 3838 coded 'DM', flying with 10 SFTS from Dauphin airfield, in the summer of 1941. Ray C Sturtivent

(Below) **Canadian Harvard IIs seen in 1941. This is a fine study of RCAF 2631, and gives excellent wing detail of the photographing aircraft alongside.** CFPU

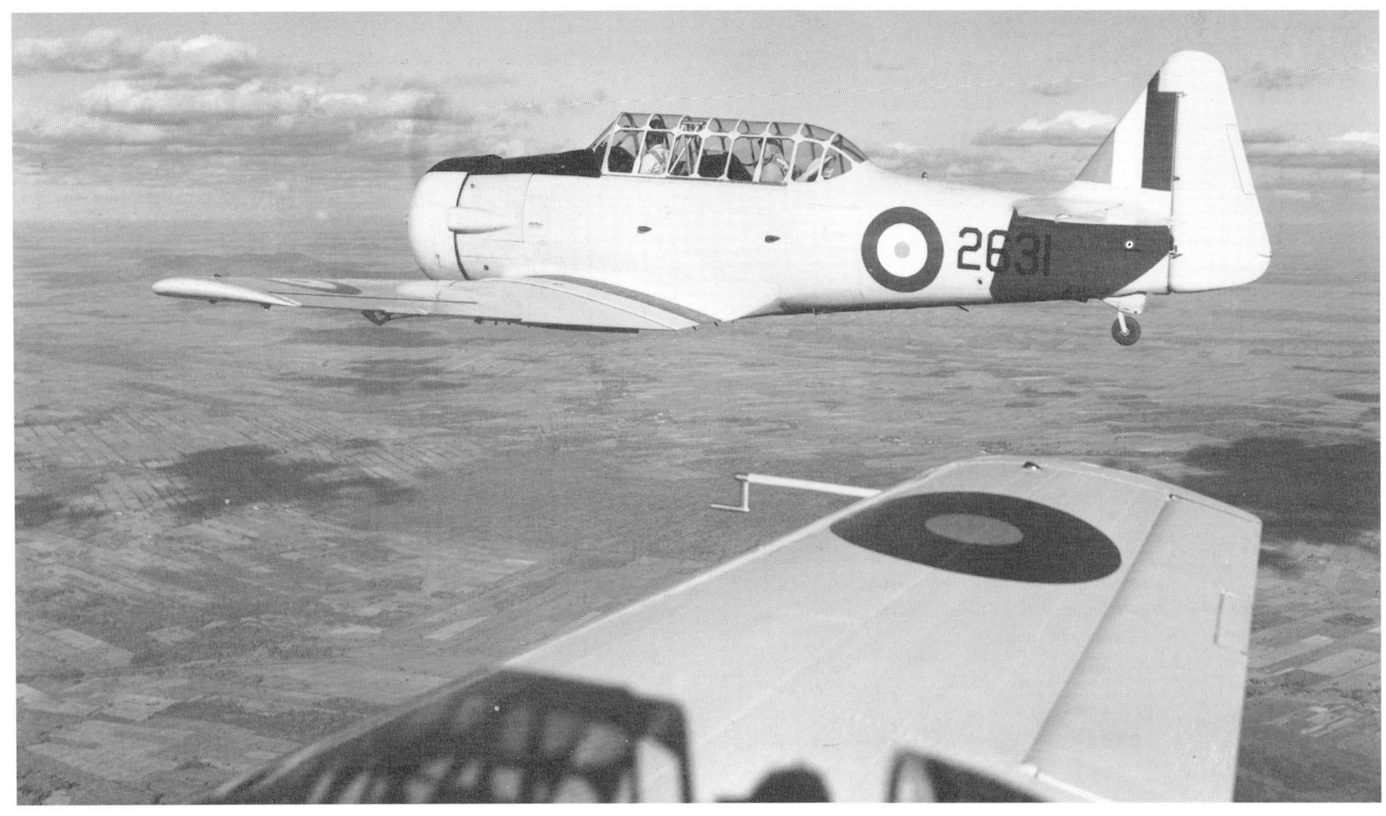

for the earlier types and, with the spread of lend-lease, the T-6 was the preferred aeroplane south of the Rio Grande. In China, the Kuomintang Government placed order after order, of which some got through to her. USAAF teams were seconded to the Chinese Air Force and carried out conversion training there. Likewise, when the Soviet Union became involved in the war, they too became recipients of the T-6, taking bulk deliveries via Lass airfield, Alaska and Siberia. The defeated French maintained a nucleus with the Vichy forces and as their North African territories (Morocco, Algeria and Tunisia) became liberated, so the type was re-introduced there; later, as France herself became liberated by the Anglo-American armies from 1944 onward, fresh batches of T-6s swelled the rejuvenated ranks of l'Armée de l'Air and Aéronavale, as well. Even the Axis powers seemed to want 'The Six', with the Luftwaffe taking over some French trainers and the licence-built Japanese 'Oak' supplanting home-built types as the war continued.

Pre-war, the tiny USAAC had established training bases at places like Randolph Field and Kelly Field, Texas; Bolling Field, Washington DC; and overseas at Hickam and Wheeler Fields, Hawaii and Clarke Field, in the Philippines; and Air Corps Reserve units from Boston, Massachusetts to Columbus, Ohio, and from Memphis, Tennessee, to Hill Field near Salt Lake City, Utah. Also, the US Navy had training units based at Naval Air Stations like Pensacola, Florida, Anacostia, and San Diego, California.

With American entry into the war, these flight training facilities mushroomed as the requirement for Air Corps pilots rose from 30,000 in December 1941, to 50,000 in October 1942. The Flying Training Command (FTC) was set up, headed by Lieutenant General Barton K. Yount. Under him there were three regional commands, Eastern, Central and Western, and in 1943 it merged with Technical Training Command. The system used by the USAAC (and later the USAAF) was to take young men in the 18–27-year-old age bracket, who had passed the Aviation Cadet Examining Board, and then process them steadily through basic training, pre-flight training, primary flight training, basic flight training and then to advanced flight training. This was followed by transitional training for selected combat aircraft. The weeding process was tough with only 20 per cent of all applicants making the grade, and it was estimated that to obtain 50,000 combat pilots, the USAAC would have to have an intake of half-a-million men.[2]

The AT-6 did not kick in until the student had reached the advanced flight training (AFT) stage, by which time he had graduated via aircraft like the Stearman PT-17 biplanes and the Fairchild PT-19 and Ryan PT-22 monoplanes to the Vultee BT-13A Valiant (affectionately known to a whole generation of pilots as the 'Vibrator' or 'Bee-Tee' or SNV by the Navy). However, in 1943 the Vultee was replaced by the AT-6 in basic flight training because it was considered just too tame and docile to teach students who would be flying mean machines like the Army Republican P-47 Thunderbolt or Navy Chance-Vought F4U Corsair. They needed something extra and 'The Six' took on this job in addition to advanced flight training.

Advanced training in 'The Six' was preceded by time in the T-6 simulator, the framework being ground-anchored for instrument familiarization and the learning of basic controls. Flaps and landing gear could be 'raised' and 'lowered' with immunity before the cadet tackled the real thing and got to know his way around the T-6 cockpit. In the sky, take-off (usually without trim) and landing loops, with the cockpit canopy usually open, were flown, with the emphasis on a 20-degree flap setting for the latter. The method taught was landing from the bottom of a glide, with the nose of 'The Six' slightly raised in the three-point position, although visibility around that great roaring radial was never easy and the aircraft had to be 'skidded' to get a snapshot view. Even so, the T-6 proved heavy on wing-tips and ground-looping was hardly a rare event. In fact the aircraft earned itself quite a reputation as the 'Terrible Texan' in some quarters, due to the number of accidents; certainly the AT-6 was a mean handful for the novice.

After the cadets had survived the introduction stage they went on to instrument flying, ground strafing and formation flying, with the three-, six- and twelve-aircraft layouts, working progressively towards taking-off and flying in the air. Some limited acrobatics was also instilled, as well as gunnery training. Navigation was taught but was fairly primitive, with

Canadian Harvard II seen in 1941. This is a fine study of RCAF 3034, parked out on a snow-bound runway in the heart of Canada. CFPU

just needle, ball, airspeed and magnetic compass to guide you, and comprised mainly of radio-range orientation and beam letdowns. Only much later (1944) was an experimental instrument landing system (ILS) put into use at Bryan Field Instrument School. The commanding officer of this outfit, Colonel John Duckworth, was credited with being the first to fit 'The Six' with a belly tank converted from P-40 wing tanks, which gave two extra hours endurance.

In late 1942, cadets at Craig Field, Alabama, set a record by flying the AT-6 for 23 million miles without a single accident attributable to mechanical failure. Another world record was established in October 1944, when at Napier Field, also in Alabama, an AT-6 completed 5,000h of continuous flying service. This aircraft averaged 3h 43min flying time per day, roughly 111½h per month and flew approximately 750,000 miles (1,200,000km), equal to seven times around the world, wearing out seven engines in the process! Another AT-6 record of a totally different kind was set up by a Craig Field machine that was credited with flying 2,000h, being involved in eleven accidents and required the replacement of seven new wings, five new landing gear struts, and six new propellers. At one period this aircraft was said to be in the air for 22h a day.

American pilots clocked up an average of 100h flying time on the various AT-6/SNJ trainers in the latter stage, a figure that contrasted sharply with the brief time the fuel-starved Japanese and German trainee pilots were expected to get by with. For example, in 1941, Japanese Navy pilots (and they were the nation's best, an élite force) spent just 30h flying in their ACT, and their elementary and intermediate flying times before this were equally brief. By the spring of 1943, even this had gone by the board and some 20 per cent of cadets went straight from basic and intermediate to combat, totally skipping advanced training.[3] Such a situation could not survive the introduction of such 'hot' machines as the Nakajima B6N *Tenzan* ('Jill'), the Yokosuka D4Y *Suisei* ('Judy') and the Yokosuka P1Y *Ginga* ('Frances'), so that the Imperial Naval General Staff was forced to authorize that all pilots should resume advanced training. However, in practice, the acute fuel situation nullified these good intentions. In 1944 the average time for the training of a naval aviator in Japan was 3 months, compared

Splendid underview of two Canadian Harvard IIs, RCAF 2660 and RCAF 2695, aloft in 1941. CFPU

All nationalities found 'The Six' a wilful and very temperamental girl to play around with. Here RCAF 3225 adopts a nose-down, tail-up posture in July 1941. CFPU

An early Harvard Mark I (Serial 1326) assigned directly to the RCAF. Ray C. Sturtivent

***(Below)* A 1941 view of RCAF Harvard II, RCAF 3001, immaculate at her new home base.** CFPU

***(Bottom)* An RAF Harvard from the Kingston Fleet Air Arm Training School, AJ 662, in the winter of 1942–43.** Harry Knight

to 3½ years pre-war. The Kyushu K10W1 ('Oak') was utilized as the standard intermediate training aircraft from 1943 onward but only 176 were ever built, about one-hundredth the output of 'The Six'.

The Germans faced similar difficulties in the final two years of the war, and the shortage of fuel and the desperate situation in the East saw a steady reduction in training hours flown by Luftwaffe cadets. The pre-war route was elementary flying school, which was split into A and B grades, but dive bomber and single-engined fighter pilots moved straight to combat types after some 200h flying, only multi-engined bomber and other types taking the C, navigational course, which was of 270h maximum. Thus by 1944, Luftwaffe fighter pilots were receiving less than 160h flying time before being thrown into the cauldron, half that of their RAF and USAAF opponents.[4] Whether or not the Luftwaffe pressed fifty or so of the captured French NA-57s into serious training use, they were certainly not a mainstay of their A/B units for any length of time.

In the USAAF, the average AT-6 training flight was of between 1½ and 2h duration. Six such sorties were flown a day with two different instructors alternating and each cadet received about 4h of flight training per day. Usually, half the day was spent in the air and the other half in the classroom; this routine was just about universal.

Fixed gunnery training flights were of shorter duration, however, lasting only about 15–30min. Colonel DeVries described it:

> The cowl gun would be loaded with 100 rounds of 0.30-calibre ammunition (half of its maximum loading). For air-to-air practice, the noses of the bullets were dipped in a waxy paint, four colours being used, a different colour for each ship in the flight. Firing at AT-6-towed sleeve (Navy) or banner (Air Corps) targets, it didn't take long to expend 100 rounds in three or four firing passes. Hits were evaluated when the target was dropped on the training airfield, the colour of the hole giving credit to the appropriate pilot. Five or more hits per target was considered 'good' for the large deflection angles such practice required. Low-deflection angles might spray the tow-ship, a definite no-no. Air-to-ground gunnery was easier to score. Each pilot had his own 10 × 10ft target.[5]

After a while it was found that fixed ring-and-bead sights were not suitable, and many AT-6s had them replaced by the N-3 sight, which was a reflector gunsight with a 70mm reticule (a 70mm lighted ring and 'pipper'). Using the 16mm gunsight aiming point (GSAP) movie camera, which could be mounted either in the Texan's port wing or in the engine cowling, enabled cadets to practise on the ground and saved fuel.

The US Navy adopted similar methods to the USAAF, and these were continued into the post-war years. The naval aviation cadet had 25 weeks of pre-flight training, 15 weeks of primary training, 22 weeks of intermediate training and 10 weeks operational training, on average. The advance training on the latter, carried out at both Corpus Christi and Pensacola, was done on the J-Bird and included instrument training, aerial gunnery, strafing and glide bombing, formation flying and night flights. The Naval aerial photography school also employed the SNJ at Chevalier Field, Florida, for this type of training. Field carrier landing practice (FCLP) was mainly conducted at Libertyville, and then the trainee moved on to brave the real thing on water!

Deck landings and take-offs were incorporated in the carrier qualification training (CARQUAL) afloat and were conducted from several small aircraft carriers, off the East coast, where the former British escort carrier *Charger* (ACV-30) and the US Navy's own *Bataan* (CVL-29) were both employed on this work, as well as the pre-war fleet carrier *Ranger* (CV-4). But such was the demand that two old Great Lakes paddle steamers were also converted to makeshift floating flight decks. These were the *Sable* (IX-81) (ex-*Chicago and Buffalo*) and the *Wolverine* (IX-64) (ex-*Greater Buffalo*). They plied the more tranquil (and safer) waters of Lake Michigan and intrepid aviators flew out from NAS Glenview in SNJs equipped with modified Grumman P/N 10149 tail hooks fitted at the Naval aircraft factory in Philadelphia, Pennsylvania, to try and land on their wooden decks and catch the arrestor wires. Many failed to do so!

An example of formation flying by the RAF Harvards from the Kingston Fleet Air Arm Training School, Ontario, in 1942. Harry Knight

Post-war these duties were taken over by the newer and faster ships, such as the light fleet carriers *Monterey* (CVL-26), *Saipan* (CVL-48) and *Wright* (CVL-49).

SNJ MEN: Captain Donald W. Monson, US Navy

Don Monson was born on 4 November 1919, on a small farm in West Prairie, Wisconsin, weighing a healthy thirteen pounds, the son of Martin H. and Anna Brudos Monson. When Don was four, the Monson family left for Viroqua, and in 1926 to Illinois. Don attended Downers Grove School before returning to West Prairie in 1928 to live with his uncle and aunt. He re-entered Downers Grove in 1931 but later joined the Civilian Conservation Corps until 1936 and finally graduated from High School two years later.

He worked for a time as clerk in Westmont, Illinois, and on various manual labouring jobs in south Chicago before joining the Electro-Motive Corporation in LaGrange. In the fall of 1941 he met Etta May McMaster, whom he was later to make his wife. The Japanese attack on Pearl Harbor in December 1941, brought changes: his brother joined the Navy and, in April 1942, while on his way to join the US Marine Corps, Don decided on the spur of the moment to apply for the new Navy V-5 Aviation Cadet Program. After time with the Civilian Pilot Training Program (CPT) at Marquette University in Milwaukee, Wisconsin, he finally got on to the Pre-Flight School at NAS Glenview.

He passed elimination and primary training, and in July 1943 was commissioned as Ensign and got his Gold Wings. He trained as a dive-bomber pilot in the Northrop BT, the Curtiss SBC-3 biplane and the OS2U. Then followed deck-landing training aboard the USS *Sable* in Lake Michigan. He married Etta at a small ceremony in NAS Glenview's chapel on 26 September 1943. He flew Curtiss SB2C Helldivers against a wide variety of Japanese targets. He was then assigned to VB-80 and shared the action and adventures of Robert Mullaney aboard the *Ticonderoga* (CV-14) and also flew from the *Hancock* (CV-19) after the former was damaged by Kamikazes. He continued in action until his last mission on 26 February 1945 against Amami Oshima, Okinawa.

After a leave period, Don joined Air Group 75 destined for service aboard the new big carrier *Franklin D. Roosevelt* (CVB-42) initially with the SB2C and later during the conversion to the Douglas AD-1 Skyraider. Duties at Training Command, Pensacola, were followed by a host of appointments, both shore-based and at sea, and he made 718 carrier deck landings in all. Meantime he and Etta had four sons and his family was his delight. His Naval career culminated in his being appointed in command of the Hydrographic Survey Ship USS *Maury* (AGS-16) on 16 January 1969. In that vessel he conducted a detailed 190-day survey of the Vietnamese coastline. Four years deskbound at the Pentagon in Washington DC brought his Navy career to an end and he retired on 1 July 1974. He currently resides at Palm Desert, California.

Donald W. Monson gave me this account of the procedures as he found them:

> I flew the SNJ as a flight instructor in Pensacola from 1947 to 1950. The first two years were spent at Whiting Field teaching every phase from primary through aerobatics. The final year was spent as a staff instructor at the instructor basic training unit (IBTU). From my old threadbare log books I note that I flew the SNJ about 1,800 hours during those years. She was a wonderful training plane.[6]

He described further and in more detail what the IBTU work with the SNJ entailed:[7]

> After about eighteen months as primary flight instructors, Bill Mackey and I were appointed to the staff of the instructor basic training unit. There we would be instructing pilots fresh from the fleet on the rudiments of becoming flight instructors.
>
> This was a new sort of ball game. At Whiting Field, flight instructors were gazed upon with awe by most of the students. At the instructor training unit, it was a different story. These guys were our peers, just in from the fleet and they knew how to fly; however, they needed to be indoctrinated in the standardized methods of flight instruction. They would have to learn to fly through every manoeuvre and talk while they were doing it. Something many returning fleet pilots might think would be 'a piece of cake' – until they tried it.
>
> I had somewhat the same attitude eighteen months earlier. But I soon learned [that] to teach flying, one must demonstrate flying through every manoeuvre, and be able to do it with precision. If designated climb speed is to be 85 knots, that airspeed needle must lock right on 85. An instructor should be able to demonstrate the standard rate of climb of 500 feet per minute. He must demonstrate a standard rate of turn of 3 degrees per second resulting in a change of direction of 180 degrees in one minute, while explaining the aerodynamics involved.
>
> Most pilots coming through instructor school passed all the necessary flight checks with no difficulty. But occasionally, a very few would report in who, for one reason or another, had very little flying ability. They had been getting by for years in a variety of ways, perhaps by opting for desk jobs involving little flying. But once they came to instructor school, they had to cut the mustard, or risk losing their wings.
>
> If a student instructor encountered difficulty in completing the course, he was given as much extra instruction as necessary to qualify him as a certified flight instructor. In most cases, this did the trick, but not always. Recommending a fellow Naval aviator for a Pilot's Disposition Board was always a last resort.

In the pre-war RAF, Arthur Gill trained (and later instructed) on the Blackburn B2, the Hawker Hart and the AVRO Tutor, which he found a delightful aircraft to fly. He did not fly Harvards until 1942 when he was checking his twin-engined Blenheim pilots after they had been a long time off flying, prior to their flying the Vengeance. Apart from his adventures in India as related, he recalled:

> I did not fly a Harvard again until January 1951 back in England, when I did a refresher course at the Flying Refresher School at RAF Finningley, having spent a year graduating at the Army Staff College at Camberley. At Finningley I first flew the Harvard 2B.[8]

Wartime entries took a different route, which featured the Harvard to a far greater extent. Norman Rose first flew on 25 October 1943, a Mark I, N 7017, at 22 FTS Thornhill, Southern Rhodesia. Later he moved on to fly the Mark II, IIA and IIB (later 2A and 2B) His training course in Rhodesia totalled 249.35h and included air-to-air firing on drogues and air-to-ground gunnery attack sorties with live ammunition, dive-bombing with practice bombs, dog fighting with cameras and low-level bombing.

Despite the problems encountered by the USAAF in trying to dive bomb in the Harvard, the main role of the RAF Harvards from the Kingston Fleet Air Arm Training School, Ontario, was training Fleet Air Arm pilots, so dive bombing practice was essential. This is the wooden pyramid target that floated offshore on Lake Ontario and which pupils 'had a go at' during the course of the training. Harry Knight

(Below) **The girls get into the act! A US Navy 'Wave' hauls a wheel block away from an SNJ in readiness for another day's flying operations, Pensacola, 1943. This photo affords some good detail of the engine, air intake, undercarriage and wheel wells on the SNJ.** National Archives, Washington DC

I don't think that kind of flying was included on the course in Canada, for example. We were lucky in Southern Rhodesia and we had perfect weather throughout. Even though Rhodesia was 5,000ft up with temperatures of 28°, it did not seem to affect the Harvard's performance much. It remained in use in the Rhodesian Air Training Group (RATG) until it closed down in 1954.

My next stop after training was 71 OTU at Fayid in the Middle East for conversion onto Hurricanes. This involved a further check on the Harvard IIB with a Greek instructor! Communication between us was hysterical as his English was minimal with a broken accent and, of course, my Greek was non-existent! How I ever made it subsequently after my pre-solo cockpit briefing in the Hurricane I'll never know! I was then posted to METS as related for rocket-firing practice on the Harvard prior to moving to No. 6 Squadron in Italy.

My next, and by far the longest, brush with the Harvard was when I went to CFS at Little Rissington in 1948. There I REALLY learnt to fly and in particular the Harvard properly. My instructor was a Fleet Air Arm pilot, Lieutenant Ray Lygo, RN, who, years later, was a Captain of the aircraft carrier *Ark Royal* and became Admiral Sir Raymond Lygo, who, after retirement from the Navy, was managing director of British Aerospace. He showed me the 'every which way' of the Harvard, including operating and landing from the back seat successfully as it wasn't the easiest of manoeuvres.

At the end of the Central Flying School course I went to No. 6 Flying Training School at RAF Ternhill in January 1949 to instruct on the Harvard. I found great job satisfaction teaching *ab initio* students to fly the Harvard, taking them through every aspect of flight and watching

them blossom into capable aviators. It was even more rewarding and with pride to see them receiving their Wings on their final day on the course. One of my first students, Cadet Ralph Toone, even finished top of the course!

During my tour with 6 FTS a batch of pilots from Iraq arrived for instrument flying and familiarization with flying in UK weather. Although they were qualified pilots in Iraq they had no experience of flying in cloud. After their refresher course on the Harvard they were to collect some Spitfires and ferry them to Iraq. Their English was pretty basic but they could get by. My chap's name was Lieutenant Aziz and it took a very long time to accomplish him on instruments. One day he was flying solo on a cross-country navigation exercise and got lost. A very faint voice was heard in Air Traffic calling for help and a homing to Ternhill. To ascertain that he could see the ground and was not in cloud, Air Traffic Control (ATC) asked him if he was VMV (which means visual meteorological conditions, i.e. in the clear and in contact with the ground, as compared to IMC, instrument meteorological conditions, i.e. in cloud). His faint, heavily accented reply was 'repeat please' and when he eventually understood came back the reply, 'No, I FBHF', which were the letters painted on his aircraft! ATC got him home eventually but not without great difficulty. All 'The Six' Iraqis were nice guys with lots of money and most sociable, but that was a long time before Saddam Hussein!

During 1949 I was detached to No. 2 FTS at South Cerney, as related, but at the end of April 1950, I took part in Exercise *Stardust* in Harvard 2B FX 213. It was unheard of to be able to low fly and beat up airfields, but the exercise allowed me to do just that! I took cadets from Ternhill in the back seat and we had a whale of a time carrying

HARVARD MEN: Squadron Leader Norman E. Rose, AFC,* AMN, RAF

Squadron Leader Norman Rise holds a unique record as the longest serving pilot in the annals of the Royal Air Force. His very long, outstanding and distinguished career of 47 years unbroken service earned him the honour of a place in the *Guinness Book of Records*: he flew military aeroplanes continuously from 1942 to 1989, achieving 11,539h in fifty-four different types.

After he retired he was honoured by GAPAN and made a 'Master Air Pilot' – a prestigious award for meritorious achievement in aviation to those who have displayed airmanship and character, and who have brought honour and respect to the profession, and is in recognition of consistently high standards of professional flying.

He was born at Kirdford, Sussex on 30 May 1924 and was educated at Reigate Grammar School. He gained his Wings as a Sergeant Pilot in Southern Rhodesia and joined No. 6 Squadron in Italy flying rocket-firing Hurricanes. When World War II ended, the squadron returned to Palestine to be involved in anti-terrorist operations. He was repatriated to the UK in 1946 to become one of the first pilots to fly the latest Meteor jet in 56 Squadron and later 245 Squadron. His experience as a fighter pilot was utilized at No. 226 OCU Bentwaters training others on Tempests, Hornets and Vampires but he was soon selected to go to the Central Flying School (CFS) to train as a flying instructor. At CFS his determination to do well resulted in one of the highest pass marks and he was posted to No. 6 FTS at Ternhill for 2½ years, where he met and married a Sergeant WAAF, his first wife Dorothy.

When his *ab initio* instructing tour was complete in 1950, his efforts were rewarded with a 'plum' posting to No. 1 (Overseas) Ferry Unit as the only NCO instructor on the Conversion Flight. For the next four years his primary job was converting ferry pilots onto new aircraft types, but he also ferried aircraft world-wide. His tenacity and courage in this work, coupled to incidents in which he saved two aircraft from possible disaster, was recognized by a recommendation for the award of the Air Force Medal (a much coveted and rare decoration given only to NCO aircrew). However, the citation was torn up at Command HQ. No reason was ever given for this unwarranted denial of such a well-earned and deserved award. Nevertheless, very shortly after he was granted a permanent commission.

After officer training he went to Singapore for what was supposed to be a ground tour. However, his QFI qualifications on Meteors and Vampires were requisitioned to teach senior officers of HQ FEAF to fly jets. He did that in his own time over and above his shift work as a Fighter Controller. Many of those senior officers owe their career furtherance and later eminence to his unselfish efforts. He was decorated with the Air Force Cross and is credited with being the only pilot to be awarded an AFC on a ground appointment.

He returned to the UK in 1957 to become a test pilot flying most of the current aircraft types in use at that time. Not long after returning from Malaysia, his first wife developed an incurable illness from which she eventually died. He married again in 1984 to his second wife, Shirley. In 1960, as the new Britannia was being introduced into RAF service, he was creamed off as a Captain. Apart from a 3-year secondment with the Royal Malaysian Air Force and a short spell on VC10s, he flew Britannias for the next 19 years with 511 Squadron and A&AEE Boscombe Down, during which time he was awarded the Bar to his AFC. At one point he was attached to BEA flying Viscounts up and down the Berlin air corridors. On 1 January 1968, he was promoted to Squadron Leader. In 1979 he took command of No. 10 AEF at RAF Woodvale, which gave

air experience to ATC cadets in Chipmunks. He made his final RAF flight on 29 May 1989 at age 65 and retired, much against his will.

He was a legendary character in the RAF, who made an indelible mark on its history. His high ideals, keen sense of humour and open heart made him much admired by his colleagues. He was a very professional and skilled pilot and an excellent leader. His passionate love of flying caused him to spurn a desk career with its promotional prospects. He was, perhaps, a little too outspoken at times – he always called a spade a spade and would not suffer fools gladly, which often gave his superiors a hard time.

In retirement Norman is a keen gardener. He is passionately fond of dogs and spends much of his time with his two golden retrievers. He made beautiful models of all of the fifty-four types of aircraft he flew. After his RAF achievement was put in the *Guinness Book of Records* his medals, flying log-book and GBR Certificate were displayed with his models in the Imperial War Museum, London; they now reside permanently in the Hall of Aviation in Southampton Museum.

out simulated strafing attacks on radar sites and airfields like Thorny Island – a wonderful break from the hum-drum task of instructing duties.

On completion of my two years on basic flying instruction I was lucky enough to be posted to No. 1 (Overseas) Ferry Unit at RAF Chivenor as a QFI to convert ferry pilots to new types and carry out check flights to maintain their currency to ferry world-wide. Here, once again, the dear old Harvard was the workhorse and backbone of 'B' Flight, the check and conversion flight. The OFU was later moved to Abingdon and then Benson. I note from my logbook that I seemed to do all the night checks and conversions on the Harvard.

In 1954 I was sent to RAF Changi in Singapore. This was the very last time I flew the trusty Harvard. The Far East Communications Squadron (FECS) 'B' Flight was established for senior officers on the strength of FEAF serving in ground appointments to maintain a minimum number of flying hours to retain their currency. My job was to check their proficiency before they flew solo as they arrived in FEAF and at periodic intervals thereafter. In 1955 the Harvards were withdrawn and were replaced by the Gloster Meteor Mark 7– but that's another story![9]

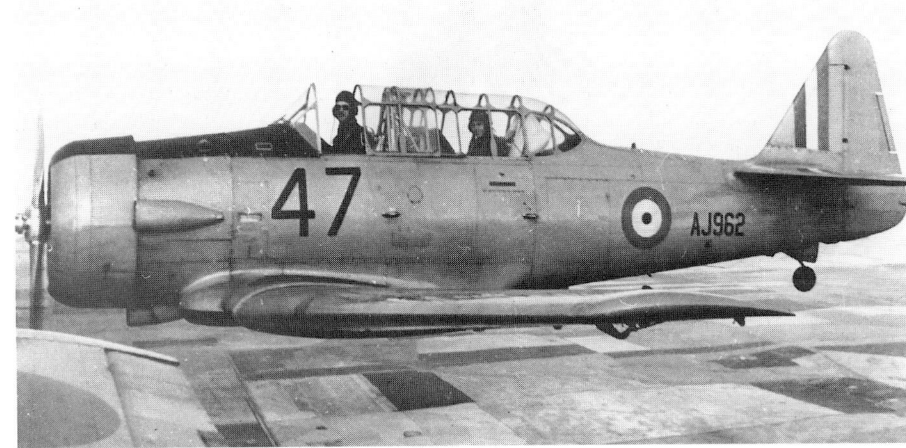

RAF Harvards serving in Canada. Under the CATS scheme RAF Harvards trained in Canada alongside their RCAF counterparts until 1944, when the British units were disbanded and their aircraft handed over to Canada. This is a Mark II Harvard AJ 962 (coded 47), which served with the RAF in 39 and 37 SFTS before being transferred to the RCAF in November 1943. RAF Museum, Hendon, London

In Canada both the Royal Air Force (up to 1943) and the Royal Canadian Air Force operated numerous Service Flying Schools. In the latter service, indeed, the Harvard held the record for longevity of aircraft in the RCAF. The first three were received at Vancouver in July 1939 and accepted at Camp Borden in August. They were still standard equipment in the summer of 1963 with No. 2 Flying Training School, Moose Jaw and No. 3 FTS at Penhold. A total of 2,063 Harvards were used by the RCAF. The breakdown is shown in the table below.

The Harvard in RCAF service
9 June 1940–14 Dec 1960

Type	*Quantity*
Harvard Mark I	34
Harvard Mark II	867
Harvard Mark IIB	859

During the war, Harvards were a familiar sight right across Canada and their characteristic rasping note was heard above many airfields. They were used as advanced trainers with Nos 1, 2, 6, 8, 9 and 13 RCAF Service Flying Training Schools at Camp Borden, Ottawa, Dunnville, Moncton, Summerside and St Hubert. In addition they were used by Nos 31, 32 and 39 RAF Service Flying Training Schools at Kingston, Moose Jaw, and Swift Current. In Canada, Harvards were also used by Nos 14, 111, 115, 123, 126, 127, 129, 130, 132, 133, 135, 163, 166 and 167 RCAF Squadrons for training and communications work.

The RAF maintained its own training squadrons in Canada right up to 1944, and one of RAF instructors at that time was Flight Lieutenant Harry Knight. He gave me this account of the RAF Harvards in Canada:[10]

I did a tour on Spitfires from May 1941 to March 1942 with No. 52 Squadron mostly based at Hornchurch, after which I was posted on rest to an instructor's course at Montrose. On completion of this, I was posted to Ternhill, a (P) AFU and then, after seven weeks, came another posting to Kingston, Ontario, Canada [No. 31 SFTS]. This was where I started to fly the Harvard giving instruction in the advanced training squadron – due, no doubt, to my operational experience. The programme concentrated on formation flying, air-to-air and air-to-ground firing, cross countries, night flying, aerobatics and dive bombing. The pupils under instruction were all Fleet Air Arm cadets! The posting lasted until June 1943, when I was posted to Trenton (the Canadian Cranwell) to train instructors to teach the same programme. This posting lasted until May 1944 when I returned to the UK to again fly Spitfires and then rocket-firing Typhoons.

Now, as to the Harvard. A very nice aeroplane to fly, quite stable with few vices other than a tendency to ground loop on landing if one was careless, due to the very narrow undercarriage. Good for aerobatics so long as correct speeds and smooth control movements were carried out and very good for formation flying. Winters out there were very severe and once the snowstorms abated, the runways were lightly cleared, then rolled, with mini fir trees marking the edges of the runways. Again, landing and taking off necessitated great care in smooth control movements, but otherwise posed no problems.

Sub-zero temperatures, however, could bring danger; on a night-flying exercise at Trenton, I

Flight Lieutenant Harry Knight, MBE, RAF (on the right) in 1945. Harry Knight

flew into freezing rain which had not been forecast, the first indication being a reduction in flying speed due to the excess weight of clear ice which formed on the aircraft (a habit of freezing rain when it strikes metal!) and controls which became very sluggish. Fortunately I was not far away from the airfield and made a hasty return and managed to put down on the runway using full power on the approach. I was very lucky, as there was over an inch of clear ice covering the aircraft which must have added at least 20mph to the stalling speed!

One other problem during the winter, in particular when flying low-level cross countries, occurred when one was 'caught short'. A facility was provided in the aircraft for such an emergency in the form of what was coarsely referred to as the 'pee-tube'. It was a tube situated in front of the seat with a rubber cup on top – the exit, of course was a hole underneath the fuselage. If one was in dire need of relief, the first problem was to undo safety harness, then parachute webbing, then followed a search through several layers of clothing before action could be initiated. Inevitably, during winter, the hole under the fuselage froze up so one was forced to fly back holding a tube full or urine, with a half-empty bladder, no straps made up (try doing that with one hand!) and possible an hour's flying left before the landing! The cold was a serious problem, of course, as we flew in temperatures often 20 to 30° below.

Air-to-air firing was carried out using a single machine-gun firing 0.303 ammo, very much a hit or miss exercise – mostly miss! One was considered to be an 'ace' if the towed sleeve was hit by even one round with the old ring and bead sight. Dive-bombing, using small smoke bombs, was also very much a guesswork exercise and 30 to 40 yards averages against a wooden pyramid target floating on the lake was good going. As you might imagine, the problem here was to restrain the student from concentrating on the target too much and reminding him of the correct height at which to pull out. Flying from the rear seat was something of a problem as the view forward was very poor but one got used to it after a while so that the problem was minimized.

Generally the weather in Ontario was good, winter or summer, and one could plan well ahead with confidence, so that there was plenty of flying to be done and in the two years I spent there, I amassed over 1,100 hours – one of the major reasons, of course, why Canada and Rhodesia were chosen for the Empire flying training scheme.

I personally enjoyed the aeroplane – its tendency to flick into a spin at the stall and the tendency to ground loop on landing being the two traits that had to be watched very carefully – otherwise a very nice aircraft. In time one's memory plays tricks of course – last year I visited the Fleet Air Arm Museum at Yeovilton and was astonished at the size of the Harvard which was on display there – no wonder that it was stable!

From the ground, the noise of the Hamilton airscrew was quite something and the civilian population never ceased to complain. Moving the pitch control from fine to coarse and back again to fine made the noise really horrendous. At Kingston, the airfield was quite close to where the St Lawrence river left Lake Ontario, the area known as the 'Thousand Islands' – it was and still is, the international line between Canada and the US. The customs post is situated on the International Bridge and it was considered to be the 'done thing' to loop a Harvard under, over and under the bridge, preferable the day before one's posting! Not that anyone I ever knew would admit to doing such a thing!

Two RAF Harvards, coded 79 and 80 (AJ 662) from the Kingston Fleet Air Arm Training School, seen over the International Bridge at Thousand Islands. Harry Knight

The Soviet 'Six'

The Soviet Union, during 1939–41 Hitler's ally, was abruptly catapulted into the war in June 1941 by the German invasion. Her own aircraft industry was forced to relocate *en masse* beyond the reach of the on-thrusting Panzers and the priority just to stay in the war was for combat aircraft of all types. With the arrival of lend-lease, the Soviet Air Force received two batches of AT-6s. During 1942 eight AT-6Cs were sent via the dangerous and deadly sea route to Murmansk, two being lost *en route*. A safer means of transport was found for the second major assignment of 54 AT-6Fs in 1945, which were delivered via the Alaska-Siberia (ALSIB) route.[11] The procedure was for 'The Sixes' to be flown up to Ladd AFB, Alaska by American ferry pilots, where Soviet ferry pilots would be waiting for a briefing before taking them on across the Bering Strait and thence westward. Another point of entry for T-6s supplied to Stalin's air force was via Iran: twenty aircraft being shipped out to Abadan airfield and then similarly transferred north. There is no record of any being returned to the United States after the war.

During the period June 1940 to November 1942, France lay under the heel of the German occupiers except for a rump ruled over by Marshal Petain's Vichy Government, which also controlled her North African colonies. These latter were the first to be freed by the Anglo-American landings of November 1942 and the clearing of Africa that followed. In the wake of

(Right) Several batches of AT-6C's were made available to the Soviet Air Force during World War II, either via Iran or Alaska. Russian flyers collected these lend-lease aircraft from British or American airfields in these countries and then flew them back to the Soviet Union, largely kept closed to outsiders, even nominal allies! Here Master Sergeant L.H. Byrd explains some points to his Soviet opposite number at Ladd AFB, Alaska. The -C already had Soviet markings fully painted up prior to transfer to keep up appearances. Post-war, the Allied aid effort was totally rubbished by Communist historians. National Archives, Washington DC

(Left) One of the more unusual adaptations of 'The Six' was the fitting of skis to this AT-6 as an experiment to produce an 'all-weather' trainer. The aircraft also featured the RAF/RCAF type exhaust heat exchanger, never adopted by the USAAF. Nothing came of this idea, but, post-war, the Swedish air force fitted several of their T-6s with skis and used them without problems. National Archives, Washington DC

The Harvard IIB became the T-2B post-war, and the final days of service for many RAF machines was with the University Air Squadrons (UAS) that existed in those days. This example is KF 735, coded 'A', carrying the marking of the Cambridge Squadron where she served between March 1954 and May 1957. Arthur Pearcy courtesy of Aubrey Pearcy

these operations French air power gradually re-asserted itself and 'The Six' was in the forefront of this renaissance.

In the autumn of 1943, three RAF Harvards were handed over to the French Air Force in Syria and two more were presented to the flying school at Blida, Tunisia, in the winter of 1944. Meantime, as allies once more, French trainees were able to learn their trade on American, British and Canadian Sixes. At these various established flying training schools, so many became familiar with the type until the cost of the course proved too much for the shattered French economy.[12]

Meantime, in April 1943, a re-training programme had been established at Marrakech, Morocco, to upgrade French

Many Harvard IIs were transferred to the French and joined the L'Armée de l'Air **training units post-war. This is the former FX 250 with F TEOB 'OB' du C.T.B. photographed at Salou de Provence, on 4 May 1957.** B. Chenel

(Below) **Post-war even the large fleet carriers were pressed into service as training carriers and here a SNJ with both hook and flaps down, coasts along the deck of the USS** Antietam **(CV-36) well past the last of the deck arrestor wires, to the intense interest of the assembled off-duty crew members lining the 'goofers' galleries around the ships bridge.** National Archives, Washington DC

veterans to fly Spitfires and P-40s, and they used a limited number of BT-9s for this after only 25h training flying time. This school moved to Meknes, Morocco, in January 1944 and by September 1945 both the BT-9s and some T-6s were reported operational there.

It was not to be until 1949 that 'The Six' became a regular feature of French air power and it was on 1 January of that year that the flying school at Marrakech in Morocco took over the duties of the by then defunct Cognac Basic School, which had operated briefly in 1944–45. The RAF transferred thirty Harvard 2s (many of them had never been out of their original shipping crates) to training schools in France that year, as shown in the table below.

RAF/RCAF-supplied Harvards in L'Armée de l'Air 1949 and 1951

	Harvard IIBs (1949)	*Harvard IIs (1951)*
FS 903	KF 376	AH 191
FT 284	KF 436	AJ 550
FT 302	KF 479	AJ 561
FT 333	KF 567	AJ 650
FT 443	KF 577	AJ 654
FT 444	KF 581	AJ 662
FX 239	KF 595	AJ 753
FX 250	KF 597	AJ 790
FX 302	KF 608	AJ 801
FX 312	KF 656	AJ 827
FX 322	KF 658	AJ 831
FX323	KF 667	AJ 897
FX 341	KF 677	AJ 918
KF 257	KF 979	AJ 937
KF 316	KF 988	AJ 950
		BW 199
		BW 203

It took a further two years, however, before sufficient numbers of T-6s (170 in all) were made available under the Mutual Defence Air Programme (MDAP) and 119 T-6Ds were sent from the USA to Morocco, being joined there by forty-five Harvard 3s via the USAF and six via the RCAF. These large numbers enabled full-time training to be undertaken at Meknes (which received forty T-6Ds between October 1951 and April 1952) and a few lingered on until Moroccan independence forced the school to move to Tours, France, in 1961. Meanwhile a Flying Instructors School was re-established at Marrakech, with another at Cazaux in 1949.

In 1952, under similar MDAP funding, the Aéronavale received a further fifty-six SNJs from the States, also to Morocco. These served mainly as trainers until 1961 when the survivors were handed over to the Moroccan Air Force. Navy pilots then had to be trained at the Air Force schools. However, a few T-6s remained on the French Navy's charge sheets until as late as 1971. 'The Six' also featured at the Rochefort and Saintes mechanics schools and at the Cazaux test centre, as well as working as squadron 'hacks' with some operational units.

CHAPTER NINE

The Wizards of Oz

Wirraway, Boomerang, Ceres

As we have seen, the three-man mission that had been sent abroad to evaluate general purpose aircraft suitable for Australian construction, in order that the growing crisis in Europe would not leave her without supply, had cocked a snook at tradition. Scorning the usual British aircraft manufacturing suppliers they had decided that the North American product would suit their needs best. Marshal of the Royal Air Force, Sir Edward Ellington, made himself very unpopular indeed when, on being invited to make an independent report, he came to the conclusion that he considered the Wirraway 'should be regarded as a temporary expedient', adding that, 'it can only be regarded as an advanced training aircraft'. But the Australian Government had already committed themselves to producing at least forty, with the possibility of a further seventy. The Air Board was most indignant at Ellington's criticism but, in fact, he only told the truth as he saw it. Criticism from Great Britain herself later became muted for, after all, in a few months she herself was buying as many of the same product as she could lay her hands on! There was also some objection within Australia itself at such an 'unpatriotic' decision, but the needs of the hour brushed them aside.

NAA sent two examples to Australia for evaluation in preparation for the setting up of the CAC production line. This is the NA-32 (NA-16-1A, c/n 32-387) with the fixed-type undercarriage. She was always known in Australia simply as the NA-16 and received the serial number A20-1.

Photo left courtesy of RAAF Museum, Point Cook

Photo below courtesy of DPR Canberra, ACT

The second machine that NAA sent out to Australia for evaluation by the CAC was the NA-33 (NA-16-2K, c/n 32-388) with the retractable undercarriage. The Australians knew her as the NA-33 and allocated the serial No. A20-2. North American Aviation

As well as NAA supplying a single example of both the fixed-undercarriage NA-32 (NA-16-1A, c/n 32-387) and the retractable undercarriage model NA-33 (NA-16-2K, c/n 32-388) Australia purchased production licences covering *all* of the single-engined variants for *both* aircraft. On arrival in Australia in 1937 they were generally known as the NA-16 and the NA-33, respectively. These two aircraft later received the RAAF serials A20-1 and A20-2, and so the first Australian-built Wirraways commenced with Serial A20-3.[1]

When the final choice was made, it was the NA-33 that had won the day, and she was given the contract designation of CA-1 by the Commonwealth Aircraft Corporation (CAC) and was also allocated the RAAF identification code A-20. The first contract was placed for an initial batch of forty CA-1s, and the name Wirraway, the Australian aboriginal word meaning 'challenge', was adopted as a very appropriate one for the fledgling company. The single wing machine gun in the NA-33 became two synchronized guns mounted in blast troughs in the upper forward fuselage, and a single machine gun on a flexible mounting was placed firing aft. Radio installations were made mandatory and some carried a camera-gun on the topside of the port inner wing section. The wing and empennage were strengthened for dive bombing but, strangely, dive brakes were not fitted at this stage. The first three A-20s were accepted into the RAAF in July 1939.

The first Wirraway (A20-3) made her maiden flight on 27 March 1939, with Flight Lieutenant H. 'Boss' Walker at the controls. After extensive testing, production was gradually built up until the outbreak of World War II in September 1939. This naturally led to increased orders to meet the demands of a rapidly-expanding RAAF.

The Wirraway Described

Although based on the NA-33, the Australians did not slavishly follow the design in every respect, but construction followed the same general outline.

Main Planes[2]

These were of aluminium alloy construction employing a single spar with channel section spar caps and sheet metal webs. Both the upper and lower spar caps were divided into sections, being spliced at each joint with a short length of similar section. The spar web was made of four sheets of aluminium alloy of varying thicknesses, which were joggled and lap-jointed. Reinforcement and rib attach angles were riveted to the faces of the spar. Flanged-type ribs extended from the spar to the trailing edge and forward of the spar to the leading edge.

The former ribs were known as trailing edge ribs. The entire assembly was covered with aluminium alloy sheet reinforced with stringers. Flanged intercostals provided support for ailerons and flaps along the trailing edge. The ribs were attached to spar and intercostals by means of formed angles. Access doors were provided on the lower surface to facilitate servicing. These could also be used, if convenient, for access to the interior for repairs.

All ribs were of pressed aluminium alloy sheet, with channel-type flanges and pressed lightening holes. The trailing edge consisted of a formed section of aluminium alloy, which was riveted to the upper skin covering and extended inboard from the aileron cut-out in each wing. Wing-tips of aluminium alloy consisted of two ribs, two intercostals, and top and bottom covering.

Bolt angles, made from aluminium alloy extruded section, formed the medium by which the other wing panels were bolted to the centre section. The centre section was also of aluminium alloy construction throughout, and incorporated riveted channel section spars and pressed channel-type ribs. Reinforcement and rib attach angles were riveted vertically across the faces of the spars. Machined aluminium alloy blocks were bolted inside the top spar caps to form the attachment for the centre section to the fuselage. The covering was of aluminium alloy sheets of varying thickness at different stations; the upper skin between the spars being reinforced by a corrugated section. The centre ribs were cut to give accommodation for the fuel tanks. Trailing edge ribs extended aft from the rear face of the front spar.

The lower surface of the centre section between the spars was made up of a removable portion, known as the fuel tank cover, which was attached to each spar by means of anchor nuts located along the inside of the lower spar caps. When this cover was bolted into position it formed an integral part of the centre-section construction. The major sub-assemblies of the complete wing assembly could be removed from the fuselage as one unit, or removed individually. Removal of the complete wing assembly or centre section could be accomplished with landing gear installed on the centre section and locked in the extended position. The wing section varied from NACA 2209 to 2215.

(Right) **Another early production model A20-21 shows the Mark I features in some detail. Note that the Wirraway followed the American practice of having the elongated radio mast stuck right in front of the pilots vision. Note also the two machine guns atop the forward fuselage firing through the prop arc. Wing-tip lights can clearly be seen also and the light bomb carriers beneath the wings.**
DPR Canberra, ACT

As a comparison with A20-21 this is A20-142 showing changes in armament and elsewhere, as well as recognition letter design. DPR Canberra, ACT

Flaps

The landing flaps were of aluminium alloy construction throughout and incorporated a 'hat' section spar and pressed channel ribs. A 'Z' section formed the leading edge, whilst the trailing edge was a standard formed section. Flaps were secured to the wings by means of a continuous type hinge. Actuating rods were attached to the flap spar by eyebolts which rotated in phosphor bronze bearings.

Dive Bomber

On the Mark III Wirraway (A20-623 onward), designed specifically as a dive bomber, special dive-bombing flaps, interconnected with the landing flaps and operated by the same hydraulic jack, were fitted. These flaps opened upwards as the flaps moved downwards.

Early Mark I Wirraways stepped up en echelon, **with A20-142 (front), A20-41, A20-28, A20-4 and A20-25 making a brave show over their main base.** DPR Canberra, ACT

Ailerons

The construction was similar to that of the flaps and incorporated a pressed channel-type spar, flanged nose and trailing ribs and channel section trailing edge suitably reinforced by gussets. Cast aluminium alloy hinge brackets were provided. Covering forward of.the spar was sheet metal, whilst fabric formed the covering for the trailing edge and also extended over the nose skin. Ailerons were fitted with three hinges. Each aileron incorporated a booster tab.

Fuselage

The fuselage frame consisted of the engine mount, the forward and aft sections, all of welded chrome-molybdenum steel tubing and steel fitting construction and the bottom section, aft of station 6, which was of aluminium alloy semi-monocoque construction. An auxiliary tail skid and jack pad were riveted to the aft end of this monocoque. An overturn structure was incorporated in the forward section of the fuselage frame, behind the front cockpit, for protection of the crew in the event of a nose-over. The firewall was a single sheet of aluminium alloy, provided with reinforcing angles about its circumference. Fuselage side panels were fabric-covered aluminium alloy frames readily detachable, being secured to the fuselage by screws.

Cockpits

The two tandem cockpits were under one enclosure, incorporating individual manually operated sliding sections at each cockpit, for entry and exit. Both sections could be locked closed or in several intermediate positions. Seats were mounted on steel tubes and were adjustable to selective vertical positions. The rear seat was reversible, being pivoted on a bearing incorporated in the fuselage frame. Provisions were made for an instrument flying hood in the front cockpit of the Mark I and Mark II training aircraft but this was not fitted in the Mark III dive bombers.

Landing Gear

This was of the single leg, half-fork, fully cantilevered design. Each unit consisted of a cylinder and piston by means of which shock absorption through air and oil was provided. The piston and cylinder were interconnected by forged chrome moly steel torsion links. A heat-treated steel fork was bolted to the lower end of the piston and carried the axle. This fork was heat treated to 160,000–180,000psi.

The gear was fully retractable inboard and forward of the wing centre-section front spar. Hydraulic power was supplied normally by an engine-driven hydraulic pump and in the event of failure of that pump or its connections, by means of a hand-operated pump. The landing gear was operated by double-acting rams, with mechanically operated spring-load latches and lockpins at the retracted and extended positions, respectively.

The landing gear could be lowered from either cockpit but, as a safety catch was incorporated in the front cockpit quadrant, it could not be raised by the rear cockpit controls. Mechanical indicators and electric warning horn were located in the front cockpit. Hydraulic wheel brakes were fitted.

The tail wheel assembly consisted of an aluminium (later magnesium) alloy wheel support casting attached to two fittings bolted to the rear end of the monocoque, a swivel-post assembly and fork, mounted on roller bearings in support casting and a pneudraulic shock strut. An 11in (30cm) diameter wheel and tyre was mounted on the axle, which was an integral part of the fork. The wheel was steerable and controlled by the rudder pedals and cables incorporated in the rudder-control system. A tail-wheel locking device was also fitted. The type pressure was 60psi. The hydraulically operated landing flaps were controlled in a manner similar to the retracting landing gear. A calibrated indicator, adjacent to the landing gear position indicator in the front cockpit, showed the position of the flaps from the Up position (0 degrees) to the Down position (60 degrees). The hand pump was used for emergency operation of landing gear and flaps.

Empennage

The rudder frame was of aluminium alloy construction and consisted essentially of a torque tube, pressed flanged ribs, channel trailing edge and metal-covered leading edge and was fabric covered. The elevators consisted of two interchangeable sections. The construction of the elevators followed the pattern of the rudder, including the fabric covering. The tailplane also comprised two interchangeable sections, each of aluminium alloy construction and consisting of a front and rear spar, pressed flanged ribs,

(Above) A fine study of a training flight of Mark I Wirraways over the outback. Note none of these aircraft have shipped their flexible mounted rear guns although the scarf rings are left in place. DPR Canberra, ACT

As a contrast with the photo above these Mark I Wirraways have both their forward-firing and rear flexi-mounted machine guns emplaced. DPR Canberra, ACT

stiffening intercostals and metal covering. The fin was of aluminium alloy construction throughout, the assembly consisting of a front and rear spar, pressed flanged ribs, stiffening intercostals and metal covering. Trim tabs were fitted to the rudders and elevators. The port and starboard sides of the tailplane were interchangeable.

Electrical System

An engine-driven generator of voltage-controlled type and control panel were fitted. A 12V battery was mounted on a shelf at the right-hand side of the firewall, below the oil tank. All wiring, with the exception of HT wires, was of glazed cotton-braided type with metal terminal lugs pressed and soldered into place. Each wire was numbered or coded with a colour designation like the wiring diagram. Two 240W landing lights were fitted to the aircraft and built in the leading edge of each wing. Navigation lights were built into wing-tips and fin; identification lights were fitted in the rear fuselage. A heated pitot static head was located on the starboard wing.

Instruments

Instrument panels were mounted on shock absorbers to prevent damage to the instruments due to engine vibration. A sub-panel was also fitted in the front cockpit below the main instrument panel, and a small panel installed aft of the rear cockpit on the port side at the prone bombing position. The main panels were directly illuminated by lamps located behind a hinged reflector covering each panel. The front cockpit instrumentation was as follows:

- air speed indicator;
- turn and bank indicator;

Flying gear for this Wirraway aircrew boarding A20-239. This photo gives a clear close up of the cockpit area and rivets and stringers on the Wirra. DPR Canberra, ACT

- rate of climb indicator;
- directional gyro;
- gyro horizon;
- altimeter;
- compass;
- clock;
- exhaust gas analyser;
- tachometer;
- manifold pressure gauge;
- engine gauge unit;
- engine cylinder head temperature indicator.

Sub-panel instruments were:

- air temperature indicator;
- suction gauge;
- connections for camera;
- engine starter switch;
- bomb jettison switch.

Rear cockpit panel instruments were:

- altimeter;
- air speed indicator;
- turn and bank indicator;
- clock;
- compass;
- tachometer.

The bomb aimer's panel (which was obviously not fitted on the Mark III dive bombers) contained:

- air speed indicator;
- altimeter.

Fuel, Oil and Hydraulic

The fuel and oil tanks, and the hydraulic fluid reservoirs were manufactured from aluminium alloy and were repairable by welding. The fuel tanks were covered with a rubber and canvas fire-proofing medium, but after aircraft No. A20-768 this protection was discontinued.

Armament

Two forward-firing 0.303 Vickers machine guns with synchronizing gear were provided and a free-swivelling, rear-facing Vickers gas operated No. 1 gun of similar calibre was mounted on an hydraulically controlled hoist in the rear cockpit (Mark I and Mark II aircraft only). The gun could move on a track in the form of a circular arc. Eight magazines, each holding sixty rounds were carried. A camera gun could be mounted on the gun hoist, in place of the gun.

Pyrotechnics included a Very pistol for signal flares, located on the right-hand side of the front cockpit; stowage for eight cartridges being provided opposite. Two forced-landing flares (Mark I and Mark II aircraft) could be dropped through launching tubes in the rear fuselage; reconnaissance flares (when used) were carried on the centre-section mechanical bomb carriers and released by the bomb-release mechanism and controls.

Eighteen bomb slips were built into the Wirraway; there were two universal carriers on each outer wing. Total normal bomb

This is A20-231, serving with No. 2 SFTS at Wagga-Wagga in 1941.
RAAF Museum, Point Cook

This Wirra, A20-41, is experiencing the usual undignified appearance caused by the unsynchronized retraction of the undercarriage. RAAF Museum, Point Cook

***(Below)* Trainee pilots from Laverton RAAF base practise the 'peel off' for dive bombing attacks in their Wirraways, February 1943.** Australian War Memorial, Canberra, ACT

load was 500lb (226kg), with two 250lb bombs under either wing, but for the overload case 1,000lb (452kg) could be carried. Light series carries were located in the trailing-edge portion of the centre section, just forward of the flaps. These carried practice bombs. A course-setting bomb sight (Mark VIII or Mark IX) was fitted below the rear cockpit floor. The Mark III dive bombers had all gun armament (including camera gun) deleted and the aft end of the cockpit was enclosed by a streamlined steel-framed Perspex canopy.

Radio – TRIIb

A transmitter and receiver were fitted in the rear cockpit, together with a trailing aerial and winch. The aerial had to extend 200ft (60m) to be effective. Other equipment carried in this cockpit included a hand-operated carbon tetrachloride fire extinguisher, readily accessible from the ground as well as from the cockpit by opening a hinged door. An F24 camera could be installed when it was desired to use the prone bombing position.

Controls

Flying controls consisted of those operating the rudder, elevators, ailerons and trim tabs. Non-corrodable flexible steel cables were used. Smooth and effective control was assured by use of sealed-type ball bearings on all pulleys, bellcranks and control surface hinge points. These were packed with lubricant on assembly and required no further lubrication.

A complete set of flying controls was installed in each cockpit, all controls being readily adjustable. A surface control lock was provided in the front cockpit. Engine controls comprised throttle, mixture and propeller control handles, all assembled in a single quadrant located on the left side of each cockpit and interconnected by rods. Hot air from the exhaust manifold shroud could be taken into the carburettor through a valve in the air mixture chamber; this was controlled by a handle with notches providing vernier adjustment. The hand fuel-pump handle was located on the left side of each cockpit, while fuel selector valve controls were adjacent. The engine starter push button was located on the instrument sub-panel in the front cockpit. The engine switch was placed ahead of the rear cockpit on the left side and was operated by mechanical linkage via a lever in the front left-hand corner of each cockpit, ahead of the throttle controls.

Engine

A Pratt and Whitney Wasp engine powered the Wirraway, driving a *three*-bladed, controllable-speed, metal propeller. The engine was a nine-cylinder, single-row R1340 S1H1G radial, and was built by CAC Engine Division under licence from Pratt and Whitney. The maximum horse power was 600 and the weight was 1,750lb (787kg). The engine could be turned with a hand-starting crank which was stowed inside the fuselage side access door.

There were nine separate Wirraway contracts issued; details of squadron allocations are given in the table below.

Wirraway strength on 12 December 1941

Unit	Strength	Location
No. 4 Squadron	12	Canberra
No. 5 Squadron	12	Laverton
No. 12 Squadron	18	Darwin
No. 22 Squadron	17	Richmond
No. 23 Squadron	12	Archerfield
No. 24 Squadron	12	Townsville
No. 25 Squadron	18	Pearce
No. 2 SFTS	36	Wagga
No. 5 SFTS	36	Uranquinty
No. 6 SFTS	36	Deniliquin
Total	209	–

Specification – Wirraway

Weight, plus fixed equipment:	4,445lb (2,015kg)
Weight, max. permissible:	6,000lb (2,720kg)
Maximum disposable load:	2,005lb (910kg). Figure for disposable load comprises guns and ammunition, bombs, radio *plus;* *Crew* – 7.5lb (3.4kg) per gallon *Fuel* – 4,455lb (2,020kg) per gallon *Oil* – 9.0lb (4.1kg) per gallon
Weight as trainer (two crew):	5,630lb (2,555kg)
Total Fuel capacity:	92 imperial gallons (including 16 imperial gallons reserve)
Oil capacity:	8¼ gallons
Dimensions:	Wing area 256ft² (23.78m²); wingspan 43ft (13.11m); overall length 27ft 10in (8.48m); height (tail down) 8ft 3½in (2.53m); airscrew clearance 9ft 8in (2.95m); track 8ft 6¼in (2.60m)
Armament:	2 × 0.303 Vickers (synchronized to fire through the airscrew), later replaced by 2 × 0.303 Brownings (under the wings on A20-356 by APU only); rear 1 × 0.303 Vickers (removed in training role)
Bomb load, normal:	500lb (230kg)
Bomb load, overload:	1,000lb (450kg)
Engine, rated power, normal:	CAC-built Pratt and Whitney S3H1-G (R-1349) radial[3] rated 550hp at 5,000ft and 2,200rpm
Engine, rated power, take-off :	600hp at 2,259rpm
Wing loading, normal:	21.8lb/in²
Power loading, normal:	9.3lb/hp
Performance:	Speed, max. at altitude (8,600ft, 2,620m) 220mph (354km/h); operating at sea level 177mph (285km/h); operating at 9,000ft (2,740m) 199mph (320km/h); operating at critical altitude 13,000ft (3,960m) 209mph (336km/h); landing, normal weight, flaps down 65mph (105km/h); landing, normal weight, flaps up 70mph (113km/h) Rate of climb, max. 1,950ft/min (595m/min) Endurance at operating speed 3.07h Range at operating speed at 450hp 640 miles (1,030km) Range at economical speed 850 miles (1,370km) Service ceiling 23,000ft (7,010m)

Into Battle

When Japan attacked southward through Malaya, New Britain, New Guinea and the Dutch East Indies from December 1941 onward, the RAAF was caught up in the general debacle that followed when British, American, Dutch and other allied forces were overwhelmed by both the speed of the advance and the superiority of Japanese equipment. Lacking any suitable fighter aircraft of their own, the RAAF were forced to throw in the trainer/GP Wirraway to act as both a makeshift dive bomber and as a fighter, a role for which she was even less suited. This brought the Wirraway up against the Japanese Navy's impressive Mitsubishi A6M, Navy Type 0, Carrier fighter, the famous Zeke, or Zero. Not surprisingly, it proved no contest!

Seven front-line squadrons of the RAAF and three reserve units were equipped with the Wirraway on 7 December 1941. No. 21 Squadron had been deployed to Malaya as early as July 1940, with a strength of eighteen Wirraways, but only a few remained as it was re-equipped with the American Brewster F2A-2 Buffalo single-engined fighter. To train new pilots in fighter tactics, an advanced flying training unit was established at Kluang with six Wirraways. These soon found themselves carrying out very different tasks as the Japanese invasion army swept down the peninsular.

The First Combat Flight of the Wirraway

The first Australian-built Wirraway, A20-47, saw combat initially in Malaya, during the desperate days of the Japanese invasion, which led to the fall of Singapore. It was a terrible situation for any combat aircraft to make her debut but it was a significant one for Australia, the RAAF and the T-6 story. Fortunately, an eyewitness account of this event can be quoted from Flying Officer H. L. Colebrook, RAAF (297188), who left his valuable account.[4]

The squadron ('Y' = Yorker Squadron) was based at Kahang, Malaya and was commanded by Flight Lieutenant J. Thompson (RAF) who was, in fact, a New Zealand officer with an RAF commission. There were eight Pilot Officers from the RNZAF; Flying Officer Colebrook, RAAF; eight Sergeant Pilots and approximately five Sergeants Air Gunners from the RNZAF; a South African Sergeant Air Gunner, and an RAAF Sergeant Air Gunner, another RAAF Sergeant NAV.BW and a Pilot Officer from the RAAF (who later won the DFC). All the ground staff were from the RAF. The unit had formed at Kulang, and then moved up to Kahang equipped with just five Wirraways, a single Tiger Moth and two Avros. Between 20 December 1941 and 1 January 1942, Flight Lieutenant Thompson and Flying Officer Colebrook made four flights in Wirraway A20-47 and attempted interceptions of Japanese bombers, but without any success. The Wirraway was no fighter plane, but their next missions were as a dive bomber. Flying Officer Colebrook recalled how:

On the 119th January 1942, we were instructed to supply all available Wirraways to attack Japs crossing the Mwar River (Western Malayan coast) in support of the A.I.F.

At 0705 on 19th January, we took off in Wirraway A20-43 in company with four other Wirraways, to rendezvous over base with three Dutch-manned Glenn Martin bombers and eight Buffalo fighters from No. 21 Squadron (RAAF). The Wirraways were capacity loaded with twenty 40lb A/P (anti-personnel) bombs and armed with the standard two forward guns and a local fixture of twin rear Vickers G.O. (gas-operated) guns. The Wirraways were also fitted with a soup-plate siren, about three feet in diameter. This was turned into wind over the target, causing a deafening screaming sound.[5]

We led the formation in at zero altitude against a launch towing two barges of troops across the river. They were strafed with forward

(*Above*) Three CAC Wirraways of No. 21 Squadron, RAAF, at Laverton base prepare for take-off and practice flights. Australian War Memorial, Canberra, ACT

(*Below*) A fine ground study of A20-202 being checked out prior to a flight gives details of underwing detail including the marked strake where the wing centre section and outer section join. Author's collection

Starboard bow three-quarter aerial study of A20-22 with all armament up and original paint scheme. DPR Canberra, ACT

guns, low levelled with bombs and strafed with the rear guns. The Glenn Martins patterned suspected HQs from 1,000ft with 250lb bombs.

Just as the target was reached eight single-engined Jap aircraft turned in to attack our aircraft but were all promptly destroyed by the escorting Buffalos. Utter confusion was caused to the Jap forces due to surprise and the effectiveness of the sirens.

Intentions on completion of the attack were that four Buffalos would escort the Glenn Martins back to Singapore and the other four Buffalos escort us back to base. Due to the general mêlée which developed over the target, the Glenn Martins left without their escort, were intercepted by Zekes en route and all destroyed.

One Wirraway was hit in the oil line by ack-ack and crash landed between the two forces. A.I.F. rescued the crew and returned them to base. Sergeant Moritz (RAAF, WAG) from another Wirraway was hit by light ack-ack and lost an eye.

One of the Buffalo fighters was also destroyed. All Wirraways were badly holed by explosive 0.50 and 0.30-calibre bullets. One Wirraway with a U/S compass became lost whilst returning and was fired on by a single-engined Jap recce aircraft. The Wirraway was not hit and returned to base. Another Wirraway landed with severed rudder wires.

Soon the Wirraways were forced to pull back to Tengah drome on Singapore Island and the aircraft were later flown to Palembang and were finally destroyed during the fall of Java.[6] Here they were used as makeshift escorts for RAAF Lockheed Hudson and Netherlands East Indies Martin B-10 bombers, which also flew forlorn missions against Japanese invasion convoys in defence of Sumatra and Java.

Meanwhile No. 24 Squadron was based out on the perimeter of Australia's island barriers and patrolling to get a first glimpse of the expected Japanese invasion forces heading for the Rabaul, New Britain, gateway to the Bismarck Archipelago, and the Japanese onrush against Papua, New Guinea, New Ireland south to the Solomon Islands. Just what they were supposed to do about it once that armada was sighted was unclear. On 6 January, two of the Wirraways sitting on the deck at New Ireland and waiting to go, got some indication of how outclassed and outnumbered they were to be.

First reports of enemy activity came in at 0805 when a flight of enemy aircraft was seen at approximately 8,000ft (2,440m) some ten miles from Vunakanu airfield. Flight Lieutenant B. H. Anderson, with Pilot Officer C. A. Butterworth, in A20-437, immediately took off before the bombs started raining down and laboriously climbed to intercept the serene and undisturbed enemy formation. A second Wirraway, A20-156, followed them up but was not sighted again.

At 0830 a formation of nine Navy Type 97 Kawanishi H6K4 (Mavis) four-engined flying boats flying in immaculate formation, seven in a 'V' and two following in a box, were observed, at an altitude of about 12,000ft (3,660m) over their airfield. Flight Lieutenant Anderson reported that:

> I was 2,000ft below the enemy aircraft which were maintaining formation. Because of motor overheating was compelled to level out.[7]

As they made an astern approach, still climbing, the Kawanishi's grew into stately silver-painted aircraft, which returned their fire from rear guns mounted beneath their tails.

> About this time enemy opened fire from rear guns, which had the appearance of cannons and tracer was evident.[8]

The Wirraway finally made an attack from astern at ranges of 300–500yd (270–450m), firing bursts of 200 rounds until all the ammunition had been expended. They seemed to make no impression whatsoever on the enemy, whose own return fire was also ineffective.

> Unable to use sufficient power to climb and maintain position, six attacks were carried out by diving and climbing underneath, slight astern and to port of formation. Range estimated 800 to 400 yards, closing until stalled, when attack was repeated. Free gun used when opportunity presented, range approximately 800 yards. From comparison of our speed, enemy speed estimated 160mph true. Camouflage was silver grey and no markings or numbers were observed.

Anderson reported on his own aircraft's performance in the action thus:

> Climb at 110mph in full fine with 35in boost, then full throttle. Cylinder head temperature gauge became u/s at 280°C, with oil temperature rising rapidly to 95° and then 100°C. At 12,000ft, oil temperature was 101° and motor commenced to smoke, and became rough. Throttling back remedied roughness, but oil temperature did not fall. Engine appeared normal on return flight and a subsequent run up did not disclose any damage or fault. Duration of flight – 50 minutes. Fuel used – 38 gallons, Oil used 2 quarts. The Vickers gun fired approximately 200 rounds bursts, functioned perfectly for 1,200 rounds. Vickers G.O. fired 500 rounds, only one stoppage.

Frustrated, they landed back with nothing accomplished. But for No. 24 Squadron, the writing was on the wall.

Japanese Decimate No. 24 Squadron at Rabaul

The full-scale Japanese air attack on the Australian base of Rabaul, which took place on 20 January 1942, proved a disaster to another RAAF Wirraway unit: No. 24 Squadron. Flight Lieutenant Tyrell, RAAF, later gave this graphic description of what took place that day.[9]

> We received two separate warnings of the approach of enemy aircraft on this occasion. A message received through naval communication channels said that approximately twenty enemy aircraft were approaching over Tabar Island, to the North East of New Ireland. The second message reported a similar number of aircraft in another direction. We thought it was the usual 'do', and went on to standby. Our instructions were to wait for an order from the Operations Room before taking off. We waited some time, but got no instructions. Then we heard the approaching drone of enemy aircraft. We waited no longer.
>
> Two Wirraways took off from Lakunai. They were piloted by Sergeant Hewitt, with whom I flew as an observer, and Sergeant Milne. Three, piloted by Sergeant C. R. Bromley (with Sergeant R. Walsh as observer), Sergeant R. A. Blackman (with Sergeant S. E. Woodcroft as observer) and Sergeant Little (with Sergeant R. Harber as observer) took off from Vunakanau. Another Wirraway, piloted by Flight Lieutenant B. H. Anderson (with P/O Butterworth as observer) was airborne at Vunakanu when the engine cut and the machine nose-dived and crashed. Anderson was severely knocked about in the head and body and Butterworth received numerous cuts and bruises. The aircraft was a complete write-off.
>
> At the time the raid warning was received two Wirraways from Lakunai were actually on patrol at approximately 15,000ft over the strip. They were piloted by P/O J. C. Lowe (with Sergeant C. Ashford as his observer) and Sergeant C. R. Herring (with P/O A. G. Claire as observer).

There were, therefore, some seven Wirraways airborne against the incoming Japanese bomber force that day. Four of them were shot down and one more was forced down, badly damaged. The surviving two landed after employing 'hide-and-seek' tactics with enemy fighters in the clouds. Flight Lieutenant Tyrell documented the uneven fight as he saw it:

> As we heard the enemy aircraft coming, away we went. We were barely 1,000ft off the deck when we saw the enemy formations above us. They were at least 10,000ft above. There was cloud over Vunakanu. It was clear over Lakunai. At that precise moment I saw a Wirraway, completely enveloped in flames, with smoke pouring out behind it, spinning down below the enemy. It crashed in the sea. I believe it was Lowe's machine. Almost immediately afterwards Herring's machine was shot down. It

Mass formation flight of a RAAF Wirraway unit instructors, clearly reveals the Wirra's plan-form well. RAAF Museum, Point Cook

crashed on the drome. Both occupants were wounded in the legs. The two patrol aircraft had gone. We were still thousands of feet below the enemy as we observed their bombs bursting.

Hewitt wisely decided to climb for position before attacking.

We tried to contact an improvised fighter R/T system at Vunakanu. We flew toward this main base but could not make contact. We climbed to about 10,000ft, at which level we saw nine enemy flying boats. They were in 'V' formation and about the same height. We faced up for an attack and where just about to go when a Zero came down on top of us.

Hewitt saw him coming and pulled our nose up hard, firing at the same time. Our aircraft stalled out of the turn. The Zero was sitting waiting as we almost stopped in the stall. With a magnificent piece of shooting he raked our bus from end to end. Cannon fire whizzed pieces out of the wing. Chunks flew off the fuselage. A small calibre bullet struck the left-hand gun through the cowling. It entered one of Hewitt's knees and bust out his shin. Hewitt blacked out temporarily. The aircraft went into a spin.

At the time I was standing up at the rear gun. I should have been strapped in but we were lacking in proper equipment of this kind. The next thing I knew was that I was hanging half over the side of the machine. Then I was flying through space. My hand fumbled for the rip cord ring. I could not find it. There was a sudden jerk. I looked up. My chute was open above me. I looked round for the Zero. It had followed Hewitt down to 4,000ft, where he pulled out of the spin. Hewitt took evasive action in clouds and shook it off. He landed at Vunakanau. The aircraft was badly damaged.

Apparently my parachute rip cord caught in the mounting in the cockpit. It was a miracle that it opened. I tried to 'spill' my chute as I approached a small clearing, but it caught in the top of a tree. I finished up astride one of the lower branches about 10ft from the ground. I was bruised and cut about. I released the harness and got to the ground. As it turned out I was about fourteen miles from the drome. I walked through the bush to a 'boong' village. The natives thought I was a Jap and wouldn't play. They either did not understand or would not speak English. I managed to make them get me two coconuts. Then I left and located a second village, where my reception was little better. One native told me of a road about a mile away and I made towards it. As I came in sight of the road a motor cycle went past but I couldn't contact the rider. Then an A.I.F. truck whizzed straight past me and stopped. Three Australians jumped out. One had a Tommy gun and two had rifles. They advanced cautiously towards me. They had been sent out to look for what was though was a Jap parachutist. I called out, 'Hold tight. I am one of you', and the tension was relieved. I was taken to Army Headquarters, and later to sick quarters, where Hewitt was overjoyed to see me.

Flight Lieutenant Tyrell had made a miraculous escape, but most of his fellows were not to be so fortunate that day. The official report continued:

Bromley's aircraft was shot down off Praed Point where it spun in near a small island. As it came down army personnel saw one of the occupants being dragged along behind it through the air. Apparently it was Walsh and it was believed his parachute caught in the cockpit in a similar manner to Tyrrell's. In his case, however, it failed to open as the cord did not break free. When recovered his body was practically unmarked. Bromley had been shot through the head and killed instantly. From a reconstruction of the combat it appeared that Bromley went straight up into the enemy formation attempting to attack from underneath. He had no chance.

The Wirraway piloted by Blackman was seen engaged in combat, but did not return. Nothing was heard of it or the occupants. Milne and Little, realizing how hopelessly outclassed they were, manoeuvred into position in the clouds. Adopting 'hide-and-seek' tactics they flew in and out of the clouds making several attacks on the superior enemy fighters. In the process their machines were badly shot up, but none of the occupants was injured. When the enemy formation had left they landed, but both their machines were unserviceable.

By the time the Japanese aircraft had droned away into the distance, there remained not so much as a single Wirraway in operational condition. Six aircrew had been killed and six injured. One of the aircraft was patched up sufficiently enough for Sergeant Milne to fly it out. He was heading for Lae when he saw that the Japanese were landing there and so he diverted to Salamaua. All the other Wirraways were blown up and set on fire, all possible equipment and stores were also destroyed before the squadron personnel left Rabaul.

Despite this experience the Wirraway, being the only aircraft available, was re-established in the combat zone with the sending of No. 4 Squadron to Berry field, near Port Moresby and from here they aided the Austalian army in halting the Japanese advance over the Owen Stanley mountains and then in the drive north.

The Wirraways were by far and away the most combat-used version of the T-6 during World War II and from the time of their initiation with No. 21 Squadron in Malaya, through to the end of hostilities, they saw action at New Guinea, New Britain and New Ireland, flying from Wau airfield, as tactical reconnaissance aircraft, but also served as target spotters, dive bombers, supply and transport aircraft, supply droppers, as well as observation machines and artillery spotters, and in as the evacuation of wounded personnel and as squadron hacks. But, of course, their greatest usefulness was in their designed training role at which they excelled. They became the main aircraft in Australia to carry out the Empire Training Scheme in that country and many thousands of young Australians were turned into combat pilots courtesy of the 'Wirra'.

The original programme of 620 aircraft had been completed by June 1942, but additional orders brought the total produced to 755 plus the two NAA built prototypes. The very last Wirraway, the 757th machine, was delivered to the RAAF in June 1946. A special dive bomber variant was produced with strengthened wings and tail assembly, but its main role was in the training of RAAF aircrew in the technique preparatory to their being equipped with the Vultee Vengeance for combat operations.[10]

Wirraway production details

Contract and type no.	*C/n*	*RAAF serial*
CAC CA-1 Wirraway I	1 to 40	A20-3 to A20-42
CAC CA-3 Wirraway II	41 to 100	A20-43 to A20-102
CAC CA-5 Wirraway II	103 to 134	A20-103 to A20-134
CAC CA-7 Wirraway II	135 to 234	A20-135 to A20-234
CAC CA-8 Wirraway II	436 to 635	A20-235 to A20-434
CAC CA-9 Wirraway II	636 to 823	A20-435 to A20-622
CAC CA-10 Wirraway II	Cancelled	–
CAC CA-10A Wirraway III	Wing assemblies	Retro-fitted Mark IIs
CAC CA-16 Wirraway III	1075 to 1209	A20-623 to A20-757

WIRRAWAY MEN: Pilot Officer Jack S. Archer, RAAF

The story of the Wirraway as a fighter aircraft is one of tragedy, but one man at least managed to turn the tables on the Zero and survived to tell the tale! The story of the only Wirraway combat kill is well worth preserving.

The incident took place on 1 January 1943. Flight Lieutenant J. S. Archer of No. 4 Squadron, RAAF, was on a routine reconnaissance patrol from Dobodura, with Sergeant J. L. Coulston as his observer, and in company with a second Wirraway from the same squadron, over Gona harbour, New Guinea, flying his favourite aircraft, *Chuff-Chuff* (A20-103). This aircraft had been allotted to No. 4 Squadron on 9 September 1940 from No. 1 Aircraft Depot and had served with that unit during the early stages of the New Guinea Campaign conducting tactical reconnaissance and supply dropping missions. They were on patrol over the anchorage, in sight of the famous wreck of a ship that had been sunk there earlier in the war. By great good fortune, Archer's aircraft, although converted to dive bombing and carrying universal bomb carriers beneath the wings, still retained her two forward-firing 0.303-calibre machine guns.

Coulston it was who first observed a third aircraft, some distance below them and at first it was taken as a 'friendly'. However, closer examination revealed to the observer the very uncomfortable fact that they had landed themselves a problem. Far from being on their side, that silhouette below them was unmistakably an enemy, and the worst kind. Coulston shouted a warning to Archer over the intercom, 'Hell, it's a [expletive deleted] Zero!' Archer could hardly believe it but there was no mistake, it was the deadliest of all their enemies. Once the Japanese pilot had sighted them both Wirraways would be doomed.

There was only one course of action, they could not fight such a powerful opponent in a fair fight, they could not run, the Zero had at least 100mph (160km/h) speed advantage over them. Archer took the instantaneous and, as it turned out, the correct decision, get him before he gets us!

Putting *Chuff-Chuff* into a dive straight down at the still unsuspecting Japanese aircraft below them, Jack got to within 200yd (180m) of him and started pressing the firing button. He left his thumb down hard on the button as the range rapidly closed to 50ft (15m). It was no good conserving ammunition, he only had one chance. As they pulled up in a tight turn at the end of the dive, Archer and Coulston saw, to their immense relief, the Zero flaming down out of the sky until it splashed in the sea below and was swallowed up. They had done it, scratch one Zero!

When interviewed after landing, Coulston said that Archer had done the only thing possible in the circumstances. Had he missed, things would have turned out very differently for everyone. Thankfully he had not. Archer was forthright when he became the centre of everyone's attention later. 'I didn't have time to think about it. I was lucky to get in the first burst. It was certainly good to see him crash into the sea.'

His squadron colleagues duly presented Jack with a whole crate of beer on his safe return to base. He had certainly earned it. Some time after this event, Archer's Wirraway was passed on to another pilot in the squadron and later returned to Australia for a refit and refurbishment. With incredible lack of sensitivity Archer's personal emblem, the wheeled Chinese Dragon, with its yellow body, outlined in red, black head and white teeth, and black and white eyes and wheels, along with the word UGH! in yellow, and his red and white 'Rising Sun' kill marking, together with his three yellow bombing mission tallies, were all painted over and replaced by a Squadron Crest. The faithful 0.303s were also removed and, unarmed, his aircraft was allocated to No. 3 Communications Squadron. She served with that unit for a while and then was placed in storage at No. 7 Aircraft Depot and forgotten.

Happily, after many years of neglect and isolation, someone had the sense to look for her and others had the sense to rescue and fully restore her to her condition as she was on that fateful day. She is now proudly displayed at the Australian War Memorial in Canberra, ACT, a fitting tribute to a famous aircraft. A unique little victory and a quick-witted Australian pilot!

***(Below)* The Wirraway's only combat victory – painting by the late Peter Connor showing the destruction of a Japanese Zero fighter over Gona harbour by Pilot Officer Jack S. Archer, RAAF.** RAAF Historical Section, Canberra, ACT

Production of the Wirraway ceased at the 135th aircraft of the CA-16 order, which had originally been for 150 aircraft.

Despite its obsolescence, the Wirraway continued to give good service as a trainer for the RAAF. An eyewitness, Sergeant Pilot I. Laming, remembered that there were two Wirraways at RAAF Townsville in October 1953, 'and I had also nicely stood a Wirraway up on its nose in Darwin a few months earlier when the brakes jammed'.[11]

Sixteen Wirraways were transferred to the Royal Australian Navy, and served between 1948 and 1953. They were utilized for both pilot and groundcrew training at HMAS *Albatross*, the RAN shore establishment at Nowra, New South Wales; Laming observed one there as late as 12 October 1953. He even asked if he could fly it, but eventually went aloft in a Sea Fury instead. Some carried the tail marking K for HMAS

This is the former A20-168, after handing over to the RAN. She received the RAN serial 972 and the tail code NW (Nowra), HMAS *Albatross*, during her service with Nos 723 and 724 Squadrons RAN. RAN Air Museum, Nowra

Sydney, or Y and later M for HMAS *Melbourne*, but no Wirraway ever deck landed on either of these carriers.

All the Fleet Air Arm Wirraways were sold after disposal to Lund Aviation Inc of New York during 1957.

The last-known RAAF unit to have operated the type was No. 23 Squadron, based at Mallala, South Australia, as late as 1959. Some 380 Wirraways had been put into long-term storage post-war and some parts were used in the production of the Ceres crop-spraying aircraft, of which more later.

Wirraway Survivors Post-War

Hardly any Wirraways were initially flown on the civilian register, post their being struck off charge by the RAAF, although a surprising number of Wirraways still exist

Wirraway's in the Royal Australian Navy

Serial no.	*Units*	*Notes*
A20-28	723 Squadron	
A20-133 and A20-139	723 and 816 Squadrons	
A20-141	805 Squadron	
A20-145	723 Squadron	SOC 18-6-53
A20-168	723 and 724 Squadrons	Tail Code NW
A20-176	723 Squadron	
A20-209, 211, 214, 225, 238, 250 and 469	723 and 724 Squadrons	
A20-490 and A20-752	723 and 724 Squadrons	752 Tail Code NW

A RAN Fleet Air Arm Wirraway at RAN Air Station Nowra in 1950, with tail code W (a contraction of NW for Nowra). No RAN Wirra ever made a deck landing although they did carry codes for the Australian aircraft carriers HMAS *Sydney* (tail code K) and HMAS *Melbourne* (tail code Y and then M) during their training days with 723, 724, 805 and 816 Squadrons RAN. RAN Air Museum, Nowra

as museum exhibits. This was mainly due to the harsh restrictions placed on such use by the then Australian Department of Civil Aviation (DCA), which effectively ruled out civilian use. Thus the majority went straight to the scrap yards. Some parts of Wirraways have been rescued from aircraft dumps down the years and form part of restoration projects which might, or might not, see completion.

Surplus Wirraway airframes were also used in the production of the Ceres aircraft (of which more later), along with many spares, but only twenty of the latter type were ever built from a planned production run of forty.

During the 1970s there was some sensible relaxation of the strict government restrictions on former military aircraft and this led to something of a minor renaissance in interest in the Wirraway. The first Wirraway rebuilt to flying standard was A20-653, which took the civilian registration VH-BFF and flew from Moorabbin airfield, Melbourne, on 4 December 1975. In 1989, VH-WIR was still flying. Seven others have been registered at one time or another, with four at least being restored to flying condition; some are still around at the time of writing. The best of the bunch are included in the Table, but there may be others in various stages of being rebuilt.

Wirraway A20-653 (coded BF-F) of No. 5 Squadron, RAAF, seen here at Bougainville in 1945. Note all-white tail common to this theatre of war and the open side hatch door in the fuselage. Squadron Leader J. Hearn, RAAF

Surviving CA-12 Wirraways

Mark	*C/n*	*RAAF serial*	*Civil reg*	*Location*
I	7	A20-9	–	Melbourne, Victoria: restoring
I	8	A20-10	–	Moorabbin Air Museum, Melbourne
I	11	A20-13	–	National Museum, Port Moresby, PNG
II	79	A20-81	VH-WWY	Caboolture, Qld: restored
II	97	A20-99	VH-JML	RAAF Richmond, New South Wales: restored
II	103	A20-103		Australian War Memorial, Canberra
II	136	A20-136	VH-CAC	Caboolture, Qld: restoring
II	223	A20-223	–	Lara, Victoria: restoring
II	224	A20-224	–	HARS, Sydney, New South Wales: restoring
II	703	A20-502	–	Ballarat Aviation Museum. Victoria
III	1101	A20-649	VH-WIR	Weeks Air Museum, Tamiami, Florida
III	1103	A20-651	–	Serviceworks, Spotswood, Victoria
III	1104	A20-652	VH-WIR	Essendon, Victoria: restoring
III	1108	A20-656	–	Tyabb, Victoria: restoring
III	1122	A20-670	–	RAAF Museum, Point Cook, Victoria
III	1137	A20-685	–	Camden Museum of Aviation, New South Wales
III	1139	A20-687	–	RAAF Museum, Point Cook, Victoria
III	1140	A20-688	–	RAAF Assoc Museum, Bullcreek, WA
III	1147	A20-695	–	Caboolture, Qld: restored
III	1156	A20-704	–	Moorabbin, Victoria: restored
III	1171	A20-719	VH-WRX	Bankstown, New South Wales
III	1174	A20-722	VH-CAC	Melbourne, Victoria

CA-12 Boomerang

The Japanese threat was a very real and immediate one to Australians in the spring of 1942. All the promised Imperial protection of the previous twenty years had either been easily destroyed by the Japanese or had never arrived at all, and their fleets and aircraft were running riot.[12] Australia lacked any front-line fighters able to challenge the Japanese Navy Zero and little hope of getting any for a considerable time. The answer seemed to be a locally built, highly-manoeuvrable and hard-hitting fighter plane.

The design staff of the CAC were called on to come up with a quick answer to this dire problem before it was too late. Their team, under Wing Commander L. J. Wackett, came up with a small fighter built around the largest and most powerful engine that was then available to them: the Pratt and Whitney R-1830 S3C4-G Wasp fourteen-cylinder radial twin 1,200hp. This engine was being constructed at Lidcombe, New South Wales, under licence for the Australian-built Beaufort medium bomber and was thus onhand. In order to save time and man-hours, existing tooling and many Wirraway components were incorporated in the design and components were built from Wirraway works drawings. Thus, the centre section, undercarriage and tail unit were almost identical to the Wirraway.[13]

The fuselage structure was of steel tube with a wooden monocoque fairing, extending from the cockpit to the rudder. A 70 Imperial gallon fuel tank of bullet-proof type was fitted in the fuselage, behind the pilot, and two 45 Imperial gallon tanks of moulded wood construction were located in the centre section. Increased range could be afforded by a 70 Imperial gallon drop tank. After aircraft No. 106, the pilot's seat and the wing-tips were also of moulded wood. The cockpit, a single-seat facility with a sliding hood, was amply protected with armour plating behind the pilot and a bullet-proof windscreen was fitted. The armament consisted of two 20mm Hispano cannon and four 0.303 Browning machine guns, all mounted in the wings. The wings, fin and tail were of all-metal stressed-skin construction, the control surfaces being fabric covered.

The design was approved on 21 December 1941, and the RAAF placed an initial order on 18 February 1942. There was no time for a prototype and 105 were ordered straight off the drawing board. Work on the first five was hastened forward to serve in lieu of a prototype for service evaluation trials. The first CA-12 (A46-1), now named the Boomerang,[14] made her maiden flight on 20 May 1942, flown by test pilot Ken Fruin, just fourteen weeks after the rough drafts had been approved.

A whole series of tests followed and resulted in a better performance than expected. A top speed of 305mph (488km/h) was attained at 15,000ft (4,572m), and the aircraft proved a sturdy, safe and highly manoeuvrable little machine, easy to fly, with a rate of climb that, at 2,900ft/min (883m/min), was better than the Hawker Hurricane I, the Supermarine Spitfire I, the Curtiss P-40N Warhawk or even the Focke-Wulf 190 F-3. And this from an aircraft that had only taken a few weeks to design, build and fly.

The main engineering problem encountered concerned the cooling of the engine, and to rectify this the third production aircraft (A46-3) was modified with the oil cooler intake incorporated within the lower lip of the cowling. At the same time a propeller spinner was added. The first two machines were retro-fitted in the same way and went to No. 2 Operational Training Unit thereafter. Mock combats against a P-40E Kittyhawk and an Bell P-39D Airacobra followed. The results proved most enlightening.[15]

(Above) Fine in-flight study of Boomerang A46-128, of No. 5 Squadron, RAAF. The massive 'spined' exhaust plume damper for night fighter work which was fitted to this mark can clearly be seen. A ring-and-bead gunsight is visible in front of the pilot. The massive comparative size of the wing-mounted 20mm cannon is very impressive. Trethewey, Oppem, Belgium

The one and only CA-14 (A46-1001), which was a converted standard Boomerang fitted with the massive General Electric turbo-supercharger. On the opposite side of the fuselage an equally large air intake was mounted. RAAF Museum

It was found that the Boomerang could turn inside a Kittyhawk and was far more manoeuvrable. The P-40s had a slight speed edge in a dive but this was compensated for by the CA-12s superior climb rate. Against the P-39, the speed difference was greater but again the CA-12 had a far better turning circle. The only chance the P-39 had was for a diving attack from a superior altitude but, once combat became mixed, the CA-12 had the superiority for the dog-fight. Performance figures are shown below.

CA-12 Boomerang – comparative performance figures 1942, trials

Altitude (ft)	*CA-12*	*P-40E*	*P-39D*
	Level performance (mph)		
SL	260	280	315
5,000	280	300	340
10,000	295	320	360
15,000	295	315	360
20,000	300	310	330
25,000	285	295	325
30,000	260	275	310
	Climb performance (ft/min)		
SL	2,500	1,850	2,000
5,000	2,500	1,850	2,000
10,000	2,300	1,850	2,000
15,000	2,080	1,400	1,550
20,000	1,550	1,000	1,100
25,000	1,050	550	650
30,000	500	150	200
Service ceilings			
	34,000	30,500	31,500

By September of that same year, a steady flow was reaching the RAAF from the CAC plant at Fishermen's Bend, near Melbourne, a site a few miles from the city centre and with its own airstrip. There were several modifications built in on the assembly line as the order progressed. The 36th machine (A46-36) had night flying ID lighting fitted under the single centre section, offset to starboard. From the 94th machine (A46-94) onward, a modified electrical starter system was installed. There was also a strengthening of the locating pins for the external belly tank. The spinner back plates also required beefing up after operational use. By June 1943, the first batch (A46-1 to A46-105 inclusive) had been completed. There proved, not surprisingly, to bear some superficial resemblance to the USAAF P-64 fighter, but CAC had reached their finished product by a totally different design route, even though the basic NAA original pedigree resulted in many common features.[16] Supplies of the standard USAAF fighter, the Curtis P-40 Warhawk (known to the RAF and RAAF as the Kittyhawk), and the British Hawker Hurricane were promised. Both of these were vastly inferior to the Zero but were expected to arrive in numbers. There was a call in government circles to abandon the Boomerang because of this but, as their delivery was by no means guaranteed in the summer of 1942, work was continued on producing the home-grown fighter as a insurance against non-supply.

Since the twin Wasp was a medium supercharged engine, giving its greatest power with the high-speed blower at about 15,000ft (4,570m), this gave a limitation to the Boomerang's performance. To overcome this, one aircraft (A46-103) was converted by the Aircraft Performance Unit (APU) to take an improved supercharger. The General Electric turbo-supercharger, one of which was obtained directly from the manufacturer, was mounted internally in the rear fuselage of the modified A46-103 aircraft. It necessitated the fitting also of a large air intake, located behind the pilot's cockpit on the port side of the fuselage. A three-bladed Curtiss electrical controllable pitch propeller was also fitted.

CA-14

This machine became the CA-14 (A46-1001) and her performance was considerably higher than that of the CA-12. Due to the severe airflow interference of the huge air intake, further improvements were made, including the fitment of sliding gills, and an engine cooling fan. The intercooler air scoop on the port side of the CA-14 was deleted, the air being directed from the engine bay via a streamlined air duct. An 18-blade cooler fan was fitted and a variable-pitch de Havilland propeller was substituted for the Hamilton. Other modifications were trialled on a modified CA-103 (A46-157) and she had a revised centre-section leading edge and was also fitted with solid (18-inch diameter) tyres. A square fin and rudder replaced the conventional Boomerang type and this greatly modified aeroplane became the CA-14A.

CA-14A

The CA-14A arrived at No. 1 APU in June 1944 for extended testing. An enormous improvement was obvious from the start and she attained a maximum speed of 348mph (556km/h) at an altitude of 28,000ft (8,530m). However, at about this time, American and British high-altitude fighters were being landed and assembled in

Specification – CA-12 Boomerang

Dimensions:	Wing span 36ft (11m); wing area 225ft^2 (20m^2); length 25ft 9in (785cm); height 13ft (4m)
Empty weight:	5,373lb (2,437kg)
Normal weight (loaded):	7,699lb (3,492kg)
All-up weight:	8,249lb (3,742kg)
Wing loading:	34.2lb/in^2
Power loading:	6.4lb/hp
Power plant:	Single CAC-built Pratt and Whitney R-1839 S3C4-G
Take off rating:	1,200hp at 2,700rpm
Military rating:	1,200hp and 2,700rpm at 4,900ft (1,490m)
Normal rating (max.):	1,100hp at 6,200ft (1,890m) and 1,000hp
Performance:	Maximum speed at sea level: 273mph (437km/h) Maximum speed at 7,400ft: 302mph (483km/h) Maximum speed at 15,500ft: 305mph (488km/h) Cruising speed (15,000ft) 190mph (304km/h) Climb from sea level 2,940ft/min (896m/min) Service ceiling 34,000ft (1,040m) Range (internal tanks only) 930 miles (1,150km) at 190mph (304km/h) at 15,000ft (4,570m) Range (with external tank) 1,600 miles (2,560km) at 175mph (280km/h) at 10,000ft (3,050m)

Australia, so that further work on the CA-14A was dropped. Meanwhile, the cancellation of the CA-11 Woomera bomber led to further orders being placed for the Boomerang, partly to keep the skilled workforce in place for future developments and partly because the little aircraft had proved herself in her new role. Two fresh orders kept the line moving along. The second batch became the CA-13.

CA-13

A whole new type number was justified by many alterations from the basic aircraft, although the name was retained for this and subsequent orders. Ninety-five CA-13s were built (A46-106/200, inclusive). With the intended night-fighter role in mind, several modifications were introduced on the CA-13. The engine, which remained the same, had the straight-through exhaust replaced with a flame-damper exhaust, designed to reduce flare and glare give-away at night. Also in this version, a new and more powerful generator was introduced for an upgraded electrical system. The metal-covered wing-tips became moulded wooden ones, and aluminium replaced fabric as the aileron covering.

The armament was unchanged, but failures in the field led to the replacement of the in-flight hydraulically operated gun-cocking system by a ground-worked mechanical system, which was more reliable. Laminated wood also replaced metal alloy in the pilot's seat. Minor alterations included an improved control column grip.

One aircraft (A46-121) was locally modified by No. 4 Squadron, RAAF, for photo-reconnaissance work. The belly tank was altered to accommodate a pair of low-altitude cameras, mounted vertically and obliquely. To keep the camera lenses clean during take-off from primitive airstrips, a highly technical device was employed by which cardboard shields were fitted on the ground and removed once airborne by pulling a piece of attached string from the cockpit! A second seat, placed inside the fuselage behind the pilot, was built to house an observer during instruction and performance tests on yet another CA-13 by the APU. A46-157 was fitted with an experimental eighteen-blade cooling fan and other aircraft had treaded tyres fitted; this feature was to become standard fitting for the third and final batch, which became the CA-19.

CA-19

Differences over the CA-13 were minimal, but this batch of forty-nine aircraft (A46-201/249, inclusive) kept Boomerangs in production until as late as February 1945 when the final machine was delivered to the RAAF. Aircraft from A46-211 onward were constructed with provision for the Fairchild F24 camera.

In total then, 250 Boomerangs, including the CA-14A, were built.

The Boomerang came into the operational picture at the time of the offensive on Salamaua in 1943. As a night fighter it was thought her limitations would not be so exposed and many were initially earmarked for nocturnal interception duties, but no Japanese aircraft was ever shot down by them. It was in a completely different field that the Boomerang eventually found her niche. Close co-operation between the Army and Air Force was in certain cases brought to a fine art by Boomerang pilots, and although lacking the performance of the latest Japanese fighters, due to other engine limitations, already mentioned, she made an extremely good bomber-interceptor, ground-strafer and Army co-operation machine. The manoeuvrability of the Boomerang proved a great asset on the strafing patrols across the mountains of New Guinea, Borneo and other jungle-clad islands.

The paint scheme carried by the Boomerang on these operations was of the 'foliage green' type, with the upper surfaces of the wings and fuselage painted in this colour to blend against a forest background when viewed from above, while the lower surfaces were duck-egg blue. RAAF roundels were carried on the upper and lower surfaces and on both sides of the fuselage and, to avoid possible confusion with the Japanese red 'meatball', the central red marking of these roundels was over-painted white. Identification markings, in grey, were on both sides at the rear end of the fuselage and standard RAAF flashes were used on the fin.

Boomerang Combat Record: 1943/45

Due to teething problems with fresh pilots and some technical problems, the first Boomerangs did not enter operational service until 2 March 1943, when the first machine joined No. 84 Squadron, RAAF, at Richmond, New South Wales. Conversion training followed subsequent deliveries and the squadron was ordered out to Horn Island airstrip on 14 April. From here they conducted their first combat sorties by mounting patrols over Merauke, New Guinea, at a range of 180 nautical miles from their base.

The first actual combat did not take place until the 16 April, when two Boomerangs, piloted by Flying Officer Johnstone and Sergeant Stammer, attacked three Mitsubishi G4M3 Navy Type I Attack (Betty) Bombers. Unfortunately the guns of one Boomerang did not work at all and, although closing to within 250yd (227m), the second failed to score any hits before the enemy bombers evaded them in cloud. There were no further aerial contacts that summer.

Two other Boomerang squadrons, Nos 83 and 85, were only utilized for coastal convoy and harbour protection duties during their lifetimes, with no opportunity to meet the enemy at all. So the Boomerang was fated to remain a fighter that never destroyed a single enemy aircraft.

Better things resulted when the Boomerang was made available to existing Wirraway squadrons engaged on close support work in the battle zone. Both No. 4 and No. 5 Army Co-operation Squadrons began using the Boomerang in the ground strafing role from 15 June 1943 onward, with excellent results. Both units continued in action during the liberation of New Guinea, New Britain, Bougainville Island and Borneo. Operation units are given in the table below.

CAC Boomerang – assigned units

Unit	*Code*	*From*	*To*
No. 2 OUT	–	10-10-42	–
No. 4 Squadron	QE	1-7-43	15-8-45
No. 5 Squadron	BF	2-11-43	15-8-46
No. 8 Squadron	ZA	19-2-44	5-8-44
No. 84 Squadron	LB	9-5-43	15-10-43
No. 85 Squadron	SH	9-5-43	27-1-45
No. 83 Squadron	MH	16-9-43	15-8-45

A number of CAC Boomerangs initially survived post-war and, although only a few were sold for civilian usage, some still remain relatively intact today. Just one is flying (VH-BOM) at the time of writing, but there are several restorations underway in both Australia and the USA. Besides those listed in the Table, some of which are part replica rebuilding projects, there are several fuselage or cockpit hulks in various store places that *might* one day be rebuilt (*see* table above right).

Surviving Boomerangs

Type	C/n	RAAF serial	Civil reg.	Location
CA-12	848	A46-2	–	CAC Fishermens Bend, Victoria
CA-12	853	A46-30	–	Australian War Memorial, Canberra
CA-12	877	A46-54	VH-MHB	Hendra, Brisbane
CA-12	924	A46-101	–	Bankstown, New South Wales
CA-13	945	A46-122	VH-MHR	Hendra, Brisbane
CA-13	962	A46-139	N32C5	Part replica, Chino, California
CA-13	988	A46-165	–	Weeks Air Museum, Tamiami, Fl.
CA-13	997	A46-174	–	Weeks Air Museum, Tamiami, Fl
CA-19	1029	A46-206	VH-BOM	Darwin: restored
CA-19	1073	A46-249	–	Melbourne: restoring

The CA28 Ceres

The huge expanses of the Australian farm lands and cattle grazing areas had for long proved arduous and time-consuming when it came to fertilizer spraying and crop-dusting with chemicals. In the 1930s and 40s little or no consideration was given to the dangers of this to plants, livestock or humans and, after the war, in common with general practice world-wide, aerial crop-spraying became common. At the end of the war, aerial crop-spraying was unknown in Australia but by 31 March 1959, well over two million acres were treated with super-phosphate, seed, insecticides, herbicides and other air-distributed materials.

Many light aircraft, both military war-surplus and civilian, were hastily converted to conduct such work, but it was found over the years that they both lacked sufficient capacity, visibility and safety for such work. Looking for fresh markets in the scaled-down post-war aviation industry, CAC saw the need for a specially-designed aircraft to carry out this task, both efficiently and safely.[17]

The CAC conducted a detailed investigation into all aspects of the problem with emphasis on cost, safety and economical operation, and the result was the Ceres Agricultural Aeroplane. By good design and the utilization of some components of

The very first Ceres, CA28-1, VH-CEA under construction at the CAC factory, 5 August 1960. The basic Wirraway fuselage accommodated the huge hopper so the re-designed pilots' cabin was elevated higher up which gave a better all-round view for the spraying. CAC Pty Ltd, Melbourne

the Wirraway trainer and dive bomber, they found that they could produce a customized and specialized aircraft to do the job at the reasonable selling price of 14,000 Australian pounds. It should be emphasized that the Ceres[18] was not a conversion from the Wirraway, but a brand-new original product; one that used design and parts from the Wirraway and, therefore, qualifies her for inclusion in these pages as a linear descendant of NAA's original prototype.

The Ceres was an all-metal, low-wing monoplane powered by the Pratt and Whitney Wasp R-1340 S3H1-G nine-cylinder radial air-cooled engine of 600hp. Agricultural loads of up to 2,327lb (1,047kg) of dust or 250 Imperial gallons of spray could be carried in her stainless-steel hopper, having a capacity of 40ft^3 (11m^3) and located over the centre of gravity (c.g.) giving her a negligible change in fore-and-aft trim. An emergency dump gate jettisoned the entire load in a few seconds. The change to liquid load was made by replacing the dust gate with an assembly carrying an air-driven pump, valve and filter. This unit had the capacity of up to 120gal/min (545l/min). Discharge was through a spay boom forming the trailing edge of the flap, which gave an effective swathe width of 90ft (27m).

Careful consideration was given by CAC to the cockpit and pilot's comfort. Footsteps and handgrips on either side enabled easy entry and exit, and the all-round vision from the high-mounted cockpit was exceptionally good for its time. The usual flight and engine instrumentation was provided with conventional flying controls, trim controls for elevator and rudder all being as standard. The flaps were operated by a cranked handle operating a screw jack, but the flaps could be left in an intermediate position during operations, lowering them for landing. Seating accommodation was made for a crew member in ferry flight mode, behind the pilot and facing aft, on some aircraft.

The wing area was 312ft^2 (28m^2), the fixed slats on the outer half of the wings and large slotted flaps resulted in excellent handling characteristics right down to the stall, which was entirely without vice. The wing loading in the normally fully loaded condition of 6,900lb (3,105kg) was 22.1lb/ft^2.

Operating and maintenance was made as simple and inexpensive as possible to fit farm budgets. The undercarriage was not retractable and no hydraulic or electrical systems were incorporated. Provision was made for the fitment of a generator and battery, however, in case an operator should require a radio or other electrical installation.

The Pratt and Whitney engine, licence-built by CAC, had established a good reputation for reliability and economy and was fitted with a three-bladed Hamilton propeller.

Specification of Ceres

Dimensions:	Wingspan 46ft 11in (28m); wing area 312ft^2 (28m^2); length overall 30ft 8½in (9m); height (level) 12ft 5in (3.7m^2); height (tail down) 11ft (3.3m); ground angle 12° 54 minutes; wheel track 12ft 6¼in (3.8m)
Fuel (max.):	80 imperial gallons (363l)
Weights and performance (duster type B)	
Empty weight (duster):	4,550lb (2,065kg)
Normal gross weight:	6,900lb (3,130kg)
Authorized max. weight (agricultural operations):	7,410lb (3,360kg)
Fuel load (normal max.):	568lb (258kg)
Fuel load (agricultural operations):	284lb (129kg)
Oil:	79lb (36kg)
Pilot:	170lb (77kg)
Hopper load (normal gross weight):	1,533lb (695kg)
Hopper load (agricultural operations):	2,327lb (1,096kg)
Wing loading (normal gross weight):	22.1lb/ft^2
Power loading (normal gross weight):	11.5lb/hp
CG range (MAC):	25.5–29.7 per cent
Take-off weight:	7,410lb (3,334kg)
Ground run distance:	435yd (391m); total over 50ft (15m): 750yd (675m)
Performance:	Rate of climb at take-off power, flaps up, 725ft/min (220m/min) Endurance: 40 gallons (181l) of fuel, 6min circuits 2h Landing (5,000lb; 2,250kg) ground run 175yd (157.5m) Stalling speed 50 knots Ferry (5,450lb; 2,452kg), cruising speed at 5,000ft (1,524m) 110 knots Rate of climb (SL) 1,520ft/min (463m/min) Range, 80 gallons (363l) fuel, no reserve, 500 nautical miles (cruise)

History

Two prototypes were built and tested before production was commenced. The performance of the prototype, Ceres Model A with a normal gross weight of 6,640lb (2,988kg), was good – maximum speed was 140 knots, cruising speed 90 knots and landing speed 47 knots. There proved little change in performance of the production Ceres, although the gross weight was increased to 7,410lb (3,334kg). The standard Ceres Model B was fitted with the Wasp geared engine and a D. H. Hamilton propeller, while model C had the same type of engine but with a 'high solidity' propeller. On aircraft No. 6 and subsequent aircraft, the cockpit enclosure was extended aft to enclose a rear passenger compartment. The extended enclosure had clear acrylic panels each side and faired at the aft end with a hinged aluminium alloy door, which swung sideways for access. The Ceres had DCA approval for a pilot and two passengers, the second passenger being accommodated in the hopper.

The Ceres was sold in very limited numbers and used for many years for crop-spray-

The Ceres – original registration and users

No.	Original reg.	Later reg.	Purchaser
CA28-1*	VH-CEA	VH-CEX	Proctors Rural Services
CA28-2	VH-CEB	–	Airfarm Associates
CA28-3	VH-CEC	–	Airfarm Associates
CA28-4	VH-CED	ZK-BPU	Aerial Farming of New Zealand
CA28-5	VH-CEF	VH-SSZ	Coondair Tintinara South Africa
CA28-6	VH-CEG	–	Airfarm Associates
CA28-7	VH-CEH	ZK-BXW	Aerial Farming of New Zealand
CA28-8**	VH-CEI	ZK-BXY	Aerial Farming of New Zealand
CA28-9	VH-CEL	ZK-BZO	Cooksons Airspread of New Zealand
CA28-10	VH-CEK	VH-SSY	Airfarm Associates
CA28-11	VH-CEM	ZK-BSQ	Wanganui Aerowork
CA28-12	VH-CEN	ZK-BVS	Aerial Farming of New Zealand
CA28-13	VH-CEO	VH-SSF	Marshall Spreading Services
CA28-14	VH-CEP	VH-DAT	Doggett Aviation,WA
CA28-15	VH-CEQ	VH-WAX	Airland Improvements
CA28-16	VH-CER	–	Marshall Spreading Services
CA28-17	VH-CET	VH-WHY	Airland Improvement
CA28-18	VH-CEX	VH-SSV	Airfarm Associates
CA28-19	VH-CEU	VH-WOT	Airland Improvements
CA28-20	VH-CEV	–	New England Aerial Top Dressing
CA28-21	VH-CEW	–	Airfarm Associates

** Aircraft rebuilt and became CA28-18.*
*** Aircraft written off.*

Inside the cockpit of Ceres showing the pilot's restricted but simplified controls. CAC Pty Ltd, Melbourne

(Below) **Ceres CA28-7 (VH-CEH) on completion. She went to Aerial Farming of New Zealand to work. Although an initial run of forty aircraft were planned, only twenty were actually finally produced.** CAC Pty Ltd, Melbourne

ing in both Australia and New Zealand. The table (above) gives some of the registrations and owners in the early years.

There is at least one Ceres carcass still in existence, CA28-14. She was displayed at the Channel Seven Vintage Museum in Perth, between 1972 and 1987, before being 'converted back' to a Wirraway (which is nonsense because she never had been a Wirraway!) and put on display at the Western Australia Museum of Aviation, in Perth. She has since been moved to Sydney, again as a 'Wirraway' restoration project! One of the six aircraft sold to New Zealand survived to be exhibited at the Auckland Museum of Transport and Techonology, the rest were written off and none returned to Australia.[19]

CHAPTER TEN

Post-War Developments

With the ceasing of hostilities, firstly against Germany in May and then against Japan in August 1945, the AT-6 suddenly faced over-production on a large scale. The three major users, the United States, Great Britain and Canada, did what democracies always do at such times and almost completely disarmed. Not for several years did it dawn on most of these nations that the communist agendas of Marshal Stalin and Chairman Mao were somewhat different and that these nations were *increasing* their arms rather than scrapping them. The result of this misplaced optimism, as far as 'The Six' was concerned, was a mass sell-off, with hundreds of trainers being disposed of at knock-down prices from 1945 onward. This included large numbers of lend-lease aircraft, which the British Air Ministry was supposed to return to the USA. On the occasions when this was done, the aircraft were quickly disposed of by either scrapping or sale, but for a great number they were sold or transferred to other nations directly, without passing back through American hands.

The fate of many British aircraft and warships post-war, this is EZ 406 'cocooned' and strapped down on the deck of a Royal Navy aircraft carrier on her way to Malta on 30 October 1947. She had previously served with No. 759 Squadron, Fleet Air Arm with code Y2Z. She was re-activated in December 1947, and joined the SF at Hal Far field, Malta, but only had a short career, colliding with a Vampire and crashing on 25 October 1948. Ray C. Sturtivent

This glut of cheap, many of them hardly used, AT-6s and Harvards, proved a boon not only to smaller air forces, now able to rebuild again for next to nothing, but also the many civilians aviation enthusiasts. Their numbers mushroomed when 'the boys came home' and started looking for easy-to-fly, reliable mounts. As the T-6 had taught most of them how to fly in the first place, what was more natural than they should turn to the huge market now available. Obtaining the aircraft was relatively cheap but running and maintaining your own personal T-6 or Harvard was very expensive and running costs were high. Thus, although this 'civilian-izing' of the AT-6 took part all over the world, it was principally done in the more affluent United States, rather than in the impoverished European and defeated Japanese areas at this period. On the other hand, in compensation, 'The Six' required relatively little conversion to make it suitable for the civilian market and the obtaining of that all–important Federal Aviation Administration (FAA) certificate that allowed them to fly.

Finally, when the penny finally dropped, a reluctant and hesitant re-arming of the Western democracies started in the early 1950s and this was to mean a new extension of life for 'The Six', not only in the United States, Great Britain and Canada, but in all nations of the Western alliance and also in the rejuvenated air forces of the former defeated axis nations, West Germany, Italy and Japan!

Civilian Usage

All manner of civilian users took 'The Six' on board in the immediate post-war era. With sell-off prices as low as US$400, in some cases there was no lack of buyers, both company and individual. The then current regulating authorities tested each conversion and those that passed were awarded either the 'memo' (category 2) certificate 2-575 (November 1945 issue), if they were former United States Military aircraft (AT-6/SNJs) and were held by North American Aviation, or, for some purely nationalistic reason, the 'restricted' certificate AR-11, if they were former Canadian-built machines, that particular certificate being held by a holding company in London, Autair Limited. The former certificate allowed for standard (commercial) licences to be issued and a civilian registration number was issued. The latter was more restrictive in scope and limited the uses to which the conversions could be legally put to. Earlier models like the NA-16, a few of which survived to join the sales scramble, all received the same certification, but in their case the issue was to the individual applicants, rather than NAA.

The result was that, by 1947, some 807 'Sixes' were on the US civil register. The uses their new owners put them to was legion. There was little the rugged Six was not adapted to at this period. Chief use was, of course, its original role, as a training aircraft, but with private companies, either specialist teaching schools across the States, or as the property of various airline companies who used them to train up their own staff and as company hacks for their executives, both business and pleasure. Another duty to which 'The Six' was widely adapted was as a crop-spraying aircraft in the Mid-West and other agricultural belts of the rural USA. The use of DDT was then fairly new and the dangers it posed were unrecognized. So former T-6s with spray nozzles and tanks full of the stuff, criss-crossed the huge acres of wheat fields and other crops discharging the chemical into the wind.

More specialized civilian usage included banner-towing or coloured smoke 'sign-

Busy post-war RAF Harvard trio working with 3FTS based at Feltwell, Middlesex; these are KF 977 (FB TA closest camera), FT 149 (FB UJ) and KF 265 (FB TR) seen here in April 1951. Ray C. Sturtivent

Seen on the deck at RAF Odiham in 1953 where she was part of the CFS, is this Harvard T2B, KF 755, coded OT on fuselage and cowling. She later went on to see brief service with both Glasgow and Liverpool University Air Squadrons from 1956, before being sold to Aviation Traders for scrap in October 1957. Ray C. Sturtivent

writing' teams for advertising, which enjoyed a brief boom at this time. One organization, the 'SkyTypers' of Los Alamitos, California, came up with a novel twist to this old concept. In the mid-1960s five SNJ-2s, painted a bright scarlet hue, were so converted. They were electronically linked together and the lead aircraft had a 'master' transmitter. On the lead's cueing, each aircraft simultaneously 'typed' its own assigned letters in the sky at a rate of nine characters per minute. Sentences and advertising slogans could thus be 'typed' ten times as fast as the traditional method.[1] Later, the same company opened another branch called SkyTypers East Inc., based at Flushing, New York, with another five SNJ-2s. Finally they bought an ex-Spanish air force T-6G to add to the fleet.

Later 65-2009 was displayed at the Seminole Air Center, Seminole, Oklahoma, while 65-2021, 65-2028, 65-2029, 79-3988 and 79-3997 became the Miller Squadron at Flushing, NY, sponsoring the Miller Brewing Company. They flew line abreast and laid down five-mile long advertisements some 1,000ft (304.8m) up in the sky. They later became the SNJ-2 Corps, still based at Flushing.

SkyTypers conversions

Type	*C/n*	*Serial*	*Civil reg.*	*Base*
SNJ-2	65-2009	BuNo 2020	N87613	Los Alamitos, CA
SNJ-2	65-2014	BuNo 2025	N61563	Los Alamitos,CA
SNJ-2	65-2021	BuNo 2021	N60734	Flushing, NY
SNJ-2	65-2026	BuNo 2037	N66082	Los Alamitos, CA
SNJ-2	65-2028	BuNo 2039	N62382	Flushing, NY
SNJ-2	65-2029	BuNo 2040	N52033	Flushing, NY
SNJ-2	79-3988	BuNo 2553	–	Flushing, NY
SNJ-2	79-3993	BuNo 2558	N60645	Los Alamitos, CA
SNJ-2	79-3997	BuNo 2562	N65370	Flushing, NY
SNJ-2	79-4993	BuNo 2568	N60833	Los Alamitos, CA
T-6G	168-395	49-3291	N29933	Los Alamitos,CA

This pristine RAF T2B is KF 694, coded PQ, seen earning her keep at Thorney Island with 3 FTS in 1954. She had a long history, with 7 FIS and 7 SFTS between January 1947 and July 1949, then with 2 FTS until 1951. She spent over five years with 3 FTS before being sold for scrap in December 1956.
Ray C. Sturtivent

These aircraft had been modified more than their certificates covered and so had to operate under 'restricted' licences. Others barn-stormed and just gave simple aerial access and pleasure to their individual owners. Enterprising film companies, happily aware of the general ignorance of the film-going public to distinguish one aircraft from another, found 'The Six' an ideal base on which to make cosmetic alterations and so present them as 'enemy' aircraft to be spectacularly destroyed by all-American aviation heroes in innumerable movies. In this, their 'starring' role, Hollywood invariably featured 'The Six' as the Japanese Mitsubishi Zero fighter. The two had manoeuvrability and a radial engine in common, and that, coupled with the best efforts of the props departments, usually sufficed!

By far the most spectacular use to which civilian 'Sixes' was put in this era, was pylon racing. These mass, low-level races were exciting, noisy, tremendous fun, and highly dangerous. They attracted large crowds thrilled by the noise and proximity of the aircraft (which looked to be going so much faster just above the ground and in spectacular turns around the markers) and gave ample adrenaline rushes to the competitors themselves. Those that forgot 'The Six' had a mean reputation, or who got a little too careless or adventurous, paid the ultimate price and there were several mid-air collisions and numerous crashes at these meetings, literally the stock-car races of the skies!

More serious competitions took place with organized air races. At first 'The Six' was considered too 'tame' for male competitors, and a special event was organized for women to race. This became the Halle Trophy Race and was run for the first time in 1947 at the resurrected National Air Races held annually at Cleveland, Ohio. Further liberties were allowed to be taken with 'The Six' for this event and the normal customizing was to reduce the two-place cockpit canopy to a single streamlined one faired into the after fuselage to reduce drag. The other obvious way to up your chances of winning was to tweak the engine, or even completely replace it with a different, and more powerful, powerplant. Thus civilian registration NX 64448 of the Vert Aircraft Company, raced (unsuccessfully) mounting a turbo-charged engine and having the canopy removed and the cockpit left open. This led some women to latch on to the fact that the solitary XAT-6E, which had been acquired post-war for racing, had the edge in speed over any standard T-6/SNJ. The adoption of the Ranger V-770-9 in-line engine was tried on at least one aircraft (an AT-6D/SNJ-5, c/n 88-16027, serial number 42-84246) and this machine with civilian registrations NX74108 was used to advertise the Sohio company's 'Wingwax' products for a while, before entering the racing scene. This conversion led to some post-war historians to assume that more than one XAT-6E had been built by Fairchild, but such was *not* the case.

Both aircraft took part in the 1947 race, with Margaret McGrath flying the original having been top qualifier at 223.325. She even hit 240mph (385km/h) on occasion but the Ranger was still the Ranger and mechanical problems forced her to pull out. This left the way clear for Ruth Johnson to win the 1947 Halle Trophy clocking up 223.602mph (359.776km/h) in a former AT-6 (NX 63770) owned by the Television Association, which had a supercharged 'Wasp' driving a three-bladed propeller. Second place was Grace Harris's AT-6 (N 90641) with a cut-down cockpit, and the following year she won the Halle and also the Kendall in 1949, despite the new rules forcing her to replace the three-bladed propeller with a two-bladed one. The converted XAT-6E was put on display at the Western Museum of Flight, Hawthorne, California.

Pushing the limits, forced these racer aircraft to fly on 'experimental' licences, which suited the former experimental XAT-6E well enough. However, initially, clipped wings were *not* permitted even here. The following year at the 1948 Cleveland show, the Halle gave way to a new event, the Kendall Trophy Race, as the women's AT-6/SNJ category event, but the previous rules still applied. However, in view of the accidents that resulted, in 1949 the Kendall rules were considerably tightened up, and only stock engines driving two-bladed propellers were permitted. This dumbed-down the race too much and the event died out for almost twenty years. However, in 1964 the National Air Races were revived, this time at Reno, Nevada, but it was a further three years before an T-6 exhibition race took place there. Its popularity led to the revival of the class, but this time for both men and women, in 1968. The new T-6 event, the Bardahi Trophy Race, kept the strict restrictions in force, however, and only 'strictly 'stock' aircraft were permitted to compete. Despite this the event continued to attract the growing numbers of 'Six' jockeys, no less than seventeen racing in 1968, who vied with each other in the authenticity (or garishness) of the paint jobs on their mounts.

Foreign Military Use: Official and Unofficial

With the advent of the Cold War between the Communist nations and their unfortunate satellites, and the Western Alliance like NATO and SEATO, the need to rebuild shattered air power in the newly-liberated nations of Western Europe and elsewhere required the provision of a large number of training aircraft. 'The Six', being both highly suitable and highly available, became the favoured option for almost every nation that aspired to any air power status in the decade that followed World War II. How these nations equipped themselves with stocks of Harvards, AT-6s and SNJs varied widely, and would require a whole book in itself to track down, if this were indeed possible. Some had batches of former American, British and Canadian trainers assigned to them, or loaned or leased to them. Others purchased batches outright from the air forces of these nations. Other countries 'came by' stocks, or even odd one or twos of 'Sixes' by more circuitous means, with secret arrangements made with dealers who bought up huge quantities of surplus aircraft and sold them on, either openly or by the 'back door'. We have already seen how the French l'Armée de l'Air and Aéronavale received both Harvard AT-6s and SNJs through official channels; they were but the start of French interest in the type, as we shall see.

But other nations trod the same, or similar paths. With the establishment of the United States Air Force as a separate military organization on 18 September 1947, the overall covering designation of both the AT-6 and SNJ was changed to just plain T-6. Similarly, Great Britain went over from roman numerals to arabic in the designation of her aircraft, the IIB becoming the 2B, for example. The Royal Canadian Air Force was supposed to follow the British lead in this but only did so slowly and, in the case of many Harvards, not at all, so the old designations mingled with the new to sow yet more confusion as types of each were moved around the globe!

RAF Harvard Mark IIA, EX 161, coded SE HA, flying with 4 FTS. She had earlier served with 22 and 2 SFTS from March 1943 onward. Her career came to an abrupt termination when she hit overhead cables on 20 January 1953, and was damaged beyond repair. Ray C. Sturtivent

British Disposals

Belgium

The Force Aéronautic Belgie (FAB) was the recipient of the first batch of RAF Harvards to be transferred by air, these being no less than fifty-six Mark IIA and Mark

IIIs, which were former South African aircraft that had arrived back in England in 1946 and been placed in storage. All this allocation was taken on charge by the Belgian Air Force between February and May 1947, at Brustem airfield, and included ten that were for use as 'spare parts' for the rest (*see* table right).

These served for several years and, in 1949, the FAB received a second batch of ten of the former RAF Mark 2Bs. They also received a single aircraft transferred from the Royal Netherlands Air Force, this was the former RAF serial FS 820 (ex-Dutch B-120), which became the FAB serial H.47. H.39 (ex- EX 292, 88-9755, 41-33275) and was on exhibition for many years at the Musée Royal de l'Armée in Brussels until 1990 when it was sold off to a private purchaser.

Belgian Harvards received from the RAF in 1949

RAF serial	FAB serial	RAF serial	FAB serial
KF 940	H.49	FX 414	H.54
KF 463	H.50	FX 466	H.55
KF 207	H.51	FX 229	H.56
KF 415	H.52	KF 483	H.57
FX 212	H.53	KF 568	H.58

H.58 (c/n 14A-2268) survived with civilian registration LN-TEX. These were followed by a third batch of ten more Mark 2Bs purchased via Rollason Aircraft in the UK, in 1950.

Belgian Harvards received from the RAF in 1950

RAF serial	FAB serial	RAF serial	FAB serial
FX 276	H.64	KF 716	H.69
KF 738	H.65	KF 737	H.70
KF 727	H.66	KF 719	H.71
KF 715	H.67	KF 860	H.72
KF 724	H.68	KF 734	H.73

In 1952–53 a fourth batch of ten followed from the Royal Netherlands Air Force, these again being ex-RAF service 2Bs (*see* table below).

The last consignment to join the Belgian Air Force from the UK were two dozen

Belgian Harvards received from the RAF in 1947

RAF serial	SAAF serial	FAB serial	RAF serial	SAAF serial	FAB serial
EZ 162	7548	H.1	EX 295	7077	H.24
EX 974	7531	H.2	EX 303	7043	H.25
EZ 335	7632	H.3	EX 371	7187	H.26
EX 660	7309	H.4	EX 439	7282	H.27
EX 937	7493	H 5	EX 461	7210	H.28
EZ 174	7555	H.6	EX 633	7349	H.29
EZ 186	7563	H.7	EX 602	7384	H.30
EX 476	7295	H.8	EX 661	7315	H.31
EX 959	7509	H.9	EX 760	7400	H.32
EX 438	7027	H.10	EX 823	7468	H.33
EX 239	7094	H.11	EX 910	7476	H.34
EX 544	7268	H.12	EX 939	7505	H.35
EX 551	7239	H.13	EX 273	7184	H.36
EX 993	7527	H.14	EX 305	7115	H.37
EZ 310	7625	H.15	EX 946	7501	H.38
EZ 214	7578	H.16	EX 292	7182	H.39
EX 542	7269	H.17	EX 318	7128	H.40
EX 181	7045	H.18	EX 567	7232	H.41
EZ 210	7605	H.19	EX 623	7344	H.42
EX 230	7007	H.20	EX 779	7409	H.43
EZ 256	7630	H.21	EZ 307	7623	H.44
EX 264	7107	H.22	EX 680	7329	H.45
EZ 292	7622	H.23	EX 994	7528	H.46
EX 251	7141	Spares	EX 546	7286	Spares
EX 254	7098	Spares	EX 547	7288	Spares
EX 275	7164	Spares	EX 550	7236	Spares
EX 393	7179	Spares	EX 821	7470	Spares
EX 448	7030	Spares	EX 940	7494	Spares

Unusual markings for this AT-6A carrying the coding BP205 with 4 BFTS.
Ray C. Sturtivent

Belgian Harvards received from Holland in 1952–53

RAF serials	Dutch serials	FAB serials	RAF serials	Dutch serials	FAB serials
FT 247	B-99	H.74	FT 210	B-105	H.79
FT 430	B-47	H.75	FS 885	B-89	H.80
FT 381	B-131	H.76	FS 730	B-128	H.81
FT 410	B-37	H.77	FT 286	B-58	H.82
FT 142	B-20	H.78	FT 390	B-139	H.83

Harvard 2As, which had become surplus to British requirements with the closing down of the Rhodesian Air Training Group. They were transferred and saw service in the Belgian Congo and the subsequent troubles there (*see* table right).

These latter aircraft were used to equip an Advanced Flying School at Kamina, where the Belgians enjoyed the same perfect all-year-round flying weather as the British had in Southern Rhodesia. These aircraft were,

Belgian Harvards received from the RAF in 1953

RAF serial	*FAB serial*	*RAF serial*	*FAB serial*	*RAF serial*	*FAB serial*
EX 419	H.201	EX 525	H.209	EX 528	H.217
EX 534	H.202	EX 753	H.210	EX 698	H.218
EX 788	H.203	EX 671	H.211	EX 197	H.219
EX 682	H.204	EX 374	H.212	EX 771	H.220
EX 655	H.205	EX 245	H.213	EX 784	H.221
EX 656	H.206	EX 379	H.214	EX 651	H.222
EX 699	H.207	EX 420	H.215	EX 657	H.223
EX 678	H.208	EX 405	H.216	EX 436	H.224

This Harvard T2B is KF 709 coded RAK:Y, seen here on the deck while serving with No. 604 Squadron at Acklington, in 1951. She went on to fly with Southampton University Air Squadron (UAS) between June and November 1952, with 14 RFS between November 1952 and April 1953, with Bristol UAS between April 1953 and September 1955 before returning to Southampton UAS between September 1955 and February 1956. She was finally struck off charge on 18 May 1956. Ray C. Sturtivent

(Bottom) **Nice clear portrait of RAF Harvard IIB, FE 267, in immaculate post-war paint scheme.** Ray C. Sturtivent

commencing July 1960, converted to the Counter-Insurgency (COIN) configuration against the Congolese rebels during the subsequent war of independence.

Disposals of all these aircraft began in 1961 and continued thereafter. Six aircraft are known to have been impressed into the Ruanda–Urundi Air Force (later the Congolese Air Corps, FAC) following the Belgian pull-out, these being the former H.22, H.23, H.34, H.35, H.203 and H.208. They fought in the subsequent civil war in 1961–62. Five machines were transferred to the South African Air Force in 1961–62, these being the former H.15, H.19, H.216, H.221 and H.223. At least twenty-six others were sold to civilian services as shown in the table right.

Fortunately one FAB example (H-21, 88-15950, 42-84169) was preserved as an exhibit at the Musée Royal de l'Armée, Brussels, as was H-19, 88-15774, 41-3400083, at the SAAF Museum, Swartkop Air Base. A Harvard III (H.14, 88-15118, 41-33966) spent her final days as an instructional airframe at the Professional School of Montmirault/LEP, Cerny La Ville, Essone, France and H.16, 88-15778, 41-34087, also ended up at Vilgenis. A Harvard IIA (H.29, 88-12127, 41-33606) was converted to resemble an F6F fighter for a time, while another (88-12046, 41-33575) ended her days at the Air France Technical School, Vilgenis, and a third (H.4, 88-12326, 41-33633) went to Air France

Belgian Harvards sold out to civilian service

FAB serial	*Civil reg.*	*FAB serial*	*Civil reg.*	*FAB serial*	*Civil reg.*
H.1	F-BJBA	H.18	00-GEQ	H.40	F-BJBL
H.3	F-BJBB	H.26	00-GEN	H.42	00-GDL
H.4	F-BJBC	H.28	00-GEO	H.43	00-GDM
H.6	F-BJBD	H.29	F-BJBI	H.45	00-GEP
H.8	F-AZFK	H.30	F-BJBJ	H.52	00-GDO
H.9	F-BJBF	H.31	00-GER	H.58	00-AAR
H.14	F-BJBG	H.33	F-BJBK	H.67	00-GDP
H.16	F-BJBH	H.36	00-GES	H.73	00-GDQ
H.17	00-GEM	H.37	00-GDX		

Sporting her wartime RAF camouflage is this Harvard IIA, EZ 452, coded 'W', seen flying with the Middle East Command's 73 OUT based at Fayid. She was struck off charge as early as 13 September 1945. Ray C. Sturtivent

***(Below)* FE 758 was one of many Harvard Mark IIBs that went to Canada on completion, and is seen in service here from a snow-clad airfield. She was shipped over to the UK in March 1944. She remained unused until sold to the Royal Netherlands Air Force in April 1947.** Canadian Government, Ottawa

Dutch Air Force B-66 (ex-FT 382) climbs straight up over the flat Dutch countryside. She had seen no RAF service prior to her transfer to Holland in June 1947.
Royal Netherlands Air Force

and then to Douala in the Cameroon between 1971 and 1977. An AT-6D, H.9, 88-14949, 41-33932, was flying until a few years ago. H.15, 88-16235, 42-84454, was being rebuilt in South Africa and another Harvard II (H.6, 88-15608, 41-34047) is, at the time of writing, being restored in France.

The Netherlands

Wartime training of Dutch pilots after the liberation commenced in 1944 with recruits being inducted at Ypenburg and then transferred to RAF Langham in Norfolk for their flying and technical training. Once a suitable field had been prepared in Holland, at Gilze-Rijen, the flying schools were transferred there in 1946. Both the Dutch Air Force (Koninklijke Luchtmacht or KL) and the Dutch Navy (Marine Luchtvaart Dienst or MLD) were equipped with the Harvard soon after the war.[2] The former took no less than 200 from both the RAF (150) and RCAF (50); the bulk of the RAF deliveries being flown directly in by 1 Ferry Unit based at RAF Pershore.

The RAF Harvards were delivered between September 1946 and March 1948 and seven were non-flying spares. They were assigned Dutch serials in the range B-1/150 (*see* the table below). The ex-RCAF deliveries were made in 1949 and underwent a full refurbishment by the Dutch company Aviolanda/Fokker at that time. They received the Les (training) classification L in the range 12-1 to 12-4. In 1964 and 1966, under a new system, the surviving air force machines were re-classified under the 043-044 and 098-099 categories.

Royal Netherlands Air Force allocations of RAF and RCAF Harvard 2Bs

RAF serial	*C/n*	*USAAF serial*	*Dutch serial*
FT 240	14A-1280	43-12981	B-1
FT 238	14A-1278	43-12979	B-2
FT 293	14A-1333	43-13034	B-3
FT 317	14A-1357	43-13058	B-4
FT 151	14A-1191	43-12892	B-5
FS 754	14AA-894	43-12595	B-6
FS 737	14-877	43-12578	B-7
FS 896	14A-1036	43-12737	B-8
FE 888	14-622	42-12375	B-9
FT 178	14A-1218	43-12919	B-10
FT 280	14A-1320	43-13021	B-11
FT 459	14A-1499	43-13200	B-12
FS 751	14A-891	43-12592	B-13
FS 831	14A-971	43-12672	B-14
FT 325	14A-1365	43-13066	B-15
FT 328	14A-1368	43-13069	B-16
FS 740	14A-880	43-12581	B-17
FT 362	14A-1402	43-13103	B-18
FT 323	14A-1363	43-13064	B-19
FT 142	14A-1185	43-12886	B-20
FT 456	14A-1496	43-13197	B-21
FT 256	14A-1296	43-12997	B-22
FT 452	14A-1492	43-13193	B-23
FS 716	14A-857	43-12557	B-24
FS 830	14A-970	43-12671	B-25
FT 234	14A-1274	43-12975	B-26
FT 231	14A-1271	43-12972	B-27

(continued overleaf)

Royal Netherlands Air Force allocations of RAF and RCAF Harvard 2Bs *(continued)*

RAF serial	*C/n*	*USAAF serial*	*Dutch serial*
FT 161	14A-1201	43-12902	B-28
FT 408	14A-1448	43-13149	B-29
FT 400	14A-1440	43-13141	B-30
FE 758	14-492	42-0955	B-31
FS 851	14A-991	43-12692	B-32
FS 908	14A-1048	43-12749	B-33
FT 420	14A-1460	43-13161	B-34
FT 340	14A-1380	43-13081	B-35
FT 134	14A-1174	43-12875	B-36
FT 410	14A-1450	43-13151	B-37
FT 425	14A-1465	43-13166	B-38
FT 437	14A-1477	43-13178	B-39
FT 177	14A-1217	43-12918	B-40
FS 915	14A-1055	43-12756	B-41
FE 750	14-484	42-0947	B-42
FE 787	14-521	42-12274	B-43
FT 212	14A-1242	43-12943	B-44
FT 229	14A-1269	43-12970	B-45
FT 345	14A-1385	43-13086	B-46
FT 430	14A-1470	43-13171	B-47
FS 912	14A-1052	43-12753	B-48
FT 222	14A-1252	43-12953	B-49
FT 308	14A-1338	43-13039	B-50
FT 448	14A-1488	43-13189	B-51
FS 824	14A-964	43-12665	B-52
FE 332	14-066	43-0529	B-53
FT 384	14A-1414	43-13115	B-54
FT 385	14A-1425	43-13126	B-55
FT 176	14A-1216	43-12917	B-56
FT 220	14A-1260	43-12961	B-57
FT 386	14A-1326	43-13027	B-58
FT 144	14A-1187	43-12888	B-59
FT 357	14A-1397	43-13098	B-60
FT 233	14A-1273	43-12974	B-61
FT 326	14A-1366	43-13067	B-62
FT 316	14A-1356	43-13057	B-63
FE 907	14-641	42-12394	B-64
FT 160	14A-1200	43-12901	B-65
FT 382	14A-1422	43-13123	B-66
FT 422	14A-1462	43-13163	B-67
FT 217	14A-1252	43-12953	B-68
FT 223	14A-1203	43-12904	B-69
FT 368	14A-1408	43-13109	B-70
FT 404	14A-1444	43-13145	B-71
FS 778	14A-918	43-12619	B-72
FT 228	14A-1268	43-12969	B-73
FT 248	14A-1288	43-12989	B-74
FT 447	14A-1487	43-13188	B-75
FS 882	14A-1022	43-12723	B-76
FS 839	14A-979	43-12680	B-77
FT 304	14A-1334	43-13035	B-78
FT 145	14A-1185	43-12886	B-79
FT 349	14A-1389	43-13090	B-80
FS 726	14A-866	43-12567	B-81
FT 148	14A-1191	43-12892	B-82
FT 406	14A-1446	43-13147	B-83
FT 454	14A-1494	43-13195	B-84
FT 458	14A-1498	43-13199	B-85
FT 242	14A-1282	43-12983	B-86
FT 249	14A-1289	43-12990	B-87
FS 910	14A-1050	43-12751	B-88
FS 885	14A-1025	43-12726	B-89
FT 136	14A-1176	43-12877	B-90
FT 225	14A-1255	43-12956	B-91
FS 774	14A-914	43-12615	B-92
FS 919	14A-1059	43-12760	B-93
FT 159	14A-1199	43-12900	B-94
FS 733	14A-873	43-12574	B-95
FS 724	14A-864	43-12565	B-96
FT 391	14A-1431	43-13132	B-97
FT 230	14A-1270	43-12971	B-98
FT 247	14A-1287	43-12988	B-99
FT 347	14A-1387	43-13088	B-100
FT 407	14A-1447	43-13148	B-101
FS 765	14A-905	43-12606	B-102
FT 419	14A-1459	43-13160	B-103
FS 728	14A-868	43-12569	B-104
FT 200	14A-1250	43-12951	B-105
FS 719	14-858	43-12560	B-106
FS 893	14A-1033	43-12734	B-107
FT 320	14A-13061	43-13061	B-108
FS 749	14A-889	43-12590	B-109
FT 167	14A-1207	43-12908	B-110
FS 775	14A-915	43-12616	B-111
FS 817	14A-957	43-12658	B-112
FS 723	14A-863	43-12564	B-113
FT 244	14A-1274	43-12925	B-114
FT 211	14A-1251	43-12952	B-115
FS 727	14A-867	43-12568	B-116
FS 717	14A-857	43-12558	B-117
FT 427	14A-1467	43-13168	B-118
FS 731	14A-871	43-12572	B-119
FS 820	14A-960	43-12661	B-120
FS 909	14A-1049	43-12750	B-121
FT 314	14A-1344	43-13045	B-122
FT 279	14A-1319	43-13020	B-123
FT 219	14A-1259	43-12960	B-124
FS 833	14A-973	43-12674	B-125
FT 146	14A-1186	43-12887	B-126
FT 171	14A-1211	43-12912	B-127
FT 730	14A-870	43-12571	B-128
FT 312	14A-1342	43-13043	B-129
FH 108	14-742	42-12495	B-130
FT 381	14A-1411	43-13112	B-131
FT 216	14A-1256	43-12957	B-132
FT 311	14A-1341	43-13042	B-133
FS 777	14A-917	43-12681	B-134
FS 880	14A-1020	43-12721	B-135
FS 913	14A-1053	43-12754	B-136
FS 771	14A-911	43-12612	B-137
FS 897	14A-1019	43-12720	B-138
FT 390	14A-1430	43-13131	B-139
FS 743	14A-1153	43-12854	B-140
FT 306	14A-1336	43-13037	B-141
FT 455	14A-1495	43-13196	B-142
FT 417	14A-1459	43-13160	B-143
FT 261	14A-1301	43-13002	B-144*
FT 268	14A-1307	43-13008	B-145*
FT 294	14A-1334	43-13035	B-146*
FT 365	14A-1405	43-13106	B-147*
FT 366	14A-1406	43-13107	B-148*
FE 395	14-129	42-0592	B-149*
FS 904	14A-1044	43-12745	B-150*

** These were not finally assigned, as the aircraft were used as spares and were never employed in any flying capacity.*

(Opposite page) **Royal Netherlands Air Force Harvard B-45 (the former RAF FT 229) catches the sunlight as she banks away from the camera, presenting a nice underview of this Mark IIB aircraft.** Royal Netherlands Air Force

(Right) **Splendid** en echelon **formation from the Dutch air force as these six Harvard IIBs fly formation. Pictured are, from top to bottom, (unknown), B-135 (43-12721), B-178 (42-12492), B-45 (43-12970) and B-66 (43-13123).** Royal Netherlands Air Force

The following ten aircraft were transferred to the MLD and received naval serials as listed: B-56 (MLD 043), B-57 (MLD 044), B-59, B-60, B-61, B-62, B-63, B-64, B-84, (MLD 098), B-101 and B-136. A disastrous hangar fire on 16 November 1961, totally wrote off B-29, B-113 and B-137. Yet ten more, B-20, B-37, B-47, B-58, B-89, B-99, B-105, B-128, B-131 and B-139, were transferred to the Belgian Air Force as related. Another eleven were eventually sold out to commercial service and received civilian registrations as shown in the Table. The rest were gradually lost through accident, scrapping and natural wastage, until the final pair of survivors (B-41 and B-66) were sold in the USA as late as 1968. Just one, the former B-136, was preserved.

Dutch Air Force Harvards sold to civilian service

Air Force serial	*Civilian reg.*
B15	PH-NIF
B-16	PH-NIZ
B-19	PH-SKK, G-AZSC
B-45	PH-SKM, G-AZKI
B-56	PH-KMA
B-61	PH-NGR, PH-NIE
B-64	PH-FAR
B-84	OO-DAF
B-97	PH-HON. G-AZBN
B-104	PH-SKL, G-BAFM
B-118	PH-TOO
B-135	PH-BKT

Forty-two former RCAF Harvards were delivered direct to the Netherlands East Indies in August 1948, but two were damaged in transit. The remainder were based at Kalidjati Flying Training School, and many fell into Indonesian hands on independence in 1950. The ex-RCAF aircraft had RAF serials when received, as shown in the table (right).

Of these aircraft, two, B-155 and B-164 (MLD 099), were transferred to the MLD. Five more aircraft received permanent or temporary civilian registrations: B-151 (PH-NIA); B-158 (PH-PPS/PH-HTC/G-BBHK); B-176 (PH-NID); B-186 (PH-NIC) and B-187 (PH-NIB). Ten more aircraft were preserved for a while: B-165, B-174, B-175, B-176, B-177, B-181, B-182, B-184, B-185 and

Ex-RCAF Harvards delivered to the Dutch Air Force 1949

RAF serial	*C/n*	*USAAF serial*	*Dutch serial*	*RAF serial*	*C/n*	*USAAF serial*	*Dutch serial*
FE 521	14-255	42-0718	B-151	FE 985	14-719	42-12472	B-176
FE 505	14-239	42-0702	B-152	FE 999	14-733	42-12486	B-177
FE 745	14-479	42-0942	B-153	FH 105	14-379	42-12492	B-178
FE 519	14-253	42-0716	B-154	FS 667	14A-807	43-12508	B-179
FE 947	14-681	42-12434	B-155	FH 133	14-767	42-12520	B-180
FE 517	14-251	42-714	B-156	FE 809	14-543	42-12296	B-181
FE 980	14-714	42-12467	B-157	FS 668	14A-808	43-12509	B-182
FE 153	14-787	42-12540	B-158	FE 998	14-732	42-12485	B-183
FE 951	14-685	42-12438	B-159	FS 960	14A-1100	43-12801	B-184
FT 289	14A-1329	43-13030	B-160	FH 139	14-773	42-12526	B-185
FS 857	14A-997	43-12698	B-161	FE 996	14-730	42-12483	B-186
FE 933	14-667	42-12420	B-162	FE 990	14-724	42-12477	B-187
FE 930	14-664	42-12417	B-163	FH 106	14-740	42-12493	B-188
FE 821	14-555	42-12308	B-164	FS 874	14A-1014	43-12715	B-189
FH 130	14-764	42-12517	B-165	FH 159	14-793	42-12546	B-190
FE 976	14-710	42-12463	B-166	FH 126	14-760	42-12513	B-191
FE 982	14-716	42-12469	B-167	FE 994	14-728	42-12481	B-192
FE 984	14-718	42-12471	B-168	FH 136	14-770	42-12523	B-193
FH 150	14-784	42-12537	B-169	FS 661	14A-801	43-12502	B-194
FE 977	14-711	42-12464	B-170	FE 307	14-041	42-504	B-195
FE 931	14-665	42-12418	B-171	FE 919	14-653	42-1240	B-196
FE 129	14-763	42-12516	B-172	FE 797	14-531	42-12284	B-197
FE 129	14-763	42-12516	B-173	FH 117	14-751	42-12504	B-198
FH 119	14-753	42-12506	B-173	FE 876	14-610	42-12363	B-199
FE 986	14-720	42-12473	B-174	FE 942	14-676	42-12429	B-200
FH 131	14-765	42-12518	B-175				

B-193. The rest were lost in accidents, scrapped or disposed of until the last one in service, B-164 (MLD 099), went in 1968.

On top of these 200 Harvards, a further twenty former RAF service aircraft were received as spare parts and were never allocated Dutch serial numbers.

Ex-RAF Harvards allocated as spares to Dutch Air Force

EX 114	EX 445	EX 750	EX 898
EX 256	EX 638	EX 808	EX 916
EX 261	EX 659	EX 819	EX 917
EX 262	EX 730	EX 885	EX 922
EX 350	EX 737	EX 893	EX 954

The Dutch Navy received fourteen allocations, most temporary, from various air force stock and designated them as the UT-6, as shown in the table (right).

Dutch Navy Harvard allocations and serials

Air Force serial	*Navy serial*
B-56	043
B-57	044
B-59	12-5
B-60	12-4
B-61	12-3
B-62	12-2
B-63	12-1
B-64	12-6
B-84	098
B-101	–
B-134	–
B-136	–
B-155	–
B-164	099

(Below) **The Royal Netherlands Air Force Harvard IIB B-66 (14A-1263, 43-13123) which later carried civilian registration N8992.**
Simon Watson

(Bottom) **Immaculate is Royal Netherlands Air Force B-184 (14A-1100, 43-12801), which was later to carry civilian registration PH-TBR as an exhibit in the Militaire Luchtvaart Museum, at Soesterberg.**
Simon Watson

Yet a further allocation of forty further Harvards from the RCAF stocks was made in August 1948; these were delivered directly to the Centrale Vlieg School (Central Flying School) at Kalidjati in the Netherlands East Indies. Two were damaged in transit, the remainder were issued with Dutch Air Force serials in the range B-401/438, inclusive. After extensive use at the Elementair Opleidings School (Elementary Training School) and the Voortgezette Opleidings School (Advanced Training School), the survivors were handed over to the Indonesian Republic upon their independence from the Netherlands in 1950.

In addition to the Dutch military, Harvards found their way into civilian usage quite independently. For example, the Dutch airline KLM used thirteen for pilot training at the Rijksluchtvaartschool, with the civilian registrations shown in the table.

KLM-registered Harvards

PH-UBD	PH-UBH	PH-UBL	PH-UBO
PH-UBE	PH-UBI	PH-UBM	PH-UBP
PH-UBF	PH-UBK	PH-UBN	PH-UBZ
			PH-UDF

Other Dutch civilian registered Harvards include those given in the table below.

Other Dutch civilian-registered Harvards

Dutch reg.	*Ex-US serial*	*Ex-RAF serial*
PH-UBG	41	–
PH-UEI	42-653	FE 456
PH-UEK	42-606	FE 409
PH-UEL	42-12532	FE 409
PH-UEM	42-637	FE 440
PH-UEN	42-468	FE 451
PH-UEO	42-12294	FE 807
PH-UEP	42-12301	FE 814
PH-UER	42-12309	FE 822

Denmark

The Royal Danish Airforce was an earlier beneficiary of ex-RAF Harvards. A batch of twenty-seven Harvard 2Bs was flown directly from the UK between December 1946 and September 1947. A further four were shipped in from Canada.

Several were transferred to the Dutch Navy including Harvard IIBs, 14-719, 42-12472, which later became civilian registered PH-NID and 14A-1184, 43-12885, which later took civilian registration PH-KLU, both going to the Pioneer Hangaar Collection at Lelystad as exhibits: 14A-1216, 43-12917; 14A-1494, 43-13195, which was later civil registered as 00-DAF.

To provide spares for these, and for technical ground training airframes, ex-South African stock from UK stores was provided, with three Mark 2As and four Mark 3s being sent.

In addition to normal training work, the Harvard was pressed into service as a courier (Basisvlucht) and communications aircraft. A photo-reconnaissance flight was based at Deelan with six camouflaged Harvards. They were also made available to train civilian pilots. Three of these Danish Harvards were sold out and received civilian registrations (310 became LN-BNN; 312 became TF-ERN; and 329 became LN-BNM), while another two were preserved (306 at Stauning and 309). The rest served for many years before being struck off charge. Others that survived for a period are given in the table below.

Royal Danish Air Force Harvards

RAF serial	*Danish serial*	*RAF serial*	*Danish serial*	*RAF serial*	*Danish serial*
FE 760	301	FT 135	312	FT 350	322
FE 798	302	FT 143	313	FT 377	323
FE 800	303	FT 154	314	FT 380	324
FE 867	304	FT 157	315	FT 398	325
FH 109	305	FT 218	316	FT 432	326
FH 114	306	FT 226	317	FE 391*	327
FS 721	307	FT 251	318	FE 592	328
FS 766	308	FT 257	319	FE 903*	329
FS 826	309	FT 291	320	FE 623*	330
FS 917	310	FT 305	321	FE 804*	331
FS 922	311				

* Ex-RCAF.

Royal Danish Air Force Harvards used for spares

RAF serial	*SAAF serial*	*Danish serial*	*RAF serial*	*SAAF serial*	*Danish serial*
EX 985	7434	351	EX 285	7075	356
EX 925	7489	352	EZ 221	7594	357
EZ 339	7629	353	EZ 150	7537	358
EX 400	7178	354	EZ 152	7538	359
EX 279	7195	355	EZ 220	7582	360

Dutch survivors

Dutch no.	*C/n*	*US no.*	*Became:*
B-19	14A-1363	43-13064	G-AZSC
B-41	14A-1055	43-12756	N8993
B-45	14A-1269	43-12970	F-AZDS Assoc French Rech. Maint en Vol Avions Historiques, Le Castellet, France
B-64	14-641	42-12394	PH-LSK
B-67	14A-1462	43-13163	Musée Royal de l'Armée, Brussels, Belgium
B-66	14A-1422	43-13123	N8992
B-69	14A-1263	43-12964	National War and Resistance Museum, Overloon
B-71	14A-1444	43-13145	PH-MLM
B-73	14A-1268	43-12969	Wings of Victory Museum, Veghet
B-82	14A-1188	43-12889	Aviodome, Schiphol airfield, Amsterdam
B-97	14A-1431	43-13132	G-AZBN
B-103	14A-1459	43-13160	Militaire Luchtvaart Museum, Soesterberg
B-104	14-868	42-12569	G-BAFM
B-118	14A-1467	43-13168	PH-IIB
B-135	14A-1020	43-12721	PH-BKT
B-158	14-787	42-12540	G-BBHK

(continued overleaf)

Dutch survivors *(continued)*

Dutch no.	*C/n*	*US no.*	*Became:*
B-163	14-664	42-12417	Thameside Aviation Museum
B-164	14-555	42-12308	Auto und Technik Museum, Sinsheim, Germany
B-165	14-764	42-12517	PH-AFS
B-168	14-718	42-12471	Stored Duxford
B-174	14-720	42-12473	N8994
B-175	14-765	42-12518	Militaire Luchtvaart Museum, Soesterberg
B-177	14-733	42-12486	MLM-Woensdrecht AB Gate Guard
B-178	14-739	42-12492	Pole display Maasbracht
B-181	14-543	42-12296	Restoring
B-182	14-808	42-12509	PH-TBR Militaire Luchtvaart Museum, Soesterberg
B-184	14A-1100	43-12801	PH-TBR Militaire Luchtvaart Museum, Soesterberg
B-193	14-770	42-12523	Westerschouwn Schelse Estuary

Ex-Dutch Indonesian AF survivors

IAF no.	*RNEIAF no.*	*Displayed at:*
B-416	B-416	Armed Forces Museum, Djakarta
B-424	B-424	Padang City Museum, Padang
B-427	B-427	Indonesian AF Museum, Adisutjipto Air Base
B-440	B-440	Indonesian AF Academy, Yogyakarta
B-442	B-442	Indonesian AF Academy, Yogyakarta
B-448	B-448	Indonesian AF Museum, Adisutjipto Air Base

Many of those that were sent to the Royal Netherlands East Indies Air Force in the Dutch East Indies came into the hands of the Indonesian Government on independence and served in the Indonesian Air Force for a period. These included the Harvard IIBs in the table above, all of which survived to become exhibits in various displays.

Sweden

The Royal Swedish Air Force equipped itself with 247 Harvards, T-6s and SNJs from various sources. In this way Sweden became one of Europe's premier users of the type. Altogether, 144 Harvard 2Bs were obtained from ex-RCAF stock, seventy-five of them reputedly via the Charles Babb Company of Montreal, Quebec, who had bought up 491 of them at rock-bottom prices earlier (*see* table below).

Sweden also added some AT-6As and SNJ-4s to her stocks later. Two of these received civilian registrations (Fv16047 became G-BDAM and Fv16144 became SE-FUZ) and several were preserved for museum displays, including serial no. Fv16109, ex FE 632, which is displayed at Linkping Air Force Museum; serial no. Fv16068, ex FE 752, at Flygapenmuseum Maalmslat Air Base; serial no. Fv16010, ex FE 831, at Luftartmuseet, Arlanda airfield, Stockholm; serial no. Fv16028, ex FE 991, and serial no. Fv16033, ex FH 138, both at Svedine Bil Och Flygmuseum, Sloinge; serial no. Fv16145, ex RCN 3223, at Jmamatlands Flyghistoriske Museum, Ostersund; and serial no. Fv16221, ex BuNo 27625, at the Museo de la Avicion Naval

Swedish ex-RAF Harvard 2Bs

RAF serial	*Swedish serial*	*RAF serial*	*Swedish serial*	*RAF serial*	*Swedish serial*	*RAF serial*	*Swedish serial*	*RAF serial*	*Swedish serial*	*RAF serial*	*Swedish serial*
FT 296	Fv16001	FE 920	Fv16025	FT 275	Fv16049	FS 958	Fv16073	FE 837	Fv16097	FE 509	Fv16121
FE 743	Fv16002	FE 648	Fv16026	FT 276	Fv16050	FE 638	Fv16074	FE 689	Fv16098	FE 688	Fv16122
FS 875	Fv16003	FE 812	Fv16027	FE 658	Fv16051	FE 630	Fv16075	FE 844	Fv16099	FE 724	Fv16123
FE 657	Fv16004	FE 991	Fv16028	FE 918	Fv16052	FE 795	Fv16076	FE 734	Fv16100	FE 660	Fv16124
FE 852	Fv16005	FH 148	Fv16029	FE 654	Fv16053	FS 966	Fv16077	FE 502	Fv16101	FE 585	Fv16125
FH 158	Fv16006	FE 565	Fv16030	FE 863	Fv16054	FS 961	Fv16078	FE 385	Fv16102	FE 692	Fv16126
FH 166	Fv16007	FT 266	Fv16031	FS 871	Fv16055	FS 673	Fv16079	FE 554	Fv16103	FE 513	Fv16127
FE 753	Fv16008	FE 849	Fv16032	FE 722	Fv16056	FS 962	Fv16080	FE 940	Fv16104	FE 511	Fv16128
FE 401	Fv16009	FH 138	Fv16033	FS 862	Fv16057	FS 666	Fv16081	FE 695	Fv16105	FE 628	Fv16129
FE 831	Fv16010	FE 653	Fv16034	FH 140	Fv16058	FS 681	Fv16082	FE 832	Fv16106	FE 437	Fv16130
FS 968	Fv16011	FE 633	Fv16035	FE 823	Fv16059	FH 154	Fv16083	FE 555	Fv16107	FE 464	Fv16131
FH 137	Fv16012	FE 694	Fv16036	FE 637	Fv16060	FS 873	Fv16084	FE 835	Fv16108	FE 564	Fv16132
FE 691	Fv16013	FS 867	Fv16037	FE 836	Fv16061	FS 878	Fv16085	FE 632	Fv16109	FE 589	Fv16133
FS 870	Fv16014	FH 163	Fv16038	FE 853	Fv16062	FE 928	Fv16086	FE 646	Fv16110	FE 833	Fv16134
FH 104	Fv16015	FT 277	Fv16039	FE 950	Fv16063	FE 312	Fv16087	FE 834	Fv16111	FE 693	Fv16135
FS 967	Fv16016	FS 672	Fv16040	FE 525	Fv16064	FT 292	Fv16088	FT 272	Fv16112	FE 741	Fv16136
FE 927	Fv16017	FE 902	Fv16041	FT 274	Fv16065	FE 723	Fv16089	FE 842	Fv16113	FE 276	Fv16137
FH 122	Fv16018	FE 524	Fv16042	FH 100	Fv16066	FE 856	Fv16090	FE 503	Fv16114	FE 562	Fv16138
FH 157	Fv16019	FE 577	Fv16043	FE 803	Fv16067	FE 851	Fv16091	FE 335	Fv16115	FE 520	Fv16139
FE 861	Fv16020	FE 651	Fv16044	FE 752	Fv16068	FE 726	Fv16092	FS 972	Fv16116	FE 272	Fv16140
FE 619	Fv16021	FE 987	Fv16045	FE 568	Fv16069	FE 661	Fv16093	FE 625	Fv16117	FH 125	Fv16141
FE 742	Fv16022	FE 796	Fv16046	FE 932	Fv16070	FE 344	Fv16094	FE 400	Fv16118	FE 328	Fv16142
FH 132	Fv16023	FE 992	Fv16047	FH 127	Fv16071	FE 327	Fv16095	FE 500	Fv16119	FE 845	Fv16143
FE 934	Fv16024	FS 957	Fv16048	FH 156	Fv16072	FE 580	Fv16096	FE 518	Fv16120	FE 792	Fv16144

Argentina, at Espora NAS, Bahi Blanca, Argentina (*see* table right).

Norway

Like many occupied countries during World War II, Norway kept fighting through her volunteers who made their way to Britain. At Winkleigh, a Norwegian training base had been set up and this continued to function until November 1945. After liberation, the Royal Norwegian Air Force flew its entire complement of twenty-three ex-RAF Harvards back to Norway, and an additional seven Harvard 2Bs were obtained from Canada. Many of these were subsequently sold to Turkey after many years good service; most of the rest were sold and scrapped.

Flygvapnet survivors preserved or sold out to civil register

Type	*Flygvapnet no.*	*C/n*	*US serial*	*RCAF serial*	*Civil reg.*
Harvard IIB	Fv16010	14-565	42-12318	FE 831	–
Harvard IIB	Fv16028	14-725	42-12478	FE 991	–
Harvard IIB	Fv16030	14-299	42-762	FE 565	–
Harvard IIB	Fv16033	14-772	42-12525	FH 138	–
Harvard IIB	Fv16047	14-726	42-12479	FE 992	G-BDAM
Harvard IIB	Fv16066	14A-1106	43-12807	FS 966	VH-JHP
Harvard IIB	Fv16068	14-486	42-949	FE 752	–
Harvard IIB	Fv16074	14-372	42-835	FE 638	–
Harvard IIB	Fv16092	14-460	42-923	FE 726	SE-FUY
Harvard IIB	Fv16105	14-429	42-892	FE 695	G-BTXI
Harvard IIB	Fv16109	14-366	42-829	FE 632	–
Harvard IIB	Fv16126	14-426	42-889	FE 692	–
Harvard IIB	Fv16128	14-245	42-708	FE 511	–
Harvard IIB	Fv16144	14-526	42-12279	FE 792	SE-FUZ
Harvard II	Fv16145	76-3497	–	3223	–
SNJ-4	Fv16221	88-13081	BuNo 27625	Argentine Navy	N1624M
SNJ-4	–	88-11825	BuNo 26966	Argentine Navy	–
AT-6A	Fv16269	76-6821	41-16443	–	SE-CHP
AT-6A	Fv16291	76-6992	41-16614	–	N13FY
AT6A	Fv-	76-6999	41-16621	–	N766CA

Crossing a tranquil sea, a trio of Royal Norwegian Air Force Harvards, 320, 319 and 351. Flyvevabnet, Flyvehistorisk Samling

Three Harvard 2Bs of the Royal Norwegian Air Force, 329, 319 and 351. Flyvevabnet, Flyvehistorisk Samling

(Above) **Seen on the grass at Vaerlose air station in camouflage markings is Royal Norwegian Air Force Harvard 2B 311.** *Flyvevabnet*, Flyvehistorisk Samling

Harvard T2B FT 309, coded M:AX, transferred to the Royal Norwegian Air Force in November 1945. Ray C. Sturtivent

Ex-RAF Royal Norwegian Air Force Harvards

RAF serial	*Norway serial*	*RAF serial*	*Norway serial*	*RAF serial*	*Norway serial*
FS 734	M-AB	FS 911	M-AM	FT 309	M-AX
FS 760	M-AC	FS 916	M-AN	FT 335	M-AY
FS 763	M-AD	FS 918	M-AO	FX 357	M-AZ
FS 768	M-AE	FT 138	M-AP	FE 435	M-BA
FS 772	M-AF	FT 139	M-AR	FE 460	M-BB
FS 834	M-AG	FT 163	M-AS	FS 965	M-BC
FS 842	M-AH	FT 221	M-AT	FE 296	M-BD
FS 887	M-AI	FT 237	M-AU	FE 621	M-BE
FS 897	M-AK	FT 252	M-AV	FS 959	M-BF
FS 907	M-AL	FT 264	M-AW	FE 992	M-BG

West Germany

Under the provisions of MDAP, the Bundeswehr, Federal Germany's new military re-armament, received impetus from NATO. A Temporary Flying Training Command was set up and the 7.351 Flying Training Wing was established at Landsberg. On 1 July 1955 no less than 135 Harvard Mark 4s from the second and third batches built by the Canadian Car and Foundry Company (which had absorbed Noorduyn) were allocated to this command. The aircraft were shipped to Belfast, Northern Ireland, and then flown across to Germany. These American-funded, Canadian-built Harvards received US serials in two batches: the first 120 had 52-8493/8612, inclusive, while an extra twenty-two received 53-4615/4636, inclusive. In West German service their received FFS serials were in the AA+600 range. The USAF 7330th Flying Training Wing was established at Furstenfeldbrück, Munich to facilitate conversion training.

(Top) A 'Lemon-bomber' of the Bundeswehr. This is AA+672 (42-8606) and companions on the mat at Landsberg. German Government

Serving with the Bundeswehr in West Germany, this is AA+666 of the Flugdienststaffel. Chaz Bowyer

Working with the Flugdienststaffel (FFS), with some allocated to the EaSLw 30 (Operational Training School for the F-84F), the Harvards continued in operation until the early 1960s and worked out of Eriding and Landsberg airfields. They were ironically christened the *Zitronenbombers* (lemon-bombers) by the German instructors and trainees because of their yellow paint scheme.

Other German Harvards were utilized as target tugs with the F1Kdo TSLw 1 at Kaufbeuren, which from 1964 trained radar-controlled flight operations. Landsbergs FFS 'A Team', the German instructors' aerobatic flying team, flew the Harvard IVs in spectacular stunts. The Harvard was finally phased out of service with the FFS in summer 1964. The final flight was made on 30 January 1962, with a flight by Oberleutnant Garske, Leutnant Kriger, Leutnant Stehil and SU Rohl. Later, at Kaufbeuren, at a suitably 'mournful' ceremony, in which a checker-nosed Harvard IV was draped in black crepe ribbon on her wing-tips, the Harvard was formally discharged!

Eight were registered to Bundesrepublik Deutschland in the summer of 1963 and received civilian registrations, as shown in the table below.

Ex-German Harvards with Bundesrepublik Deutschland civilian registrations

CCF c/n	*USAF*	*FFS no.*	*Civilian reg.*
CCF4-465	52-8544	AA+615	D-FABU
CCF4-484	52-8563	AA+678	D-FACA
CCF4-499	52-8578	AA+624	D-FABE
CCF4-509	52-8588	AA+633	D-FACI
CCF4-514	52-8593	AA+603	D-FABO
CCF4-524	52-8603	AA+629	D-FACE
CCF4-537	53-4618	AA+628	D-FABI
CCF4-550	53-4631	AA+635	D-FABA

Luftwaffe machines transferred to Portugal or sold to civil register

Type	*C/n*	*US serial*	*GAF no.*	*FAB no.*	*Civil reg.*
Harvard 4	CCF4-464	52-8543	BF+068	1766	G-BUKY
Harvard 4	CCF4-465	52-8544	AA+615	–	D-FABU
Harvard 4	CCF4-483	52-8562	AA+053	1753	G-BSBG
Harvard 4	CCF4-486	52-8565	BF+079	1774	–
Harvard 4	CCF4-491	52-8570	AA+622	–	–
Harvard 4	CCF4-498	52-8577	BF+065	1762	–
Harvard 4	CCF4-499	52-8578	AA+624	–	D-FABE
Harvard 4	CCF4-509	52-8588	AA+633	–	D-FACI
Harvard 4	CCF4-514	52-8593	AA+603	–	D-FABO
Harvard 4	CCF4-517	52-8596	BF+078	1769	–
Harvard 4	CCF4-520	52-8599	BF+059	1754	–
Harvard 4	CCF4-529	52-8608	BF+064	1740	C-FWBS
Harvard 4	CCF4-537	53-4618	AA+628	–	F-AZFC
Harvard 4	CCF4-538	53-4619	BF+050	1747	G-BGPB
Harvard 4	CCF4-539	53-4620	AA+637	1755	ZS-WLL
Harvard 4	CCF4-543	53-4624	AA+690	1748	ZS-WSE
Harvard 4	CCF4-548	53-4629	BF+055	1741	G-HRVD
Harvard 4	CCF4-550	53-4631	AA+635	–	F-AZAT
Harvard 4	CCF4-555	53-4636	AA+689	1788	G-BSBB

A Swiss Air Force Harvard 2B (left) shares the attention of these naval cadets at an open day. Author's collection via Swiss Air Force

A former RCAF Harvard 2B of the Swiss Air Force. Author's collection via Swiss Air Force

Others saw varied and elongated subsequent careers: first, in the Portuguese Air Force, then in the PLAF of Mozambique, and finally, in South Africa as civilian aircraft, as shown in the table left.

One aircraft (serial CCF4-465, 52-8544) was preserved as an exhibit at the Luftwaffe Museum, Germany; a second (CCF4-499, 52-8578) is in the Fliegendes Museum Augsburg, Germany; a third (CCF4-486, 52-8565) is in the Museo do Ar, Sintra Air Base, Portugal; a fourth (CCF4-491, 52-8570) is in the Norwegian AF Museum, Gardermoen Air Base, Norway; a fifth (CCF4-517, 52-8596) is in the Museo do Ar, Sintra Air Base, Portugal.

Portugal

Another major European user of former RAF Harvards was Portugal. Britain's 'oldest ally' had always maintained strong links with the UK and the Commonwealth and this link was kept up post-war, despite the fact that a right-wing dictatorship was in power. The initial batch of sixteen Harvard 3s was not supplied until March 1956, and were all ex-Royal Navy aircraft. They received Forca Aerea Portuguesa (FAP) serials as shown in the table (top right).

These served with the Aviacao Naval (Portuguese Navy) who gave them serials in the range 1701/1799, and some lasted for many years, but in 1969 a further large delivery was made to the FAP of former South African Air Force Harvard 2As, as shown in the table (bottom right).

These aircraft were allocated the FAP serials 1501/1559, inclusive. Portugal was fighting rebels in her African territories at this time and during the wars in Angola, Mozambique and Guinea, the Harvards and T-6s were used as light bombers in the classic COIN role. Some were still in use as late as August 1974 and many fell into the hands of their former enemies, on Portuguese withdrawal from the area.

Back home, the Harvard again saw combat when, on 11 March 1975, two of them carried out the bombing of a Lisbon military barracks during an abortive right-wing *coup d'état.* The last operational machine was struck off charge in 1978 and many were sold out at that time. Nine received civilian registrations, as shown in the table right.

Two of these were returned to the UK for preservation as Royal Navy Harvards:

Ex-Royal Navy Harvard 3s in Portuguese service

USN/RAF serial	*FAP serial*	*USN/RAF serial*	*FAP serial*	*USN/RAF serial*	*FAP serial*
BuNo 51392	1654	FT 966	1659	EZ 451	1665
EZ 421	1655	EZ 403	1660	EZ 312	1666
EZ 407	1656	FT 971	1661	EZ 281	1667
EX 976	1657	EZ 341	1662	EZ 438	1668
FT 965	1658	EZ 303	1663	EZ 420	1669
		EZ 401	1664		

Ex-South African Air Force Harvards in Portuguese service

RAF serial	*SAAF serial*	*RAF serial*	*SAAF serial*	*RAF serial*	*SAAF serial*
EX 211	7004	EX 287	7168	EX 841	7428
EX 227	7020	EX 271	7171	EX 881	7424
EX 229	7022	EX 361	7174	EX 884	7426
EX 446	7029	EX 392	7185	EX 873	7430
EX 467	7039	EX 443	7202	EX 892	7431
EX 408	7043	EX 488	7220	EX 915	7439
EX 182	7051	EX 495	7223	EX 894	7441
EX 196	7052	EX 561	7224	EX 890	7445
EX 205	7060	EX 580	7248	EX 869	7450
EX 302	7084	EX 475	7296	EX 911	7485
EX 117	7096	EX 472	7301	EX 935	7504
EX 260	7103	EX 634	7319	EX 973	7518
EX 263	7106	EX 688	7333	EZ 144	7571
EX 267	7110	EX 693	7334	EZ 201	7588
EX 314	7124	EX 599	7335	EZ 207	7591
EX 169	7131	EX 636	7350	EZ 226	7613
EX 170	7132	EX 695	7363	EZ 224	7614
EX 171	7133	EX 600	7382	EX 582	7243
EX 252	7142	EX 608	7388	EX 584	7244
EX 330	7150	EX 706	7407		

Taking off from their home base near Lisbon, two Harvards of the Portuguese Air Force, with second and third pairs following them up in the background. Some Portuguese Harvards saw combat when they took part in an attempted coup d'état in 1975, bombing barracks in Lisbon. Portuguese Air Force Official

Portuguese Air Force Harvard (1606) at her home base. Portuguese Air Force Official

1657 (ex-EX 407) at the Fleet Air Arm Museum, Yeovilton; 1513 (ex-EX 884) was restored at Cranfield, Bedfordshire; and 1662 (ex-EZ 341) was preserved as a Portuguese exhibit at Sintra.

Another source of supply for the Portuguese was Belgium. A total of ten civilian registered, former South African Air Force Harvards were transferred from Belgium in 1962, being seven 2As and three 2Bs, as shown in the table below.

Ex-Belgian Harvards in Portuguese service

RAF serial	SAAF serial	Belgian serial	Civil reg.
EX 623	7344	H.42	00-GDL
EX 779	7409	H.43	00-GDM
KF 415	–	H.52	00-GDO
KF 715	?	H.67	00-GDP
EX 371	7187	H.26	00-GEN
EX 461	7210	H.28	00-GEO
EX 181	7045	H.18	00-GEQ
EX 661	7315	H.31	00-GER
EX 273	7184	H.36	00-GES
KF 568	?	H.58	00-AAR

Many of these Portuguese Harvards were also sold to the civilian register abroad and a few still fly today (*see* table right).

Several went as museum exhibits, as shown in the table below.

Ex-Portuguese Harvards in museums

Serial	Location
1512	Museo do Ar, Sintra Air Base
1513	Georgia Historical Aviation Museum, Stone Mountain,GA
1527	Museo do Ar, Alverca Air Base
1546	Museo do Ar, Sinfta Air Base
1656	Fleet Air Arm Museum, RNAS, Yeovilton, Someset, UK
1657	Fleet Air Arm Museum, RNAS Yeovilton, Somerset, UK
1737	Museo do Ar, Montijo Air Base
88-15698	SAA Museum Society, Johannesburg, RSA

Switzerland

A few survived for a while after service, and among these were FE 590 (c/n 14-201, 42-664), which became U-332 and was preserved as an exhibit at the Museum de Schweizerischen Fliergertruppe, Dubendorf Air Base, as did the former U-328, an ex-RCAF Harvard IIB (FE 811, 14-545, 42-12298), and FE 824 (c/n 14-324, 42-

Ex-Portuguese Harvards with civilian registrations

RAF serial	FAP serial	Civilian reg.	RAF serial	FAP serial	Civilian reg.
EX 287	1560	G-RCAF	EX 894	1504	G-ELLY
EX 302	1545	G-BICE	EX 915	1502	G-JUDI
EX 392	1554	G-BGOU	EX 935	1508	G-BGOR
EX 600	1559	G-BGOV	FT 971	1661	G-BGOW
EX 881	1506	G-SUES			

This Italian Harvard, coded AA 42, features silver fuselage and yellow wings and is seen in 1972. Aeronautica Militare, Rome

Ex-Portuguese Harvard survivors

Type	FAP no.	C/n	US serial	Ex-serial	Fate
Harvard III	1502	88-14722	41-33888	SAAF7439	G-JUDI
Harvard III	1504	88-14661	41-33867	SAAF7441	–
Harvard III	1506	88-14552	41-33854	SAAF7424	LN-WNH
Harvard III	1508	88-14880	41-33980	SAAF7504	G-BGOR
Harvard IIB	1512	–	SAAF	RAF EX	–
Harvard III	1513	88-14555	41-33857	SAAF7426	N15WS
Harvard IIA	1522	88-10677	41-33557	SAAF7244	N36CA
Harvard IIA	1523	88-9696	41-33253	SAAF7333	–
Harvard IIB	1527	–	SAAF	RAF EX	–
Harvard III	1529	88-14659	41-33865	SAAF7431	N3770D
Harvard IIA	1535	88-9725	41-33262	SAAF7183	G-TSIX
Harvard IIA	1545	88-9755	41-33275	SAAF7084	G-BICE
Harvard IIB	1546	–	SAAF	RAF EX	–
Harvard IIA	1551	88-10560	41-33449	SAAF7039	N37642
Harvard IIA	1554	88-10108	41-33365	SAAF7185	–
Harvard IIA	1559	88-12044	41-33573	SAAF7382	N44334N
Harvard IIA	1560	88-9723	41-33260	SAAF7168	N42BA
Harvard III	1656	88-16712	42-84931	EZ 407	–
Harvard III	1657	88-15044	BuNo 51938	EX 976	–
Harvard III	1661	88-14748	42-44554	FT 971	N13HP
Harvard III	1662	88-16336	42-84555	EZ 333	G-ELMH
Harvard 4	1705	–	USAF	–	Store
Harvard 4	1737	–	USAF	–	–
Harvard 4	1780	–	USAF	–	Store
Harvard III	–	88-15698	41-34067	SAAF7601	ZS-WLP
Harvard III	–	88-15744	41-34073	EZ 200	N8539L

787), which became U-322 and flew as civilian registered D-FHGK.

In 1947 the Fliegerabwehrtruppen (Swiss Air Force) took delivery of forty Noorduyn-built Harvard IIBs, which were surplus to RCAF requirements. They were allocated the Swiss serials U-310/340, inclusive. They were first shipped to the Netherlands where the Dutch firm Aviolanda/Fokker gave them complete overhauls at their Amsterdam and Schipol works, respectively. The Swiss utilized these aircraft as blind-flying instructors and thus they never carried any armament at all. They served well from 1949 until the last was discarded in 1968. Two aircraft and four engines survived as preservations.

Italy

Italy was the first of the former Axis powers to receive stocks of Harvards and T-6s. On 10 May 1949 a total of thirteen Mark 2As were sold by the USA to Italy, and were subsequently delivered in dribs and drabs, as they were brought out of mothballs from No. 15 MU at RAF Wroughton and shipped across to Italy. These were ex-South African stocks returned under lend-lease after being 'recaptured' by the Americans in 1946. To these was added a solitary Mark 2, which was an ex-RCAF aircraft. They received the AMI serials MM 53038/53051, inclusive and served at the Scuola di Lecce (Lecce Flying School) (*see* table above).

Ex-SAAF/RCAF Harvards in Italian service

RAF serial	*SAAF serial*	*RAF serial*	*SAAF serial*	*RAF serial*	*SAAF serial*
EX 258	Ex-RCAF	EX 332	7151	EX 504	7258
EX 258	7101	EX 390	7189	EX 581	7247
EX 269	7112	EX 397	7180	EX 731	7375
EX 278	7169	EX 466	7038	EX 835	7458
EX 301	7083	EX 489	7221		

A further twelve former RCAF Harvards were delivered to Italy in the mid-1950s, as shown in the table below.

Ex-RCAF Harvards transferred to Italy

AJ 564	3079	3107	3308
3822	3081	3125	3312
3077	3091	3271	3325

Yugoslavia

In March 1945, the British agreed to supply Marshal Tito's communist forces with ten brand new Harvard IIBs to train up the new Yugoslavian Air Force, following the liberation of that country. A flying training school was established under the auspices of the Mediterranean Allied Air Forces, and the Harvards were flown out to the Adriatic by 12 FU from Melton Mowbray airfield.

Ex-RAF Harvard IIBs in Yugoslav service

FT 152	FT 339	KF 302	KF 429	KF 474
FT 174	KF 283	KF 305	KF 471	KF 477

None of these aircraft was returned by the Tito Government after the war, but one (the ex-RAF FT152, 14A-1192, 43-12893) still survives as an exhibit in the National Aviation Museum at Belgrade.

The Royal Hellenic Air Force, which escaped from Greece after the German invasion in 1941, was re-grouped in Egypt and recruits were trained with RAF units in Southern Rhodesia. This photo shows two Harvard Is N7013 and another, with Greek cadets undergoing instruction. Later, as Squadron Leader Norman E. Rose recalled, some became instructors also, despite the language difficulties! Ray C. Sturtivent

Greece

Once the British had helped defeat the communist uprising in Greece, which followed the German pull-out in 1945, the rebuilding of the Royal Hellenic Air Force could commence. In 1947 a large batch of thirty-five former South African Air Force Harvard IIAs (which had only just returned to the UK) was allocated to Greece and delivered between March and August of that year.

Ex-South African Harvard IIBs in Greek service

RAF serials	*SAAF serials*	*RAF serials*	*SAAF serials*	*RAF serials*	*SAAF serials*
EX 177	7136	EX 308	7118	EX 552	7229
EX 221	7014	EX 313	7123	EX 558	7235
EX 223	7016	EX 320	7130	EX 568	7285
EX 228	7021	EX 340	7071	EX 579	7249
EX 236	7089	EX 347	7158	EX 612	7389
EX 249	7139	EX 382	7175	EX 615	7339
EX 253	7097	EX 431	7275	EX 617	7361
EX 257	7100	EX 441	7274	EX 624	7345
EX 259	7102	EX 442	7207	EX 647	7358
EX 282	7196	EX 471	7298	EX 729	7373
EX 291	7199	EX 486	7218	EX 736	7370
EX 299	7081	EX 494	7222		

Additional Harvard IIBs were sent in several batches in both 1947 and in 1949, totalling thirty aircraft. Seven of these were from RAF stocks in the Middle East – most of these had been converted for target towing.

Ex-RAF MEC Harvards in Greek service

FX 201	KF 189	KF 621	KF 743	KF 956*
FX 204	KF 203	KF 631	KF 752	KF 957*
FX 235	KF 295	KF 655	KF 908*	KF 962
FX 275	KF 34	KF 697	KF 91	KF 963
FX 413	KF 48	KF 72	KF 933	KF 967
FX 421	KF 54	KF 74	KF 939	KF 973*

Turkey

The Turkish Government, as one of the most exposed member of NATO during the Cold War, was anxious to build up her air force and not rely on her allies totally. From 1955 onward, two batches of Harvards were sent to help in this task. The Royal Norwegian Air Force despatched seventeen of her former RAF Mark IIBs to Turkey (*see* table below).

The first batch was followed in the winter of 1957–58 by eight Mark II Harvards, which had just been struck off charge by the RCAF (*see* table bottom).

Ex-Norwegian Air Force Harvards in Turkish service

RAF serial	*Norway serial*	*RAF serial*	*Norway serial*	*RAF serial*	*Norway serial*
FE 296	M-BD	FS 887	M-AI	FT 237	M-AU
FS 734	M-AB	FS 907	M-AL	FT 252	M-AV
FS 760	M-AC	FS 965	M-BC	FT 264	M-AW
FS 763	M-AD	FT 138	M-AP	FT 309	M-AX
FS 772	M-AF	FT 163	M-AS	FX 357	M-AZ
FS 834	M-AG	FT 221	M-AT		

Ex-RCAF Harvards in Turkish service

AH 187	AJ 565	AJ 791	AJ 848	AJ 940	AJ 970	BW 188	BW 207

Turkish Air Force Harvard coded 83, one of the former Norwegian air force aircraft taken over from 1955. Turkish official photo

Israel

In 1948 the United Nations overthrew the British Mandate in Palestine, which had been keeping an uneasy but even-handed peace between the Jews and the Arabs in that region for several decades, despite terrorist atrocities against British forces and civilians. This resulted in British withdrawal from this region and, again, both sides were immediately at each others throats, and that has continued to the present day. Although most sources state that the Israeli Defence Force Air Force only acquired a single RAF Harvard at this time (Ex-FE 452, which became Israeli serial number 4X-ARA), they actually utilized more, including at least one AT-6A obtained in 1946 (serial 1165, 78-7245, 41-16867), which was later preserved at the Ha-aretz Sciences et Technology Museum in Tel Aviv. Those aircraft that they employed in combat at this time were rapidly armed with two 0.50-calibre forward-firing machine guns, one in each wing, plus a 0.303 machine gun on a flexible mounting aft. These aircraft were also adapted to carry makeshift bomb racks and toted eight 110lb bombs or four 100lb bombs into battle; alternative loading was eight rockets.

They continued to serve on and eight years later were once more pressed into full combat service during the 1956 conflict with her Arab neighbours. The Harvards attacked Egyptian tank columns during this war, but they proved very vulnerable to modern battlefield AAA fire and were pulled out after taking severe damage. They stayed on as trainers until pensioned off as late as 1965.

One that went on to fly later for a period was the former RCAF Harvard IIB (FE 452, 14-186, 42-649), which became civilian 4X-ARA.

Egypt

Fifteen Canadian-built Harvard Mark 4s were acquired in 1955. By this time CCandF had been taken over by the Avro Canada Company and among the contracts it inherited was one from NAA to supply these fifteen aircraft. There was an embargo on the sale of combat aircraft to Egypt at this time, but this was ignored. Permission to go ahead was granted by the Canadian Prime Minister in July 1955, and he expressed the naïve view that these aircraft 'could not be made into effective combat aircraft', despite the evidence of the Indian Air Force, the Korean War and the French in Algeria being well-known. The batch was completed by Avro Canada between December 1955 and February 1956, and they arrived in Egypt during the Suez crisis, which was a political gaffe of the highest order. They served in the Egyptian Air Force for a number of years.

***(Above)* Pictured here in 1951, two Harvards of the IDF, 1105, coded 05, and 1113, coded 13.** IDF – Israeli Air Force Historical Branch

Line-up of eight Israeli T-6s at the operational base in 1953. IDF – Israeli Air Force Historical Branch

Syria

Twenty former 'Sixes' were on the strength of the Syrian Air Force at one time or another, ten of which were Noorduyn-built Harvard IIBs of ex-RAF stock, which came from surplus South African stocks in 1954–56. These aircraft had been given civil registrations to enable renovation work to be conducted on them by Field Aircraft Services (SA) Pty Limited at Rand airport. Two known RAF serials were

FT 392 and KF 151. A single aircraft, serial number 44 and listed as a AT-6D, survives in the Syrian War Museum at Damascus.

Ex-Canadian-built Harvard Mark IIBs in Syrian service

C/n	*C/n*	*C/n*	*C/n*	*C/n*
14-1124	14-1382	14-2036	14-2149	14-2433
14-1362	14-1432	14-2107	14-2162	14-2502

Lebanon

The Lebanese Air Force obtained ten Harvards of various types, which it managed to assemble from various British sources. In 1952 a dozen came from RAF disposals stock via the British company Airwork Limited. They received the Lebanese Air Force serial numbers L121/132. Four more came to them from tired old former Middle East Command disposals in 1954 and were given the serial numbers L133 (ex-KF 287), L134 (ex-KF 350), L135 (ex-KF 391) and L 136 (ex KF 394).

Jordan

Similarly another Arab state, Jordan, took delivery of a trio of ex-RAF Harvard 2Bs (serials FS 855, FT 409 and KF 579) which had been retired from service after anti-Mau Mau operations with 1340 Flight in Kenya, early in 1956.

Iraq

When Iraq was still a kingdom and friendly to the West, Britain supplied six Harvard 2Bs in 1951 to equip the Iraqi Air Force Flying School just outside Baghdad.

South Africa

By far and away the largest user of the Harvard outside the UK and Canada, the South African Air Force used them in a variety of roles for far longer than almost any other nation. From the time of her first delivery of three Mark I Harvards in 1940, through the enormous deliveries of the war years, and on into the post-war years, the Harvard proved the mainstay of her air operations. Her stocks were raided by many other nations down the years, as we have seen, and towards the end many former SAAF Harvards, even in the most unlikely condition, found unlikely homes in the forces of former bitter enemies like Mozambique, as well as friendly nations. Up to now they have been scattered far and wide across the globe. Ironically, after getting rid of hundreds from her own itinerary, she was forced to re-purchase back at least some of her original stock from Belgium to keep operations going.

No less than 633 Harvards, both Mark IIA and Mark III, were consigned by ship to South Africa between 1942 and June 1946. All were un-crated, assembled, given SAAF serials and then widely distributed throughout the country, both at flying training schools and to squadrons. Apart from losses due to accidents, etc., the bulk of these survived and in the winter of 1946–47, 178 IIAs and 102 IIIs were re-assigned their RAF serials, and crated and shipped back to the UK, even though many were 'officially' USAF property. Once back in England, the bulk were put straight into store. Many were re-allocated to other nations, as we have

Mark I Harvards in SAAF use

RAF serial	*SAAF serial*	*RAF serial*	*SAAF serial*	*RAF serial*	*SAAF serial*
N7002	1304/IS349*	N7091	IS341	P5921	1302
N7042	IS 348	N7103	IS345	P5928	1301
N7046	IS347	N7185	IS343	P5931	1303
N7079	IS342	N7193	IS344	P5966	IS346

* *Instructional airframes only.*

A Harvard of the Lebanon Air Defence Force, the former RAF FS 881, seen here on her sale in June, 1957. She had formerly served with Nos 587, 691 and 612 Squadrons, RAF, before being sold via Avex Engineering in February 1957. Simon Watson

The largest user of the Harvard in Africa down the years was the South African Air Force. Having received hundreds of all marks during the war she went on operating them, in an anti-terrorist role as well as a trainer, right into the 1980s and beyond. This is a Harvard IIA, with SAAF serial 7037, the former RAF EX 454, featuring the characteristic highlighted SAAF block numbering. Ray C. Sturtivent

seen, but many more were just left to rot. In 1947 the USA 'recaptured' those that remained but they remained on the charge of the SAAF and served well for decades. From their ranks further allocations were made overseas, including the Netherlands (1947) and Portugal (1969); others went across the border to the Southern Rhodesian Air Force as early as 1949. Some former SAAF Harvards, after seeing service in the Dutch and Belgian Air Forces, were 'available' at the end of the Congo war and were taken back into the fold and given brand-new serial numbers; but none appear to have been utilized. Down the years time has taken its toll, but through sales and 'wastage' South African Harvards are now to be found all over the world in private hands.

Ex-RAF Harvards in SAAF service

RAF serial	*SAAF serial*	*RAF serial*	*SAAF serial*	*RAF serial*	*SAAF serial*	*RAF serial*	*SAAF serial*	*RAF serial*	*SAAF serial*	*RAF serial*	*SAAF serial*
EX 208	7001	EX 226	7019	EX 462	7037	EX 200	7055	EX 331	7073	EX 240	7091
EX 209	7002	EX 227	7020	EX 466	7038	EX 201	7056	EX 334	7074	EX 231	7092
EX 210	7003	EX 228	7021	EX 467	7039	EX 202	7057	EX 285	7075	EX 235	7093
EX 211	7004	EX 229	7022	EX 478	7040	EX 203	7058	EX 294	7076	EX 239	7094
EX 213	7005	EX 352	7023	EX 473	7041	EX 204	7059	EX 295	7077	EX 114	7095
EX 214	7006	EX 355	7024	EX 477	7042	EX 205	7060	EX 296	7078	EX 117	7096
EX 217	7007	EX 356	7025	EX 408	7043	EX 207	7061	EX 297	7079	EX 253	7097
EX 215	7008	EX 417	7026	EX 474	7044	EX 342	7062	EX 298	7080	EX 254	7098
EX 216	7009	EX 438	7027	EX 181	7045	EX 367	7063	EX 299	7081	EX 255	7099
EX 217	7010	EX 444	7028	EX 178	7046	EX 366	7064	EX 300	7082	EX 257	7100
EX 218	7011	EX 446	7029	EX 179	7047	EX 338	7065	EX 301	7083	EX 258	7101
EX 219	7012	EX 448	7030	EX 206	7048	EX 364	7066	EX 302	7084	EX 259	7102
EX 220	7013	EX 542	7031	EX 183	7049	EX 349	7067	EX 232	7085	EX 260	7103
EX 221	7014	EX 454	7032	EX 180	7050	EX 351	7068	EX 233	7086	EX 261	7104
EX 222	7015	EX 455	7033	EX 182	7051	EX 337	7069	EX 238	7087	EX 262	7105
EX 223	7016	EX 457	7034	EX 196	7052	EX 339	7070	EX 234	7088	EX 263	7106
EX 224	7017	EX 458	7035	EX 198	7053	EX 340	7071	EX 236	7089	EX 264	7107
EX 225	7018	EX 459	7036	EX 199	7054	EX 335	7072	EX 237	7090	EX 265	7108

(continued overleaf)

Ex-RAF Harvards in SAAF service *(continued)*

RAF serial	*SAAF serial*	*RAF serial*	*SAAF serial*	*RAF serial*	*SAAF serial*	*RAF serial*	*SAAF serial*	*RAF serial*	*SAAF serial*	*RAF serial*	*SAAF serial*
EX 266	7109	EX 363	7162	EX 483	7215	EX 544	7268	EX 692	7321	EX 730	7374
EX 267	7110	EX 283	7163	EX 484	7216	EX 542	7269	EX 713	7322	EX 731	7375
EX 268	7111	EX 275	7164	EX 485	7217	EX 540	7270	EX 733	7323	EX 734	7376
EX 269	7112	EX 272	7165	EX 486	7218	EX 545	7271	EX 735	7324	EX 740	7377
EX 270	7113	EX 277	7166	EX 487	7219	EX 433	7272	EX 627	7325	EX 594	7378
EX 304	7114	EX 280	7167	EX 488	7220	EX 469	7273	EX 628	7326	EX 595	7379
EX 305	7115	EX 287	7168	EX 489	7221	EX 441	7274	EX 629	7327	EX 596	7380
EX 306	7116	EX 278	7169	EX 494	7222	EX 431	7275	EX 679	7328	EX 597	7381
EX 307	7117	EX 286	7170	EX 495	7223	EX 432	7276	EX 680	7329	EX 600	7382
EX 308	7118	EX 271	7171	EX 561	7224	EX 464	7277	EX 681	7330	EX 601	7383
EX 309	7119	EX 281	7172	EX 562	7225	EX 443	7278	EX 685	7331	EX 602	7384
EX 310	7120	EX 360	7173	EX 556	7226	EX 465	7279	EX 686	7332	EX 605	7385
EX 311	7121	EX 361	7174	EX 560	7227	EX 543	7280	EX 688	7333	EX 606	7386
EX 312	7122	EX 382	7175	EX 559	7228	EX 541	7281	EX 693	7334	EX 607	7387
EX 313	7123	EX 398	7176	EX 552	7229	EX 439	7282	EX 599	7335	EX 608	7388
EX 314	7124	EX 276	7177	EX 554	7230	EX 456	7283	EX 603	7336	EX 612	7389
EX 315	7125	EX 400	7178	EX 570	7231	EX 539	7284	EX 611	7337	EX 613	7390
EX 316	7126	EX 393	7179	EX 567	7232	EX 568	7285	EX 614	7338	EX 618	7391
EX 317	7127	EX 397	7180	EX 557	7233	EX 546	7286	EX 615	7339	EX 622	7392
EX 318	7128	EX 288	7181	EX 569	7234	EX 555	7287	EX 616	7340	EX 737	7393
EX 319	7129	EX 292	7182	EX 558	7235	EX 547	7288	EX 617	7341	EX 738	7394
EX 320	7130	EX 289	7183	EX 550	7236	EX 553	7289	EX 619	7342	EX 751	7395
EX 169	7131	EX 273	7184	EX 574	7237	EX 563	7290	EX 621	7343	EX 757	7396
EX 170	7132	EX 392	7185	EX 566	7238	EX 571	7291	EX 623	7344	EX 749	7397
EX 171	7133	EX 362	7186	EX 551	7239	EX 548	7292	EX 624	7345	EX 750	7398
EX 173	7134	EX 371	7187	EX 565	7240	EX 549	7293	EX 630	7346	EX 755	7399
EX 176	7135	EX 372	7188	EX 572	7241	EX 564	7294	EX 631	7347	EX 760	7400
EX 177	7136	EX 390	7189	EX 573	7242	EX 476	7295	EX 632	7348	EX 769	7401
EX 247	7137	EX 391	7190	EX 582	7243	EX 475	7296	EX 633	7349	EX 770	7402
EX 248	7138	EX 394	7191	EX 584	7244	EX 479	7297	EX 636	7350	EX 771	7403
EX 249	7139	EX 395	7192	EX 578	7245	EX 471	7298	EX 638	7351	EX 774	7404
EX 250	7140	EX 399	7193	EX 583	7246	EX 470	7299	EX 639	7352	EX 776	7405
EX 251	7141	EX 274	7194	EX 581	7247	EX 478	7300	EX 640	7353	EX 705	7406
EX 252	7142	EX 279	7195	EX 580	7248	EX 472	7301	EX 642	7354	EX 706	7407
EX 303	7143	EX 282	7196	EX 579	7249	EX 593	7302	EX 643	7355	EX 775	7408
EX 380	7144	EX 284	7197	EX 577	7250	EX 610	7303	EX 645	7356	EX 779	7409
EX 381	7145	EX 290	7198	EX 575	7251	EX 625	7304	EX 646	7357	EX 781	7410
EX 341	7146	EX 291	7199	EX 576	7252	EX 396	7305	EX 647	7358	EX 782	7411
EX 333	7147	EX 293	7200	EX 499	7253	EX 626	7306	EX 648	7359	EX 787	7412
EX 336	7148	EX 445	7201	EX 503	7254	EX 637	7307	EX 666	7360	EX 798	7413
EX 353	7149	EX 443	7202	EX 496	7255	EX 644	7308	EX 664	7361	EX 799	7414
EX 330	7150	EX 407	7203	EX 497	7256	EX 660	7309	EX 694	7362	EX 802	7415
EX 332	7151	EX 429	7204	EX 502	7257	EX 668	7310	EX 695	7363	EX 803	7416
EX 365	7152	EX 460	7205	EX 504	7258	EX 659	7311	EX 701	7364	EX 804	7417
EX 343	7153	EX 447	7206	EX 505	7259	EX 667	7312	EX 704	7365	EEX 805	7418
EX 346	7154	EX 442	7207	EX 507	7260	EX 662	7313	EX 715	7366	EX 864	7419
EX 345	7155	EX 450	7208	EX 508	7261	EX 665	7314	EX 716	7367	EX 872	7420
EX 354	7156	EX 449	7209	EX 506	7262	EX 661	7315	EX 717	7368	EX 878	7421
EX 350	7157	EX 461	7210	EX 509	7263	EX 635	7316	EX 732	7369	EX 879	7422
EX 347	7158	EX 451	7211	EX 256	7264	EX 604	7317	EX 736	7370	EX 880	7423
EX 368	7159	EX 480	7212	EX 440	7265	EX 663	7318	EX 739	7371	EX 881	7424
EX 348	7160	EX 481	7213	EX 453	7266	EX 634	7319	EX 718	7372	EX 882	7425
EX 344	7161	EX 482	7214	EX 434	7267	EX 687	7320	EX 729	7373	EX 884	7426

Ex-RAF Harvards in SAAF service *(continued)*

RAF serial	*SAAF serial*	*RAF serial*	*SAAF serial*	*RAF serial*	*SAAF serial*	*RAF serial*	*SAAF serial*	*RAF serial*	*SAAF serial*	*RAF serial*	*SAAF serial*
EX 886	7427	EX 809	7462	EX 953	7497	EX 991	7532	EZ 119	7567	EZ 197	7602
EX 841	7428	EX 811	7463	EX 954	7498	EZ 131	7533	EZ 123	7568	EZ 199	7603
EX 847	7429	EX 813	7464	EX 955	7499	EZ 136	7534	EZ 132	7569	EZ 205	7604
EX 873	7430	EX 815	7465	EX 808	7500	EZ 137	7535	EZ 143	7570	EZ 210	7605
EX 892	7431	EX 819	7466	EX 946	7501	EZ 142	7536	EZ 144	7571	EZ 229	7606
EX 883	7432	EX 820	7467	EX 947	7502	EZ 150	7537	EZ 145	7572	EZ 237	7607
EX 885	7433	EX 823	7468	EX 948	7503	EZ 152	7538	EZ 146	7573	EZ 232	7608
EX 895	7434	EX 922	7469	EX 935	7504	EZ 134	7539	EZ 147	7574	EZ 236	7609
EX 899	7435	EX 821	7470	EX 939	7505	EZ 154	7540	EZ 149	7575	EZ 209	7610
EX 901	7436	EX 817	7471	EX 960	7506	EZ 135	7541	EZ 155	7576	EZ 294	7611
EX 902	7437	EX 871	7472	EX 964	7507	EZ 169	7542	EZ 158	7577	EZ 289	7612
EX 904	7438	EX 874	7473	EX 969	7508	EZ 172	7543	EZ 214	7578	EZ 226	7613
EX 915	7439	EX 903	7474	EX 959	7509	EZ 173	7544	EZ 215	7579	EZ 224	7614
EX 889	7440	EX 909	7475	EX 970	7510	EZ 180	7545	EZ 216	7580	EZ 189	7615
EX 894	7441	EX 910	7476	EX 986	7511	EZ 159	7546	EZ 217	7581	EZ 189	7616
EX 900	7442	EX 912	7477	EX 987	7512	EZ 161	7547	EZ 220	7582	EZ 187	7617
EX 914	7443	EX 916	7478	EX 988	7513	EZ 162	7548	EZ 230	7583	EZ 315	7618
EX 858	7444	EX 917	7479	EX 945	7514	EZ 163	7549	EZ 184	7584	EZ 254	7619
EX 890	7445	EX 918	7480	EX 963	7515	EZ 164	7550	EZ 185	7585	EZ 211	7620
EX 893	7446	EX 920	7481	EX 967	7516	EZ 165	7551	EZ 196	7586	EZ 251	7621
EX 898	7447	EX 924	7482	EX 972	7517	EZ 166	7552	EZ 200	7587	EZ 252	7622
EX 855	7448	EX 923	7483	EX 973	7518	EZ 168	7553	EZ 201	7588	EZ 307	7623
EX 857	7449	EX 876	7484	EX 975	7519	EZ 171	7554	EZ 203	7589	EZ 309	7624
EX 869	7450	EX 911	7485	EX 977	7520	EZ 174	7555	EZ 206	7590	EZ 310	7625
EX 850	7451	EX 919	7486	EX 978	7521	EZ 175	7556	EZ 207	7591	EZ 314	7626
EX 921	7452	EX 929	7487	EX 979	7522	EZ 176	7557	EZ 213	7592	EZ 321	7627
EX 875	7453	EX 932	7488	EX 980	7523	EZ 178	7558	EZ 219	7593	EZ 338	7628
EX 887	7454	EX 925	7489	EX 981	7524	EZ 179	7559	EZ 221	7594	EZ 339	7629
EX 816	7455	EX 927	7490	EX 985	7525	EZ 181	7560	EZ 231	7595	EZ 256	7630
EX 829	7456	EX 931	7491	EX 990	7526	EZ 182	7561	EZ 235	7596	EZ 259	7631
EX 831	7457	EX 934	7492	EX 993	7527	EZ 183	7562	EZ 240	7597	EZ 335	7632
EX 835	7458	EX 937	7493	EX 994	7528	EZ 186	7563	EZ 247	7598	EZ 336	7633
EX 836	7459	EX 940	7494	EZ 138	7529	EZ 193	7564	EZ 191	7599		
EX 837	7460	EX 950	7495	EX 989	7530	EZ 195	7565	EZ 192	7600		
EX 838	7461	EX 952	7496	EX 974	7531	EZ 118	7566	EZ 194	7601		

Harvard EX 399, coded FB-80, was shipped straight out to South Africa in December 1942, and subsequently served as SAAF 7193. Ray C. Sturtivent

Line-up of SAAF Harvards, with 7569, the the former RAF EZ 132, in the foreground. Ray C. Sturtivent

To this massive total has to be added one lone ex-British Harvard 3, which after service with the Royal Navy in the USA had been handed back and then received the civilian registration N69675. She was sold to the SAAF in August 1952 and was assigned the serial number 7663. Ten T-6s were also acquired from North American sources and were numbered 7690/7699, inclusive. One machine that was shipped direct to South Africa and later served with the SAAF (serial 7321) and then the Southern Rhodesian Air Force, serial number SR50, was later sold out to the civil register and flew for a time as ZS-WEJ and has been restored once more to flying condition. The five other Harvard 3s that South Africa bought back again were as shown in the table below.

As well as a trainer *par excellence*, the SAAF utilized the Harvard in the COIN role quite considerably, with missions being flown against SWAPO guerilla gangs in South-West Africa (now Namibia) and against Mozambique-backed guerrilla raids into South Africa herself.

A number have been sold out for civilian service and others preserved. SAAF serial 7729, a Mark III Harvard, was for many years on display at Fort Klapperkop Military Museum but was then transferred to the South African Airways Apprentice School. Another (SAAF serial 7569), a veteran from the Central Flying School and based at Dunnottar, Transvaal, was renovated in 1987, receiving yellow outer wings to an all-metal fuselage of the Joint Air Training Scheme and became a regular CFS aircraft at air displays all over South Africa.

Southern Rhodesia

Home for most of the war and for a long period afterwards, to the RAF's EAT scheme, a huge number of surplus Harvards were on hand for the formation of Southern Rhodesia's own air force when it was re-formed in February 1949. An initial batch of twelve Harvard Mark IIs were transferred, as shown in the table below.

Re-purchased Harvard 3s in SAAF service

RAF serial	Original SAAF serial	Belgian serial	New SAAF serial
EX 405	–	H.216	7732
EX 657	–	H.223	7730
EX 784	–	H.221	7728
EZ 210	7605	H.19	7731
EZ 310	7625	H.15	7729

Ex-RAF Harvards in Southern Rhodesian service

AJ 607	AJ 667	AJ 718	AJ 741	BD 131	BD 134
AJ 621	AJ 706	AJ 720	AJ 752	BD 132	DH 430

Next, in April 1949, a second batch of nine former SAAF Harvard 2As were similarly transferred (*see* table right).

In August 1951, a batch of eleven Harvard 2Bs were shipped out from the UK on extended loan. After only a year or so they were transferred to the RAF and used in the Rhodesian Air Training Group (*see* table middle right).

The Harvard 2Bs above were exchanged for twelve Harvard 2As in 1952–53, of which one (serial number 753) was returned to the RAF in June 1952 (*see* table bottom right).

Ex-SAAF Harvards in Southern Rhodesian service

RAF serial	*SAAF serial*	*RAF serial*	*SAAF serial*	*RAF serial*	*SAAF serial*
EX 210	7003	EX 433	7272	EX 749	7397
EX 213	7005	EX 463	7278	EX 755	7399
EX 240	7091	EX 692	7321	EX 838	7461

RAF Harvards on loan to Southern Rhodesia 1951–53

FX 265	FX 335	KF 223	KF 331	KF 401	KF 625
FX 308	EX 393	KF 326	KF 398	KF 420	

Ex-RAF Harvard 2As in service in Southern Rhodesia

EX 160	EX 373	EX 401	EX 519	EX 522	EX 786
EX 246	EX 385	EX 414	EX 520	EX 753	EX 845

Mozambique

With the Portuguese pull-out, a number of Harvards and T-6s of various marks were obtained from both abandoned FAP aircraft and from surplus Luftwaffe stock. They were used for a number of years by the Fremlo and the Mozambique Air Force. They were unable to keep them operational, however, and they were parked out in the open at Maputo Airfield, where they steadily rotted away. Despite this a great many still survive in various stages of repair. In 1988, Brian Zeederberg bought them up and had them transferred to South Africa. Three aircraft (serials 1727, 1731 and 1751) were subsequently sold to the South African Airways apprentice school. Of the others, all three were sold out to the civil register at a price of about £15,000 apiece: serial 1762 being sold in Durban, serial 1748 in Johannesburg, and serial 1854 in Cape Town. The South African Airworks company Fields, at Rand Airport, renovated at least a dozen Harvard Mark IVMs, which ended up at Syferfontein where they were rebuilt to civilian requirements for world-wide distribution.

Zaire

The tiny Zaire Air Force managed to accumulate a total of sixteen trainers, either T-6s or Harvard 2Bs, from various sources.

Fine study of EX 523 (coded 'P') and EX 778 (coded '60') flying over Southern Rhodesia while serving with 20 SFTS. The former subsequently served with 5 and 4 FTS and crashed at Meilloo on 16 July 1948, while the latter served with 4 FTS and was sold for scrap in November 1953. RAF Museum, Hendon, London

New Zealand

Although the RNZAF had taken delivery of sixty-seven Mark II Harvards directly from the United States, another thirty-eight were taken from British Purchasing Commission allotments and sent to reinforce them in 1942. A third batch consisted of fifty-two Mark IIAs and forty-two Mark IIIs in 1943–44. The last assignments were three Harvard IIBs in 1944, and one brought back from post-war RNZAF use in occupied Japan. This gave a total of 196 aircraft, some of which were handed over the Royal New Zealand Navy.

Ex-RAF Harvards in RNZAF service

RAF serial	*RNZAF serial*	*RAF serial*	*RNZAF serial*	*RAF serial*	*RNZAF serial*	*RAF serial*	*RNZAF serial*	*RAF serial*	*RNZAF serial*	*RAF serial*	*RNZAF serial*
AJ 855	NZ 968	AJ 876	NZ 989	EX 187	NZ 1009	EX 585	NZ 1030	EX 905	NZ 1066	EZ 301	NZ 1084
AJ 856	NZ 969	AJ 877	NZ 990	EX 188	NZ 1010	EX 586	NZ 1031	EX 906	NZ 1067	EZ 329	NZ 1085
AJ 857	NZ 970	AJ 878	NZ 991	EX 189	NZ 1011	EX 587	NZ 1032	EX 907	NZ 1068	EZ 330	NZ 1086
AJ 858	NZ 971	AJ 879	NZ 992	EX 190	NZ 1012	EX 588	NZ 1033	EX 908	NZ 1069	EZ 331	NZ 1087
AJ 859	NZ 972	AJ 880	NZ 993	EX 191	NZ 1013	EX 589	NZ 1034	EX 941	NZ 1062	EZ 332	NZ 1088
AJ 860	NZ 973	AJ 881	NZ 994	EX 192	NZ 1014	EX 590	NZ 1035	EX 942	NZ 1063	EZ 333	NZ 1089
AJ 861	NZ 974	AJ 882	NZ 995	EX 193	NZ 1015	EX 591	NZ 1036	EX 943	NZ 1064	EZ 359	NZ 1090
AJ 862	NZ 975	AJ 883	NZ 996	EX 194	NZ 1016	EX 592	NZ 1037	EX 944	NZ 1065	EZ 360	NZ 1091
AJ 863	NZ 976	AJ 884	NZ 997	EX 195	NZ 1017	EX 741	NZ 1038	EX 997	NZ 1071	EZ 361	NZ 1092
AJ 864	NZ 977	AJ 885	NZ 998	EX 326	NZ 1018	EX 742	NZ 1039	EX 998	NZ 1072	EZ 362	NZ 1093
AJ 865	NZ 978	AJ 886	NZ 999	EX 327	NZ 1019	EX 743	NZ 1040	EX 999	NZ 1073	EZ 363	NZ 1094
AJ 866	NZ 979	AJ 887	NZ 1000	EX 328	NZ 1020	EX 744	NZ 1041	EZ 177	NZ 1079	EZ 439	NZ 1095
AJ 867	NZ 980	AJ 888	NZ 1001	EX 329	NZ 1021	EX 745	NZ 1042	EZ 242	NZ 1074	EZ 449	NZ 1096
AJ 868	NZ 981	AJ 889	NZ 1002	EX 421	NZ 1022	EX 746	NZ 1043	EZ 243	NZ 1075	EZ 453	NZ 1097
AJ 869	NZ 982	AJ 890	NZ 1003	EX 422	NZ 1023	EX 747	NZ 1044	EZ 244	NZ 1076	EZ 455	NZ 1098
AJ 870	NZ 983	AJ 891	NZ 1004	EX 423	NZ 1024	EX 748	NZ 1045	EZ 245	NZ 1077	EZ 456	NZ 1099
AJ 871	NZ 984	AJ 892	NZ 1005	EX 424	NZ 1025	EX 865	NZ 1058	EZ 246	NZ 1078	KF 113	?
AJ 872	NZ 985	EX 184	NZ 1006	EX 425	NZ 1026	EX 866	NZ 1059	EZ 297	NZ 1080	KF 403	NZ 1100
AJ 873	NZ 986	EX 185	NZ 1007	EX 426	NZ 1027	EX 867	NZ 1060	EZ 298	NZ 1081	KF 407	NZ 1101
AJ 874	NZ 987	EX 186	NZ 1008	EX 427	NZ 1028	EX 868	NZ 1061	EZ 299	NZ 1082	KF 410	NZ 1102
AJ 875	NZ 988			EX 428	NZ 1029			EZ 300	NZ 1083		

Like South Africa, the Royal New Zealand Air Force, as a participant in the EATS, received direct shipments of Harvards direct from the NAA plants in the USA. This is NZ 1051, seen here while she was serving with the CFS at Wigram air base near Christchurch. Ray C. Sturtivent

At the end of their useful lives, these were taken off charge and disposed of. Several went to museums including: NZ 1102 to the RNAZ Museum at Wigram Airfield near Christchurch, New Zealand; NZ 944 (ex RAF serial AH 918) went to the Museum of Transport and Technology, Auckland, New Zealand; NZ 1012 went to the Ashburton Aviation Museum; NZ 1033 went to the New Zealand Sport and Vintage Aviation Museum, Masterton, New Zealand; NZ 1034 and NZ 1060 went to the RAAF Museum, Point Cook, Victoria, Australia; NZ 1083 to the RNZAF Historic Flight at Woodhouse Air Base, New Zealand; NZ 1087 to the Taranaki Transport and Technology Museum, New Plymouth, New Zealand; NZ 918 was put on a pole for display at Pahiatua, New Zealand; NZ 1050 as a pole display at RZAF Base Wigram; NZ 1077 was displayed on a pedestal at Ashburton, New Zealand; NZ 1009 and NZ 1015 went to the RNZAF Historic Flight at Wigram Air Base; NZ 1060 went to Ferrymead Museum of Science and Technology, Christchurch.

Some others saw service on the civilian registers for a good many years and a few still fly today.

One of the preserved RNZAF Harvards, this is NZ 1050 pictured here at Point Cook air base and Museum. Simon Watson

India and Pakistan

The handover of power in India in September 1947 led to a splitting-up of the former British India into the countries of India and Pakistan, largely on religious grounds, and both these nations quickly established their own forces and, from time-to-time, engaged in wasteful and futile wars against each other. Thus the first actual combat actions in which 'The Six' actually took part (Wirraway derivatives excepted of course) were by those in Indian and Pakistan service. Initial ex-RAF allocations to these nations was as shown in the Table, with India receiving a total of eighty-two aircraft all ex-RAF stock *in situ*. They were later given the IAF serials in the HT (= Harvard Trainer) 200 range. They saw considerable

Ex-RNZAF Harvard survivors

Type	*RNZAF no.*	*C/n*	*US serial*	*Civilian reg.*
Harvard II	NZ 918	66-2711	–	-
Harvard II	NZ 944	66-2757	RCAF 3009	–
Harvard II	NZ 946	66-2759	–	–
Harvard II	NZ 977	76-3834	–	ZK-XII
Harvard IIA	NZ 1006	88-9263	41-33157	VH-TEX
Harvard IIA	NZ 1007	88-9264	41-33158	VH-HAR
Harvard IIA	NZ 1009	88-9266	41-33160	–
Harvard IIA	NZ 1012	88-9269	41-33163	–
Harvard IIA	NZ 1015	88-9272	41-33166	
Harvard IIA	NZ 1023	88-10252	41-33395	VH-CRC
Harvard IIA	NZ 1024	88-10253	41-33396	VH-ZNF
Harvard IIA	NZ 1025	88-10254	41-33397	–
Harvard IIA	NZ 1033	88-12032	41-33561	ZK-SGQ
Harvard IIA	NZ 1034	88-12033	41-33565	–
Harvard IIA	NZ 1037	88-12036	41-33565	ZK-ENA
Harvard IIA	NZ 1038	88-13187	41-33714	VH-AYO
Harvard IIA	NZ 1040	88-13189	41-33716	–
Harvard IIA	NZ 1041	88-13190	41-33717	–
Harvard IIA	NZ 1044	88-13193	41-33720	–
Harvard IIA	NZ 1050	88-13907	41-33766	–
Harvard IIA	NZ 1051	88-13908	41-3376	–
Harvard IIA	NZ 1052	88-13909	41-33768	ZK-MJN
Harvard IIA	NZ 1053	88-13910	41-33769	–
Harvard IIA	NZ 1056	88-14177	41-33800	VH-NAH
Harvard IIA	NZ 1057	88-14178	41-33801	–
Harvard III	NZ 1060	88-14493	41-33840	VH-SFY
Harvard III	NZ 1061	88-14494	41-33841	NH-PEM
Harvard III	NZ 1065	88-14889	41-33917	ZK-ENF
Harvard III	NZ 1066	88-14672	41-33878	ZK-ENE
Harvard III	NZ 1068	88-14674	41-33880	–
Harvard III	NZ 1069	88-14675	41-33881	–
Harvard III	NZ 1075	88-15870	41-34116	VH-HVD
Harvard III	NZ 1076	88-15871	41-34117	ZK-ENB
Harvard III	NZ 1077	88-15872	41-34118	–
Harvard III	NZ 1078	88-15873	41-34119	XK-ENG
Harvard III	NZ 1079	88-15611	41-34050	N101NZ
Harvard III	NZ 1082	88-16143	42-84362	ZK-USN
Harvard III	NZ 1083	88-16144	42-84363	–
Harvard III	NZ 1085	88-16324	42-84543	VH-SNJ
Harvard III	NZ 1086	88-16325	42-84544	–
Harvard III	NZ 1087	88-16326	42-84545	–
Harvard III	NZ 1090	88-16504	42-84723	VH-AUR
Harvard III	NZ 1091	88-16505	42-84724	ZK-ENC
Harvard III	NZ 1092	88-16506	42-84725	ZK-WAR
Harvard III	NZ 1096	88-17004	42-85223	ZK-END
Harvard III	NZ 1098	88-17010	42-85229	XK-ENJ
Harvard III	NZ 1099	88-17011	42-85230	ZK-ENK
Harvard IIB	NZ 1100	14A-2103		–
Harvard IIB	NZ 1102	14A-2110		–

action during the fighting over Kashmir, which commenced on 28 October 1947.

Two of the IAF Harvards were quickly adapted as ground-strafing close-support aircraft working out of Srinagar airfield during the battles at Ambala on 31 October, and so useful did they prove that another pair of similar conversions quickly joined them there. In order to keep these aircraft airborne, Dakotas had to airlift aviation fuel up to the front line, which had to be laboriously transferred to buckets and used to top up the Harvards' fuel tanks. Their next combat sortie took place on 5 November, all four conversions being used as spotter planes. They played a significant part in that they located and then guided an Indian armoured column from the Banihal Pas to Srinagar over a two-day period. Their work enabled a major Indian attack to be launched in that area on 7 November. Five days later, this advance became bogged down by stiff Pakistani opposition near Rampur. Two of the Harvards conducted repeated ground-attack missions at Domel, Kotli, Mirpur and Uri, resulting in the fall of the latter on 13 November. Three days later, Uri was again their target and they bombed and strafed the strategic Pakistani defences at the critical Milepost 67.

Many Harvards saw wartime service in British India, either with training units or attached to squadrons as 'hacks'. This is FS 948, with unusual markings. Assigned to DGA CF, she was one of many former RAF aircraft assigned to the Indian Air Force after independence. RAF Museum, Hendon, London

The Indian Air Force used their Harvards as combat aircraft from the very start, and during the war with Pakistan over Kashmir they were in the thick of the fighting. Here two IAF Harvards are seen early in the fighting. Indian Air Force Official

RAF Harvard assignments to the Indian Air Force 1947

FE 354	FS 782	FT 115	FX 455
FE 374	FS 787	FT 121	FX 458
FE 424	FS799	FT 123	FX 460
FE 429	FS 803	FT 128	FX 464
FE 482	FS 806	FT 131	FX 472
FE 483	FS 927	FT 132	FX 473
FE 597	FS 934	FT 179	FX 478
FE 616	FS 939	FT 180	FX 482
FE 664	FS 940	FT 181	FX 486
FE 685	FS 944	FT 185	FX 490
FE 711	FS 948	FT 187	FX 492
FE 775	FS 949	FT 192	KF 100
FE 883	FS 956	FT 195	KF 101
FE 952	FS 986	FT 202	KF 102
FE 954	FS 987	FT 371	KF 115
FE 974	FT 101	FX 401	KF 119
FH 113	FT 103	FX 445	KF 122
FS 693	FT 106	FX 447	KF 123
FS 697	FT 112	FX 448	KF 135
FS 700	FT 114	FX 451	KF 137
FS 707		FX 454	

After the cease-fire, the bulk of the IAF Harvards reverted to their more normal role of pilot training. They continued to carry out this job faithfully for many years. In 1963, the survivors were concentrated at the AFFC. A fresh supply of thirty-six former RCAF Harvard IVs arrived in 1963.

By 1973 there were still some flying alongside the HJT-16 Kiran jet trainers at the AFA. The last IAF Harvard finally bowed out in 1975, after almost three decades of dedicated service.

A single survivor (serial HT 291, ex-FS 787, 14A-927, 43-12626) is preserved at the Indian Air Force Museum, Pelam Air Base.

In a similar manner, Pakistan received the allocation of twenty-nine ex-RAF Harvards, as shown in the table below.

RAF Harvard assignments to the Pakistan Air Force 1947

FE 373	FS 711	FT 122	FX 485
FE 413	FS 783	FT 182	FX 497
FE 272	FS 791	FT 188	KF 110
FE 687	FS 931	FT 191	KF 116
FE 708	FS 947	FT 194	KF 212
FE 766	FS 953	FX 456	KF 125
FE 879	FS 993	FX 457	KF 144
FS 702			

CHAPTER ELEVEN

The T-6 Renaissance

The AT-6 became the T-6 when the USAAF became the USAF in November 1947. 'The Six' had taken over the primary trainer role as well at this time and trainees clocked up 20h of dual control now, instead of just 8–12h in the gentle PT-17, before going solo. Like the Harvard, 'The Six' seemed in terminal decline. With jets now beginning to fill the skies, who would need a propeller-driven trainer designed in the 1930s? Well, as it turned out, just about EVERYBODY!

War-surplus stocks were eagerly bought up by such companies as Bellanca, of Newcastle, Delaware, A. E. Ulmann and Associates, and TEMCO in Texas, as well as by the NAA themselves, and given various types of upgrade to make them re-saleable. It was not just NATO and SEATO nations that benefited. Under the Rio Pact, Latin American nations were able to join in the scramble for T-6s. Brazil took delivery of 100 machines, a mixed offering that included 6As, 6Bs, 5Cs and 6Ds. Some of these were later locally upgraded to T-6G standards and then so-listed by the Brazilian air force, refurbished up to AT-6D standards!

North American were earlier in the field, thus getting two bites at the same cherry! Under USAAF contract AC-19192, a mixed batch of sixty-eight 'Sixes', T-6C/SNJ-4s, were given a refurbishment at the Inglewood plant and then assigned brand-new serial numbers in the range 48-1301/1368, inclusive. The same treatment was subsequently meted out to batches of T-6Ds and T-6Gs. Bellanca modified a batch of thirty T-6Ds for the Royal Iranian Air Force in 1949. In this case, their original serials were retained when they were delivered in the first two months of 1950. TEMCO similarly upgraded ten T-6s for the Italian Air Force in July 1950 and followed up with similar orders for both the Philippines and Thailand, all under the MDAP auspices. The USAF undertook such upgrade work themselves in some instances, while other foreign recipients took delivery of the aircraft 'as they were' and carried out their own modifications once they got them back home. Cases in point were l'Armée de l'Air and Aéronavale aircraft (sixty T-6Ds), Italy (thirty) and Portugal (twenty of all types)

With the formation of the Western Union, in the face of imminent Soviet invasion, followed by the establishment of the North Atlantic Treaty Organization (NATO) and the South-East Asia Treaty Organization (SEATO), all formed against the common communist threat, the T-6 suddenly found herself back in demand again. To enable every participant air force a degree of training ability, in order to build up against a common foe, a latter-day lend-lease was set up in the United States. This was the Mutual Defense Assistance Pact (MDAP), which in theory meant all the nations helped each other, but which in practice meant the USA, Great Britain and Canada assisted their impoverished brethren.

When NATO was established in August 1949, Canada committed herself to again undertake her World War II role of training host to many of the other eleven member nations. Some 6,000 post-war military pilots learned to fly in the Harvard in Canada. An early indication of the way the tide was turning came in 1949.

Not a NAA idea but a private attempt to re-work the T-6 into a COIN aircraft by a private venture. This is the T-6S Bacon Super, which featured wing-tip fuel tanks, bubble canopy, a tricycle landing gear, new engine and other modifications. Good though she looked the idea did not catch on, there were just too many upgraded T-6s on the market at cheaper prices. She found some brief success as a film substitute for a Soviet Yak fighter as shown here. Arthur Pearcy collection courtesy of Audrey Pearcy

Greece

A batch of thirty-five AT-6Ds was assigned to Greece by the USA, but before they were delivered, unlike many of the British Harvards, these aircraft were given a complete refurbishment and upgrade. So complete was this make-over that they were awarded new air force serial numbers (49-2722/2756, inclusive) as if they had been *new* aircraft (which caused enormous confusion later) and a new designation, as the T-6D.

So successful was this upgrade that it was planned to similarly convert another

NAA had continued to develop the T-6 during the war, and would continue doing so post-war. However, designers had already combined all the desirable features found wanting into a new concept for the US Navy. Here it all was with a double bubble canopy for all-round vision for both pupil and instructor, and a whole series of innovative emergency simulations to keep both fully stretched! This was the North American X-SN2J-1 and she could combine these training qualities with that of a scouting aircraft as well. Sound as the idea was, there proved to be no takers, although many of these ideas were later to feature in the more commercially successful Trojan design. Rockwell International

1,200 aircraft to the T-6D standard; however, this idea was dropped with the adoption of the T-6G programme instead.

While the US Training Command still had hundreds of 'Sixes' on their books, a large number of these were in storage around the country. More than 400 of these were taken out, dusted down, given a make-over and also sold abroad under the MDAP programme.

T-6G/SNJ-7

A new standard of upgrade was introduced in 1949, which led to yet another new designation for what was, in fact, a rebuild operation performed on several different Marks of varying age and origins. The changes went much further than with the T-6Ds and again resulted in the allocation of completely new USAF serial numbers to them all. The initial funding came from the cancellation of 100 of the aborted Fairchild T-31 trainers. The success of the T-6G also led to the demise of the Douglas T-30 and the Temco T-31 projects. This programme was demand-led by America's allies and put the USAF in a somewhat difficult position. Aircraft that had been disdainfully sold off wholesale for next to nothing scant years before, now had to be bought back at twenty times their sell-off price! The simple reason for this was that the USAF no longer had sufficient aircraft still left in store to meet the new demand.

The alterations carried out to 'G' standard were as follows:

- The rear cockpit was modified with the rear seat being raised in height by 6in (15cm).
- The cockpit layout was simplified by the deletion of the centre uprights from the side panels.
- An extra 30 US gallons of fuel was added in two 15 US-gallon bladder type wing tanks in the outer wing panels, to extend endurance and range.
- The hydraulic system was modified and upgraded. There was direct actuation of both landing-gear and wing flaps. The pilot only had to shift the gear handle to Down and the full landing-gear functions were automatically carried out. Thus the hydraulic pressure gauge could be eliminated.
- Up-to-date radio equipment for VHF and UHF reception/transmission was fitted and the RC-103 and AN/ARN-5

instrument landing systems appeared in many. Cockpit instrumentation was refined and updated with varying intercom fittings.

- An F-type tail wheel was shipped to aid steering in yet another effort to minimize ground-looping. This locking/steerable system enabled the pilot to make the wheel free-swivelling by neutralizing the rudder pedals and pushing the control stick forward.

- A much more prominent DF casing was installed abaft the cockpit on top of the rear fuselage.

- All refurbished aircraft that emerged as T-6s were painted yellow all over in the way that the Harvard always had been.

This work was carried out at several NAA locations, but also by other contractors at the following locations: North American Aviation's Downey, California plant; North American Aviation's Columbus, Ohio plant (the old Curtis–Wright plant bought a couple of years before), and they also brought some T-6Fs up to T-6G standard as the T-6H (later re-designated as the T-6G-NH); North American Aviation's leased Dallas, Texas plant (including 100 assembled from spare T-6 parts); North American Aviation's Fresno, California plant; the US Navy (under the projected SNJ-7 programme fifty were planned but only six produced) at NAS Pensacola, Florida; Canadian Car and Foundry plant, Fort William, Quebec (upgraded Harvard IV/4s costed by the USAAF and allegedly designated as the T-6J-CCF).[1] They also built brand-new Harvard 4s from 1951 onward. Canadian aircraft could always be identified by the elongated starboard engine exhausts and lower profile ADF antenna. Despite the work involved, conversion could be quick: the first T-6G being delivered only forty-four days from signature of contract.

The T-6G extended the life of 'The Six' by yet another decade. Even in the USA, the last USAF Texan did not retire until 17 September 1956, when a ceremony was

CATS T-6 Texan (84-588) pictured at Templehof airfield, Berlin, on 6 September 1947. Arthur Pearcy courtesy of Audrey Pearcy

Breakdown of T-6G conversions

Charge no.	*Plant*	*Designation*	*Total*	*USAF serials*	*Assigned*
NA-168	NAA Downey	T-6G-NI	641	49-2897 to 49-3537	USAF
NA-182	NAA Downey	T-6G-NT	50	50-1277 to 50-1326	ANG
NA-182	NAA Columbus	T-6G-1-NA	824	51-14314 to 51-15137	USAF/MDAP
NA-188	NAA Dallas	T-6G-NA	100	51-15138 to 51-15237	MDAP
NA-188	NAA Downey	T-6G-NA	7	51-16071 to 51-16077	MDAP
NA-195	NAA Fresno	T-6G-NF	11	51-17354 to 51-17346	USAF
NA-197	NAA Fresno	T-6G-NF	50	52-8197 to 52-8246	MDAP
NA-197	NAA Fresno	T-6G-NF	60	53-4555 to 53-4614	ANG
–	USN Pensacola	SNJ-7*	1	BuNo 112383	USN
–	USN Pensacola	SNJ-7B**	2	BuNo 27850 and 12229	USN
–	USN Pensacola	SNJ-7-C***	3	BuNo 90678, 90743 and 112314	USN
–	CC&F Ottawa	Harvard IV	143	57-17089 to 57-17231	MDAP
–	CC&F Ottawa	Harvard IV	120	52-8493 to 52-8612	MDAP
–	CC&F Ottawa	Harvard IV	22	53-4615 to 53-4636	MDAP (6 for USAF)
–	CC&F Ottawa	Harvard 4	270	RCAF 20210 to 20479	RCAF

** As Prototype (SNJ-4-7BX).*
*** As Gunnery Trainers (SNJ-5-7X).*
**** Fitted with Arrestor hooks for carrier landings (SNJ-6-7CX).*

held at Bartow Air Force Base in Florida. Eighteen months later, on 14 March 1958, the last SNJ also bowed out from Barrin Field, Alabama (sometimes called 'Bloody Barrin' due to the number of fatal T-6 accidents there during the war). In the USA alone, some 50,000 Army Air Force and 40,000 Navy pilots had been trained up to that time. T-6s continued to see some active service Stateside for longer than this, however, as they were gainfully employed by 35 Air Rescue Squadron of the US Civil Air Patrol on into the early 1960s.

Aside from those that served with the USAF Training Command and rejuvenated Air National Guard units at home and overseas, and the RCAF Harvard 4s, which joined Canadian units, allocations of all these aircraft overseas to foreign recipients were led by NATO countries, but gradually the T-6Gs spread around the globe. Of those officially supplied, not all were MDAP supported: some were purchased, others assigned, yet more reached their destinations second-, third- or even fourth-hand by very circuitous and dubious routes. It will in all probability never be fully known just how many other T-6s of all types circulated around in remote corners of the globe or how they got there. For example, some fifty-six former RCAF Harvard IVs were sold out to the civilian register at the end of their useful lives.[2]

In summary then, smaller air forces could build up their stocks of 'The Six' by the following methods:

- direct purchase of war surplus stocks via dealers;
- direct purchase of NAA and other company upgrades;
- under MDAP and similar assistance schemes;
- under various official governmental agreements like the Rio Pact;
- by inheriting abandoned or ceded aircraft from ex-colonial powers (Portugal, Spain, France, Great Britain, the Netherlands, Belgium, South Africa and Southern Rhodesia all 'contributed' in this way down the years);
- by sale, re-sale or transfer between second-, third- and even fourth-hand users.

In the process, these 'Sixes' could be modified under official schemes, upgraded by companies privately, upgraded by their own air forces or be refurbished by speculators. In all a wondrously labyrinthine trail that almost defies unravelling. Anyone who tries should invest in a large bottle of aspirin, and be aware that, no matter what comes out at the end of it, the nit-pickers and acid reviewers will always ignore the revelations and find *something*, however petty, to hang their egos on!

Superb aerial view of 49-3143 of TA-143 of the NA-168 batch shows off all the T-6G modifications.
Rockwell International

Austria

Although a strict neutral in the Cold War, the Austrian Air Force acquired at least one (and probably more) T-6G (serial number 4C-TE, 168-295, 49-3191), which is preserved at the Heeresgeschichtiches Museum in Vienna.

Belgium

Under MDAP, Belgium took delivery of sixteen T-6Ds to add to her establishment of Harvards. Along with the earlier Harvards, many of these were sent to the training school established at Kaminia, Belgian Congo, where they were armed and used to combat the Congolese rebel insurgents.

Denmark

Also a member of NATO, between 1951 and 1953 the Royal Danish Air Force received twenty-one T-6Ds and some ex-Canadian IIBs under MDAP and by transfers from Norway. They received Danish Air Force serials in the 31/300 range. Four survived as museum exhibits, they are: serial 329 (ex-FE 905, 14-639, 42-12392), which was on display at the Newark Air Museum, Nottingham, UK; serial 306 (ex-FH 114, 14-748, 42-12501), on display at the Dansk Veteranflysamling, Stauning, Denmark; serial 309 (ex-FS 826, 14A-966, 43-12667), on display at the Danmarks Flyvemuseum, Billund, Denmark; and serial 324 (ex-FT 380, 14A-1420, 43-13121), on display at the Historiske Forening Museet, Karup, Denmark. A fifth, serial 310, the former Norwegian Harvard IIB (ex-FS 917, 14-A-1057, 43-12758), flew for a while as civilian registration LN-BNN.

This is a Canadian-built Harvard 4, RCAF 20300. Canadian Government, Ottawa

CC&F-built Canadian Harvard T4, RCAF 20279 coded CB-T, serving with No. 417 Squadron, RCAF. Ray C. Sturtivent

Norway

In 1950 the Royal Norwegian Air Force took delivery of four T-6Ds under MDAP to supplement her ex-RAF Harvard fleet.

Portugal

Under the provisions of MDAP, the Forca Aerea Portuguesa (FAP) took delivery of twenty-five T-6Gs in 1951, to which were added another twenty surplus AT-6As and AT-6Bs, which arrived aboard the escort carrier *Corregidor* in October 1951. The Aviacao Naval (Portuguese Navy) received eight former US Navy SNJ-4s in 1956 and these were given FAP serials I-1/6, inclusive. Some later Marks of SNJ arrived later.

In addition to normal training requirements and duties, some of these aircraft were modified to LT-6G standards, with underwing gun pods and bomb racks, and operated in the COIN role during the vicious little wars in Portugal's colonial possessions like Angola, Mozambique and Guinea before they finally withdrew from Africa – the last being in action as late as 1974. All had been phased out by 1978 and a great

(Opposite page, top) **Royal Canadian Air Force CC&F-built Harvard 4 with low-profile antenna; RCAF 20414 pictured in 1956.** CFPU

(Opposite page, bottom) **Fine overhead forward view taken in 1961 of a CC&F-built Harvard 4, RCAF 20300.** CFPU

(This page, top) **Royal Canadian Navy Harvard 4, RCAF 3108, coded 903.** Ray C. Sturtivent

(Above) **Under lowering skies this Canadian-built Harvard 4, coded RCAF 385, makes a striking study.** Air Portraits

number reached the civilian market and a few of them are still flying.

Serial 1608 (77-4176, 41-217) was later exhibited at the Albatros Flugmuseum at Stuttgart airport for a time from 1992.

Former Forca Aerea Portuguesa T-6/SNJ survivors

Type	*FAP no.*	*C/n*	*US serial*	*Civilian reg.*
AT-6A	1608	77-4176	41-217	D-FOBY
AT-6A	1620	76-6698	41-16320	N77TX
AT-6D	–	88-15878	41-34607	N8541B
AT-6D	–	–	–	N8539G
SNJ-4	I-1	88-10293	BuNo 10288	N3747X
SNJ-4	I-2	88-11041	BuNo 26667	N37477
SNJ-4	I-3	88-12122	BuNo 27179	N85398B
SNJ-4	I-4	88-12847	BuNo 27511	N3747Z
SNJ-4	I-5	88-13037	BuNo 27581	N378474
SNJ-4	I-6	88-13585	BuNo 27849	N6171A
SNJ-4	I-7	88-13630	BuNo 51363	N22518
SNJ-4	I-8	88-14253	BuNo 51611	N22519
SNJ-5	–	88-15308	BuNo 43643	N1049A
SNJ-5	–	88-18065	BuNo 90787	N45000
SNJ-6	–	121-42368	44-81646	N8540P

Serials 1737, 1769 and 1774 were sent to the Museu do Ar, at Montijo Air Base in 1985, all in flyable condition.

Italy

To supplement the Harvards she had received, Italy took delivery of four T-6s on 12 January 1951, four more on 16 February and one more on 14 March, all direct from the United States. They were distributed to training schools at Alhgero and Elmas air bases in Sardinia, which had a strength of six aircraft at Lecce. The following year saw a considerable increase in T-6 strength under the auspices of NATO and thirty T-6Gs were received from the USA (with some AT-6Fs refurbished and listed as T-6Hs). In 1953–54 two Canadian built Harvard 4s

Ex-Portuguese T-6G survivors

T-6G	1707	182-729	51-15042	France	G-BGHU
T-6G	1710	182-750	51-15063	France	N8048J
T-6G	1715	182-29	51-14342	France	N4434M
T-6G	–	182-30	51-14343	France	N8048E
T-6G	–	182-735	51-15048	France	N42JM
T-6G	–	197-97	53-4601	France	N4269E
T-6G	–	197-106	53-4610	France	N4269X
T-6G	1769	–	USAF	–	FAP 1769
T-6G	1774	–	USAF	–	FAP 1774
T-6G	–	182-5	51-14318	USAF	N1384Z
T-6G	–	195-2	51-17355	USAF	N4269P
T-6G	–	195-6	51-17359	USAF	N1385K
T-6G	–	195-10	51-17363	USAF	N1385H
T-6G	–	197-3	52-82199	USAF	N1385B
T-6G	–	197-40	52-8236	USAF	N4269R
T-6G	–	197-54	52-4558	USAF	N4269Q
T-6G	–	–	–	USAF	N8048N

An RCAF instructor makes an examination of his aircraft, Harvard 4 RCAF 20264, prior to take off in 1964. CFPU

Italian T-6s, coded AA*32 and AA*42 with all-metal finish save for yellow outer wing panels. Stato Maggiore dell Aeronautica, Rome

Trio of Italian T-6s, coded AA*51, AA*62, and AA*45, in all-yellow finish. Stato Maggiore dell Aeronautica, Rome

(Below) **Port rear (top) and port frontal (bottom) three-quarter view of Italian T-6G, serial number 53669, AA*56, with the old-type 'football' D/F pod abaft the cockpit.** Stato Maggiore dell Aeronautica, Rome

were received (52-8493 and 52-8494), again listed as T-6Hs.

These large deliveries enabled the establishment of the Scuola Centrale Insruttori di Volo (SCIV, Central Instructors Flying School) at Foggia, with eight T-6s, five of which were operational. They were also assigned to the Scuola Addestramento Aviogetti (SAA), as well as the CAV dell' Accademia Aeronautica at Pomigliano d'Arco airfield. On 1 June 1956, fifteen T-6C and G types, modified for ground attack, formed 525 Squadriglia Scuola. The Italian 'Sixes' were also used to train radar-operators at the Scuola Cacchia Ogne Tempo (SCOT, All-speed Fighter School).

From 1956, the T-6s were concentrated in 202° Gruppo at Cagliaria and the Scuola di Lecce. On 30 April 1957, the SCIV became independent and transferred to the Grottaglie (TA) air base the 200° Gruppo di Volo (with 410, 411 Squadriglia equipped with the T-6).[3]

Head-on view of an Italian T-6G making a low-level pass over her base.
Stato Maggiore dell Aeronautica, Rome

'The Six' served in the Aeronautica Militare until the mid-1970s in ever-decreasing numbers. There were sixty on strength in 1962, and this had fallen to fifty-five a year later, of which thirty were operational. The same story was told in other units. With the 670° Squadriglia del CAT based at Decimomannu Air Base, the T-6 was used for advanced training, reconnaissance, navigation and liaison. Of sixty aircraft on the strength of SCIV at this time, a breakdown revealed the following: seven T-6C (four operational); twelve T-6D (nine operational), thirteen T-6G (twelve operational), five T-6H.2 (five operational) and twenty-five T6-H.4M (twenty-one operational).

Home-built training aircraft like the L-18C and the L-21B gradually replaced 'The Six' in the early 1970s. The 'official' farewell flight of an Italian T-6 took place on 13 February 1979, when Colonel Sergio Ponzio of 53 Stormo flew serial number 166.12 into the history books. However, his thunder was stolen when, five days after this event, an anonymous colonel from No. 330 Gruppo made his very own *un*official flight in a T-6.

Large numbers of former Italian 'Sixes' made their way onto the civilian market after this date, and they include those shown in the table (below left), some of which are still flying today.

Many others were initially preserved in museums or as gate guards, or put on display; *some* of these still exist today.

Italian civilian registered machines

Type	*Italian serial*	*C/n*	*Serial*	*Civilian reg.*
AT-6D	MM-53418			N1364N
T-6G	MM-53655			N1364J
T-6G	MM-53664	188-90	51-15227	G-BKRA
Harvard 4	MM-53785	CCF4-288	51-17106	I-TSIX
Harvard 4	MM-53802	CCF4-		F-AZCM
Harvard 4	MM-53833	CCF4-		VH-USR
Harvard 4	MM-53844	CCF4-407	51-17225	N587CB
Harvard 4	MM-53846	CCF4-		G-BIWX
Harvard 4	MM-53795	CCF4-		G-BJST
Harvard 4	MM-53816	CCF4-363	51-17181	N1363W
T-6G	MM-54099	182-155	51-14469	G-BRBC
T-6H	MM-54135			N604R
T-6H	MM-54136			N8021R
Harvard 4	MM-54137	07-30	RCAF 3064	G-CTKL
Harvard 4	MM-	CCF4-384	51-17202	HB-RAJ
Harvard 4	MM-	CCF4-387	51-17205	N52494
Harvard II	MM-	75-3439	RCAF 3165	N3231H
Harvard 4	MM-	CCF4-		I-RYGA

Italian displayed aircraft

Type	*Italian serial*	*Was on display at:*
T-6H	MM-53670	Castello di Annone
T-6H	MM-53679	Scuola Specialisti, Capua.
T-6H	MM-53818	Gate guard, Viterbo AB
T-6H	MM-53822	Raccolta Della Base di Rivolto, Rivolto AB
Harvard 4	MM-53823	Museo Dell'Aria, Castello di San Pelagio
T-6H	MM-53825	Guidonia
T-6H	MM-53835	Cascino
T-6D	MM-53864	Camp Darby
T-6G	MM-54097	Museo Storico Dell Aeronautica, Vigna di Valle AB, Rome
T-6G	MM-54098	Grazzanise
T-6G	MM-54106	Raccolta Della Base de Cameri, Cameri AB
T-6G	MM-54114	Museo Nazinonale Della Scienza and Della Technica, Milan
T-6H	MM-54143	Raccolta Della Base di Gallarate, Gallarate AB
T-6H	MM-54144	Assoc pour la Sauvegarde des Avions Anciens, Orion, France
T-6H	MM-54146	Museo Della Guerra, Rome
T-6H	MM-54149	Castel del Rio
T-6H	MM-54292	Conegliano D'Otranto

A few others survived various changes of hand to either end up in civilian store pending restoration, as spares for other rebuilds or as projects. Some of these are shown in the table below.

Other Italian survivors

AT-6C	MM-53432
T-6G	MM-53652
T-6G	MM-53758
T-6H	MM-53692
Harvard 4	MM-53796
T-6H	MM-53806
T-6H	MM-53820
T-6H	MM-53828
Harvard 4	MM-53835
T-6H	MM-54099

Yugoslavia

Although a communist nation, under Marshal Tito Yugoslavia did not slavishly follow the Stalinist line and thus means were found to assist her in many ways that were not obvious. The Yugoslav Air Force was, therefore, able to supplement her 'retained' former RAF Harvards with some former US Air National Guard T-6G-NHs in the mid-1950s.

Greece

A total of fifty-two T-6Gs were delivered to the Royal Hellenic Air Force under the MDAP agreement. On the striking off charge of these aircraft, two of them (serial number 49-3424 168-548, 49-3424 and serial number 93500, 168-644, 49-3500) were put on exhibition for a time in the Royal Hellenic Air Force Museum at Tatoi Air Base.

Spain

Spain had first received the Texan with a large consignment of sixty AT-6Ds, which were shipped via US escort carriers to the port of Santander and taken out of their protective cocoons and made ready for operations at the nearby air base between August and October 1954. They were assigned the Spanish serial numbers E.16-1/60, inclusive. They were used in the training role at the Matacana and Villanubla training establishments. The first Spanish Air Force unit to equip with these machines was No. 74 Agrupacion Aerea. Some of this batch were modified for ground attack and liaison duties and equipped No. 3 Cazabombardeo Tactico (Tactical Ground-Attack Squadron or CT).

A second batch, also of sixty aircraft, arrived in 1958. These were the rebuilt T-6Gs and they received the Spanish serials E.16-61/120, inclusive. They were straightforward replacements for the first batch of aircraft at both training schools and No. 3 CT. They saw similar service in the Spanish against guerrilla forces. They served in this role right through the next decade, finally being replaced by Mirage F-1Cs in 1974. The survivors still flew reconnaissance and observation missions, however, for a further two years. In 1976 they were finally withdrawn to Spain and assigned to No. 90 Escuadrillas Grupo based at Getafe. Others served a squadron hacks and the during their last years of service the few that remained were re-classified as CE.6s.

Meanwhile, a third delivery of seventy former US Navy SNJ-4, -5 and -6 aircraft

A Spanish T-6D, E16-120, s/n coded 742 120, 431 (5) No. 39 JHCA. Spanish Air Force Official

Sahara during the war with rebel forces in Spanish Morocco when the Ejercito del Aire threw in the retired AT-6Ds to act in the ground-support role. Many were totally refurbished by the American company Charlotte Aircraft Engineering almost up the equivalent of T-6G standard.

In the case of the COIN configuration, aircraft were taken in hand at the AISA plant at Carabancehl. Here, two wing-mounted Breda 7.7mm machine guns were carried and under-wing racks, which could carry either twelve Oerlikon ATG rockets or ten 221lb (99kg) bombs, were fitted. These aircraft were re-designated as C.6 (Caza) attack aircraft. In 1961 sixteen of these C.6s formed No. 7 Buchones del Ala and flew from Villanubia to Jerez for use

had been received between 1959 and 1963. They were assigned the Spanish serials E.16-21/190 and were used as trainers, and with the famed aerial formation team, at Matacan and other Spanish training bases. A final batch of T-6Gs arrived in Spain from France, where they were surplus to Armée de l'Air requirements. They received the Spanish serials E.16-191/201, inclusive. They were employed with 741 and 742 Escuadrones based at Matacan field before being transferred to San Javier and joining 743 Escuadron, where they lingered on until finally replaced by CASA C-101 trainers.

'The Six' was not yet dead in Spain, not by a long chalk! The Spanish Air Force Aerobatics team Esquadrilla da Fumaca

(Above) **A Spanish T-6, s/n E16-6, coded 29-41, 89-2a IHCA in 1965.** Spanish Air Force Official

(Below) **A Spanish Air Force T-6D, s/n E16-100, 431 (7) 3a IHCA.** Spanish Air Force Official

(Smoke Squadron) used them with considerable flair and *élan* for a number of years giving precision performances. It was not until 31 June 1982 that the last Spanish Air Force T-6 made her farewell flight.

Surplus ex-Ejercito de Aire Harvards, T-6s and SNJs dominated the civilian scene for many years after this as large numbers were sold out, to be re-sold and re-sold down the years. Accidents and old age have taken their toll of these, but a large number can still be seen flying today.

Ex-Spanish Harvards and AT-6s sold out to civilian usage

Type	*EA no.*	*C/n*	*US serial*	*Civil reg.*
AT-6D	C6-12	88-17155	42-17155	N49961
AT-6D	C6-24	121-41580	44-80858	N107FG
AT-6D	C6-27	88-17849	42-86068	N4086T
AT-6D	C6-30	88-17923	42-86142	N4996M
AT-6D	C6-45	88-15143	42-44709	N4292C
AT-6D	C6-60	88-15992	42-84211	N42897
Harvard IIA	C6-166	88-10633	41-33513	N7044J
AT-6D	E16-168	–	–	–
AT-6D	C6-178	88-17478	42-85697	N29947

Two of these aircraft ended their days as museum exhibits: E16-168 was on display at the Museo del Aire, at Cuatro Vientos Air Base in 1988, and C6-178 was displayed at the Cavanaugh Flight Museum at Addison airfield, Dallas, Texas from 1993.

Three of these aircraft became museum exhibits: C6-150 at the Kentucky Aviation Museum, Louisville, Kentucky from 1993; C6-155 at the Museo del Aire, Cuatra Vientos Air Base, Spain; and c/n 121-42070, BuNo 91074 at the Air Combat Museum, Springfield, Illinois from 1990.

Ex-Spanish SNJ-5s sold out to civilian register

C6-130	88-15239	BuNo 52026	N29941
C6-132	121-42104	BuNo 91088	N29930
C6-134	88-16224	BuNo 43942	N3931Z
C6-141	88-15737	BuNo 43756	N350HT
C6-142	88-14705	BuNo 51811	N5FJ
C6-150	88-16056	BuNo 43884	N29937
C6-153	88-15838	41-34588	N39403
C6-155	121-41833	BuNo 90982	–
C6-156	88-13635	BuNo 51368	N29BS
C6-157	88-13581	BuNo 27845	N29910
C6-161	88-15307	BuNo 43642	F-AZDM
C6-162	88-14713	BuNo 51819	N2965S
C6-163	88-16496	BuNo 84825	VH-XAN
C6-171	88-15187	BuNo 51999	N29678
C6-174	88-16210	BuNo 43928	N817NP
C6-176	88-17562	BuNo 90634	N29965
–	88-16784	BuNo 84923	N3931R
–	88-16857	BuNo 84936	N64KP
–	88-17002	BuNo 84991	N29940
–	88-18189	BuNo 90841	N3145J
–	121-42036	BuNo 91040	N1944D
–	121-42047	BuNo 91051	N2686D
–	121-42070	BuNo 91074	N39313

Ex-Spanish T-6Gs sold out to civilian register

EA no.	*C/n*	*US serial*	*Civilian reg.*	*EA no.*	*C/n*	*US serial*	*Civilian reg.*
C6-66	168-336	49-3232	N2449	E16-108	168-470	49-3356	N94SC
C6-67	168-424	49-3320	N4996H	E16-111	168-482	49-3368	N799MU
C6-75	168-461	49-3347	N5449N	E16-114	168-496	49-3382	N5451E
C6-100	168-481	49-3367	N4995C	E16-115	168-525	49-3401	N4995P
C6.167	168-415	49-3311	N3931Y	E16-116	168-571	49-3437	N8084G
C6-170	168-682	49-3269	N61MH	E16-120	168-464	49-3350	N49RR
C6-175	168-189	49-3085	N29935	E16.173	168-319	49-3215	N29938
C6-181	168-349	49-3245	N28955	E16-188	168-160	49-3056	–
C6-182	168-16	49-2912	N299CM	E16-191	182-142	51-14456	F-AZCV
C6-186	168-107	49-3003	N39311	E16-193	168-141	49-3037	F-AXCO
C6-187	168-138	49-3034	N29939	E16-197	168-583	49-3449	N29931
C6-195	168-175	49-3071	N2996Q	E16-198	182-591	51-14904	EC-DUM
E16-69	168-430	49-3326	N100XK	E16-200	197-64	53-4568	N153NA
E16-71	168-456	49-3342	I-TSEI	E16-201	197-20	52-8216	EC-DUN
E16-79	168-440	49-3336	N25KP	–	168-81	49-2977	N29963
E16-82	168-431	49-3327	N2205G	E16-	168-91	49-2987	N2757G
E16-84	168-490	49-3376	N49NA	–	168-142	49-3038	N66TY
E16-85	168-434	49-3330	N5115D	–	168-170	49-3066	N49388
E16-86	168-451	49-3337	N7337	–	168-263	49-3159	N43AW
E16-92	168-466	49-3352	N49939	E16-	168-409	49-3305	N332CA
E16-94	168-472	49-3358	N8301V	–	168-463	49-3368	N6G
E16-95	168-473	49-3359	N5830R	–	168-477	49-3363	N44CT
E16-98	168-479	49-3365	N365TA	–	182-657	51-14970	N25WT
E16-103	168-554	49-3430	N45CT	–	–	49-3829	N27409
E16-106	168-587	49-3453	LX-PAE	–	–	–	N2055G

A Spanish T-6D, C6-187, coded 744 187, 431 (17) 3a IHCA. Spanish Air Force Official

No less than eight former Spanish T-6Gs went to various museums, thus: C6.167 to Weeks Air Museum Tamiami, Florida from 1989; E16-111 to the US Air Force Museum at Wright-Patterson Air Base, Ohio, from 1998; E16-97 and E16.188 to the Museo del Aire, at Cuatro Vienntos Air Base, from 1988; E16-63, E16-110 and E16-114 to the Patrimoine Aeronautique Nationale, at Findel airfield, Luxembourg from 1983; and the former 168-463, 49-3349, to the Combat Air Museum, Topeka, Kansas from 1991.

Turkey

The first consignment of 100 AT-6Cs was received by the Turkish Air Force on 2 August 1948. They were allocated the Turkish Air Force serials 7251/7359, inclusive.

On 7 October 1957, eleven T-6Gs were received as part of a batch assigned under MDAP and these received the Turkish serials 7396/7399 and 7501/7505, consecutively. In 1958 further batches arrived from the States. On 13 January twenty-one T-6Gs were unloaded and assigned Turkish serials 7508/7528, inclusive, while on 5 May the final group of nineteen T-6Gs was received and these aircraft were given the Turkish serials 7529/7547, inclusive.

These aircraft joined a further twenty-four ex-RCAF Harvards as shown in the table below.

Ex-RCAF Harvards transferred to Turkey

2508	2953	2993	3235	3278	3343
2513	2965	3021	3244	3307	3779
2562	2989	3038	3260	3321	3788
2672	2990	3127	3266	3329	3831

For the next quarter of a century these trainers served under the Turkish flag, gradually reducing in numbers until the final one was struck off charge in 1976.

A T-6G, serial 7504, now resides on display at the Turk Hava Muzesi at Ataturk Air Basse, near Istanbul.

Morocco

Morocco was the recipient of fifty T-6s of various Marks, many of them received direct from the USA under MAP or similar schemes and served in the Royal Air Maroc (RAM). A solitary surviving T-6G (serial Y61305, ex L'Armée de l'Air 114720, c/n 182-75, 51-14388) was recovered in 1975 and put into storage in France. Two former Aéronavale machines were utilized as instructional airframes (RAM-1 and RAM-2) at the RAM Engineering School at Anfa air base near Casablanca. Another, Y61501, 168-87, 49-2983, was found on a dump in Tunisia and taken back to France for restoration.

Mozambique

The Peoples Liberation Air Force (PLAF) inherited by various means at least sixteen aircraft, an odd Harvard III and T-6Gs, but mainly ex-Portuguese, ex-German or ex-French, American and Canadian-built Harvard 4s (T-6Js), but were unable to maintain them very well. Most ended their days rotting away at Maputo airport until bought by South African dealers. Some were restored to flying condition in civilian use for a time, and just a few are still currently flying (*see* table below).

Mozambique Harvard 4s survivors list

C/n	*Serial*	*PLAF no.*	*FAP no.*	*Luftwaffe or SAAF*	*Civilian reg.*
88-15069	41-33962	–	7700	SAAF 7530	ZS-WLQ
182-694	51-15007	1681	1681	115007	G-BSBD
CCF4-425	52-8504	1727	1727	AA+638	ZS-WLU
CCF4-442	52-8521	1730	1730	AA+652	G-TVIJ
CCF4-448	52-8527	1731	1731	AA+658	ZS-WLR
CCF4-451	52-8530	1751	1751	AA+660	ZS-WLS
CCF4-483	52-8562	1753	1753	AA+053	G-BSBG
CCF4-498	52-8577	3101	1762	BF+065	–
CCF4-511	52-8590	1736	1736	AA+058	G-BSBF
CCF4-520	52-8599	1754	1754	BF+059	–
CCF4-529	52-8608	1740	1740	BF+064	C-FWBS
CCF4-539	52-4620	1755	1755	AA+637	ZS-WLL
CCF4-543	52-4624	1748	1748	AA+690	ZS-WSE
CCF4-548	53-4629	1741	1741	BF+055	G-HRVD
CCF4-555	53-4636	1788	1788	AA+689	G-BSBB
CCF4-	–	1780	1780		–

Tunisia

The Tunisian Air Force received twelve T-6s by direct inheritance from the L'Armée de l'Air disposals as the French withdrew from their former African colonies in 1963. They saw desultory usage until lack of spares made them redundant.

Congo/Zaire

Twelve Canadian-built Harvard 4s served with the F A Congolaise during the 1960s. At least one of these (AT 845, c/n CCF4-408, serial 51-17226) was seen in a derelict condition at N'dolo airport near Kinshasa as late as October 1993. Two former Belgian aircraft, destined for Katanga, were purchased from the COGEA company in 1961 and there may well have been other 'pre-emptive acquisitions' from Katanganese orders.

Biafra

During their brief struggle for independence from Nigeria, French mercenary pilots flew a few T-6s in combat missions against regular army forces in the period 1967–70. They are said to have been instrumental in the destruction of at least one Nigerian Air Force MiG-17 'Fresco' jet fighter (not in air-to-air combat, but by ground-strafing it must be added!). Twelve T-6Gs have been mentioned, but in fact eight former L'Armée de l'Air machines were purchased in 1967 and never got further than Lisbon docks before were they were impounded, stored at various locations then either scrapped or sold off.

Biafran T-6Gs impounded at Lisbon 1967

C/n	*Serial*	*French serial*	*Last sighting*
182-457	51-14770	114770	Cascais, Portugal
182-481	51-14794	114794	Museo do Air, Sintra AB, Portugal
182-487	51-14800	114800	Cascais, Portugal
182-560	51-14873	114873	Le Ferte-Alais
182-646	51-14959	114959	Cascais, Portugal
182-678	51-14991	114991	Cascais, Portugal
182-733	51-15046	115046	Cascais, Portugal
182-770	51-15083	115082	Cascais, Portugal

Katanga

After the bloody disorder that followed the Belgian withdrawal from the Congo in 1962, the comparatively rich province of Katanga declared independence and attempted to acquire a number of former Belgian and Italian Harvard and T-6Gs to arm themselves. No clear records have survived the civil war that followed, but at least two ex-Belgian aircraft were obtained via the COGEA company in 1963 although these were taken over by the Congolese Air Force. Katanga also purchased twelve former Italian T-6Gs through agents in 1963. Likewise the USA was approached in 1964 for further T-6Gs but these do not appear to have ever been delivered. Further ex-Belgian aircraft were purchased by COGEA in 1961–62 but the bulk of these were taken over by the Congolese, and many have languished in stores and dumps ever since.

An Israeli T-6, s/n 001, banks away from the camera during an air display during the open day at Hatzim Air Force Base in 1999. Simon Watson

Israel

A total of twenty-one T-6s were received from various sources, mainly the USA. Like the earlier Harvards they were equipped for combat duties with two 0.50-calibre machine guns in the wings and underwing racks for up to eight 110lb bombs. Used for liaison duties, they were also utilized in direct combat against Egyptian armoured columns during the 1956 war. They took a lot of damage from ground fire and had to be withdrawn. The survivors carried on as trainers until 1965, when they were struck off charge.

A number survived for a time as exhibits in the IDAF Museum at Hazerim AB, these included IDAF serials 08, 10, 14, 24, 25, 39, 48, 54, 92 and 102. An ex-IDAF Harvard IIB (c/n 14-186, 42-649, FE 452) flew for a time as civilian registration 4X-ARA. A former IDAF AT-6D, 88-17025, 42-85244 with civil registration 4X-ARC was also preserved at the IDAF Museum.

Iran

Following on the 1949 Bellance upgraded T-6Ds, the Shah's Imperial air force further expanded rapidly with the oil revenues. A total of twelve further T-6D trainers were delivered to the Imperial Iranian Air Force between 1950 and 1953. Several former US Air National Guard T-6G-NHs were received in the mid-1950s also under the MDAP programme.

Saudi Arabia

A number of war-surplus AT-6Bs found their way into the inventory of the Royal Saudi Air Force. A solitary survivor (serial 84-7640, 41-17262) remains in the Saudi Air Force Museum Collection at Riyadh, Saudi Arabia.

Yemen

A pair of former Saudi Arabian T-6s were acquired in 1955 by the Imam, who used them as part of the Royal Flight for several years.

Pakistan

Under the SEATO alliance agreement, the Pakistani Air Force received a total of forty-one T-6Gs. A solitary survivor (serial T4200) was an exhibit in the Pakistan Air Force Museum, at Pershawa Air Base from 1979.

India

The Indian Air Force took delivery of thirty-six former RCAF Harvard 4s under a 'free transfer' mutual aid agreement in 1963, to supplement her ailing fleet of ex-RAF Harvards.

***(Above)* A painting of a Royal Saudi Air Force T-6G, s/n C13.** Royal Saudi Air Force

Ex-RCAF Harvard 4s transferred to India 1963

20214	20278	20322	20397
20234	20279	20335	20416
20245	20281	20356	20430
20250	20282	20358	20434
20252	20285	20383	20447
20260	20291	20386	20452
20266	20293	20393	20458
20270	20312	20394	20460
20271	20320	20395	20462

A T-6G of the US Far Eastern Air Force (FEAF) in flight over the Tachikawa Air Base, near Tokyo. FEAF Base Photo Lab, via Tadashi Nozawa

Japan

The very first T-6, of a total supply of 175 T-6 Ds and Gs to carry the Red 'meatball' of the Rising Sun of the re-established Japanese Air-Self Defense Force, was serial number 2861-29. She was handed over at Camp Matushima in the Miyagi Prefecture in 1954 and received the JASDF serial TA-100. The 'US Air Force' tail marking had the forward vertical stroke of the 'U' removed neatly turning it into 'JS Air Force', which the perpetrators thought was near enough! As eleven of these aircraft were subsequently returned to the USAF this may have been a remarkable piece of prediction on someone's part! In 1951 eleven T-6Fs were supplied under MAP. A further twenty-six former USAF Training Command T-6G-NTs were allocated under the MDAP programme code 5T502. Deliveries continued up to 1958 – many to the Japanese Maritime Defence Force (JMDF), and most remained in service for the next eighteen years before being pensioned off.

A number of these have been preserved as open-air displays at various air bases around the country. When the author visited the Gifu AFB in 1999, the serial 52-

Upgrades for the Nationalist Chinese Government. The lines are full again in 1949 as NAA re-work re-purchased T-6Ds with the latest technology for overseas customers. The aircraft in the foreground carries the number AT-60058 on her tail, that at the head of the line on the right, AT-60184. Rockwell International

0100 (a T-6G) was in a row of such machines, but they had all badly weathered and looked neglected.

Preserved Japanese T-6s

Type	*JMDF no.*	*Location*
SNJ-5	6192	Kuushu Gakuin University
T-6G	52-0018	Kyushu Gakuin University
T-6G	52-0002	Ashiya AB.
T-6G	52-0011	Shizuhama AB
ABT-6G	52-0022	Iruma
T-6G	52-0074	Hamamatsu AB
T-6G	52-0075	Nara-shi Officers School
T-6G	52-0080	Matsushima AB
T-6G	52-0082	Komatsu AB
T-6G	52-0099	Tokorozawa Aviation Museum,Tokyo
T-6G	52-0100	Gifu AB
T-6G	52-0128	Kumagaya AF Technical School
T-6G	72-0132	Seki-Shi (Naka Nihon Koku Senmon Gakko College)
T-6G	72-0178	Nyutaburu AB

A few others survived and were sold off to civilian use for some years, including: an SNJ-4 (88-11104, BuNo 26690) as civilian N89015; an SNJ-5 (88-17551, BuNo 90623) as N89013; SNJ-5 serial 6205 (88-18286, Bu 90868) as N9013A; SNJ-5 serial 6193 (121-41633, BuNo 90917) as N1038A; SNJ-5 serial 6210 (121-41642, BuNo 90926) as N2266W; a T-6G (182-600, 51-14913) as N257DB; an SNJ-5 (88-16676, BuNo 84865) as N89014, which is now with the Confederate Air Force.

China (Taiwan)

In 1951 the Nationalist Chinese Government, exiled to the island of Taiwan (Formosa), obtained a total of twelve T-6s (by various private agents in the States), which were used exclusively for training purposes. These supplemented the twenty AT-6Ds received under lend-lease during the war.

Indonesia

Using the second-hand disposal market, and buying through various trading agencies, the Indonesian Air Force 'acquired' fifteen T-6s of various Marks in the years 1951–55. These supplemented the ex-Dutch Harvards they had 'inherited' with independence in 1950.

Laos

Eight T-6s were supplied to the Laotian Air Force under MAP. Thanks to the chaotic conditions prevailing at the time, they saw little direct action but combat patrols were flown against the Communist Pathet Lao guerrilla forces from time to time and against the Viet-Cong supply lines, where they cut through Laotian territory during the Vietnam war.

Thailand

A large number of T-6s served with the Royal Thai Air Force (RTAF), no less than seventy-four being received directly from the United States under SEATO auspices between 1948 and 1957. Thirty of these were T-6Fs, which were delivered under MAP in June 1951. Many were adapted as ground-attack aircraft, being

Display Royal Thai Air Force T-6F, 121-42518, 44-881796, at Bien Hoa Air Museum, Bangkok. Royal Thai Air Force

Surviving Royal Thai Air Force aircraft

Type	*Thai serial*	*C/n*	*US serial*	*Civilian reg.*
T-6G	185	182-17	51-14330	CATC Bangkok
T-6G	–	182-241	51-14554	RTAF Museum
T-6G	–	182-244	51-14557	RTAF Museum
T-6G	51-14630	182-317	51-14630	'Tango One' Team
T-6G	51-14647	182-334	51-14647	'Tango One' Team
T-6G	51-14662	182-349	51-14662	'Tango One' Team
T-6G	51-14666	182-353	51-14666	RTAF Museum

(Below) **A T-6G of the Royal Thai Air Force, serial 4314, with Cobra motif on her fuselage.** Royal Thai Air Force

(Bottom) **The air force of the Philippines was also a beneficiary of the re-worked T-6D, receiving a large batch re-built by TEMCO in the early 1950s. This is the former 42-10162 carrying Philippine Air Force markings and serials.** Ray C. Sturtivent

easy to fly, and they saw considerable service with Nos 1, 2, 3, 4, 5, 6 and 7 Wings RTAF. Three Attack Groups were formed from these units. Those used for training served with the RTAF training school based at Don Muang, near Bangkok, and they stayed in service until as late as 1978.

An AT-6F (121-42518, 44-881796) is preserved at the Royal Thai Air Force Museum, Don Muang and three T-6Gs also survive as exhibits there, while another three are allocated to the famous 'Tango One' Thai AF display team. A seventh machine was at the Civil Aviation Training Centre, Bangkok.

Philippines

The TEMCO upgrades of 1950–51 were joined later by eight T-6Gs, which were sent to the Philippines Air Force who used them in their training configuration for a number of years. These were all supplied by the USA under MAP arrangements, which had promised a total of twenty-five aircraft. One of these aircraft (serial 150162/662), survives today as an exhibit in the Philippine Air Force Museum, at Villamor Air Base, near Manila.

South Vietnam

After the former French colony of Indo-China was split up, following the French withdrawal, Vietnam was further subdivided between the communist north and the democratic south. As help against continual aggression and intrusion from Hanoi, in what was to escalate into the Vietnam War, the Saigon Government appealed for help from the United States. Between 1954 and 1956, under MAP, a total of fifty-five T-6s were acquired from the States to serve as advance trainers. The Vietnamese Air Force (VNAF) had inherited the former French Air Instruction Centre at Nha Trang Air Base on 7 July 1955. The first T-6Gs, painted overall bright yellow, flew in there soon after and the 912th, 918th and 920th Air Training Squadrons operated there until training was switched to the USA.

South Korea

Like Vietnam, but earlier, the former Japanese dependency of Korea had been split between the communist north and the southern Republic of Korea (ROK) in the immediate aftermath of World War II. The resulting war and stalemate that followed the invasion by the North saw the establishment of the ROK's own Air Force and a consignment of thirty T-6D and T-6G trainers was sent by the United States from 1953 onward. They also received seven T-6Fs under MAP in 1956. A T-6G (serial number 117354, 51-17354), was preserved at the Korean War Museum in Seoul at the end of their life in 1974, while a T-6D (88-15997, 42-84216) ended up at the US Air Force Museum, Wright-Patterson Air Base, Ohio, in 1994.

Argentina

Some former US Navy SNJ5s and SNJ-5Cs saw service with the Argentine Navy (Armada) under the Rio agreement. One of these (serial number 0462, 88-17660, BuNo 90662) was later placed in the Museo de la Aviacion Naval Argentina, at Espora NAS, Bahia Blanca.

Brazil

A mixed-bag of 100 machines was received under the 1947 MDAP auspices. These T-6D upgrades were given blanket Forca Aerea Brasileira (FAB) serials in the ranges 1397/1435, inclusive, and 1447/1506, inclusive, and joined their surviving lend-lease sisters. Subsequent deliveries of SNJ-4s, SNJ-5Cs and SNJ-6s for the Brazilian Navy and -Ds and -Gs for the FAB, incorporated FAB serials in the 1600/1700 range. Many were upgraded to give them COIN capability and served as such for a long period. Some also went to the Brazilian Navy (Brasileira Armada).

As recounted, those subsequently locally upgraded to T-6s were used in the COIN role earlier and these were supplemented by T-6Gs, which also served in the liaison and observation Esquadrilla of the Forca Aerea Brasilia. An outstanding user of the T-6 was the Esquadrilla de Fumaca (Smoke-trailing Squadron) of the FAB, which employed them in their display team from 1956 until their replacement by T-24 jet trainers on 7 February 1963. They were painted in striking colours: brilliant white with red wing tips, black underbellies and a horizontal red light flash down either side of the fuselage.

A few FAB 'Sixes' survived to fly for a while as civilian machines and others have been preserved on display (*see* table below).

Serial 88-9360 and seven others were converted to crop-spraying aircraft; the latter flew as, PT-KSW, PT-KSY, PT-KSZ, PT-KTB, PT-KBF, PT-KTG and PT-KZY.

At least one aircraft, an AT-6D, FAB1633, was transferred to Paraguay. There are ten in museums: AT-6Ds, 88-14780, 88-18266, 42-86485, 121-4227, 44-81564, and two others, were later preserved at the Museu Aerospacial, Campo dos Afonsos, Rio de Janeiro; while two further AT-6Ds are on display at the Museu de Armas e Vellculos Motorizados Antigos, Bebeduroro; and one is displayed at the Museo Aeronáutico da Fundascau, Sao Paulo.

Ex-Brazilian civilian registered and preserved aircraft

Type	*FAB serial*	*C/n*	*US serial*	*Civil reg.*
AT-6D	FAB 1264	88-12472	42-4224	N310JH
SNJ-4	FAB 1406	88-9589	BuNo 10030	PT-KVD
AT-6A	FAB 1497	78-7233	41-16855	PT-KSZ
AT-6A	FAB 1506	78-7005	41-16627	PT-KVG
SNJ-6	FAB 1631	121-42356	44-81634	N390TB
AT-6D	FAB 1639	121-41757	44-81035	–
T-6G	FAB 1658	168-306	49-3202	–
T-6G	FAB 1672	168-494	49-3380	N40280
SNJ-5C	FAB 1703	88-15370	BuNo 43669	PT-KRD
SNJ-5C	FAB 1704	88-15385	BuNo 43684	–
SNJ-5C	FAB 1706	88-17199	BuNo 85038	–
SNJ-6	FAB 1712	121-43045	BuNo 112187	PY-KVE
AT-6D	–	88-14780	42-44586	N205SB
SNJ-4	–	88-9360	BuNo 09845	PT-KTH

Bolivia

As well as some AT-6Fs, several former US Air National Guard T-6G-NHs were received in the mid-1950s under the MDAP programme. The Fuerza Aerea Boliviano sold off one AT-6F (serial FAB 366, 121-43104, 44-82382) in 1990 to the civilian register and she flew for a time as N6617X. She also sold a T-6G (serial FAB 369, 168-448, 50-1284) to the civil register, where it flew as N1284.

Chile

By way of privately re-manufactured aircraft, the Fuerza Aerea Nacional de Chile obtained twenty-seven T-6Ds in the first months of 1950. Also, under the terms of MAP programmes ten T-6Gs were supplied to the Chilean Government by 30 June 1957. This number was supplemented by the purchase of an additional thirteen aircraft by September of the same year. At the end of their useful lives the survivors were sold off or scrapped, but two were preserved: an AT-6G (serial 285) in the Museo Aeronautico, Los Cerillos Air Base; and one (serial 264) as a gate guard at Los Condores Air Base.

Colombia

Colombia received a batch of former US Navy SNJ-5s, which they used for many years until the mid-1970s. One of these

The Chilean Fuerza Aerea Nacional de Chile operated both T-6Ds and T-6Gs post-war from various sources. Serial 239 was one. National Archives, Washington DC

(serial number 777, 88-16469, BuNo 44020) was sold out to the civil register and flew for a time as HK-2049P.

Cuba

The Bastista regime appealed for help in fighting the communist guerrilla forces under Fidel Castro. Great Britain refused to help but under MAP some brand-new AT-6Fs, and at least two T-6Gs, reached them before the overthrow of the Government in 1959.

Dominica

The very last batch of T-6Gs to be distributed overseas under the MAP agreement consisted of twenty-six aircraft assigned to the Cuerpo de Aviacion Dominicana to replace her aged lend-lease fleet.

Ecuador

In 1955 the United States supplied the Government of Ecuador with seven T-6Ds, and a further seven T-6Gs followed during the years up to 1957.

Haiti

A T-6G of the Fuerza Aera D'Haiti, obtained originally in March 1957 and which had served until 1982 (serial number 3209, 168-313, 49-3209), later flew as civilian registered G-DDMV; and an SNJ-5 (serial number 86099, 88-17880, BuNo 90732) flew for a while as N22410.

Honduras

In readiness for further deliveries under MDAP, Honduran pilots were sent to train on the T-6G-NA at the USAF training facility at Hondo, Texas. On completion of this, a single aircraft from this small batch of seven was handed over to return home to continue the work at the end of 1955.

In March 1956, Honduras received six former USAF Training Command T-6G-NTs under MDAP programme code 6T430. Several former US Air National Guard T-6G-NHs were received in the mid-1950s, also under the MDAP programme.

It is also thought that twelve T-6Gs were received by Honduras under the Rio agreement, and they were given serials 201/212, inclusive. One former Fuerza Aerea Hondurena with the FAH serial number 211 (168-102, 49-2998) was sold out to the civil register in December 1982 and flew for many years as N128WK. Another, serial number FAH 208 (182-603, 51-14916), was sold to the civil register and flew for a time as N27817. There were also at least two SNJ-4s, one of which (serial number 202, 88-12827, BuNo 27491) later flew as civilian N127VF in US Marine Corps colours, from 1984 onward.

Guatemala

In the same manner as Honduras under MDAP, Guatemalan pilots were sent to train on the T-6G-NA at the USAF training facility at Hondo, Texas. Again, of these a single aircraft was handed over to return home to continue the work at the end of 1955.

In November 1955, the Cuerpo de Aeronáutico Militar Guatemalteca received a consignment of twelve former USAF Training Command T-6G-NTs under the MDAP program 6T261. Several former US Air National Guard T-6G-NHs were received in the mid-1950s, also under the MDAP programme.

Mexico

The Fuerza Aerea Mexicana received a consignment of twenty 're-manufactured'

A large number of T-6s of various marks found their way to Mexico and served with the Fuerza Aerea Mexicana through direct purchase orders, via agents, lend-lease and MAP. Here is a line up of AT-6Ds at the Military Aviation School, Base No. 5, at Zapapan, Jalisco near Guadalajara. Santiago Flores Ruiz

T-6Ds as early as 1950 to bolster her lend-lease trainers. Many were flown at the Military Aviation School established at FAM base No. 5 at Zapapan, Jalisco near Guadalajara.

Nicaragua

Like Honduras and Guatemala, under the terms of the MDAP Nicaraguan pilots were sent to train on the T-6G-NA at Hondo, Texas. Similarly, a single aircraft was handed over in 1955 for continuation of local training.

In November 1955, the Fuerza Aerea de la Guardia Nacional de Nicaragaua received an allocation of thirteen former USAF Training Command T-6G-NTs under the MDAP program 6T175. Several former US Air National Guard T-6G-NHs were received in the mid-1950s also under the MDAP programme.

Paraguay

Seldom mentioned in reference books on 'The Six' is the fact is that, post-war, Paraguay equipped her Fuerza Aerea Nacional del Paraguay with quite a number of such aircraft to supplement the thirty-four lend-lease aircraft she had received earlier. Some were directly supplied under the Rio Pact from the United States, while others were obtained from surplus Harvard IIAs from SAAF (which they listed as T-6s) and ex-RCAF stocks. Some came from discards by other nations like Brazil. The Paraguay Navy (in a totally land-locked country) is also credited with receiving some former Flygvapnet SNJ-4s the same way. They include the aircraft listed in the table (*right*), some of which were sold out and later served in the civilian register for a while.

Uruguay

In 1955 ten T-6D/SNJ-5s were received by the Uruguay Government. A total of ten T-6Gs were subsequently delivered in 1957, all under Mutual Aid Programmes. A single Fuerza Aerea Uruguaya SNJ-5 (88-16466, BuNo 44104) was sold out to the civil register, and had a number of owners, flying for a time as N3642F.

Venezuela

A batch of twenty 're-manufactured' T-6Ds were received from the United States in the summer of 1949 to supplement their lend-lease allocations. The following FA Venezolana aircraft were preserved in museums: a T-6 at Maracay; another (serial 2506) was on display at Sucre Air Base; an AT-6A (76-6445, 41-16107) was on exhibit at the Museo Aeronautico, Maracay Air Base; also an ex-L'Armée de l'Air, ex-RCAF Harvard II (81-4128, ex-BW 203).

NA-198

Yet a further order for what would have become the SNJ-8 was placed by the US Navy on 3 July 1952. Having given up on their upgrading of the SNJ-4, -5 and -6 to T-6G standards, they decided to build from new to meet the new specification.

SNJ-8

NAA manufacturing numbers were allotted to 240 aircraft in the range 198-1/240, inclusive, and the US Navy's Bureau of Ordnance allocated BuNos 137247/137485, inclusive, but with the stalemate situation in Korea and reduced demand, the whole order was cancelled and there never was an SNJ-8.

FT-6G

As part of the NA-168 charge allocation at the North American Aviation plant, Downey, California, one aircraft was converted as a specific fighter trainer and designated as the FT-6G. This was an attempt to produce a counter-insurgency (COIN) aircraft on the cheap and featured underwing gun pods mounting 0.30-calibre machine guns, rocket launchers and bomb racks. Provision was made to carry a 50 US-gallon external fuel tank under the fuselage centreline, and this could be substituted for a napalm tank for combat operations.

LT-6G

The lone FT-6G was followed by a further fifty-eight machines, which had the dual

Ex-Paraguay Air Force survivors

Type	*FAP no.*	*Ex-serial*	*C/n*	*US serial*	*Civilian reg.*
AT-6D	0101	FAB1633	88-17125	42-85344	N3173L
Harvard IIA	0102	SAAF7040	88-10542	–	N3171A
AT-6A	0103	–	78-7095	41-16717	N61167
Harvard IIA	0104	SAAF7083	88-10585	–	Restoring
Harvard IIA	0106	–	78-7094	41-16716	VH-WWA
T-6	0107	SAAF	–	–	VH-YPY
T-6	0108	SAAF	–	–	VH-TOA
Harvard IIA	0109	SAAF7500		–	VH-DGP
SNJ-4	0111	–	88-9352	BuNo 09837	N3172N
Harvard IIA	0116	SAAF7320	88-12353	–	N3171P
Harvard IIA	0119	SAAF7229	88-10675	–	N3171R
Harvard IIA	0123	SAAF7324		–	N3172H
Harvard IIA	0124	SAAF7699	–	–	Restoring
T-6	0143	–	–	–	N3172J
T-6	0147	–	–	–	N3172M
T-6G	–	SAAF7694	–	–	N522LU
T-6G	–	SAAF7695	–	–	N98FP
T-6G	–	SAAF7690	–	–	N97FP
AT-6G	–	–	–	–	N725SD
AT-6G	–	–	–	–	N826G
AT-6G	–	–	–	–	N836G
AT-6G	–	–	–	–	N7721Z
AT-6G	–	–	–	–	N26YP
AT-6G	–	–	–	–	N26WR
SNJ-3	–	BuNo unknown	–	–	N625JT

roles of liaison/trainer T-6Gs. These were given the 'L' prefix to denote their role and were, in fact, dedicated forward air control (FAC) aircraft. They received the NAA charge numbers 168-692/750, inclusive, and were allotted fresh USAF serial numbers in the range 49-3538/3596, inclusive.

Born out of the inability of the few Stinson L-5s spotter planes to adequately perform this job, they were converted to carry the extra and specialized equipment to enable them not only to spot enemy troop movements and dispositions, but to ground mark them with smoke rockets, so that the fighter-bombers they called up could strike their targets quickly and accurately. Their radio equipment was designed for both air-to-ground and air-to-air contact in order to home friendly forces, be they ground attack planes or artillery, immediately on to their targets.

Modification from the T-6G format included equipping them with the AN/ARC-3, the AN/ARN-6 and the SCR-522A radios giving them unrivalled (for their day) coverage and reach. Six racks for triple rocket-launchers were carried, three under each outer wing panel, and two 0.30-calibre machine guns were pod mounted, one under either wing. These could be removed to increase speed over the ground, which became a factor in subsequent employment.

They were issued to the USAF Training Command but most soon found themselves transferred to Korea from 1950 onward. Vastly outnumbering the UN forces on the ground, the North Korean and Red Chinese armies could mass huge numbers of troops and launch them in human waves, thus overwhelming UN defensive positions. The arrival of the LT-6G redressed the balance by giving prior warning of such concentrations. Their story is fully recorded in the following chapter.

As late as 1989, there were four surviving 'Sixes' from the USAF Korean war era still surviving: two T-6Ds (42-84216 and 42-86163) and two T-6Fs (44-82527 and 44-82536).

Many of those LT-6G-NAs that either survived Korea or were made surplus from the USAF, also ended up abroad. In other cases foreign governments had assigned T-6Gs similarly converted to meet their own COIN requirements. These included the following.

Iran

Under the pro-Western rule of the last Shah, the Imperial Iranian Air Force took delivery of forty-four COIN-configured T-6Gs (plus four RLT-6Gs, whose special designation prefix is unclear – reconnaissance, maybe?). They were employed in combat against Kurdish insurgent forces, and after the Ayatollah's revolution, gradually fell into disrepair and decay.

Turkey

Under the NATO Mutual Air Programme, sixteen former LT-6Gs were received by the Turkish Air Force on 7 September 1957. They were given the new serials 7277/7292, inclusive. On 7 October of the same year a second consignment arrived that consisted of three further LT-G6Gs, which were given the serials 7393/7395, inclusive.

Cambodia

Under United States Government allocations in 1959, the Cambodian Government took delivery of twelve LT-6G ground-attack aircraft, but such was the shambles in that country that they saw little useful employment against the Khmer Rouge guerrillas, who ultimately overthrew the government and massacred a large part of the populace.

A unique aircraft in more than one respect. This is the only T-6 floatplane, and was the Republic of Korea's (ROK) first military floatplane as well. She was a T-6F of the 6147th which crashed at Kwangji in December 1950, after running out of fuel in bad weather conditions (*see* story). She was salvaged at Chinhae and the centre float from a World War II Japanese Nakajima A6M2-N, Navy Type 2 Fighter Seaplane ('Rufe') was incorporated along with wing floats made from F-80 Shooting Star wing-tip fuel tanks. The ROK designated her as the KN-1 and she flew for several months before again crashing and being finally written off. National Archives, Washington DC

South Korea (ROK)

Following the work of the USAF Mosquitoes, it was natural that the Republic of Korea should seek to avail herself of similar aircraft for her own air force. Two dozen LT-6Gs were supplied by the United States Government up to the end of 1958.

There was also a unique machine, an abandoned USAF AT-6F, which was salvaged in 1950 from its crash site at Kwangji. In an experiment, the ROK fitted this aircraft with F-80 wing-tip fuel tanks, as substitute outboard floats, and a single centreline float, and she became the only amphibious 'Six' ever to see the light of day (although NAA had original scouted this configuration as one of their alternatives during the 1930s, but it was never taken up). As the NA-16/T-6 floatplane, this aircraft flew for a short period from August 1951 onward before again being written off and scrapped.

France

By far the most intensive user of T-6Gs modified to the ground-attack role was

L'Armée de l'Air, specifically in the long-drawn out operations against guerrillas in Algeria. To deal with the growing insurgency in that vast territory, it was decided in 1956 to establish a special Ground Support Light Aviation Command. Initially they were to be equipped with available aircraft drawn from existing training aircraft suitably converted for this role. Types thus considered were home-produced like the Morane 733 Alcyon, the Sipa 12 and the Sipa 21, as well as the existing stocks of T-6Ds with the training schools in Morocco. From April of that year many T-6Ds were hastily modified and sent to Algeria, where they quickly proved more durable and suitable for this work than the French-built trainers. The French decided to concentrate on the T-6D only.[4]

The requirements for the combat usage of the T-6D fell into two broad requirements:

- close co-operation between air and ground forces;
- observation and reconnaissance being coupled with the ability to quickly call up tactical aircraft and ground-attack aircraft to deal with highly mobile and elusive enemy forces with the minimum of delay.

In January 1956, No. 330 Light Aviation Crew Instruction Centre had been set up at Aulnat. The mission of this unit was to train teams for the air-policing of Algeria. On transfer to Reghala, near Algiers itself, jet-experienced pilots were trained in flying prop-driven aircraft with navigator/observers for the newly established Escadrille d'Aviation Legere d'Appui (EALA, Ground Support Light Squadrons). Between 1951 and 1953, eleven Ordinary Reserve Training Centres were formed in all the Air Regions of France as a reserve of ground-attack trained personnel that could be called upon in the event of such a subversive war as was now under way in Algeria. Both air and ground personnel were trained up in the flying and maintenance of T-6s. In 1956 these units were re-designated as Escadrilles de Reserve d'Aviation Legere d' Appui (ERALA, Tactical Light Aviation Reserve Squadrons). This ensured a continuous flow of correctly trained personnel to the forward operational squadrons. Their mission statement included bombing, strafing, rocket-firing sorties, in addition to observation and photo-reconnaissance duties.

Ex-RCAF Harvards transferred to France

AH 191	AJ 831	2685	2897	3169
AJ 561	AJ 897	2740	2932	3171
AJ 584	AJ 918	2748	2977	3240
AJ 650	AJ 937	2752	3002	3241
AJ 654	AJ 950	2761	3074	3256
AJ 662	BW 199	2784	3075	3804
AJ 724	BW 203	2785	3095	3814
AJ 753	2518	2808	3101	3815
AJ 790	2587	2817	3129	3820
AJ 801	2589	2820	3139	3826
AJ 827	2593	2890		

The French found two main handicaps in so employing their T-6Ds. First, these selfsame aircraft were in high demand in their original role as trainers and so only limited numbers could be released – these proved quite inadequate as the crisis worsened. Second, the T-6D was not really the right aircraft for the COIN role, for the maximum armament that could be carried, one 7.62mm calibre machine gun and two light bomb racks under the wings, was insufficient fire power to deal with increasingly sophisticated and well-armed opposition.

Fortuitously, the French need for a more suitable aircraft coincided with the availability of the upgraded T-6G, which was being offered for sale in the USA. At least two consignments (of twenty-four and twenty-nine aircraft, respectively) of these were T-6G-NFs. There were also fifty-one Canadian-built Harvard 4s. No time was lost, and in March 1956 the first French order was placed for 150 T-6Gs at the bargain unit price of US$2,000. These 150 aircraft were sealed against the elements and transhipped across the North Atlantic aboard US Navy escort carriers disembarking at the port of Bordeaux. This first order was followed by a second batch of 150 more, and then more, until, by the end of 1958, the French had imported a total of 693 T-6Gs. The French were no less impressed by the snarling noise their new charges emitted and christened them 'Tomcats' because of it.

On arrival in France the procedure was for the T-6Gs to be taken in hand for considerable modification to fit them for their new duties. These changes were:

- removing the single nose-mounted machine-gun and improving fire-power by the provision of gun pods and light bomb racks under each wing; two alternative armament configurations were used:
- two 7.5 mm MAC machine guns in pods under wings;
- four bomb racks for 110lb (50kg) bombs;
- four 68mm SNEB rockets and six T-10 rockets;
- four 7.5mm MAC machine guns in pods under wings;
- two racks for 110lb (50kg) bombs;
- four 68mm SNEB rockets and six T-10 rockets;
- new radio equipment was fitted for ground-air communication and intercom work;
- armour was placed around the sides and the floor of both cockpits;

Also, in the summer of 1958 the all-yellow colour paint and colourful EALA artwork was stripped off and they reappeared in an all-aluminium finish with a black anti-glare panel along the nose in front of the pilot. Some later had span-wise yellow panels repainted on the upper surfaces only, where they were not visible for targeting from the ground, but they *were* visible to searching rescue aircraft from the air when a Tomcat was unfortunate to come down in the trackless desert.

Essential as all these changes were, the overall increase in the aircraft's laden weight decreased performance and, despite the 600hp of the Pratt and Whitney R-1340 Wasp, 'The Six' was never a racehorse! It also made flying more delicate. Maximum speed before conversion was 204mph (326km/h) with a range of 808 miles (1,292km); with the T-6Gs extra fuel tank that brought capacity up to 140 US gallons.

Nonetheless in the early days these conversions were put to widespread use in Algeria, where the Armée de l'Air worked under the command of the 5th Air Region, which covered the whole of French North Africa (Morocco, Algeria and Tunisia). Algeria itself was split into three regions, with a Ground Support Light Aircraft Group (GALAG) assigned to each one, (GALAG-1, western; GALAG-2, central; and GALAG-3, eastern).

During the period of their maximum employment, between 1955 and 1962, no less than thirty EALA Escadrille of T-6Gs had been formed, the bulk of which were working over these zones. During this time the EALA ran up some impressive mission sorties and other statistics. A total of 742,530h flying was clocked up, 75 per cent of which was operational. The operational missions soared from less than 1,000 in January 1956, to in excess of 10,000 by March 1957. During 1958 the T-G combat sorties mounted by the first twenty-six EALAs set-up, conducted 106,512 missions during the first 10 months of operations and racked up 115, 000h flying. They worked out of 2,600ft (800m) long desert air strips, some seventy-two of which were established at strategic points around the country, so the 'Tomcats' were also able to respond to calls from the army within a short timeframe.

The enemy was by no means impotent and, as the Americans had discovered in Korea and were later to find in Vietnam, Eastern-bloc armaments of increasing sophistication steadily reached them, so the low flying and vulnerable T-6Gs were frequently hit and often lost. In total, 255 French aircrew were lost in these missions.

Increasingly the French looked for a more powerful aircraft to carry out the Tomcat's role, and this was found in another North American Aviation product, the T-28 Trojan, also being phased out of USAF training service. Known to the French as the Fennec (French equivalent of the British 'Desert Rat'), these types began to take on more of the combat roles in later years, although they never totally replaced the T-6G. In 1959, with the arrival of sufficient T-28 conversions, the fourteen operating Escadrilles were paired into seven Escadrons. Of these seven larger groupings, four were equipped with the T-28, while the remaining three retained the Tomcat. Composition of a T-6G Escadrille had been twelve operational aircraft plus one reserve aircraft. In all, ten of the original twenty-four squadrons operational in Algiers remained on combat operations until the end of the conflict in 1962.

No further French use was envisaged for these very specialized aircraft as the French withdrew from all their colonial possessions in North Africa, and the bulk went into storage and were later either sold or scrapped. They still attracted the attention of some air forces, however, and, as we have seen, in 1965 they appeared again flying for Portugal, India, Spain and (ironically enough) Morocco and Tunisia. The national carrier, Air France, purchased twelve of them for pilot training. A few more were broken up for spares, which were crated and shipped back to the United States. A few re-appeared by devious routes in the skies over both Biafra and the Congo during their bitter little wars in the 1960s. Many, many more found their way into civilian use world-wide, and from the list in the table below, many are still flying today.

A number of former French T-6Gs ended up in museums as follows: a L'Armée de l'Air T-6G (serial number 01289) went to the Yugoslavian National Aviation Museum at Belgrade Airport in 1990 and was put on display as 'TT-152'; another (serial number 93432) went to the Associatione des Amateurs d'Aeronefs de Collection at Les Ailes de France, Luneville, in 1990; and two (serial number 114351 and serial number 114522) went to the Musée de l'Air et Espace, Le Bourget airfield, Paris in 1990.

Ex-French T-6Gs sold out to civilian service

Ex-French no.	*C/n*	*US serial*	*Civilian reg.*	*Ex-French no.*	*C/n*	*US serial*	*Civilian reg.*	*Ex-French no.*	*C/n*	*US serial*	*Civilian reg.*
092901	168-5	49-2901	–	114707	182-394	51-14707	–	114959	182-646	51-14959	Biafra
093432	168-556	49-3432	F-AZGS	114718	182-405	51-14718	–	114979	182-666	51-14979	–
011289	168-503	50-1289	–	114720	182-407	51-14720	Morocco	114991	182-678	51-14991	Biafra
114314	182-1	51-14314	F-BOEN	114726	182-413	51-14726	N92761	115007	182-694	51-15007	G-BSBD
114333	182-20	51-14333	N5599L	114734	182-421	51-14734	N9705N	115017	182-704	51-15017	–
114342	182-29	51-14342	N4434M	114740	182-427	51-14740	–	115033	182-720	51-15033	–
114343	182-30	51-14343	N8048E	114761	182-448	51-14761	N9739T	115042	182-729	51-15042	Portugal
114351	182-38	51-14351	–	114770	182-457	51-14770	–	115046	182-733	51-150-46	Biafra
114367	182-54	51-14367	F-AZHD	114790	182-477	51-14790	–	115048	182-735	51-15048	Portugal
114374	182-61	51-14374	–	114791	182-478	51-14791	N8044H	115049	182-736	51-15049	F-AZAS
114387	182-74	51-14387	F-AZEF	114794	182-481	51-14794	Biafra	115060	182-747	51-15060	–
114388	182-75	51-14388	–	114799	182-486	51-14799	N92778	115063	182-750	51-15063	N8048J
114391	182-78	51-14392	–	114800	182-487	51-14799	Biafra	115082	182-769	51-15082	–
114394	182-81	51-14394	N394NA	114794	182-481	51-14794	Biafra	115082	182-770	51-15083	Biafra
114401	182-88	51-14401	–	114799	182-486	51-14799	N92778	115102	182-789	51-15102	–
114429	182-116	51-14429	N896WW	114811	182-498	51-14811	–	115113	182-800	51-15113	F-AZAU
114522	182-209	51-14522	–	114827	182-514	51-14827	N92796	28216	197-20	52-8216	EC-DUN
114526	182-213	51-14526	G-BRWB	114839	182-526	51-14839	–	28231	197-35	52-8231	–
114594	182-281	51-14594	–	114842	182-529	51-14842	N8FU	34572	197-68	53-4572	–
114668	182-355	51-14668	–	114848	182-535	51-14848	F-AZBQ	34579	197-75	53-4579	–
114674	182-361	51-14674	F-AZEZ	114849	182-536	51-14849	N9701Z	34592	197-88	53-4592	G-BTKI
114684	182-371	51-14684	–	114871	182-558	51-14871	–	34593	197-89	53-4593	–
114688	182-375	51-14688	–	114873	182-560	51-14873	Biafra	34594	197-90	53-4594	–
114694	182-381	51-14694	N7865	114898	182-585	51-14898	F-AZIB	34601	197-97	53-4601	Portugal
114696	182-383	51-14696	F-BMJO	114904	182-591	51-14904	EC-DUM	34610	197-106	53-4610	Portugal
114700	182-387	51-14700	–	114915	182-602	51-14915	–	34611	197-107	53-4611	–

CHAPTER TWELVE

The Mosquitoes Bite

Korea

Mosquitoes, with red upper wing panels and some with red tails, sit at their Korea base in April 1951. A rescue C-47 sits in the background. The Mosquito Association Inc

The story of the Mosquitoes in Korea is an incredible one but one that remains largely untold and unknown, as with so much of that conflict. It is also the story of the 6147th TAC Control Group in the main, although, of course, there were many other Sixes in Korean skies outside this group. The totally unprovoked invasion of South Korea by the Communist North on 25 June 1950 initially looked like succeeding, with the ROK forces and their few allied helpers penned in to a small area around Pusan on the south-eastern tip of the peninsular. Fortunately, due to the absence of the Soviet Union delegate, who was thus unable to veto it, the United Nations stood firm against aggression and allied forces were rushed to the area. Among them were a few individuals with no clear mission orders other than to find out where the enemy advance was next coming.

On July 9 1950, two young pilots, First Lieutenants James A. Bryant and Frank G. Mitchell flew two L-5 spotter aircraft to 'a loose gravel runway about the width of a country road and not much else', that was dignified by the title Taejon Airstrip (K-5). First Lieutenant Harold E. Morris greeted them at this desolate spot, already threatened by the communist advance and, within a few more days, the first commander of the 6147th, Major Merrill H. Carlton, arrived along with Captain John D. Lytle. Meanwhile First Lieutenants L. E. Trout and B. G. Turner each flew a T-6 from Japan to Taejon and the unit was established.[1]

The need to make better use of the allied air force's tactical aircraft was paramount. Two major problems presented themselves in this early period. First, lack of information for the fighter-bomber pilots concerning friendly and enemy troop dispositions. The Tactical Air Control Parties (TACP) on the ground had restricted capabilities due to the length of the lines of communications and the inadequacy of facilitates, and consequently could not be kept fully informed. In addition, lengthy delays in organizing the strikes resulted in reduced or totally ineffective results. Second, was the need to maximize the use of every available aircraft during this period of bad weather conditions. Fuel was wasted idling or looking for targets in the crud, and missions had to be aborted because of this, or were so brief that they were useless.

Lieutenant Colonel Stanley P. Latiolais, A-3 Operations, 5th Air Force, therefore made the suggestion, with the approval of Major General Earl E. Partridge, CO, Fifth Air Force, that the T-6 be used as an eye-in-the-sky over the immediate points of contact and in the rear areas to establish tactical reconnaissance and tactical control with friendly air forces. A single T-6 was despatched to Lieutenant Colonel John McGinney, the Air Liaison Officer with the US 8th Army, but he was unable to use her in actual air operations. With the establishment on 6 July of the JOC Operations Section at Taejon the impetus was begun. Initial strength requested was just one Operations Officer and five pilots!

Two of the pilots, Bryant and Mitchell, with call-signs 'Angelo Fox' and 'Angelo George' flew individual 3-hour missions in support of the US Army's 24th Infantry Division, which were attempting to stem the flood. The US 5th Air Force established a Joint Operations Centre (JOC) but things took a while to settle in, and initially many of the F-80 fighter-bomber pilots had received no briefing on the work of the airborne direction L-19s. Nonetheless, good directions were made and enemy

A little mishap! LTA-558 comes to rest in a very undignified position after chalking up the unit's 44th landing accident in September 1952. The Mosquito Association Inc

armour and concentrations around Unsan were hit hard, despite the fact that one aircraft was jumped by a Yak-3 fighter.

The vulnerability of the L-5 was already an established fact. The ROK Air Force had lost L-5s, and the 24th Infantry Division were losing their L-5s and L-4s in numbers in their role as artillery spotters. Major Carlton made a strong appeal for the use of the T-6 instead. As the official history stated, 'Members of the unit preferred flying the T-6 for this purpose. Therefore the L-5s were practically pushed off the stage as soon as the T-6s were made available.'

The T-6 made her debut as an airborne controller on 10 July 1950. On that day three missions were flown with aircraft fitted with the ARC-3 radio set. The first mission was flown by Lieutenant Harold Morris, with the advantage of fine weather for once, who located enemy tanks moving along the Chongju-Unsan road. He called in a flight of RAAF F-51s and directed them in, continuing to do so even when his radio dropped out, by waggling his wings. Bryant and Mitchell were both airborne that day and they located forty-two enemy tanks in a closely-packed column on the main road. The T-6s called in the F-80s who made runs firing rockets and strafing with 0.50-calibre machine guns; a total of seventeen communist tanks were destroyed and the column was forced to disperse.

Taejon only lasted as a forward base for a few days before it was overrun by the enemy, in torrential rain. One T-6 was an early loss when the pilot was forced to bail out before reaching the airstrip due to the appalling weather. A new base was set up at Taegu (airstrip K-2) and additional aircraft and personnel continually arrived there; by July there were twelve T-6s on the unit's strength with twenty-seven pilots, including three US Navy CPO pilot observers. Due to the pace of the enemy advance, the unit was only able to fly some twenty-six missions before Taegu then had to be evacuated. The first sorties were flown with no prior briefing as to the latest positions of friendly or enemy units, no operational procedures and no defined mission requirements. Still the basic rationale of the force was there, to fly over the fluid front line, find the enemy, pinpoint his location and direct friendly fighter-bomber strikes against him to try and

Mosquitoes line both sides of a dusty air strip in mid-summer, while in the background a Marine Corps F4U Corsair prepares for take-off. The Mosquito Association Inc

halt his advance. This they did, working initially under the 51st Provisional Fighter Squadron with F-51s.

On the 15 July, the 5th Air Force HQ designated the unit's missions for the day as 'Mosquito Able' and 'Mosquito Baker', etc., up to 'Mosquito How', to cover various ground force areas. These call-signs, reflecting the work of the T-6s, stuck very quickly, and unofficially the unit became generally known as the 'Mosquito' Squadron and the T-6 controllers and members of the 6147th as the 'Mosquitoes'. So a legend was born.

In the beginning there was considerable difficulty with the 'cluttering' of the VHF channels. A major cause of this was the lack of common frequency for fighter groups and the lack of compliance with radio-telephone procedures on the part of pilots. In addition, only four of the available eight channels were being utilized.

There was also the problem of just whose baby the Mosquitoes were anyway! At the end of July, the 6132nd Tactical Air Control Group arrived from the Zone of the Interior. The Mosquitoes were scheduled to become part of this organization but their commander protested 'There is no place in my organization for aircraft!' The unit therefore remained an undesignated one under the direct operational control of 5th Air Force HQ and supported by the 51st, until official activation on 1 August. A manning table was drawn up by Major Carlton on the basis of flying five sorties for six flying periods during 15 hours of the day, or thirty missions per day.

The first T-6 had been assigned to the unit without a crew chief and without any forms except 'Form 1'. The next two aircraft were accompanied by their crew chiefs, but without any tools! The fuelling unit at Taejon comprised an army truck, a hand-pump and five Korean labourers. No tools or aircraft parts were available! Radio parts were obtained only through exchanges with cargo plane crews flying into the airstrip. Oil was so low in the first T-6 to arrive that six gallons were needed to fill the reservoir. The oil was filled by personnel transporting the oil physically a gallon at a time over 100yd (90m).

A crashed C-47 provided the unit with their first radio equipment and tools, and this kept two T-6s flying. Similar salvage work produced a generator and other parts, which enabled the third aircraft to also be placed in commission. The fourth T-6 arrived with a crew chief *and* a set of spark plugs! This offset the loss of the second T-6, which made a belly-landing on a dry river bed tributary of the Naktong River. The aircraft was a write off but a salvage team managed to get out to the wreck and bring back critically needed parts. The first radio mechanic, Staff Sergeant Orville Tracey Jr, did not get assigned until 14 July.

At Taejon the crews slept under the wings of the T-6s in readiness for instant evacuation should the enemy break through to the airstrip. Gradually things got sorted. While at Taejon, the crew members were given their pre-mission briefings at JOC in Taejon City itself. The bulk of the information received was based on reports received from the previous Mosquito missions with G-2 EUSAK providing ground situation reports when possible. Interrogation of crew members was accomplished by personnel at JOC – the pilots physically reporting immediately after completion of each mission.

After the unit moved to Taegu airstrip, operations and intelligence were concentrated in a combined section that 'occupied a small room in a battered building on the edge of the strip'. In this constricted area (8 × 10ft), shared by the Troop Carrier Operations, it is little wonder that, as the official history recorded, 'much confusion prevailed throughout the day with all phases of operations and intelligence being conducted simultaneously'.

The daily routine was for Major Carlton to be driven in a jeep to JOC at 0330h to obtain an overlay of the latest JOC situation map. The information was posted on the map in the small operations–intelligence room at the strip, prior to departure of the first mission. From then until the last T-6 came back home at the end of the day, each mission functioned as briefer for the succeeding one. Interrogation was done at first by direct phone communication with JOC, and later the debriefing was hastily carried out by airmen of the unit and the report then transmitted to JOC.

Mosquito fighting gear – Lieutenant-Colonel Holman and Bob Grant in their flying suits having just returned from a mission over Communist lines, 1953. The Mosquito Association Inc

However, as the Mosquito pilots brought in the most current and the most reliable information, JOC Intelligence came more and more to rely on them for the latest front-line dispositions and the boot was on the other foot. The Mosquito unit was, from the very beginning of its existence, functioning as the intelligence of JOC, as well as accomplishing its mission of providing tactical air control for UN fighter-bomber squadrons.

During the period 9 to 31 July 1950, some 269 sorties were flown totalling 670

Seen over the rugged Korean landscape over which their missions were fought, this is LTA-594 flown by First Lieutenant Hanson, seen near the K-55 airstrip in the spring of 1956. The Mosquito Association Inc

hours 20min flying time. The maintenance crews ensured that, despite the primitive conditions and intensity of operations, there was never more than one T-6 out of service at any one time. Two aircraft, both T-6Ds, were lost in this period, serial 080 over Taejon when Lieutenant Morris ran out of fuel and had to bail out, and serial 942, also piloted by Morris, for the self-same reason, and he had to belly-land. He survived both incidents.

Covered over from the Korean dust and dirt, Mosquito TA-583 features an all-silver finish with a black anti-glare panel atop the front fuselage. She has her propeller spinner still in place and has a drop tank. Behind her sits a Marine Corps Chance Vought F6U Corsair fighter-bomber. The Mosquito Association Inc

Many deep-penetration missions were flown in these early days, simply because the pilots had no specific information on where the front line was that day. Although missions of this type were increasingly to become a vital element in the Mosquito game-plan, these early sorties took place because the pilots were deep in enemy air space before they realized it. Fortunately, the destruction of two Yak fighters by F-80s north-east of Taejon on the 21st, eliminated any aggressive intent against the T-6s by the North Korean air force, but the threat of flak damage was very real.

Some of the more outstanding early missions deserve recording.

On 24 July First Lieutenants John W. Planiac and Wayne Upell Jr were carrying out a reconnaissance in the Hamchang area. Conditions were far from ideal with low overcast and the T-6 was forced to fly down to an altitude of just 50ft (15m).

First Lieutenant Sid McNeil poses with the 'Scream'n' Rebel', TA-579, in his full flying outfit. The location was the K-47 airstrip in 1953. The Mosquito Association Inc

Communist ground fire was a daily occurrence and often it was accurate. Here LTA-548 has taken some very unfriendly metal into the fuselage at the wing joint, but still got home safe if not sound! The Mosquito Association Inc

They spotted an area near a hairpin bend on the main road where the branches and leaves seemed a different hue to that of the surround foliage. They had spotted a concentration of hidden enemy tanks. Despite intense 20mm anti-aircraft fire, they stayed over the target and called in a flight of four F-80s, each armed with four rockets, who worked over the tanks methodically, destroying three of them.

Next day, First Lieutenant James H. Bryant and Second Lieutenant Billy D. Brown sighted a North Korean supply column with some twenty-three large trucks moving along the main Mungiong road. They homed in a flight of four F-51s who strafed the column, torching at least six of the vehicles and their contents.

On the 29 July, First Lieutenant Upell and Second Lieutenant Roger S. Wilkes were working over the Hadong area, when they sighted about fifteen enemy tanks and fifty vehicles of various types on the road between Chinju and Hadong and Ponggie Ri to Konyang. Upell and Wilkes called in no less than ten different fighter-bomber flights to deal with this concentration and, as a result, at least four tanks and twenty-five of the vehicles were taken out. A bridge at Ponggie Ri was destroyed as a bonus.

July 30 saw First Lieutenant Edward G. Palm working over the Yongdong–Hwanggan area and he sighted eight artillery pieces and a large number of vehicles two miles north-east of that town. An F-80 flight was directed in against these targets and they were well hit with rockets and strafing, resulting in damage to all the artillery pieces and destruction of four trucks. On the same mission they located a second target of about 1,500–2,000 communist infantry five miles south-east of the town and these were likewise worked over.

Various high-ranking Air Force and Army officers took observation missions over the enemy lines with the Mosquitoes as their fame began to grow, among them Major General Partridge (as a pilot), Lieutenant General Walton H. Walker and Lieutenant General James H. Doolittle. War correspondents Lionel Hudson and Hal Boyle (Associated Press) also hitched rides and wrote stories on the unit's work.

The 6147th Tactical Control Squadron (Airborne) came of age in August 1940 and gradually its main roles and functions were defined and established. These were:

- close support of friendly units in defensive positions;
- location of areas of enemy build-ups;
- finding 'refugee' groups in order that they might be led to safety;
- location of camouflaged objects;
- spotting large enemy movements.

Special missions included:

- deep penetration reconnaissance;
- search missions for lost friendly aircraft;
- leaflet drops in support of psychological warfare;
- briefing missions in which VIPs and

journalists were flown along enemy lines;

- night and pre-dawn missions to harass the enemy and minimize his nocturnal movements – reports from ground units on interrogations of captured communist officers confirmed that the enemy feared the presence of even a single T-6 in the area at night.

All these missions, in the (usually) unarmed and totally unarmoured T-6, were hazardous to say the very least. Exposure to ground fire of all types and from light automatic weapons up to the heaviest calibre weapons was there right from the very start and the dangers steadily increased as the Soviet Union and Red China built up the North Korean's weapon stocks. From the very first missions then, the T-6s were taking hits and returning to base with holes in the fuselage, wings and empennage (sometimes through the pilots cockpit itself).

By the end of August, the 6147th strength had increased to fifty-five pilots, of which seventeen had already completed a normal tour of duty of fifty missions. A total of 1,012 sorties were flown by the 6147th that month, ranging from seventeen sorties flown on 4 August to forty-one on 20 and 21 August, a daily average of 33.3 missions. The strength of the Mosquitoes was built up from twelve aircraft at the beginning of August (eleven T-6Ds and one T-6F) to twenty-seven machines (seventeen T-6Ds, ten T-6Fs). Pilot numbers had increased to a total of fifty-five with forty-four observers.

Losses also grew, of course, and five aircraft were written off in this period:

- 9 August, T-6D (serial 44-80951) crashed on take off from K-2;
- 12 August, T-6D (serial 42-86011) crashed on landing when tail assembly was badly battered by enemy ground fire;
- 20 August, T-6F (serial 44-82521) failed to return from a mission over Uiryong with Second Lieutenant Ernest J. Reeves and Master Sergeant Herschel I. Bushman aboard;
- 22 August, T-6D (serial 42-86132) crashed into Soham San in bad weather, piloted by Second Lieutenant Robert McCormick and Second Lieutenant Charles P. Wenzl (both bodies were recovered and identified);
- 28 August, T-6F (serial 44-82563) hit by enemy fire over Uihang, crash-landing in friendly territory.

Some very extensive damage was taken in the inner wing panel from Communist gunners on this Mosquito. It burst hydraulic pipes, but she still managed to get home.
The Mosquito Association Inc

In return they had been instrumental in the certain destruction of 183 communist tanks, 119 trucks and 778 other vehicles (plus fifteen oxcarts!). Gradually the basic T-6s were supplemented and eventually almost totally replaced by the LT-6G, specially modified for Forward Air Control (FAC) use, with air-to-ground and air-to-air radios, racks for a dozen white phosphorous smoke rockets and underwing pods equipped with the 0.30-calibre forward-firing gun. These were soon removed as the temptation to use them on the enemy by the young pilots tended to override their primary function of spotting and target direction.

September saw a continued period of communist pressure on the United Nations toe-hold of Pusan and, under cover of atrocious weather conditions, the enemy threw all they had to drive the allies back into the sea once and for all. Taegu itself was constantly under threat of both artillery bombardment and being over-run by the enemy at any time, and for a while it was touch-and-go. The 6147th earned its reputation for tenacity during this critical period for, as the threat grew from the north and north-east, units began to withdraw from K-2. By 5 September the 6147th was the sole remaining combat air unit still operating from the strip and the next day they were told to pull out and withdraw to K-1 Pusan Air Strip (East). Some elements, amidst appalling road conditions, did make the move and some T-6 missions were flown from K-1, but half the unit held on and continued flying from K-2. Even on 11 September, when it seemed that the strip's capture was imminent, the T-6s continued to fly from Taegu and next day the whole unit elected to move back there and continue the fight.

The precision called for during this first period of close-in ground fighting was to become a hallmark of the Mosquitoes. They used 1:50,000 scale maps to pin-point targets within 100yd (90m), which made it imperative to know exactly which side of a disputed ridge was occupied by friendly forces. One outstanding example of this work by the Mosquitoes was seen at the 'Walled-city' at Kasan, some 7 miles (11km) north of Taegu, and two adjacent ridges. Nor was the enemy spared by the arrival of darkness, for, on at least one occasion, the Mosquito pilots homed in a flight of B-26 medium bombers by exposing his landing lights over the target zone.

Observers had mainly been Air Force personnel at the start but gradually others took over this duty and in the main left the flying to the Air Force. Three US Navy CPOs were the first such to fly missions, co-ordinating strikes by carrier aircraft, and they were joined by ground-force officers and enlisted men. Many of these observers were selected by divisional commanders on the basis of previous combat air experience in World War II. Not only Americans were to fly as observers, and as the months went by the force became more and more an international one with British, Canadian, Australian and South African officers all joining the team.

Like all aspects of supply, the unit lacked efficient maps when it began operating, the only maps available being AAF Aeronautical ones, 1948 issue, which were blanks (black and white) with a minimum of contour lines, place names and grids. Only through what was termed 'aggressive search' on the part of the squadron personnel, and the generosity of other air and ground units, were the Mosquitoes able to procure even a minimum number of proper maps with which to properly do their job. During the siege period around Taegu and Pusan, the Army Map Service (AMS) ground-force maps of 1:250,000 scale were considered the most practical because of their greater detail. However, in accordance with direction from higher headquarters, the Air Force grid system was used in reading co-ordinates. In the Air Force grid system the standard AAF Aeronautical Approach Chart of 1:250,000 scale was used. Each chart (1 degree and 45 minutes east–west and 1 degree north–south) was divided into twenty-eight squares, each

First Lieutenant Gunn in flying gear but with unconventional headgear, poses by LTA-551 at the K-55 airstrip in 1955, just prior to flying to Itazuke on the way home. The Mosquito Association Inc

Looking rather forlorn without her wings and dignity, LTA-587 displays her buckled prop and battered empennage as honourable war wounds to a jeep full of unsympathetic GIs. The Mosquito Association Inc

156 by 15 minutes in area and designated by numbers 1 through 28; each square was further sub-divided into nine squares each 5 by 5 minutes in area and designed by letters 'a' through 'i'; each sub-square was further subdivided into five squares each 2½ minutes in area (one such sub-square in the middle of four) designated by numbers reading from left to right horizontally. This system had obviously been developed for use on the standard AAF chart and thus made the AMS map impractical for this purpose, even though, in most cases, the Mosquito pilots preferred the latter! Maps considered most useful for tactical air control included the AMS 1:250,000 and 1:50,000 maps and the AAF Aeronautical chart 1:250,000 scale, July 1950 edition.

As a means to minimize map consumption and losses on the part of crew members who were handicapped because map kits were not available, transparent plastic chart cases were prepared by the section. The boards served the twofold purpose of preserving charts and enabling flying personnel to mark significant information with grease pencils. The plastic material was obtained at FEAMCOM. Always a critical problem was the lack of grease pencils, overlay paper and other basic intelligence supplies.

In anticipation of the conversion of maps of all military branches to the Universal Transverse Mercator (UTM) grid system announced by higher headquarters, which was to come into effect from 1 September, all crew members were given an orientation on the method of its use, and quantities of UTM maps were requisitioned. From 18 August an intelligence officer and four airman intelligence specialists joined the squadron providing the Mosquitoes with a staff of some semblance of an S-2 Section for the first time. Major projects were then put in hand including the setting up of five major charts, which included:

- mosaic map of 1:50,000 scale keeping current information on all targets in the immediate front both live and dead, location of enemy troop concentrations, direction of enemy movements and area of build-up in supplies and material;
- an area-control map of 1:250,000 scale giving the latest locations of ground controllers;
- a ground situation map of 1:250,000 scale giving the current information on location of friendly and enemy units;
- a flak chart, giving latest intelligence on active enemy flak and anti-aircraft positions;
- a 1:250,000-scale map showing enemy lines of communications and points of interdiction.

The Mosquitoes proved to be, without doubt, the prime provider of information for 5th Air Force Intelligence. Through their continuous operations from an hour before sunrise to an hour or more after sunset, it was the Mosquitoes that at all times were in position to give current and first-hand information on the following:

- location of enemy troop concentrations;
- directions and trends of enemy build up in supply and material;
- latest tactics utilized by the enemy, particularly camouflage;
- probable points of interdiction and lines of communication;
- changes in the situation of a given area;
- evaluation of the effectiveness of friendly air and ground action against the enemy, both in tactics and type of ammunition used.

On 28 August, Captain Thomas Plourde, G-3 EUSAK was assigned by his headquarters as ground liaison officer (GLO) with the squadron. His assignment enabled the exchange of intelligence resulting in a benefit to both the squadron and S-2 and G-3 JOC.

Captain Fitzgerald piloting LTA-594 over the Korean hills makes for a fine study of the Mosquito. Note the yellow wing-tips and extended anti-glare blacking atop the aircraft's nose. The Mosquito Association Inc

Keeping them flying proved a constant headache, but one in which improvization and ingenuity held the field, and as a result of sterling work by the ground crews 100 per cent of the aircraft assigned to the unit was kept in commission twenty days of that month. The number of T-6s on hand during those twenty days ranged from a minimum of twelve aircraft to a maximum of twenty-nine. One aircraft came back with two bullet holes in her left fuel tank from enemy ground fire. A tank was removed from one of the wrecked T-6s and re-installed in the aircraft which had been hit. The plane was in commission again within three days ready for its next mission.

The pressure on the Pusan perimeter was finally eased on 16 September, when General Douglas McArthur led an United Nations amphibious landing far in the rear of the communist lines, at Inchon, the port of the ROK capital, Seoul, just below the 38th parallel. Faced with this unexpected exposure of their forces to being cut off, the communists began to hastily pull back and this North Korean retreat quickly turned into a rout. The changed conditions of the pursuit led to a more fluid battlefield for a time, and this affected the Mosquitoes role accordingly. Now their prime missions became:

- location of withdrawing enemy units and directing air strikes at them;
- cover for the advancing columns of the 1st Cavalry and 2, 24 and 25 Infantry Divisions, and 1 and 2 ROK Corps;
- dropping of 300,000 'safe conduct passes' to civilians caught up in the fighting as the communists fled northward.

The allied advance continued steadily with the two United Nations armies linking up and then pushing on into the aggressors' home territory. By 24 November almost the whole of North Korea was freed and the UN forces were approaching the frontier with Red China, along the Yalu River. It was at this point that the Red Chinese entered the fray with massive land forces, which they threw in regardless of loss. The tide turned once more.

For a brief period, the 6147th operated out of K-16, which was Seoul City Airport after its liberation, and then moved further north to work from K-24, which was an airfield close to the North Korean capital of Pyongyang. Despite the bitter weather of the Korean winter, initially the unit only had tented accommodation, but later they were able to re-house themselves in a North Korean tank school, which they christened 'The Castle'.

It was around this time, October 1950, that the unit's unique 'Mosquito' Patch was brought into being, originally the brainchild of First Lieutenant James J. Brockmyer, an observer on detached duty from the 25 Infantry Division. An enemy counter-offensive again forced a hasty relocation south on 3 December and once more they had to shift base back to K-16 in the middle of arctic conditions of snow and ice. Despite the atrocious weather, described as 'Siberian', the 6147th continued to function and conducted some of their most outstanding missions, which included the following:

Another hit which could have proven fatal! The starboard trailing edge and flap on 'Beetle Bum' (named after the racehorse in a popular song of the time) present a sorry sight, but she landed okay. The Mosquito Association Inc

- On 5 December 1950, covering the evacuation by sea of UN Forces from Chinnampo, south-west of Pyongyang.
- On 13 December 1950, deep reconnaissance against an enemy road-block 30 miles (48km) north of Seoul.
- On 16–22 December 1950, a series of night-reconnaissance missions ('the night route') to check enemy movements along the main supply road near the existing front lines.
- On 14 December 1950, a mass reconnaissance mission with no less than twenty-five T-6s airborne at the same time. This special operation followed a period of 36 hours of low ceiling, snow showers and poor visibility along the front line, which the enemy used to his advantage in moving troops up for a massive assault. The UN command had been blinded so, as soon as the weather lifted sufficiently, the whole available T-6 strength was mobilized. Pilots and observers had been standing by all day waiting for their chance and, within forty minutes of take-off, every aircraft was over its assigned target zone.
- On 24 December 1950, they oversaw the daring rescue of thirty-four UN POWs.
- Several missions were flown taking members of the Korean Military Advisory Group, Korean Liaison Officer and GHQ, Far Eastern Command, over pre-designated areas of the battle zone.
- Special weather condition sampling missions.

This outstanding work did not go unnoticed or unrewarded. At a special presentation at the K-37 Taegu West airstrip, held on 4 February 1951, Major General Earl E. Partridge, Commander of the US 5th Air Force, presented the Mosquitoes with the Distinguished Unit Citation as a result of their 'heroic, unique and valorous action in Korea during the period 9 July to 25 November 1950'. Two days later they even got some publicity back home when the distinguished broadcaster Edward R. Murrow,

This time it was the leading edge of the Mosquito's wing that had a North Korean shell pass straight through it, peppering the rest of the wing as it exploded.
The Mosquito Association Inc

told listeners to the Columbia Broadcasting News about the work of the Mosquitoes.

> Those Mosquitoes can only be compared to scouts, in the days of Indian fighting on the Western plains. They literally track tanks across a river, up a valley and under the trees. Much of the time they work at an altitude of a hundred feet or less.
>
> Those old T-6 Mosquitoes couldn't live against air opposition, and they are vulnerable to ground fire, even from light, automatic weapons. They have taken their losses, and now, as a unit, have received a Presidential citation. They are a gallant crew of aerial scouts, with uncanny ability to penetrate enemy camouflage. Their low-level flying and spotting have not been equalled since men began to use flying machines to make war.[2]

On 28 March 1951, the 6147th received a new commanding officer when Colonel Merrill H. Carlton was relieved by Lieutenant Colonel Timothy F. O'Keefe, former Deputy of Operations at FEAMCOM, Tachikawa AFB, Japan. Typical of the new intake was Lieutenant John E. Persons and he described his induction to the Mosquitoes this way:

> Lieutenant Robert C. Mathis (later General) and I arrived at Pyong Tec on May 16 1951. I recall that we went over to the mess hall, and the centre of attention was a pilot that had bailed out about six weeks earlier and had just made his way back to unit that day. I don't recall his name, but his story was absolutely spell-binding. He was moved a few miles north after capture, a couple of forced marches, and they had been at that holding location for several days. He realized that he and the group would be moved further north in the next few days, and any escape had to be done soon. He developed a habit of going out to the edge of the area to urinate every night, and he proved trustworthy to the guard, who watched him less and less carefully every night, and he went further and stayed longer every night. This selected night, he took off and made it. It seems that he led and assisted in a quick armoured movement to the area of the camp and reclaimed some if not all of the prisoners that he had left in the camp. Wonderful story!
>
> There was a Major Raines there who had been an instructor at Perrin AFB when I went through basic there in 1948–49. A Lieutenant Ediburg who had been in the 51st with us, also (last seen as a Colonel in 1975).
>
> Having taken training in the T-6, I had no difficulty checking out, and flew the requisite number of missions, ten I think, as an observer with an experienced pilot. Then I 'drew' a marvellous Army Captain who was a civilian pilot with considerable capability in the T-6. We all added to that skill as we flew with him. I had about twenty missions in the F-80s in the 51st FS, and I ended up with the full tour, so I must have had eight-odd missions in the 6147th. The front was slowly moving north, and about the time I left, had stabilized where it would essentially remain.
>
> We were fortunate not to be troubled with as much well-emplaced anti-aircraft weaponry as later developed, although they had begun to put some good guns on the north side of the Iron Triangle by the time I left.
>
> The first month was pretty much routine, covering those division fronts that were on the western side of the dividing line between 'A' Flight and 'B' Flight. I don't remember when it went to a Group – maybe before I got there, but I don't think so.
>
> I had just finished two long missions that netted me about 9 hours, total. I flew 135 hours in June that year. I was a volunteer who had arrived in Okinawa in November of 1949, and was nearing rotation without the benefit of a full tour – which is why I volunteered. Mathis and I were the first of the 'quota' set up from 15th Air Force. I escaped being Base Flight Maintenance Officer at NAHA and Bob escaped Generals Aide for General Sterley. We were both doomed to return with twenty-odd missions in Korea.[3]

The missions continued and grew even more varied and diverse, if that was deemed possible! In the ghastly Korean climate, one hazard in the summer months was malaria. A chore added to the Mosquitoes duties was being fitted up as a spraying aircraft to fight these pests. Half-a-dozen machines, identified by their checked-pattern engine cowls, were so fitted out and utilized, Mosquitoes against Mosquitoes, *someone* must have had a sense of humour! One spin-off was to provide material for George Wunders syndicated cartoon strip 'Terry and the Pirates', actual operations being even more dramatic than anything a fiction writer could dream up themselves!

One Scots officer, Lieutenant Kenneth Wilson from Edinburgh, with the Royal Scots Regiment, flew as an observer more than any other UN soldier, he clocked up no less than 232 missions – an all-time record. His total number of missions averaged one a day for the length of his time with the 6147th. He could have left off when he hit 100 missions, be he stayed on voluntarily.

The first piggyback pickup was made by a T-6 with one of the Mosquito pilots. An Air Control Party working with an ROK unit from a front-line airstrip radioed for help in evacuating a wounded Air Force Sergeant,

Fred L. Gentry. A crew comprising Lieutenant Carroll L. James and Lieutenant John Corey of the 1st Cavalry, landed after jettisoning their belly tanks and other gear, just as the North Koreans put in another attack and overran the 1,200ft (365m) long strip. The ROKs and two officers got Sergeant Gentry into the plane and they took off under heavy fire from the enemy on the airstrip, as well as from other communist troops in surrounding areas. Because of the extra load and the short runway, the T-6 plunged through a power line at the end of the strip but, although damaged, did not crash and got their man safely home.

The 6150th TAC Squadron carried out this assignment. Their job was to go out in teams supported by the Mosquitoes and send back radio reports on enemy positions and likely targets. The team leader was always a combat-experienced Mosquito pilot assisted by a radio operator and a radio mechanic. Travelling up close, and sometimes mere yards away from the target area, these teams spotted targets for allied artillery, radioed the information to the Mosquitoes (on one occasion first to C-47s, which then relayed the message to the Mosquito pilot), which then came in to spot and dot the target with smoke rocket, and directed the fighter-bomber strikes that followed. The Mosquitoes were the only Air Force unit to receive front-line pay, as its men were as constantly exposed to as many dangers as the 'Dough Boys' down in the mud.

Another mission that was rather different was Operation *Candy Bar*! Lieutenant James Topping was on a routine patrol when he spotted some isolated American troops on a 3,000ft (914m) mountain close to Waegwan. They waved to him and he dipped his wings in acknowledgement. They radioed him, 'Do you have a candy bar on you?' Topping replied, 'No; but hold on'. He then flew back to his base where he and his aerial cameraman, Top Sergeant Raymond T. Wittum, collected two dozen Hershey bars and flew back to the mountain where they made their drop with an improvised parachute.

By July 1951, the front line had established and settled down to a long period of 'trench warfare', more akin to the attrition of the First World War than anything seen since. From just below the 38th parallel, south-east of Panjunjom, ROK, the fortified positions snaked north-east, east and then north-east again across the Korean peninsular, reaching the sea again between

Sad farewell to a gallant T-6. Sooner or later even the best aircraft had to admit the end of the road had been reached, as is the case here with the battered carcass of what remained of LTA-587 being low-loaded and carted away. The Mosquito Association Inc

Unique close-up view of the target-marking rockets in place under the wing of a Mosquito at K-47 airstrip in the summer of 1952. These rockets were not armament in the conventional sense because they were used to mark targets for the fighter-bombers to hit. The Mosquito Association Inc

Kosong and Kansong in North Korea. There followed a period of intense and costly blow and counter-blow along this line, known as the 'Stalemate' war. It lasted from July 1951 for two long and wearisome years. Losses were heavy on both sides, while the line changed but little. Meanwhile 'truce' talks began in July 1951, at Kaesong, then moved to Panmunjom in October 1951. They continue to this day!

The whole front line ran across the mountainous spine of Korea and whomever controlled the torturous ridges and crests controlled the narrow valleys. Soon Mosquitoes were familiar with them all and their names: Siberia Hill, Bunker Hill, Gibraltar and The Hook in the south-west; T-Bone Hill, Big Noria, Pork Chop Hill and Old Baldy to the north; Luke's Castle, Punchbowl and Heartbreak Ridge to the east; and, most infamous of all, the Iron Triangle, Chorwon-Pyongang and Kumhwam, an area in the centre of the lines where the communists repeatedly tried to break through the Main Line of Resistance (MLR) with enormous number of troops.

One such redoubt was at Papasan, described by Sidney Johnston as, 'a Gibraltar in the key defences of North Korean Forces (NKF)'. This area became the watching brief and continuous battle ground of the 6147th, now grown into a Tactical Air Control Group, with 6148 TAC Squadron at its heart. While the endless peace negotiations went on, the communists built up their three armies in the area with Chinese and North Korean regular divisions generously equipped with Chinese and Russian armour and equipment. In the spring of 1953, the communists finally committed them in the Battle of the Kumsong Bulge.

At Chunchon, which was to be their permanent base for some time,[4] a reorganization took place. The unit was expanded to become the 6147th Tactical Control Group and now comprised two TCS (airborne) squadrons, the 6148th and 6149th, with the 6150th as the TCS (ground) squadron handling all aspects of the ground support including the tactical air control parties (TACP). These latter units were three-man teams (a Mosquito pilot officer, a radio mechanic and a vehicle mechanic) equipped with radio jeeps. Their role was to co-ordinate both the airborne Mosquitoes and the relay aircraft. At this period also the first LT-6Gs arrived and steadily re-equipped the two airborne squadrons.

The Mosquitoes were airborne daily trying to keep on eye on this massive build-up and warn the thinly-stretched UN forces of when and where it might blow; when it came at White Horse Mountain in the Chowon valley, they performed as valiantly as ever. The main thrust came through at Osong-San Mountain (1,062ft or 323m), which was called Old Papasan in the area known as Papasan at Kumhwa. The initial communist assault was overwhelming and, despite heavy losses (10,000 men on a single day), they rolled over the defenders wiping out the 555th Field Artillery Battalion and pounding over the ROK's tough 25th Infantry Division. The dead and dying of both sides lined the flanks and slopes of Old Papasan and the Mosquitoes could hardly believe the carnage they saw as they swooped low over the area on mission after mission. Strike after strike was directed to try and hold the onslaught, and the Mosquitoes also directed heavy UN artillery fire on massed communist forces whenever the opportunity presented itself. It was an intense and dramatic period.

Smoke rocket installation on a Mosquito. Three of the rockets have been fired on a previous mission. The pod houses a 0.30-calibre machine gun. This aircraft was one of the few that carried such armament or indeed any armament at all. The use of machine guns was discontinued early in the war because it distracted the crews from their primary mission of reconnaissance and strike direction. The Mosquito Association Inc

Many fierce actions were fought during this time, but just a few incidents will have to serve as typical of the dangers and hazards of the Mosquitoes' work during this period.

Sidney F. Johnston, Jr, was the Tactical Air Control Party running the air-to-ground flight from the trenches at Kumhwa with the 9th ROK Division during the last big battle in July 1953. He later was to recall what happened:

> On the 15th July, Army Major Fishpaw and I observed an estimated 10,000 CCF/NKF troops with trucks/artillery/tanks crossing and moving down the Kumhwa-Kumson Valley right at us. With the few troops in the line with us, it was impossible to stop that many in the trenches on a man-to-man basis. The answer was artillery and air power. After much air-to-air talk asking for help – this F-84 flight flew by, circled (no ordnance available) and went for help – they couldn't believe that many enemy troops were out in the open! Well, the F-84s came back with lots of help and I gave them first hand credit as being the major contributor in stopping the battle at Kumhwa – in that, if they had not returned to help, I do not think I would be here today. Then too, the present DMZ would most probably be somewhere

south of the 38th Parallel, possible south of Seoul! For over thirty years I have been trying to locate the F-84 flight leader that did so much to stop the CCF/NKF and saving our fanny!

He finally succeeded in tracking him and, by a remarkable coincidence, that man turned out to be Lieutenant Colonel Randy Presley, USAF, who had been Johnston's classmate, with the same instructor, and they had sat together in that class every day during their Air Force basic pilot training days in the T-6, as well as in jet fighter school later! This is Randy's own pilot account of that eventful day and just how the Mosquitoes helped stopped the last communist offensive dead in its tracks.

On the morning of June 15 1953, I was leading a flight of four F-84s on an early light recon mission in an area about fifteen miles north of the front. We were given an area to recce looking for trucks that were coming off the road from night movement and going into camouflage. We covered our area from one end to the other on this day and could not find a thing so we dropped our bombs on a few small buildings at a crossroads and shot up a few other outhouse type buildings and started home. As we were joining up while crossing the front, I hear a Limey flying a T-6 almost screaming for some fighters to come into his area. Since we were not far away, we turned over to his area. He said he had 4,000, then 10,000 troops coming down the valley in open offensive. I couldn't believe it since I had about fifty missions by this time and I had hardly ever seen a handful of people out in the open anywhere in North Korea. Sure enough when we found him, he was right. We made a couple of circles around the valley and watched the show since we didn't have any ordnance left. There were troops lined up line abreast, tanks, drums and bugles, and the whole bit! Since there was nothing we could do and we were getting low on fuel we then headed for K-2.

When we landed I was met by a staff car with a two star flag on the front bumper. I asked my crew chief what was going on and he didn't know. He said they wanted to know where 447 parked and they were waiting for me. I started filling out the Form 1 and a Lieutenant Colonel aide came over and told me to forget the paperwork and hurry up. I got out and started taking off my G-suit and the general said, 'Hell, son, get in the car and don't worry abut that thing'. I had no idea what I had done and was scared to death. On the way to the group ops the general and aide kept quizzing me about what I had seen at the front. I told them about the show and when we got to ops everyone in both groups was there, brass that is. They brought my other three wingmen in and had us explain it all to everyone for about thirty minutes. Then they took us into the group briefing room and there were seventy-two pilots and I had to tell them the story. The general (whose name I can't remember because he was from 5th Rear in Taegu) then told me that I was going to lead the group back to the area. For a brand new spot first lieutenant this scared me more than any combat I ever saw.

In less that an hour after I landed we were on our way back to the front again, this time with three squadrons of twenty-four F-84s each. Sure enough, the British Mosquito pilot was still on station and by this time a raft of F-86 fighter-bombers from K-13 had already gotten there and filled the valley with smoke. We rolled in for one pass only, strafed on the bomb run, dropped a couple of 1,000 pounds and left before we got run over by the whole group from K-13 coming back again.

Before noon that day I had flown three missions and they said that three was enough. I heard that some of the F-86s from K-13 flew two missions that day without ever shutting the engine off or getting out of the plane. They taxied up to a refueller and then to a bomb dolly where they put on two 500 pounders and didn't rearm the guns. During that offensive I think I flew eight missions in three days. If you were there then you probably flew all day long every day.[5]

The hazards of the Mosquitoes' job increased once the lines had settled down and the North Koreans and Red Chinese began installing their Russian-supplied anti-aircraft artillery in substantial numbers. There were many hits taken and the rule was never to fly straight in the T-6 for any length of time in case they 'drew a bead' on you. Concentration on the job in hand could sometimes lead to this essential survival technique being overlooked, and it could be with fatal results. One of the most extraordinary rescues involving a shot-down Mosquito observer was the rescue of the 25-year-old British First Lieutenant W. P. R. (Peter) Tolputt, who was flying with the unit on loan from the 14th Field Regiment, Royal Artillery, First British Commonwealth Division. The story can be told from several angles by the many Allied participants, not least Peter Tolputt himself, and is a remarkable one.[6] The basic facts are contained in Peter Tolputt's 'Evasion and Escape Report', made on 28 May 1952 at the 6147th Tactical Control Group HQ.[7] It is interesting also for the detailed description it gives of how the Mosquito observers went about their dangerous task and how these very brave individuals were equipped.

I was flying as observer in a T-6 aircraft on a reconnaissance mission across the US IX Corps front. The TACP in the Thunderhead 'A' sector requested that we make a low level reconnaissance of three possible gun and mortar positions. The time was approximately 271401. The target was in the vicinity of CT-6747. I was wearing:

heavy infantry boots;
one pair of thick woollen socks;
OD trousers;
summer flying suit with a red scarf;
L-2 flying jacket;
peaked cap.

Well laden with rockets, LTA-538 (49-3538) lifts off on another mission. Peter Tolputt

(Above) **A Mosquito makes a pass over a Tactical Air Control Party. These were the Air Force men on the ground in the front line who worked with the Mosquitoes in the control of close air support. They were equipped with special jeeps with radio installations identical to that of the Mosquito.** The Mosquito Association Inc

A bomb blast on a close air support mission in the vicinity of strong point, a sharp ridge known as 'Old Baldy', 1952. The Mosquito Association Inc

In addition I carried:

45 cal automatic in holster on web belt;
1 extra 45 ammo clip;
1 hand-held flare;
1 first-aid kit;
1 jack knife;
1 mail drop streamer;
1 EandE barter kit containing blood chit;
1 pack cigarettes;
lighter;
map case and map;
1 pack chewing gum;

wristwatch;
headset;
seat-type parachute;
URC-4 radio in carrying vest;
3 morphine syrettes (British issue).

We acknowledged control's request and received artillery clearance and headed north across friendly lines at approximately 4,000ft above terrain, about 5,000m east of target location. We turned west 2,000m north of our target, losing altitude at a rapid rate. We turned south and passed over the target at approximately 600ft. When just past and south of Target, both crew members heard 30mm fire, seemingly coming from left and behind the aircraft. A very brief exchange of comment concerning the fire ensued between the pilot and observer over the interphone. No later words were passed between pilot and observer. Almost immediately after this a very sudden burst of flame appeared in front of me and possibly on the left side. I was aware immediately that my moustache had been singed. I immediately opened the canopy, unfastened my shoulder harness, but forgot to unhook my headset. I stood up in a half crouch in the cockpit and pulled my parachute rip-cord before I left the aircraft. I now believe that the pilot chute pulled me out of the aircraft on the left side. I estimate the altitude at this time to have been approximately 400ft. I don't remember falling through the air at all, the next thing I remember was that the ground was six feet under me. I hit the ground on the sloping side of a hill with considerable impact.

In a later letter to his parents, written at K-47 on 28 May, Peter filled in more details.

It was the third time I'd been hit – once in front of Comwel Division with a bullet through the canopy, once in front of 40 Division with a bullet through the propeller and this last time, also in front of 40 Division. Believe it or not the pilot was McBride again, and we were hit because we didn't take enough evasive action. We were doing a recce for 40 Division, looking for gun and mortar positions, starting about 1400h. We passed over our target at 600ft and then had some 20mm cannon fire coming up behind us and to the left. McBride said, 'Do you hear that?' I said, 'Yes – it's twenties' and he said, 'Lets get out of here'. That's the last we ever spoke to each other, for a moment later the cockpit in front of me was enveloped in a sudden bursting sheet of flame.

My next few actions were done entirely by instinct. I somehow opened the canopy, undid my shoulder harness, forgot to uncouple my headset leads and then crouched up in my seat. Then I must have got a flap on because I pulled my ripcord whilst still in the aeroplane. This, in actual fact, was my saving, because I judged the plane to be only 400 feet up – below normal parachuting level! The pilot chute on the end of the main canopy, which is sprung loaded, must have shot out into the slipstream and literally dragged me after it. My chute opened and the next thing I knew was that the ground was coming up to meet me only six feet away. I landed in some bushes on the steep side of a hill, coming in much too fast of course because it was too low for the chute to be working properly.

Only damage was a twisted knee, but I looked down and saw blood all over my left side. I immediately looked around and saw that I was surround by Chink hills on three sides with my red and white parachute plainly visible on the ground beside me. Most of the pockets of my flying suit had been unzipped so I lost all their contents, plus my watch which was torn off my wrist. So I had no way of knowing which was north or south except by a vague guess from looking at the sun. Just then I heard another Mosquito circling high overhead so I set up the little 400 dollar escape radio we all carry. I spoke on it and picked up the Mosquito strong and clear. He told me I was about 1,000yd from friendlies and about 75yd from the Chinks, and said that there was a helicopter on the way to pick me up. Meanwhile our plane had spun into the ground and blown up – the tail was the only recognizable bit still showing. McBride must have been killed instantly.[8]

The other Mosquito was flown by Lieutenant John W. Payer, USAF. He remembered the incident thus:

On 27 May 1952, I was on my 'day off', saw a Red Cross show and decide to fly a mission. Got a new observer for a check out. As the wheels came up, the call of the closest control was of a 'plane down'. I went to my site and worked the rescue as I was the only 'group' plane up and of course was fully loaded. Guess about three hours at max power, and red lights on! In the group, we took some re-worked 'G's'. The beating that engine took – never hurt it.

Many people worked on the rescue, I have no true number of fighters I had waiting for direction and the guns that got the plane did not last very long. The North tried to get Pete with a tank but one of the fighter flights spotted him and requested permission to take care of it. The Army was apparently spotting my smoke target and really did a super job with ground fire from them. The volunteers that came in apparently had a path cleared through no-man's land by their artillery.

I never got to identify the various units nor to be able to get a casualty count; but I do know that the area was either out of ammo, because the North's ground fire was reduced, or they were not risking giving their positions sway. Almost peaceful!!

I had just checked out the pilot (McBride) and he was a good friend of mine and I had flown with Pete Tolputt and respected his coolness – it made it much easier to run the rescue. His voice sounded relieved after we got the area secured.[9]

Peter was not feeling that cool at the time, as he told his parents.

Then mortar fire, artillery and small arms fire started – machine-guns were firing only three feet above my head making the Chink keep his head down. Just then our own boys intercepted a Chink radio message saying that I must be taken alive at all costs. That accounts for why they didn't plaster the area around my parachute with machine-gun fire when I was fully visible to them all the time. Soon after this a flight of Mustangs and a flight of Shooting Star jets appeared on the scene and reported in to the Mosquito – all this radio chatter is done on the same wavelength as that of the downed pilot's little radio, so I was able to hear it all going on. John Payer, the other Mosquito pilot, did a most wonderful job – he made countless low passes over me firing marker rockets followed by the fighters firing their machine guns. The artillery also saw the markers and crept their fire slowly towards me, till eventually it was landing two hundred yards away and the machine gun fire was going three feet above my head. Then, suddenly, a patrol of fourteen Americans appeared on the scene.[10]

Lieutenant Alfred H. Gale was serving, with the primary duty of air observer, at 40th US Divisional Artillery Headquarters. He described the action from another perspective, which was recorded thus:

Early in the afternoon of 27 May 1952, Al Gale and his pilot, First Lieutenant James F. 'Sandy' Sanders were flying a routine artillery observation mission in their L-19 aircraft, covering the eastern half of the 40th Division sector near Kumwha in east-central Korea. They soon observed a Mosquito flying over the Chinese lines at about 500ft altitude crossing much of the division sector from east to west. The Mosquito was attracting a large amount of ground fire and its pilot was taking violent evasive action (sic). As it appeared that the Mosquito was going to get clear of the hostile fire, at about 1455h it did a wing-over and went vertically into the ground in the vicinity of 689452. The pilot, First Lieutenant Charles L. McBride, was apparently hit and died in the crash.

Al was amazed to see a parachute open and immediately hit the ground about 100yd in

> front of the Chinese position and 1,000yd from our lines. The chute had landed in the sector of another Divert plane but Al's pilot flew as close to the area as possible without interfering with the other plane. Al soon heard a call in a distinctly British accent on the UHF survival radio channel. The call was immediately answered by another Mosquito piloted by Air Force Captain John Payer, who was in the area training a new observer. Captain Payer immediately took charge of the operation and diverted some F-51s and F-80s to hit the area around the survivor, keeping the Chinese away.[11]

Peter later told me that:

> These guys were wonderful – each time they saw a bunch of Chinese leap out of their foxholes to come and grab me, they would peel off in turn and fire unkindly missiles and 50-calibre.[12]

How did things appear from the ground? Although John had reassured Peter that a helicopter was on its was to pick him up, both men knew full well that there was just 'no way' any helicopter could get anywhere near the downed observer and not be destroyed herself. He had to be got out of his dire situation on foot or not at all!

First Lieutenant Arthur Belknap, leading Easy Company 224th Infantry, were dug in on a nearby mountain-top and watched this drama unfold before their eyes. Arthur made contact with the commander of the 223rd company, to his east and in whose sector the Mosquito had crashed, and was told that the 223rd had no intentions of sending out a patrol to rescue the downed observer. (The 223rd Regiment's Command Report for May 1952 makes no mention of this activity though it happened less than a thousand yards in front of their Item Company's position.)

Recognizing the urgency – who would reach the injured observer first, the Chinese or the Americans, Lieutenant Belknap obtained approval for a rescue mission and called his platoon leaders to find volunteers for a patrol. At 1525h the special patrol crossed the Main Line of Resistance (MLR) and headed towards the Chinese lines.

By 1530 additional air cover and medical support had been requested. However, a call for more air cover was unnecessary since the Mosquito hovering overhead was already providing good cover for his fellow crewman on the ground. With the Chinese Communist troops deterred from leaving their own positions by the US artillery and air strikes, Lieutenant Belknap's patrol hurried across no-man's-land toward Peter. Belknap's volunteers were:

- Second Lieutenant Edward C. 'Shy' Meyer, Weapons Platoon Leader, who had just arrived five days earlier;
- Sfc Peter T. Croghan, US Infantry, 3rd Platoon Squad Leader, who was the patrol rear guard;
- Sfc John G. Dolenshek, US Infantry, the Mortar Section Leader, who was point man;
- Sfc William J. Hughes, RA, Infantry, assigned to one of the rifle platoons;
- Sfc Roger E. Lumire, US Infantry, Weapons Platoon Sergeant;
- Sfc Lorennzo E. Velasques, RA, US Infantry, assigned to 3rd Rifle Platoon;
- Sgt Roy J. Black, US Infantry, assigned to the Weapons Platoon;
- Sgt Benjamin J. Conness, US Infantry, assigned to the Weapons Platoon;
- Sgt Charles H. Kanovsky, RA, US Infantry, assigned to one of the rifle platoons;
- Sgt Robert Lawrie-Smith, National Guard, Army Medical Service, Medic assigned to rifle platoon;
- Sft Ramon B. Pina, US Infantry, assigned to one of the rifle platoons;
- Cpl John H. 'Jack' Appleby, US Infantry, Company Headquarters;
- Cpl Edmond J. Dussert, US Infantry, assigned to one of the rifle platoons;
- Cpl Neal J. Froese, Jr, US Infantry, Radioman assigned to one of the rifle platoons;
- Pfc Jack L. Tidd, RA, Army Medical Service, Medic assigned to the Weapons Platoon.

The then Lieutenant Belknap (now a retired colonel) remembered that as the

LTA-571 and LTA-594 leave airstrip K-47 for an early morning mission in 1952. The former has a red tip to her vertical tail surface while the whole of the latter's rudder is red. Both still retain their spinners.
The Mosquito Association Inc

LTA-573 firing her rockets. One missile (ringed right) can be seen speeding toward the target area.
The Mosquito Association Inc

patrol approached the downed airman, the leading patrol members were engaged by enemy fire from the right front (north-east). And when the patrol reached Lieutenant Tolputt (co-ordinates 689452) at 1610h, the patrol came under fire from the left front (east-north-east). Sfcs Velasques, Dolesnshek and Hughes and Cpl Appleby …

> … returned the fire and suppressed the enemy while the patrol medics got the evacuation of Lieutenant Tolputt underway.
>
> Since Lieutenant Tolputt had twisted his knee on landing and suffered a head wound in the aircraft, he was helped back to friendly lines intermittently on a litter and by patrol members in pairs supporting him.

All through their return to friendly lines, the patrol continued to exchange …

> … fire with the pursuing enemy forces approaching from the west, north and east. During the same period the patrol was receiving support from the covering aircraft, Divisional Artillery and Regimental and Company mortar and machine-gun units. Yet none of us were afraid – we were simply terrified! Sfc Dolenshek had the stock of his rifle shattered by an enemy bullet. His fingers and cheek were scratched by wood splinters but no bullet wound. Sfc Velasques suffered a bullet burn to the forehead – and nothing more.
>
> For Lieutenant Myer and most other patrol members the most traumatic time was on their return toward friendly lines when they received a radio call from the adjacent company (Item Company, 223rd Infantry). They were in an unmarked mine field! Stunned, the patrol members spread out further and moved quickly toward Easy Company's hill. Colonel Belknap remembers well being knocked on his arse by Sfc Velasques just as he was about to step on a personnel land mine.
>
> Sgt Roy Black also recalls the great cover they received from Air Force strafing when they were *en route* to Peter Tolputt's position and from Division Artillery barrages that hit the hills behind them as they returned to their lines. 'The artillery passing overhead was sweet music to us – we knew we weren't out their alone.' Roy also remembers well the beer that General Joe Cleland brought in on the chopper that evacuated Peter.

Peter told his parents that on the return the patrol was …

> … firing behind us as we left, because a Chink patrol was only two minutes behind us.

Peter also told me how the patrol had…

> … all volunteered to carry out a fighting patrol in daylight into and amongst the Chinese. Brave chaps and interestingly, the patrol was led by a green youngster just out of West Point, who went on to become a Five Star General, and, as Chief of Staff, handed over to Colin Powell just before the Gulf War.[13]

Al Gale recorded how …

> … the patrol re-entered Easy Company positions at 1650h. Behind friendly lines a helicopter picked up Peter and evacuated him to a MASH hospital. After preliminary medical treatment he returned to K-47 airfield at Chun Chon.

Said Peter:

> We stumbled into friendly lines where a helicopter was waiting for me. I was whisked on to it and taken south to an American hospital. There they couldn't believe I'd jumped from 400ft and made it! They asked me what was wrong and I told them my head was damaged. So they immediately took my trousers off!

For their 'outstanding courage, determination and devotion to duty' each member of

MOSQUITO MEN: Lieutenant W. P. R. 'Peter' Tolputt, Royal Artillery

Peter, whose remarkable adventure is recounted in these pages, was born in British Guiana, the son of a regular soldier. He was educated in England, '... at a prep school whose buildings were blown up to make way for Mr Kodak's head office in Hemel Hempstead'. Also at Felsted School 'and my house building was also blown up (after I left it) as the lead on the roof was worth more than the building!' He went off to enter Wadham College, Oxford and then entered the army, serving with the Royal Armoured Corps from 1944 onward. Peter was commissioned into the 8th King's Royal Irish Hussars (now defunct). The post-war regiments were too expensive for young second lieutenants whose pay was the same size as the compulsory mess bill! Peter, therefore, in 1948 got himself transferred to the Royal Artillery. 'A very good move. Though we were known as the Nine Mile Snipers and Poor, Proud and Prejudiced, they were in fact a grand bunch of people, and very professional from the lowest rank upwards.'

From 1949 Peter served at Hong Kong at the time the victorious communist armies were expected to invade it at any time. ('We would have lasted about twelve hours against the Chinese hordes, some predicted less!') He was then attached to Combined Operations and went to sea with the Royal Navy when they conducted shore bombardments of the Malay Peninsular with the object of dislodging Communist terrorists.

Then, in 1951, Peter's unit was sent as an Artillery Regiment to support the 1st Commonwealth Division in Korea, his particular battery looking after the Royal Norfolk Regiment in the line. 'By this time the line had become fairly static and the Comwel Div, with English, Scots, Canadians, Australians and New Zealanders tended to be grouped near the line of the Imjin River. Our role was mass defensive fire to reel Chinese attacks, especially at night, plus round-the-clock harassing fire on to pre-selected co-ordinates with doubtful results, except to deter the Chinese rear echelons from hanging out the washing!'

Peter felt that life could be more exciting than this and when word went round that a volunteer was wanted to join the USAF and the colonel selected a name from those applied, he was the lucky one. Peter told me:

For close support from the air, the mountainous terrain made ground observation less than successful, so in the same way the artillery had spotter aircraft to control the guns, the flyers used air controllers to guide their air strikes. Which was were I came in. The USAF had two squadrons doing this job, and as the style of work was nipping in and nipping out quickly, we aptly named them Mosquitoes (not to be confused with the far more famous Mossies of the RAF in World War Two). Our 'Mosquitoes', however, were Harvards –good old Harvards, which Americans called T-6 'Texans', T of course being for trainer. They were, however, ideal for the role, slow, very manoeuvrable at low altitudes and with good visibility and a great reputation for reliability.

Different to the aircraft called in to do the strikes – they were first generation jets, like the F-80 Shooting Star, the F-84 Thunderjet and the F9F US Navy Panthers. We did, however, also use piston-engined aircraft – AD-4 Douglas Skyraiders, P-51M Chance Vought Corsairs and a few Royal Navy Sea Furies from carriers off the coast. The Skyraiders and Mustangs were best for the job. Our two squadrons provided at least one aircraft circling each corps area during all daylight hours, awaiting orders from a group controller at division or brigade HQ. (He would be a 'rested' flyer who would know how to advise and handle ground troop requests.) Over the radio we would be

(Above) **Near miss for rear seat Mosquito man Lieutenant Peter Tolputt, RA, British Army. The next hit he took proved even more hairy!** Peter Tolputt

(Left) **The Mosquito rear-seat observers were a truly international assembly of men with a common cause. Here Lieutenant Peter Tolputt, who made a remarkable adventure after crashing close to Communist lines, is seated on the wheel of a Mosquito. Others of his team are, seated on the wing (left) Lieutenant William Watson, New Zealand; (right) Captain Philip Plouffe, Canada and, standing, Lieutenant Albert Bull, Canada.** USAF via The Mosquito Association Inc

given a target – say a mortar position, a troop concentration, whatever. The co-ordinates would either then be marked by coloured smoke from artillery or we had to target mark with some of the twelve white phosphorous (WP, 'Willy Petes') marker rockets we carried.

An inbound flight of normally four aircraft would be allotted to us, with whom we would establish radio contact, arrange an air rendezvous, do some talking about the target and then control the ground attack as we best saw its likelihood of success. There was a marked variation in the flying quality of the fighter-bombers we controlled. Best of all, by far, were the South Africans in P-51s; then came the Navy and Marine guys from aircraft carriers in the Yellow Sea, with Skyraiders or Corsairs, who were very accurate. Then there were the F-9Fs, then the P-51, F-80 and F-86s from the USAF and then, the Royal Navy Sea Furies who, embarrassingly, seemed to hold back, much to my chagrin when being joked at debriefing! Lastly came the South Korean (ROK) Air Force, when anything might happen and anything but the target might be hit!

I flew, I think, sixty-one sorties and managed to avoid being hit by ground fire except on three occasions. The first one, which caused some amusement, was one small round from a Chinese Burp gun, which entered via my cockpit roof, thus demonstrating that the ground-based pot shooter was at a higher altitude than myself! The second occasion was also minor – triple A which did no good to the engine – a 9 cylinder radial – and we returned minus one cylinder, but the tough old engine just ran rough and deposited rather a lot of oil.

The third occasion was more serious; when doing a pre-strike recce prior to a target marking run we were hit by 20mm ground fire. This unfortunately put us ablaze very quickly and an urgent departure was required. Sadly my fellow crew didn't jump – I think he was already dead at the wheel – so I was left on my own and amongst the Chinese. It was obvious they were under orders to capture and not kill me (a downed flyer at that stage of the Korean War was regarded by them as a tremendous propaganda coup), so we played cat and mouse.

After this experience Peter spent three years as a Company Commander in Colonial Troops, the East African Rifles, during the Mau Mau emergency, before finally leaving the service in 1959. Peter then ran his own garage in Bath for seventeen years as a SAAB distributorship. He sold that and, with his yacht based at Lymington, he turned his hobby into a business. Peter obtained the necessary qualifications and ran a RYA approved offshore sailing school and yacht charter operation for several years. In turn that was sold off and Peter became a professional skipper 'for unpleasant millionaires in large shiny yachts, so dumped that fairly soon. Hung up my wellies and built a professional photo darkroom doing quality colour enlargement work for exhibitions and the like.'

Peter later suffered a heart attack and double pneumonia. On his recovery from that Peter now lives in Alton, Hampshire and 'earns his pocket money' restoring old pictures.

the patrol received the Silver Star, the third highest medal awarded for gallantry in action by the United States Army. John Payer received the DFC for his excellent work also that day. All these awards were very well deserved!

John Payer recalled:

I'll never forget those days and most of all the next morning. I was working briefings and the chopper was bringing Pete back from the MASH. So, I went to meet it, but Pete didn't wait – he jumped out of the chopper and drug his leg that had been hurt for a long distance to hug me, and he was a cool Brit!![14]

***(Above)* How the GIs brought Mosquito man Lieutenant Peter Tolputt, RA, British Army, out from under the enemy's noses.** Peter Tolputt

Lieutenant Peter Tolputt, RA, British Army, rescued Mosquito rear-seat man, shakes hands with one of his rescuers. Peter Tolputt

Mosquito LTA-578 climbs out of the area after marking the target to allow the fighter-bombers space to strike at the enemy. The Mosquito Association Inc

When the fighting eventually stopped, the 6147th TCG had established an enviable record. Over 117,471 combat flying hours the T-6s had carried out a total of 40,354 sorties. During that time they had lost forty-two aircraft, but only thirty-three aircrew had been killed in all that time. Their good work had enabled the fighter-bombers and artillery to decimate the best part of eight North Korean and Chinese divisions, create mayhem to five Chinese tank divisions and led to the certain destruction of 563 artillery pieces, 5,079 road vehicles of all types; twelve locomotives and eighty-four strategically important bridges were taken out.

Both the UN and the communist forces eventually agreed a 2½-mile (4km) wide buffer zone right across Korea on 27 July 1953. Since then the North has never ceased to probe and prod and direct an unending stream of 'hate' against their ROK neighbours. They still maintain huge standing armies poised to strike again, while their own people starve by the million. The war has faded from the memories of all but a few, but the threat is just as real today. As for the effects on future wars, the Mosquitoes expertise was unrivalled. However, as always with democracies, and as the late Jefrey L. Ethell succinctly put it:

> When the final Mosquito mission, number 40,354 was flown in 1953, a wealth of knowledge on the forward air control mission disappeared from military studies and the lessons would have to be learned all over again ten years later in another part of the Far East.

The Mosquitoes' (also known as the 'Mighty Mites') job did not end in 1953, however, for the war could have resumed at any time subsequent to that. Although hostilities were not in place, the watch had to be maintained. Before the armistice was signed, the Mosquitoes were working from Chunchon air base (K-47) but subsequently they moved back to Osan Air Base, (K-55) in August 1954. The main activities of the group during this period were to train new aircrews and observers and maintain their combat effectiveness just in case.

MOSQUITO MEN: Colonel Kenneth W. Beckstrom, USAF

Lieutenant Colonel Ken W. Beckstrom was assigned to the 6147th Tactical Control Group, with the job of Special Project Officer to Colonel Harry B. Young, while the unit was at K-47. After some time here, Beckstrom assumed command of the 6147th Tactical Control Group on 29 November 1954 at Osan.

Colonel Beckstrom originally gained his Bachelor of Science degree in engineering at Montana Sate College, where he majored in physics in 1949. He and his wife, Maureen, were later to establish their home at the township of Vaugh, Montana. Ken Beckstrom became a member of the Army Air Corps in 1940. His first assignment was to attend the Pan American navigators' school, a civilian institution, at Coral Gables, Florida. In March 1941, Ken went to Panama as a navigator. After Pearl Harbor, Beckstrom's next assignment was out into the south-west Pacific, where the action was at its hottest. He flew combat missions on B-17s, some forty in all, both bombing and reconnaissance missions, over such areas as New Britain and the main Japanese base of Rabaul. After thirteen months he returned to the United States and took part in an experimental school, which was set up to determine the feasibility of training navigators and bombardiers.

Ken proved it could most certainly be done and duly graduated as a pilot. He then attended a familiarization course on the B-24 and later went over to England to join in the 'other war' in Europe with the 8th Air Force, again though, flying with a B-17 unit. He flew no less than twenty-three combat missions over Germany, and on a dozen of them was the squadron leader.

With the arrival of V-E Day, Ken Beckstrom, now a full Colonel, returned to the United States once more and was appointed as a design and development engineer in the engineering division at the Wright-Patterson Air Base in Ohio. Here he remained until 1949. Colonel Beckstrom then went to the Air Command Staff School and, after his graduation from there, was assigned to the Pentagon in the Research and Development Directorate, where, for eight months, he was the acting chief of the equipment division.

Lieutenant Colonel Ken W. Beckstrom (standing) was assigned to the 6147th Tactical Control Group, with the job of Special Project Officer to Colonel Harry B. Young, while the unit was at K-47. After some time here, Beckstrom assumed command of the 6147th Tactical Control Group on 29 November 1954 at Osan. This photo was taken in December 1954. Colonel Kenneth W. Beckstrom

He became the Deputy Chief and left in July 1953. His next assignment well suited him for the Mosquito commander's role, for he went to the Army Command and General Staff College at Fort Levenworth, Kansas.

In 1954 he was assigned to 6148th Tactical Control Squadron as its Commander and moved to Kimpo (K-14) with that unit, before finally returning to the States on 7 July 1954. Colonel Beckstrom currently lives in Albuquerque, New Mexico and is an active member of the Mosquitoes Association there.

CHAPTER THIRTEEN

The Great Revival

Civilian Usage

The initial post-war disposals brought, as we have seen, the first great civilian boom in the T-6, but thereafter numbers steadily declined as the expense of running these aircraft was, and remains, considerable. Over the six decades that have followed, there have been peaks and troughs as available airframes and engines declined, and then were revitalized as fresh disposals took place. Thus a series of 'waves' of availability as different Air Forces discarded their 'Sixes' was reflected in increases in civilian registrations for a while. The mid-1940s was the first boom; the second came a decade later when the United States, Canada and the United Kingdom finally abandoned the type as a military trainer. The next boom came with similar disposals of Italian, French, Spanish and Portuguese T-6s and Harvards, and the most recent boost came with the final disposal of what remained of South Africa's still sizeable fleet in the 1990s. So, from a figure of 805 American civilian registered aircraft in 1947, the numbers declined to 317 by 1952, then rose to 424 in 1977 and then to 586 in 1986. By 1989 numbers stood at about 400 in the USA alone and in 1997 there were an incredible 900+ registered world-wide, with many more in museums and undergoing restoration!

Building Your Own T-6

Not content with the usual rebuilding and renovating, at least one American enthusiast went one better and built from scratch his own T-6. Nor did he stop with just one machine either! The gentleman concerned was Dr Gerald A. 'Doc' Swayze of Mesquite, Texas. He had long been a 'Six' man, taking part in T-6 races for many years. Now he wanted to go one better. He gave me his first-hand account of just how this came about.

He had looked hard for a suitable aircraft to renovate but found none that really came up to his requirements.

> It was impossible to find one that didn't have zinc chromate peeling off on all the interior surfaces. Very few of them are clean and dent-free enough to look good with a polished aluminium exterior. Besides, I had always wanted a new T-6 and for that I had been born too late![1]

How to rebuild a 'Six'. The sleek lines and polished perfection of 'Doc' Swayze's 'How Sweet It Is' (N3682F) seen here on her maiden flight. She went on to win the 1972 Grand Champion Warbird accolade. Courtesy of Dr Gerald A. 'Doc' Swayze

While continuing with his search for perfection, Dr Swayze was at the 1968 Confederate Air Force Airshow and it was here that he first saw Gunther Balz's beautiful N-9G Bearcat.

> This airplane gave me the inspiration I needed to begin the project that had been teasing my brain. Why not build a new T-6 with new surplus parts?

To most people this would have presented a daunting, almost impossible, task, but the 'Doc' went about it in a professional and logical way, step-by-determined-step. His first move was to buy an old hulk because, as he told me:

> In order to put together a new T-6, I would have to first tear an old one apart to see how to do it.

And so Swayze purchased N3682F, whose engine was run out and done for. She was a former SNJ-5B (c/n 88-17662, serial 42-85881, BuNo 90664), which had been flown by Walter H. Hackett, of Niles, Ohio and from whom the Doc purchased her in 1969. If nothing else he felt he might make use of some of her better-preserved parts and make new ones, particularly non-moving castings.

Doc Swayze then set about hunting down the many parts he needed by instituting a nationwide search. Most of what he needed he found from Don Wise and Southwest Aero Sales. After diligent search he found no less than *five* brand-new starboard wings, three of which were pristine and still sitting in their Dallas crates. Three of them were still coated with cosoline and in mint condition. What he could not acquire was a new port wing and so he bit the bullet and authorized the re-manufacture of a used one, which cost him $3,000 outright. He managed to locate and purchase a new rear fuselage section, which had been in store. Unfortunately it was covered in scratches from decades of careless handling and Doc decided to completely re-skin the whole thing.

Swayze was also fortunate in locating a new wing centre section and wing fuel tanks. He also fitted entirely brand-new spare parts in the centre section, landing gear, wheels and brakes complete. His next hurdle was the powerplant.

> New engines were not to be found and I wanted to custom-build one anyway. How I ever got lucky enough to find Mr Faxel and Mr Cleveland of Fort Worth Engine Overhaul I don't know. They did a magnificent job with the R-1340An-1.

He described their work as producing, 'the smoothest, most economical 1340 with respect to both fuel and oil consumption, that I have ever sat behind'.

Doc estimated that it would take him at least three years work, starting from scratch, to complete his project. He was still a practising MD, with a wife and family, and he later confessed that it would have probably taken him twice that long had he not had the enthusiastic help of Mr Redell Gross, who had been his pit-man and crew chief from his racing days.

If building your own aeroplane was difficult with regard to the structure itself, when it came to the internal electrics, the exercise turned into a real nightmare. Determined to do the job himself Doc took courses in electrical soldering and applied himself to learning how to read and interpret electrical diagrams. He described the wiring up of his aircraft as the 'real monster' in the whole project.

> It took four months and when later assembled all the goodies worked with the proper switch – that was a surprise. I really thought it would burn.

There were other hazards to overcome, not the least the patience of his then wife, Francine!

> Much of the work was done at home. The garage was scattered with parts. The study, upstairs, served as a storage area for completed parts and subassemblies. The cabinet in the den was fully of completed small parts. Most of the time there were T-6 parts on the bar in the breakfast area.

The Doc's wife was, at that time, a school teacher of first- and second-grade pupils, and, being used to the untidy ways of small children was quite tolerant of her own 'child', but there were limits!

> Once, while doing the electrical system (wires were all over the kitchen amidst dripping little balls of solder) I saw her standing, hands on hips, tight-lipped with her right foot tapping the floor. She got over it after I retreated with my wires. I was finished anyway!

His second wife, Linda, 'dearly loves AT-6s (enough said!)'.

Swayze admitted to me that he would probably not have completed the task he had set himself had he not had enormous help from a team of volunteers that included Redell, Tom Ryan, Frank Goodloe, Jim Walters and Dave Groark. Eventually the aircraft came together beautifully, and, on 14 May 1972, after an inspection by Bob Card, it flew like a dream. Named *How Sweet It Is* and with burnished aluminium body and wings, brilliantly polished yellow cowling and red-and-white horizontally striped rudder, she took to the air. In 1972 and again in 1973, his creation won the Grand Champion Warbird award.

> We did a green and yellow one, 6437D, which was finished in 1983, but was not taken to Oshkosh. It was painted in the pre-World War II colours of the carrier *Ranger*.

Far from being deterred by the mammoth task and the due reward, Swayze went on to build a further *six* T-6s in the same dedicated manner, one of them a former SNJ-5, a sister to his own machine, 5486V for Dave Groark. She was painted in the colour scheme of the pre-war carrier *Saratoga*. Completed in June 1987, she scooped the third National Award for best T-6 at Oshkosh that same year.

In October 1997 *How Sweet It Is* was acquired by Ralph C. Parker, of Wichita Falls, Texas who flew her until 1996.

A different approach to the rebuild was taken by Bill Melamed. The 1989 Grand Champion was again a T-6 in 1989, when a CCandF Harvard 4 (20247), built in 1955, took the honour. She had originally served with No. 4 Fighter Training Squadron, RCAF at Penhold, Alberta, and had logged 4,191 hours flying time. She had an accident in 1958, but was totally repaired and overhauled, receiving a new right elevator, wing flaps, centre section, vertical stabilizer, starboard wing and hydraulic assemblies – virtually a rebuild. She continued to serve at Penhold, logging up a staggering 6,512 hours flying and going through six engines. She was not finally struck off charge by the RCAF until 28 February 1966, when her wings were removed, engine and prop put into separate storage and the rest of the aircraft moth-balled.

Later this aircraft was ferried down to Chino, California, and then went back into storage for another two decades, until Bill Melamed, a Los Angeles enthusiast, purchased her and undertook her restoration. He took her to John Muszala of Pacific Fighters and her engine was given a total overhaul, while inspection of her original control surfaces, fabric showed them to still be in a near-perfect state. This aircraft was special in that she was built almost totally from authentic original parts, rather than newly manufactured ones. However, the CAA insisted on the removal of the original radio and equipment and its replacement with modern equipment in the interests of safety. This was mounted on a removable panel and the other 97 per cent of the aircraft was original. She was given an authentic yellow paint job, with day-glo pink cowling and rudder and scooped the award with ease.

together to form the 'upper wing', complete with fully-operational ailerons, of this monstrosity. This 'wing' was affixed to the upper surface of the wing of the other SNJ with spars and cross-members in the traditional manner. The cockpit canopy had to be sacrificed in the process. The object was to produce a crop-duster aeroplane, but professional conversions like the Ceres did not feature in this experiment.

The chemical tank was made from an old fuel belly tank, which was 'stuffed' into the aircraft's rear cockpit. Receiving the civil registration N6435D, this machine

decades ago, Andrew first learned to fly at Shoreham and he got the bug at that time. He has subsequently become a leading player in the sale of aircraft of all ages and was Chief Executive of Southern Air Ltd at Shoreham, which distributes Enstrom and McDonnell Douglas helicopters as well as carrying out restoration work.

Andrew was the first in the UK to obtain a Certificate of Airworthiness in the Transport Category for a North American product. Such was his determination that he persevered, even though it took him four years to do it. Once achieved, it

An immaculate Harvard IV (ex-FT 239, G-BIWX) is pictured taxiing at West Malling airfield, 26 August 1985.
RAF Museum, Hendon, London

Bacon Super T-6S

A rather more spectacular T-6 rebuild was done by Gordon Israel in 1957. She featured a tricycle landing gear, a bubble canopy and wing-tip fuel tanks a.k.a the *Thunderchief*. She was no mere show-plane, despite her exotic appearance and clocked up an impressive 216mph (345km/h), rather faster than a standard T-6.

T-6 Biplane

Another bizarre conversion was carried out by Robert C. Stroop of Selma, Alabama, in the United States. He had two SNJ-5s in 1966, and from one of them (c/n 88-17079, BuNo 42-85289) he stripped the outer wing panels and wing-tips, bolting them

actually flew at a maximum speed of about 90 knots, but what it lacked in hustle it more than made up for in lift, taking off in less than two hundred feet. Equally her rate of descent, unless held by full power, was 'spectacular'. Nonetheless she worked for J. F. Carter of Monroeville, Alabama on regular agricultural work, between 1963 and 1970.

Transport Command, Shoreham-by-Sea

That such dedication to the loving reconstruction of 'The Six' is by no means confined to the United States is shown by the splendid work undertaken by Andrew and Karen Edie of Transport Command based at Shoreham Airport. More than two

enabled the hiring out of his T-6G, *Romeo Alpha*, G-BKRA, from Shoreham on a 'hire or reward' basis. Andrew told me that, without the help of a dedicated team it would have taken him even longer.

> I was fortunate enough to get real help and assistance in tracking down the original NAA drawings which were essential from C. E. 'Rocky' Ruckdahel from North American Rockwell. I also had the unique help of Al Allen whose expertise was invaluable in confirming the build standard.[2]

Al had spent his entire career, apart from war service with the US Eighth Air Force when he flew thirty combat missions in B-17s, with North American and was in on the T-6 story from almost the start. After his discharge from the service, Al returned

(Above) **The AAE&E's immaculate and long-serving T2B (ex-KF 183) seen here at Middle Wallop on 23 July 1982.** RAF Museum, Hendon, London

Civilian pilots were, alas, no less immune from the T-6's foibles than wartime trainees. Many famous names have met their end in 'The Six' over the past half-century, others were fortunate enough to walk away. Here is the former SNJ-5 (BuNo 43818, 88-15903, 41-34632) with civil registration N6628C of SNJ-5 Inc, Rolling Meadows, Illinois, in a sorry state after a hard knock. Author's collection

to Inglewood and was involved in the T-6G scheme and so knew his stuff perfectly.

The T-6G that Andrew had purchased had originally been built in 1941 and was one of those that NAA had touted for on the war-surplus market post-war in order to re-manufacture them for resale, offering $400 to private owners of such aircraft to fly them back to Inglewood for the work to be done. She received a new radio, new electronics, long-range fuel tanks and also the new serials of 188-90, 51-15227, when she emerged in 1951. Further alterations were carried out under the MDAP scheme in December of that year, and in February 1952 she was allocated to the Italian Air Force. On arrival in Italy she was given the Italian serial MM 53664 and coded RM-9. She worked with the 1° Reparto Volo Regionale (RVR) at Orio Al Serio Air Base, Bergamo, until 1973, when she was struck off charge and put into storage. In 1981 she was one of several such aircraft auctioned under the MDAP terms by the US Defense Logistics Agency at Camp Darby, Livorno. After the sale she was transported via France and shipped over to the old Supermarine factory at Woolston, Southampton, where she arrived on 21 November 1981, where she was again stored, unconverted. In October 1982, she was transhipped over to Sandown, Isle of Wight, where Terry S. Warren undertook her restoration. On 18 June 1983 she was completed to a US Navy SNJ dark-blue colour scheme with a yellow cowl, and serial 51-15227, registered to Andrew Edie. She appeared on 19 August 1983 with her British civilian registration G-BKRA. She took part at air shows at Duxford in September 1985, and again at Middle Wallop in July 1988.

From October 1985 to October/August 1987 she was operated by Pulsegrove Ltd, at Shoreham, and between August 1987 and 1988 by Malcolm D. Faiers of Nympsfield, but Andrew renewed his association with her in 1991 and has operated her ever since. In 1991 she won the Ted White Trophy at the Great Warbirds Air Display held at West Malling.

Andrew told me:

> I found the wiring up relatively easy. As for availability of spare parts I use Lance Aviation of Dallas who can get me almost anything I want at a reasonable price. The Pratt and Whitney R-1340-AN-1 radial was given a total overhaul by Covington Aircraft Engines, of Oklahoma and a new nine-foot Hamilton Standard propeller was fitted. The RAF used to cut the prop down by several feet but I find she flies better in the original configuration.[3]

She flew in her colour scheme for many years, but in 1999 Andrew and Karen carried out deeper research and Martin Pengelly at Landrake, Saltash, was able to supply them with the exact US Navy specification for SNJs that were allocated out to fleet units in the latter part of the war, and Andrew had her re-painted and coded accordingly. She now works hard flying enthusiasts (this author among them) and conducts flight training, PPL type conversions, Aerobatic training and trial lessons.

The 'Noisy North American' tag still refuses to die, however, although nowadays it seems to be confined to chickens! On 3 April 1998, the local *Argus* newspaper carried a story in which a local farmer, Shaun Hazelden, complained about it:

> My hens don't like it, they stop laying. They rush into one corner, and then the other, clucking like mad. They see it up there and can't understand the noise. I think they're worried it might be a great hawk or something.[4]

Whether an April Fool story or not, Andrew and Karen take their responsibilities very seriously and the Chief Flying Instructor of the Warbird Flying Club, Mike Chapman, issued the following guidelines to all Harvard pilots on 4 June 1999:

> **To all Pilots and Instructors.**
> T6 Operation – Noise Minimization.
> We have received a number of complaints about the noise generated by the Harvard propeller. The following power/rpm settings produce the

How the Italian T-6Gs arrived in England. This is the former Italian MM 53652 after being undocked. Originally built in 1941 she was one of those purchased for $400 post-war and returned to the NAA Inglewood plant for modernization and re-sale. With new radio, electronics and long-range fuel tanks she re-emerged in 1951 with the new serial number 51-15227. Following further updating in December 1951, she was assigned to Italy under the terms of MDAP, serving for a while with the 1° Reparto Volo Regionale (RVR) at Bergamo/Orio Al Serio airfield. After being retired in 1973 she was put into store there and then auctioned-off under the MDAP terms in 1981 by the US Defense Agency at Camp Darby (Livorno). After purchase she was shipped via France with three sister aircraft, arriving at Woolston, Southampton, on 21 November 1981, as pictured here. Andrew & Karen Edie

Andrew Edie was not content with just one renovation and took on a further five Harvard IV's and one T-6G (G-BSBB to G-BSBG) which were recovered from Mozambique and put through the renovation line at Thruxton Flight Centre. Here is the splendid results of one of them, G-BSBE in the colours of USAAF TA-521 and serial 52-8521. Andrew & Karen Edie

least noise without extreme performance penalties:

take-off	1850–1900 30' (do not exceed 30' at this rpm)	
rejoin	1700	as required <24'.

These are recommendations only and depend upon pilot currency, runway length and conditions, wind direction and wind gusts notwithstanding all-up weight and temperature.

Thank you for your co-operation in the 'neighbourly' operation of the aircraft.

Not content with the sterling work done with *Romeo Alpha*, Andrew and John Woodhouse set about rebuilding a further five Harvards, which they recovered from Mozambique in a difficult salvage operation. These aircraft (with British civil registrations G-BSBB/BSBG, inclusive) have been likewise transformed at the Thruxton Flight Centre 'production' line and have re-appeared in various guises, all with equal authenticity. As Andrew told me, 'Whenever possible I always like to use the real parts for the restorations'. Karen

(Above) **Andrew Edie's Transport Command T-6G, in her first paint scheme. She is seen here preparing for take-off from Old Warden airfield, Bedfordshire, piloted by Adrian Read with the author in the back seat, on 19 September 1998.** Peter C. Smith

(Below) **Restoration project AJ 693 went to Canada on completion and served in 31 SFTS until she crashed into Lake Ontario on 29 September 1943. On her subsequent post-war recovery a lot of hard work was required to get her back into even this shape.** John A. Pritchard

T-6/HARVARD MEN: CFI Michael John Chapman

The Chief Flying Instructor with the Warbird Flying Club, and the man with the most T-6/Harvard flying hours under his belt in the UK today, is Michael John Chapman. I was privileged to meet and talk with him at Shoreham in between his taking *Romeo Alpha* into the sky.

Michael was born on 5 March 1951, and was educated at Surbiton County Grammar School, Surrey between 1962 and 1969. His interest in aviation started early and he joined the Air Training Corps, reaching Warrant Officer rank. This was followed by two years as a civilian instructor. Michael also gained gliding qualifications and a PPL on an RAF Scholarship. A keen sportsman, he represented Surrey Wing in shooting, boxing and athletics and attained RAF marksman standard in the former.

Michael initially started work as a market research assistant for Hawker Siddeley Aviation, at Kingston, Surrey in 1970, but moved to New Zealand for three years and worked at the Ford Motor Company at Wiri. On return to the United Kingdom, he worked in telecommunications between 1974 and 1975. Michael then became a preventive officer with Customs and Exercise at Gatwick Airport, which after Heathrow is the second busiest airport in the world. He was most successful in the field of detection and became an anti-drug smuggling specialist, but he resigned in 1988 in order to pursue a full-time career in aviation.

Michael's career here began with commercial employment on short/medium haul multi-sector operations with the SAAB 340s, and between 1989 and 1995 he conducted instructional flying based mainly at Shoreham. He completed CPL/IR/ATPL studies and examinations during this period and was employed as a instructor on the Harvard at Southern Air.

I asked Michael if, when he first approached the Harvard, had he known of her reputation? 'Yes, I was well aware of the Harvard's notoriety', he replied, 'but, I treated her with due respect and caution and never had any trouble. I do not owe her any wing-tips at all!'[5]

Certainly he has built up a formidable knowledge of 'The Six' down the years, with a total flying time of 4,920h including 1,950 hours as QFI. This total has been clocked up on a wide variety of types, including the Hunting Percival Provost, Beagle 206 Basset, de Havilland Tiger Moth, and the Chipmunk, as well as the SAAB 340 and the BAe 146, but pride of place must go to his 700 plus hours on the T-6/Harvard.

Michael manages to have other interests than flying, believe it or not, and lists reading, walking, history, current affairs and DIY among them.

confirmed to me also that 'Andrew likes things to be exactly right!' Nor has all this work dampened his ardour for 'The Six'. Despite the almost total time-consuming dedication involved, Andrew confided to me that, 'I'd like to do another one, from scratch, and *really* get it right!'[6]

Typical of the high standard of work done in the UK is a Harvard IIB, G-AZBN, which I was also fortunate enough to be able to examine and photograph in detail at Shoreham. She is a 1943 Noorduyn Aviation built aircraft (serial 43-13132 under contract 14A-1431) and was the former RCAF and then RAF serial FT 391. She stayed in storage for a long period until her transfer to the Royal Netherlands Air Force in October 1947, when she became their B-97. She served for many years until discharged in 1969 to C. Honcoop at Veen, under civil registration PH-HON and was purchased in 1971 by Sir William Roberts of Shoreham (later Strathallan). She was lovingly restored to her RAF colours in 1978. She was part of the Strathallan Collection between March 1971 and 1981, and then was owned by Colt Executive Aviation at Staverton between July of that year and September 1986, when she was taken over by Ashbon Associates at Duxford airfield, then the Old Flying Machine Company and J. N. Carter of Swaygate, Hove in 1992. She is currently (April 2000) at Shoreham undergoing upgrading and has a current permit to fly, with a total airframe time of 3,155 hours and a total engine time of 784 hours since the last major overhaul. She is up for sale for £85,000, which would have made Dutch Kindleberger (always the man for a deal) sit up sharply and take notice!

Clubs, Associations and Display Teams

A whole T-6 culture now exists with clubs and associations that regularly perform and show at meets and airshows in the USA, UK and other nations. As famous aerial photographer Steven D. Eisener once told me, 'Air shows in the United States now draw a greater yearly attendance than football games, believe it or not'.[7] Great air-meets like Oshkosh see T-6s assemble by the hundred. In Australia, the Antique Aeroplane Association of Australia features in its numbers not just the Wirraway, Boomerang and Ceres but also the Harvard, T-6 and SNJ in flying condition. One notable Wirraway flown at such meets was that owned by Stephen Death of Albury, NSW, while one Australian-owned Harvard frequently seen was that owned by John Barnes of Melbourne and flown by Steve Chapman. Others featured with the Western Warbirds based at Jandakot airfield, Perth. A Ceres was still being commercially operated and flown as late as March 1979, when VH-SSF was seen at Bathurst, NSW, belonging to Airfarm Associates.

In New Zealand the Warbirds Harvard Team operated to great acclaim, from 1988 onward featuring at the annual Warbirds over Wanaka airshow. They featured NZ1078 (all yellow), NZ1072 (in standard RAF green/brown camouflage) and NZ1065 (red empennage, outer wings and after fuselage, blue forward fuselage and wings, with Kiwi national markings in the roundels). Their displays included variations of barrel rolls, masked loops and combined loop and barrel rolls, closing with their speciality, a roll and brake positioning approach. Of course, several serve with the RNAZ Historic Flight, based at Wigram AB, Christchurch.

In the United States such T-6-rich groups as the Confederate Air Force abound, and there is a thriving T-6 Owners Association along with the Warbirds of American organization. In the late 1940s, Swede Ralston's Air Circus was a great draw both in the USA and Canada, with 'Swede' and Al Vaughan flying a pair of Harvards laying down complex smoke patterns and shapes in the sky for their audiences. In the late 1980s, yet another popular group appeared, the 'North American Team', a three-man outfit of Ben Cunningham (T-6G), Steve Gustafson (T-6F) and Alan Hanley (SNJ-5) which put on some stunning displays.

The National Air Races held annually at Reno, Nevada, still feature 'The Six' in a big way, and she still has her own special Pacing Class. Classified as an antique aircraft by the Experimental Aircraft Association as a Warbird, the T-6/SNJ/Harvard is as popular as ever at events from coast-to-coast, the highlight being the Annual EAA fly-in at Oshkosh, Wisconsin of course. The EAA also has T-6s/SNJs and Harvards strongly featuring in the classics category. The Sport Aviation Association section is based at Franklin, Wisconsin and a European branch at Welwyn Garden City, Hertfordshire. Stony Stonich got the North American Trainer Association up to 400 pilot members in the USA, and in conjunction with the Warbirds of America encourages proper maintenance, promotion and safety aspects of T-6 restoration, flying and exhibition. Now headquartered at Brush Prairie, Wisconsin, they publish their own magazine *Texans and Trojans* to keep enthusiasts up to date with the latest on the AT-6, T-28, TF-51 and TB-25 training aircraft. The Mosquito Association, based at Albuquerque, New Mexico, is famous for its high membership and loyalty of the LT-6G and AT-6 veterans of the Korean War and have regular reunion meetings. Another event at which the T-6 participated was the Hawthorne Air Fair. The Warbirds of Virginia flew at Roanoke in the 1970s and 1980s.

Happy ending. The ear-grating roar of a Harvard brought back from the grave marks the culmination of years of hard work in this restored Harvard. John A. Pritchard

The 50th anniversary of 'The Six' was marked with special celebrations including the North American Trainer Associations major event at Kenosha, Wisconsin between 23 and 27 July 1988, when almost 150 T-6 derivatives flew in for what was then the largest gathering of its kind. They were commemorating a unique aircraft, one that has seen service in no less than thirty-four different countries.

In the United Kingdom there are The Fighter Collection, at the Imperial War Museum collection, Duxford, near Cambridge; the Warbirds of Great Britain, Blackbushe; Anthony Hutton's Fighter Collection based at the former Battle of Britain airfield of North Weald, near Harlow, Essex and he also was responsible for the Harvard Formation Team based there.

The Harvard Formation team was established in 1983 and their debut was at the Great Warbirds Air Display that same September. The team were sponsored by Terrapin Construction of Milton Keynes, and regularly took part and won the Cranfield Air Races and Air Show, held near the author's home. There was a special 'Harvard' Trophy to be won at this event. One of its most famous members was the pop star, Gary Numan.[8] The team travelled worldwide between May and October giving spectacular formation displays.[9] The British Warbirds Fighter Meet takes place at North Weald also and, being close to London, is very well attended.

Regular Harvard fly-ins were also a feature at Bassingbourn barracks, near Royston, Hertfordshire and were always well attended.

Another firm favourite team (not least with this author) is Transport Command based at Shoreham, West Sussex. They have nineteen Qualified Flying Instructors (QFIs) who fly for them,[10] all are commercial pilots and most fly for airlines: Britannia, British Airways, Airtours, Virgin, Flightline, etc., and they even have a university professor. Their display pilot is Rod Dean, who is deputy head of general aviation at the Civil Aviation Authority (CAA). They also have other enthusiasts who fly regularly on a self-fly hire basis, and have lots of enthusiasm and experience.

Typical of these is Mark Johns of Hove. He first started flying the Harvard back in 1993 and out of a total flying time of 4,500 hours has spent 150 hours on the type. He works at Gatwick on the GB Airways Boeing 737, 300 and 400 fleet. Mark first learnt to fly gliders with the Sussex College of Hang Gliding in 1984 and put in about 500 hours. He commenced flying fixed-wing aircraft in 1988 at Southern Air and obtained his PPL in 1989, converted to CPL in 1990. Between 1989 and 1992 he flew as observer on helicopter pipeline patrol for Esso Petroleum. Mark gained his instructor rating I in 1990 and flew some 2,000 instructional hours at Southern Air between 1990 and 1997, as well as flying Cessna 310s on private charter operations. He obtained ATFL in November 1996 and undertakes occasional ferry work, his longest ferry flight being from the UK to New Zealand in a Piper Lancia.

Bill Perrins is another stalwart with Warbird Flying. As a boy, this son of a former RAF pilot (who flew many hours on Harvards) used to spend every spare moment of his time at the local airfields dreaming he might one day get to fly for a living. Now he does just that! In 1973 he was awarded a 'Flying Scholarship' which gave him 30 hours flying in a Cherokee, and he managed to bolt on the extra 5 hours required to get a private pilot's licence! In 1974 he entered the RAF to train as a pilot, which took ages due to a backlog. He spent several months flying Chipmunks giving experience flights to Air Cadets (thus going full circle) and towing gliders. Eventually he ended up flying Vulcan bombers based at RAF Waddington, a posting that included involvement during the 1982 Falklands War.

He then became a QFI and at the end of the 6-month course Bill won the 'Clarkson' trophy for aerobatics. He then spent two years at RAF Linton-on-Ouse instructing basic students of RAF, Royal Navy and Middle East air forces on the Jet Provost Marks 3 and 5. In 1985 he was posted to RAF Brawdy in Wales where, in addition to being involved in the UK orientation course for foreign military pilots, there was regular instruction for potential forward air controllers. This enabled Bill to fly the Jet Provost 4, Hawk and Chipmunk all in one day!

After this tour Bill flew Tornado F3 air defence missions from RAF Leeming in North Yorkshire, but continued Chipmunk flying in his spare time with the Air Experience Flights from nearby RAF Finningley. Bill and a friend bought a Bucker Jungmann and he was also first introduced to the Harvard Mark 2 of a friend who also flew from Breighton airfield. On leaving the RAF in 1994, he flew commercial airliners: Boeing 757s for Monarch and Boeing 757s and 767s for Airtours. In order to keep up his skills, Bill helped out at the bi-annual North Weald formation school, which involved teaching PPLs formation-flying in a safe and disciplined environment. The majority of the work was on Yak 52s (large numbers of which were coming in), Harvards, Chipmunks and Zlins. He then moved to Virgin Atlantic as a Boeing 747-200 'classic' pilot. This involved a move south, but Bill had converted his RAF QFI qualification to a CAA rating and so he now flies the T-6 from Shoreham with real enthusiasm. Bill has to date (April 2000) clocked up a total flying time of 7,700 hours, of which 738 is tailwheel flying and 97 was on the Harvard.

Andy Shuttleworth was another who started visiting his local airfield at the tender age of eleven, while his brother was taking his PPL. He became a fixture there cadging rides whenever possible at the expense of his homework. He joined the ATC and got to ride in Chipmunks, before going solo at the age of sixteen in a powered glider. His PPL followed a year later.

After school and polytechnic Andy worked in industry for two years before 'giving in to the inevitable' and taking his commercial licence. In the interim he had become an instructor specializing in tailwheel flying mainly on Tiger Moths and Chipmunks with the Cambridge Flying Group, taking his initial instrument instructors course on the latter.

Smoke-laying as they sweep over the airfield at Cranfield, Bedfordshire, at the 1988 Airshow, the Harvard Formation Team make a brave show. Charlie Wooding, courtesy of Terrapin International, Milton Keynes

Bill then worked for Suckling Airways at Cambridge from 1991 to 1993, flying a Dornier 228 and was promoted to captain, flying thus for a further two years, but he continued to instruct and fly for pleasure in his own time, mainly on tail-wheel aircraft. In 1995 he moved to the Air Transpiration Division of the Ford Motor Company, Fordair, and flew the MD 87. He currently flies the MD 87 and until recently the BAe 125. Andy has just taken a Gulfstream IV course.

During his time with Fordair Andy maintained his interest in vintage aircraft and developed his aerobatic flair, flying the 'Plane Sailing' Catalina for a short while before it met with its unfortunate accident. He now flies the T-6 with Andrew and Karen at Shoreham and considers himself lucky to be able to do so. In Andy's own words, 'The T6 is a superbly rewarding aircraft to fly and it really is a privilege to have this opportunity.' Andy has currently amassed a flying hour total of 6,350 hours (April 2000).

Other large organizations worldwide include the Harvard Club of South Africa, while Canada has a long tradition of outstanding aerobatic teams that utilize the Harvard. Two, then-serving officers with the RCAF, Flight Lieutenants Lou Hill and Ray Greene formed the first 'official' team flying RCAF 3034 (GG-Q) and RCAF 3337 (DB-O) in 1947/48. They were followed by a group of four Canadian instructor pilots (Bob Ayes, Ray Embury, Frank Pickles and Eernie Saunders) who called themselves the Centralia Formation Aerobatics Team, but this became the more friendly Easy Aces in 1952 flying a varied assortment of Harvards and AT-16s. After a lapse of some years, 1959 saw the formation of the Goldilocks team (named as a name-play on the more formal Golden Hawks team, which flew gold-painted Sabre jets that were distinctive and their displays quite outstanding).[11] The Goldilocks aerobatic team put on impressive displays (including their lunatic Crazy Formation) between 1962 and 1964 until officialdom stopped their funding and, after 1,529 successful shows, sternly closed them down!

Another team of the 1960s was the Goldenaires, formed by Tom Conroy. In 1973, as a tribute to the Goldilocks team, a civilian

Perhaps the most famous 'civilian' to learn to fly the Harvard was HRH The Duke of Edinburgh, husband of Queen Elizabeth II. A former Royal Navy man, the Duke learnt to fly post-war and is pictured here going solo at the controls of a Noorduyn-built Harvard IIB KF 729 over Windsor Castle. This particular aircraft was with the RAF Home Command Examining Unit based at White Waltham and did not fly until 1953. This photo was taken from another Harvard, piloted by Flight Lieutenant C. R. Gordon. Ray C. Sturtivent

team called the Harvard Demonstration Team was formed flying four Mark 4 Harvards until 1978. Finally, the Western Warbirds teams began display flying at the Calgary Stampede in 1974 and had no less than twelve Harvards on their strength at that date and has grown year-on-year since then.

Film and TV Work

The number of motion pictures that feature 'The Six', usually disguised as something quite different (with varying success ranging from poor to indifferent), are legion. Modified cockpits, engine cowlings, wingtips and rudders and a wide variety of paint jobs and markings turn the T-6 into all manner of 'enemy' and 'friendly' doubles, usually the Mitsubishi Zero, but also the Republic P-47 Thunderbolt and others. However, one of the first (and historically the best) films made (in which the T-6

(Below) **A preserved T-6G of the Italian Air Force, coded HT 291, under tow.** Simon Watson

Pictured here in Arizona, this AT-6C (Registration N16730) is beautifully painted up in the colours of a crack Luftwaffe World War II Fw.190 fighter unit. Pima Air & Space Museum, Tucson

played herself for once!) was Paramount's *I Wanted Wings*, made in 1940. The stars of the film were Ray Milland, William Holden, Brian Donlevy, Veronica Lake and the AT-6s based at Kelly and Randolph Fields near San Antonio, Texas, where the lead ship was thrown about the sky for the benefit of the cameras by film stunt pilot Paul Mantz. The Canadian Directorate of Public Relations persuaded Warner Brothers to make a semi-documentary film on training, starring James Cagney in *Captains Of the Clouds*. A list of some of the more famous films (and the T-6's role) is as follows:

- *I Wanted Wings* – AT-6;
- *Captains of the Clouds* – Harvard;
- *Tora, Tora, Tora* – Japanese Zero fighter and Kate torpedo bomber;
- *Battle of Midway* – Japanese Zero fighter and Kate torpedo bomber;
- *Black Sheep Squadron* – Japanese Zero fighter;
- *A Bridge too Far* – P-47 Thunderbolt, Hawker Typhoon and Focke Wulf Fw.190;
- *The Great Escape* – miscellaneous parked German aircraft;
- *The Empire of the Sun* – Japanese Zero fighter.

Museum Exhibits

The number of 'Sixes' resident at museums the world over is also very large. As always, aircraft come and go, are put on display and taken out of display, often without notification, so the rule, as always, is *check before you go*! But any T-6 enthusiast has a better chance of seeing his or her favourite aircraft than any other Warbird whatever, no matter what part of the world they search. The listings included in this book, and this section's selection of accompanying photographs can, necessarily, only provide a 'snapshot' of the rich fare that has been, and still is, the Harvard collections.

To movie makers, 'The Six' is rarely what she seems. Here is an SNJ of the Japanese Maritime Self-Defense Force, pictured at Shimofusa Air Base, 'disguised' as a Zero fighter for a Nipponese film on that famous aircraft. Courtesy of Tadashi Nozawa

APPENDIX I

Harvard 2B Engine Data

	RPM	BOOST (LB/IN²)	TEMPERATURE (°C) CYL.	OIL	MIXTURE CONTROL
Max. take-off (5-min. limit)	2,250	+3	260	85	RICH
Max. climb (continuous)	2,200	+1½	260	85	RICH*
Max. cruising (continuous)	1,925	–½	230	85	RICH*
Max. weak (continuous)	1,850	–2	230	85	Up to the throttle
Desired temperatures diving			205	50/70	

The maximum rpm was 2,650; 2,250rpm was to be only exceeded for 20s and then with the throttle not less than one-third open.

*At altitude it was sometimes necessary to advance the mixture control to avoid over-richness.

Oil pressure:
- maximum: 100lb/in²
- normal: 70–90lb/in²
- minimum cruising: 50lb/in²
- minimum idling: 10lb/in².

Temperatures:
- minimum for take-off: oil + 40°C/cyl. 120°C
- minimum before take-off: cyl. 205°C
- maximum for stopping engine: cyl. 205°C.

Fuel pressure:
- normal: 3–5lb/in².

Flying limitations:
- Maximum speed in knots:
  diving: 225
  undercarriage lowering: 130
  undercarriage locked down: 145
  flaps down: 110.
- Full use of ailerons could be made up to 165 knots; thereafter they were to have been used with care, particularly when 'g' was applied.
- Certain conditions of loading would have brought the C.G. behind the aft limit and before flight it was checked that the loading was in accordance with the then current loading diagram.

APPENDIX II

NAA Charge Number List

CHARGE NO	DATE	DESIGNATOR	CUSTOMER	QUANTITY	FACTORY SERIAL
NA-16	–	NA-16	–	11	NA-16-1
NA18	13/05/1935	NA-18	Argentina	–	NA-18-1
NA-19	10/03/1935	BT-9	USAAC	42	NA-19-1,-3,-5/11,-20/34,-50/67
NA-19A	–	BT-9A	USAAC Reserve	40	NA-19-4, -12/19, -35/49, -68/83
NA-20	–	NA-16-2H	Honduras	1	NA-16-2 (Ex NA-19-2)
NA-22	–	NA-22	USAAC	1	NA-16-1
NA-23	01/12/1936	BT-9B	USAAC	117	NA-23-85/201
NA-26	20/10/1936	BC-1	Canada	1	26-202
NA-27	01/12/1936	NA-16-2H	Fokker	1	27-312
NA-28	14/12/1936	NJ-1	USAAC for USN	40	28-313/352
NA-29	22/12/1936	BT-9C YIBT-10 BT-9C	USAAC Reserve USAAC USAAC	32 1 34	29-353/384 29-385 29-505/538
NA-30	–	YIBT-10	–	–	
NA-31	02/08/1937	NA-16-4M	Sweden	1	31-386
NA-32	10/03/1937	NA-16-1-A	Australia for CAC	1	32-387
NA-33	10/03/1937	NA-16-2K	Australia for CAC	1	33-388
NA-34	19/03/1937	NA-16-4P	Argentina	30	34-389/418
NA-36	16/06/1937	BC-1	USAAC	177	36-420/504, 596/687
NA-37	02/09/1937	NA-16-4R	Japan	1	37-539
NA-38	28/09/1937	NA-16-4M	Sweden	1	38-540
NA-41	23/02/1938	NA-16-4	China	35	41-697/731
NA-42	09/12/1937	NA-16-2A	Honduras	2	42-691/692
NA-43	09/12/1937	NA-16-1Q	Brazil	–	Cancelled
NA-44	09/12/1937	NA-44	Canada	1	44-747
NA-45	14/12/1937	NA-16-1GV	Venezuela	3	45-693/695
NA-46	02/12/1938	NA-16-4	Brazil	12	46-972/977, 1991/1996
NA-47	16/12/1937	NA-16-4RW	Japan	1	47-699
NA-48	23/02/1938	NA-16-3C	China	15	48-732/746
NA-49	07/02/1938	NA-16-1E	United Kingdom	200 200	49-748/947 49-1053/1252
NA-50	09/02/1939	NA-50	Peru	7	50-948/954
NA-52	28/09/1938	SNJ-1	USN	16	52-956/971
NA-54	03/10/1938	BC-2	USAAC	3	54-688/690
NA-55	–	BC-1A	USAAC	83	55-1548/1630
NA-56	18/04/1939	NA-16-4	China	50	56-1453/1502
NA-57	21/02/1939	NA-57 (BT-9B)	France	230	57-1253/1452, -1518/1547

CHARGE NO	DATE	DESIGNATOR	CUSTOMER	QUANTITY	FACTORY SERIAL
NA-58	28/04/1939	BT-14	USAAC	251	58-1655/1905
NA-59	–	AT-6	USAAC	94	59-1631/1639, -1906/1990
NA-61	25/05/1939	NA-16-1E	Canada	30	61-1503/1517, -1640/1654
NA-64	05/09/1939	NA-64	France	230	64-2033/2232. -3018/3047
NA-65	25/09/1939	SNJ-2	USN	36	65-1997/2032
NA-66	17/11/1939	Harvard II	United Kingdom	600	66-2234/2833
NA-68	30/11/1939	NA-50A (P-64)	Siam	6	68-3058/3063
NA-69	30/11/1939	NA-44	Siam	10	60-3064/3073
NA-70	09/01/1940	Cancelled	–	–	
NA-71	18/01/1940	NA-16-3C	Venezuela	3	71-3074/3076
NA-72	13/01/1940	NA-44 (BC1A)	Brazil	30	72-3077/3096, -4757/4766
NA-74	07/08/1940	NA-44	Chile	12	74-4745/4756
NA-75	03/06/1940	Harvard II	Canada	100	75-3048/3057, -3418/3507
NA-76	05/06/1940	Harvard II	United Kingdom	450	76-3508/3957
NA-77	28/06/1940	AT-6A SNJ-3	USAAC USN	517 120	
NA-78	01/10/1940	AT-6A SNJ-3	USAAC USN	1330 150	
NA-79	–	SNJ-2	USN	25	78-3983/4007
NA-81	11/07/1940	Harvard II	United Kingdom	125	81-4008/4132
NA-84	06/12/1940	AT-6B	USAAC	400	84-7412/7811
NA-85	–	SNJ-3	USN	–	To NA-78
NA-88	10/04/1941	AT-6C AT-6D SNJ-4 SNJ-5	USAAF USAAF USN USN	2970 2604 2400 1357	
NA-119	10/01/1944	AT-6D	USAAF (for Brazil)	81	119-40086/40166
NA-121	11/02/1944	AT-6D AT-6F	USAAF USAAF	800 956	121-41567/42366 121-42367/43322
NA-128	01/06/1944	Cancelled			
NA-168	05/10/1949	T-6G	USAF	641	168-1/371, -387/440, -450/500, -511/560, -571/620, -631/680, -681/691
		LT-6G	USAF	59	168-692/750
		T-6G	ANG	50	168-372/381, -441/450, -501/510, -561/570, -621/630
NA-182	08/02/1951	T-6G	USAF	824	182-1/824
NA-186	22/06/1951	T-GJ	USAF	–	Design data
NA-188	11/04/1951	T-6G	USAF	100 7	188-1/1-100 188-101/107
NA-195	19/03/1952	T-6G	USAF	11	191-1/11
NA-195	19/03/1952	T-6G	USAF	11	191-1/11
NA-197	16/06/1952	T-6G	USAF	50	197-1/50
FO-8002		T-6D to T-6G	ANG	60	8002-1/60
NA-198	03/07/1952	Terminated	USN	240	

AT-6D/SNJ Listings (The '88' Series List)[1]

SNJ-4 (NAVY)

Sequence no.	*Customer no.*	*Factory no.*	*Sequence no.*	*Customer no.*	*Factory no.*
1310–1325	26427–26442	88-10322–88-10337	3254–3302	27230–27278	88-12266–88-12314
1358–1428	26443–26513	88-10370–88-10440	3323–3344	27279–27300	88-12335–88-12356
1666–1740	26514–26588	88-10678–88-10752	3389–3416	27301–27328	88-12401–88-12428
1771–1910	26589–26628	88-10883–88-10922	3473–3522	27329–27378	88-12495–88-12554
1991–2030	26629–26668	88-11003–88-11042	3603–3652	27379–27428	88-12615–88-12664
2071–2110	26669–26708	88-11083–88-11122	3693–3742	27429-27478	88-12705–88-12754
2181–2220	26709–26748	88-11193–88-11232	3803–3852	27479–27528	88-12815–88-12864
2301–2340	26749–26788	88-11313–88-11352	3913–3962	27529–27578	88-12925–88-12974
2421–2460	26789–26828	88-11433–88-11472	4023–4072	27579–27628	88-13035–88-13084
2501–2540	26829–26868	88-11513–88-11552	4113–4162	27629–27678	88-13125–88-13174
2676–2745	26869–26938	88-11688–88-11757	4223–4272	27679–27728	88-13235–88-13284
2786–2855	26939–27008	88-11798–88-11867	4333–4382	27729–27778	88-13345–88-13394
2896–3016	27009–27129	88-11908–88-12028	4463–4512	27779–27828	88-13475–88-13524
3061–3110	27130–27179	88-12073–88 12122	4553–4575	27829–27851	88-13565–88-13587
3163–3212	27180–27229	88-12175–88-12224			

AT-6D (USAAF)

Sequence no.	*Customer no.*	*Factory no.*	*Sequence no.*	*Customer no.*	*Factory no.*
4208–4222	42-43847–42-43861	88-13220–88-13234	4797–4876	42-44146–42-44225	88-13809–88-13888
4273–4332	42-43862–42-43921	88-13285–88-13344	4947–5006	42-44226–42-44285	88-13959–88-14018
4403–4462	42-43922–42-43981	88-13415–88-13474	5057–5096	42-44286–42-44325	88-14069–88-14108
4513–4552	42-43982–42-44021	88-13525–88-13564	5167–5206	42-44326–42-44365	88-14179–88-14218
4596–4604	42-44022–42-44030	88-13608–88-13616	5257–5302	42-44366–42-44411	88-14269–88-14314
4632–4746	42-44031–42-44145	88-13644–88-13758			

SNJ-4 (NAVY)

Sequence no.	*Customer no.*	*Factory no.*	*Sequence no.*	*Customer no.*	*Factory no.*
22–151	05527–05656	88-9034–88-9163	1201–1234	10224–10257	88-10213–88-10246
302–319	05657–05674	88-9314–88-9331	1251–1309	10258–10316	88-10263–88-10321
320–466	09817–09963	88-9332–88-9478	4605–4631	51350–51376	88-13617–88-13643
511–600	09964–10053	88-9523–88-9612	4747–4796	51377–51426	88-13759–88-13808
726–735	10054–10063	88-9738–88-9747	4877–4890	51427–51440	88-13889–88-13902
746–765	10064–10083	88-9758–88-9777	4911–4946	51441–51476	88-13923–88-13958
776–795	10084–10103	88-9788–88-9807	5007–5056	51477–51526	88-14019–88-14068
806–825	10104–10123	88-9818–88-9837	5097–5146	51527–51576	88-14109–88-14158
836–855	10124–10143	88-9848–88-9867	5207–5256	51577–51626	88-14219–88-14268
1101–1140	10144–10183	88-10113–88-10152	5303–5352	51627–51676	88-14315–88-14364
1151–1190	10184–10223	88-10163–88-10202			

AT-6D (AIR FORCE)

Sequence no.	Customer no.	Factory no.	Sequence no.	Customer no.	Factory no.
5373–5412	42-44412–42-44451	88-14385–88-14424	6219–6222	41-34123–41-34126	88-15231–88-15234
5483–5502	42-44452–42-44471	88-14495–88-14514	6268–6287	41-34127–41-34146	88-15280–88-15299
5548–5593	42-44472–42-44517	88-14560–88-14605	6337–6348	41-34147–41-34158	88-15349–88-15360
5564–5683	42-44518–42-44537	88-14676–88-14695	6381–6560	41-34159–41-34338	88-15393–88-15572
5720–5787	42-44538–42-44605	88-14732–88-14799	6601–6634	41-34339–41-34372	88-15613–88-15646
5813–5832	42-44606–42-44625	88-14825–88-14844	6635–6640	41-34447–41-34452	88-15647–88-15652
5878–5897	42-44626–42-44645	88-14890–88-14909	6691–6710	41-34483–41-34502	88-15703–88-15722
5948–5987	42-44646–44-44685	88-14960–88-14999	6781–6813	41-34543–41-34575	88-15793–88-15825
6058–6077	42-44686–42-44705	88-15070–88-15089	6865–6884	41-34606–41-34625	88-15877–88-15896
6128–6147	42-44706–42-44725	88-15140–88-15159	6914–6931	41-34655–41-34672	88-15926–88-15943
6198–6218	42-44726–42-44746	88-15210–88-15230			

SNJ-5 (NAVY)

Sequence no.	Customer no.	Factory no.
5413–5462	51677–51726	88-14425–88-14474
5503–5527	51727–51751	88-14515–88-14539
5594–5643	51752–51801	88-14606–88-14655
5684–5703	51802–51821	88-14696–88-14715
5788–5812	51822–51846	88-14800–88-14824
5833–5857	51847–51871	88-14845–88-14869
5898–5922	51872–51896	88-14910–88-14934
5988–6037	51897–51946	88-15000–88-15049
6078–6102	51947–51971	88-15090–88-15114
6148–6197	51972–52021	88-15160–88-15209
6223–6247	52022–52046	88-15235–88-15259
6288–6290	52047–52049	88-15300–88-15302
6291–6312	43638–43659 (41-34373–41-34394)	88-15303–88-15324
6349–6380	43660–43691 (41-34395–41-34426)	88-15361–88-15392
6561–6580	43692–43711 (41-34427–41-34446)	88-15573–88-15592
6641–6670	43712–43741 (41-34453–41-34482)	88-15653–88-15682
6711–6730	43742–43761 (41-34503–41-34522)	88-15723–88-15742
6741–6760	43762–43781 (41-34523–41-34542)	88-15753–88-15772
6814–6843	43782–43811 (41-34576–41-34605)	88-15826–88-15855
6885–6913	43812–43840 (41-34626–41-34654)	88-15897–88-15925

AT-6C (BRITISH-DA8)

Sequence no.	Customer no.	Factory no.	Sequence no.	Customer no.	Factory no.
167–301	EX 100–EX 234	88-9179–88-9313	946–955	EX 355–EX 364	88-9958–88-9967
609–618	EX 235–EX 244	88-9621–88-9630	996–1005	EX 365–EX 374	88-10008–88-10017
629–638	EX 245–EX 254	88-9641–88-9650	1046–1055	EX 375–EX 384	88-10058–88-10067
649–658	EX 255–EX 264	88-9661–88-9670	1089–1100	EX 385–EX 396	88-10101–88-10112
669–678	EX 265–EX 274	88-9681–88-9690	1141–1150	EX 397–EX 406	88-10153–88-1062
689–698	EX 275–EX 284	88-9701–88-9710	1191–1200	EX 407–EX 416	88-10203–88-10212
709–718	EX 285–EX 294	88-9721–88-9730	1235–1250	EX 417–EX 432	88-10247–88-10262
736–745	EX 295–EX 304	88-9748–88-9757	1514–1665	EX 433–EX 584	88-10526–88-10677
766–775	EX 305–EX 314	88-9778–88-9787	3017–3060	EX 585–EX 628	88-12029–88-12072
796–805	EX 315–EX 324	88-9808–88-9817	3111–3130	EX 629–EX 648	88-12123–88-12142
826–835	EX 325–EX 334	88-9838–88-9847	3303–3322	EX 649–EX 668	88-12315–88-12334
856–865	EX 335–EX 344	88-9868–88-9877	3523–3542	EX 669–EX 688	88-12535–88-12554
901–910	EX 345–EX 354	88-9913–88-9922	3743–3762	EX 689–EX 708	88-12755–88-12774

AT-6C (BRITISH DA-8) *(continued)*

Sequence no.	Customer no.	Factory no.	Sequence no.	Customer no.	Factory no.
3963–3982	EX 709–EX 728	88-12975–88-12994	4891–4910	EX 789–EX 808	88-13903–88-13922
4163–4182	EX 729–EX 748	88-13175–88-13194	5147–5166	EX 809–EX 828	88-14159–88-14178
4383–4402	EX 749–EX 768	88-13395–88-13414	5353–5370	EX 829–EX 846	88-14365–88-14382
4576–4595	EX 769–EX 788	88-13588–88-13607			

AT-6D (BRITISH DA-8)

Sequence no.	Customer no.	Factory no.
5371–5372	EX 847–EX 848 (41-33820–41-33821)	88-14383–88-14384
5463–5482	EX 849–EX 868 (41-33822–41-33841)	88-14475–88-14494
5528–5547	EX 869–EX 888 (41-33842–41-33861)	88-14540–88-14559
5644–5663	EX 889–EX 908 (41-33862–41-33881)	88-14656–88-14675
5704–5719	EX 909–EX 924 (41-33882–41-33897)	88-14716–88-14731
5858–5877	EX 925–EX 944 (41-33898–41-33917)	88-14870–88-14889
5923–5947	EX 945–EX 969 (41-33918–41-33942)	88-14935–88-14959
6038–6057	EX 970–EX 989 (41-33943–41-33962)	88-15050–88-15069
6103–6112	EX 990–EX 999 (41-33963–41-33972)	88-15115–88-15124
6113–6127	EZ 100–EZ 114 (41-33973–41-33987)	88-15125–88-15139
6248–6267	EZ 115–EZ 134 (41-33988–41-34007)	88-15260–88-15279
6313–6336	EZ 135–EZ 158 (41-34008–41-34031)	88-15325–88-15348
6581–6600	EZ 159–EZ 178 (41-34032–41-34051)	88-15593–88-15612
6671–6690	EZ 179–EZ 198 (41-34052–41-34071)	88-15683–88-15702
6731–6740	EZ 199–EZ 208 (41-34072–41-34081)	88-15743–88-15752
6761–6780	EZ 209–EZ 228 (41-34082–41-34101)	88-15773–88-15792
6844–6864	EZ 229–EZ 249 (41-34102–41-34122)	88-15856–88-15876

AT-6D (USAAF)

Sequence no.	Customer no.	Factory no.	Sequence no.	Customer no.	Factory no.
6971–7010	42 84202–42-84241	88-15983–88-16022	8002–8061	42-85233–42-85292	88-17014–88-17073
7071–7110	42-84302–42-84341	88-16083–88-16122	8102–8181	42-85333–42-85412	88-17114–88-17193
7141–7160	42-84372–42-84391	88-16153–88-16172	8202–8261	42-85433–42-85492	88-17214–88-17273
7172–7191	42-84403–42-84422	88-16184–88-16203	8302–8381	42-85533–42-85612	88-17314–88-17393
7242–7281	42-84473–42-84512	88-16254–88-16293	8422–8536	42-85653–42-85767	88-17484–88-17598
7332–7371	42-84563–42-84602	88-16344–88-16383	8557–8626	42-85788–42-85857	88-17569–88-17638
7412–7451	42-84643–42-84682	88-16424–88-16463	8667–8736	42-85898–42-85967	88-17679–88-17748
7512–7551	42-84743–42-84782	88-16524–88-16563	8777–8856	42-86008–42-86087	88-17789–88-17868
7592–7651	42-84823–42-84882	88-16604–88-16663	8877–8936	42-86108–42-86167	88-17889–88-17948
7702–7741	42-84933–42-84972	88-16714–88-16753	8977–9046	42-86208–42-86277	88-17989–88-18058
7802–7841	42-85033–42-85072	88-16814–88-16853	9087–9156	42-86318–42-86387	88-18099–88-18168
7862–7871	42-85093–42-85102	88-16874–88-16883	9187–9256	42-86418–42-86487	88-18199–88-18268
7892–7951	42-85123–42-85182	88-16904–88-16963	9297–9331	42-86528–42-86562	88-18309–88-18343

SNJ-5 (USN)

Sequence no.	Customer no.	Factory no.
6941–6950	43841–43850 (42-84172–42-84181)	88-15953–88-15962
7011–7050	43851–43890 (42-84242–42-84281)	88-16023–88-16062
7111–7130	43891–43910 (42-84342–42-84361)	88-16123–88-16142
7161–7171	43911–43921 (42-84392–42-84402)	88-16173–88-16183
7192–7221	43922–43951 (42-84423–42-84452)	88-16204–88-16233
7282–7311	43952–43981 (42-84513–42-84542)	88-16294–88-16323
7372–7401	43982–44011 (42-84603–42-84632)	88-16384–88-16413
7452–7477	44012–44037 (42-84683–42-84708)	88-16464–88-16489
7478–7491	84819–84832 (42-84709–42-84722)	88-16490–88-16503

SNJ-5 (USN)

Sequence no.	*Customer no.*	*Factory no.*
7552–7571	84833–84852 (42-84783–42-84802)	88-16564–88-16583
7652–7691	84853–84892 (42-84883–42-84922)	88-16664–88-16703
7742–7781	84893–84932 (42-84973–42-85012)	88-16754–88-16793
7842–7861	84933–84952 (42-85073–42-85092)	88-16854–88-16873
7952–7991	84953–84992 (42-85183–42-85222)	88-16964–88-17003
8062–8101	84993–85032 (42-85293–42-85332)	88-17074–88-17113
8182–8201	85033–85052 (42-85413–42-85432)	88-17194–88-17213
8262–8301	85053–85092 (42-85493–42-85532)	88-17274–88-17313
8382	85093 (42-85613)	88-17394
8383–8421	90582–90620 (42-85614–42-85652)	88-17395–88-17433
8537–8556	90621–90640 (42-85768–42-85787)	88-17549–88-17568
8627–8666	90641–90680 (42-85858–42-85897)	88-17639–88-17678
8737–8776	90681–90720 (42-85968–42-86007)	88-17749–88-17788
8857–8876	90721–90740 (42-84088–42-86107)	88-17869–88-17888
8937–8976	90741–90780 (42-86168–42-86207)	88-17949–88-17988
9047–9086	90781–90820 (42-86278–42-86317)	88-18059–88-18098
9157–9186	90821–90850 (42-86388–42-86417)	88-18169–88-18198
9257–9296	90851–90890 (42-86488–42-86527)	88-18269–88-18308

AT-6D (HARVARD III) RAF

Sequence no.	*Customer no.*	*Factory no.*
6932–6940	EZ 250–EZ 258 (42-84163–42-84171)	88-15944–88-15952
6951–6970	EZ 259–EZ 278 (42-84182–42-84201)	88-15943–88-15962
7051–7070	EZ 279–EZ 298 (42-84282–42-84301)	88-16063–88-16082
7131–7140	EZ 299–EZ 308 (42-84362–42-84371)	88-16143–88-16152
7222–7241	EZ 309–EZ 328 (42-84453–42-84472)	88-16234–88-16253
7312–7331	EZ 329–EZ 348 (42-84543–42-84568)	88-16324–88-16343
7402–7411	EZ 349–EZ 358 (42-84633–42-84642)	88-16414–88-16423
7492–7511	EZ 359–EZ 378 (42-84723–42-84742)	88-16504–88-16523
7572–7591	EZ 379–EZ 398 (42-84803–42-84822)	88-16584–88-16603
7692–7701	EZ 399–EZ 408 (42-84923–42-84932)	88-16704–88-16713
7782–7801	EZ 409–EZ 428 (42-85013–42-85032)	88-16794–88-16813
7872–7891	EZ 429–EZ 448 (42-85103–42-85122)	88-16884–88-16903
7992–8001	EZ 449–EZ 458 (42-85233–42-85232)	88-17004–88-17013

APPENDIX IV

Royal Canadian Air Force NAA Trainer List

The Harvards/T-6s that served in the Royal Canadian Air Force (and Navy) came from four separate plants (North American at Inglewood and then Dallas, Noorduyn near Montreal and post-war from Canadian Car & Foundry at Fort William, now Thunder Bay) at different times and each group had a different serial batching system dependent on whether they were built under RCAF, RAF or USAF orders.

TYPE (CHARGE NO.)	C/N	NO.	SERIALS
NA-26	26-202	1	3345
NA-44	44-747	1	3344
Harvard Mark I (NA-49)	49-768	1	3560
Harvard Mark I	Ex-RAF	1	A83 (Inst A/F)
Harvard Mark I	–	1	A100 (Inst A/F)
Harvard Mark I	–	1	A102 (Inst A/F)
Harvard Mark I (NA-61)	61-1503–61-1517, 61-1640–61-1654	30	1321–1350
Yale (NA-64)	64-2033–60-2232, 64-3018, 64-3047	119	3346–3464
Harvard Mark II (NA-66)	66-2234–66-2746	513	2501–3013
Harvard Mark II	66-2747–66-2766	20	AH 185–AH 204
Harvard Mark II (NA-75)	75-3048–75-3057, 75-3418–75-3507	100	3134–3233
Harvard Mark II (NA-76)	Ex-French	259	AJ 538–597, AJ 643–662, AJ 683–702, AJ 723–737, AJ 753–767, AJ 788–802, AJ 823–836, AJ 847–854, AJ 893–910, AJ 912–986
Harvard Mark II (NA-81)	81-4008–81-4027	20	3014–3033
Harvard Mark II	81-4028–81-4108	81	3761–3841
Harvard Mark II	81-4109–81-4132	24	BW 184–BW 207
Harvard Mark II	–	1	A429 (Inst A/F)
Harvard Mark IIB	07-01–07-100	100	3034–3133
Harvard Mark IIB	07-101–07-210	110	3234–3343
Harvard Mark IIB	in the lease-lend block ranges 14-002–733, 14-734–800, 14A-801–1500	639	FE 268–352, 383–412, 433–467, 498–527, 553–592, 618–662, 688–695, 721–765, 790–877, 902–951, 976–999, FH 100–106, FH 117–166, FH 661–681, FS 857–878, FS 957–978, FT 265–301
Harvard Mark IIB	Ex-lease-end*	10	20200–20209
T-6D (loaned)	Ex-USAF**	100	In the range of 41-34177–44-81634
Mark 4	CCF4-1–CCF4-270	270	20210–20479

* Lend-lease AT-16s returned to USAF post-war but re-purchased for RCAF.

RCAF SERIAL	USAF SERIAL	ORIGINAL SERIAL
20200	42-12552	FH 165
20201	43-12810	FS 969
20202	42-12531	FH 144
20203	43-12517	FS 676
20204	43-12511	FS 670
20205	42-12347	FE 860
20206	42-12347	FE 988
20207	42-792	FE 595
20208	42-12409	FE 922
20209	42-12334	FE 847

**Six loaned T-6Ds crashed and were written off while in RCAF service and had to be replaced. These, and their replacements, were as shown below.

USAF SERIAL LOST	REPLACED BY MARK 4 SERIAL
41-34335	RCAF 20331
42-84650	RCAF 20468
42-85165	RCAF 20364
42-85174	RCAF 20457
44-81078	RCAF 20315
44-81433	RCAF 20316

Mosquito Nomenclature – Korea

(originally compiled by Sidney F. Johnston Jnr)

'A' frame	Korean backpack frame
'Blue'	One of eight channels on Mosquito VHF radio
'Cluster'	Position surrounded by the enemy and under attack
'Diploma' TACP	UN French tank regiment; TACP CT 496298
'Double bend in the railroad'	CT 4646
'Exile control'	IX Corps, Artillery HQ, RACP Cmdr and AF ALO at CT 532378
'Format TACP'	Capital ROK Division CT 732370
'Green'	One of eight channels on Mosquito VHF Radio
'Guard'	One of eight channels on Mosquito VHF Radio
'Hatpin Alpha'	Regiment TACP CT 398325
'Hatpin' TACP	45th Division, Chorwon CT 442332
'Itemizable' TACP	Regiment with the US 2nd Division CT 508344
'Itemize' TACP	2nd American Division CT558308
'No-name Mountain'	Hill next to K-47 at Chunchon (Also 'No-mans Mountain')
'Old Joe'	Joe Chink/Korean enemy soldier
'Orange'	One of eight channels on Mosquito VHF Radio
'Primary'	Target priority
'Purple'	One of eight channels on Mosquito VHF Radio
'Railroad Horse Shoes'	CT 4646
'Red'	One of eight channels on Mosquito VHF Radio
'Remote' TACP	9th ROK Infantry Division CT 671328 (Kumhwa)
'Satuhi-rie-by-the-sea'	R & R place? Sokchori (or) Tongchori DT 6529
'Secondary'	Target priority
'Siggie-Reid'	President of South Korea in the 1950s
'String out'	Fighter bombers in trail, usually 20s apart
'Washing-machine Charlie'	Small North Korean scout aircraft
'White'	One of eight channels on Mosquito VHF Radio
'Yellow'	One of eight channels on Mosquito VHF Radio
Able Dog	Douglas AD Skyraider, Navy/Marine Corps Attach/Dive bomber
Able Easy 12	Army-Engineer Airstrip No 12
Able-easy twelve	AE-12 Army dirt airstrip, CT 535255
Ace hole	'MiG-15 Alley Tourist Centre', fighter base of F-86s at K-14 Seoul

AFAC	Aireborne Forward Air Controller
A-Frame Cowboy	Korean civilian
Air burst	Shells exploding above the ground in barrage
Air-drop	Supplies delivered to cut-off troops by parachute
Alligator Ridge	Geographic position CT 335384
ALO	Air Liaison Officer
Angels reference ——	Aircraft altitude
A-OK	Everything is alright
APs	Armour piercing
Artie	Armour-piercing artillery
Ass-hole	Bad job, person, place, order, mission
Automatic fire	Machine gun
Back to the Barn	Return home to base
Baker Adam	Bust your Ass! – get moving
Baker Tare	Map coordinates
Baker-baker	Bomb burst
Baker-baker tango	Bomb burst on target
Bandits	Hostile aircraft
BC scope (TAC)	Artillery, target spotting scope lens
Bed-check Charlie	North Korean night harassment aircraft
Belly buster	Airsick
Belly up	Aircraft flipped over on landing
Bent out of shape	Enemy fire damaged TACP equipment
Big'I'	Intelligence Officer
Big Brothers	B-29s
Big Daddy	Wing/Group Commander
Big Indian	AF Intelligence de-briefing
Big Stuff	Large calibre artillery
Bird Dog	Looking for Targets
Black out	Cut off all night illumination
Blackberry	TACP Ground-Air controller
Blood relative	Same type aircraft
Blue boy	Army infantryman
Blue Sky Mission	C-47 radio monitor aircraft
Boomerang Ridge	CT 46142
Bought the farm	Killed
Box cars at Kumsong	CT 724485
Break	Pulling aircraft 90 degrees plus
Break off	Leave, depart the target
Break over friendlies	Turn plane for home
Bring it up	Fighter-bomber flight close up, finger-tip
Bugging out	Leave in haste!
Bunker busting	Dropping large bombs on enemy OPs
Bunker palace	Sandbag quarters well-protected
Cap-rock Division	25 ROK Infantry Division
Cats eyes	Night travelling lights on cambet jeeps, trucks, etc.

Charlie Charlie Fox	Chinese Communist Forces
Charlie Nancy	'CN'; radio-beacon in front line at K-47 Chunchon
Charlie Sugar	Map coordinates
Charlie Tare	Map coordinates CT
Check-in	Make radio contact with
Chicks	Fighter-Bombers
Chorwon Valley	CT 4630
Clobbered	Hit in combat, in bad condition
Close call	Near miss
Closing down	TACP team cutting off radio contact
Collecting calories	TACP eating 'C' rations
Collecting vitamins	TACP at Army Ordnance being issued small arms prior to a fire fight (combat)
Combat exemptions	Family commitments
Crying at Mamas	Talking to the chaplain
Crystal Ball	Radar
Cut-a-Chogie	Run for safety
Daddy	Squadron commander
Dear John	Bad news from unfaithful wife/girlfriend
Deep six	Under water
Dog Tare	Map coordinates (DT), east of Charlie Tare to coast
Dog's Head	CT3539 to CT 3639
Double Bin at Imjin Gan River	CT 1505
Eyeball	In sight
Eyeball	T-6 Mosquito Observer, usually an Allied Army artillery FO
Farmer's weather	Rain, steady drizzle for days
Fear-of-eight	'Lazy-Eight' flight pattern or T-6 criss-crossing over target
FETAC	Code identification and number. Far East tactical air code
Field phone	Army battery-operated telephones
Fire ball	Secondary burst explosion
Fire bomb	Napalm
Fire-fight	Ground combat; infantry battles
Firefly	Night missions, C-47 or B-26 dropping flares/bombs at night
Fishtail Lake	Geographic position CT 495448 (Poyang-Ho Lake)
Flak	Ground to air weapons, air burst from AAA
Flak suppression	Artillery firing on known Ack-Ack sites
Flak suppression	Artillery fire on known enemy AAA sites prior to an air attack
Flight surgeon bar stock	Post mission whisky at squadron de-briefing
Fly boy	Army for Air Force pilots
Footlocker cleanout	Missing in combat; processing of personal items to send back home
Fox-hole hermit	TACP team under constant enemy fire
Friendlies	Allied aircraft
FUJIGMO (pronounced FIG'MO)	'F— you Jack, I got my orders'
Gaggle	Unorganized aircraft in flight
Gook	North Korean or Chinese soldier
Goon-balloon	C-47 transport
Grapevine ridge road	CT 705380
Ground fire	Fired upon by ground positions
Ground pounders	Army personnel
Ground protection fire	Friendly arms fire help
Hard-hat flyboy	TACP duty in front lines
Heavy arty	Bomb strike by B-29s
Hell bent	In a hurry
Hell bent for leather	Flying back to base at maximum speed; heading for foxhole at TACP
Hell's acre	Large bad place
Hell's kitchen	Bad place to be
HIVAR	5in smoke rocket used by the T-6 from 1953
Hog leg	0.45 pistol in holster
Honey bucket	Toilet
Honey house	Outside latrine
Hooch	Korean house
Horror stories	Bad mission, combat damage
Hose it down	Strafe target
Hot target	Lots of combat action
Huba-huba	TACP; run like hell for cover
In sight	Can see
Incoming fire	Usually explosive shells
Iron Triangle	Korean war zone: Chorwon–Kumhwa–Pyongggang CT 4334–CT6583–CT5152
Jane Russell Mountains	(at 1062) CT 660410 (north) and CT 662403 (south)
Jeep trail	Road only good enough for a Jeep (GP, general-purpose vehicle)
Jeepny	Army car
Jerry-can	5-gallon fuel container (first used by Rommel's Panzers in North Africa)
Joe-San	Oriental girl
K-16 trip	Airbase at Seoul; used as processing centre to go Stateside or Japan
KIA	Killed in Action
Kilo-four-seven	K-47 airstrip, Chunchon
King-four	K-4 airbase, Taeju
KSC	Korean Service Battalion; worker
Kumhas-san Mountain	West Chorwan valley CT 426272
Kumsong Bulge	Last Korean war battle CT 7852 and CT 7952 (apex)
Lamp-lighter	flare drops C-47/C46 at night in the MLR-controlled by Mosquito TACP
Land of the big PX	USA
Lead	First aircraft of fighter-bomber flight
Line crossers	Enemy patrol in vicinity
Little brothers	T-6s, L-20s, L-5s
Long-range Arty	Army 240mm guns
Lost his numbers	Condition unknown
Love-love	Land-Line telephone
Mag Boy	Military adviser to Allied forces in combat
Maggie's drawers	Missed hitting the target
Margaret O'Brien Ridge	Mountains (at 1062) CT6640
Marking round	Artillery shell smoke on the target
MASH	Mobile Army Support Hospital
M-D	Mail delivery
Meat wagon	Ambulance
Mike Charlie	Mission control
Mike tare	Mobile target; trucks, tanks, vehicles moving
Mike-mike	Millimetre

MLR	Main line of resistance
Motar Ridge	part of mountain 1062, CT 629445
Mosquito	Combat T-6 aircraft
Moving in	Setting up base
Moving out	Clearing from the area
Nape	Napalm
Negative	Cannot do, do not understand
Nuggest control	IX Corp HQ TACP 1953, after cease-fire in July '53
Number ten	Not good, BAD!
Old Man	Squadron Commander
Old Papasan Mountains	(1062) 'Osong-San' at Kumhwa, Korea, CT 649459
On fire	Aircraft burning
On the move	Moving out
On top	Above the clouds
One-o-five	105mm artillery gun
OP Harry	Oscar Pappa Harry (CT 536393)
Oscar Papa (OP)	Observation Post
Outgoing fire	Friendly ground fire aimed at enemy
Outhouse Hill	Bad place to be
Overrun	Enemy gone by TACP ground position
Paper work	Damage assessment
Parrot's Beak	Geographical location CT 4142
Patches number one	T-6 with most battle damage
Pedal pushers	Person on bicycle
Penis-in-the-river	CT 8542
Pong Yang Express	North Korean CCF truck/troop convoys heading south from Pyongyang
Pork Chop Hill	Geographical location CT 2837 to 2937 south CT 2936
Pounding	Continuous delivery of ordnance on target
PSP strip	Runway made out of metal webbing
Punch bowl	Geographic position Songhwang Dang and Madaeri: CT 3826
Put them in the smoke	Drop bombs on the marking round explosion
R and R	Rest and recuperation
Rag Bunker!	Tent near the battle front
Rattlesnake Road	CT 7238
Red neck	Army artilleryman (they wear red scarfs)
Republic Airlines	F-84 squadron
Res-cap	Rescue mission
RES-CAP	Air and ground support during rescue missions
Rocket battery	105mm rocket launchers
Roger	Will do, understand
ROK	Republic of Korea (South Korea)
RON	Remain over night
Round-the-clock	Direction of bomb strike
Sampan	Small oriental boat
Seduce the camel	Smoke a cigarette
Shack job	Night in a Korean whorehouse
Shit-and-git	'Fire your rockets and clear the target area' before incoming strike arrives
Shoe man	Infantry
Silk landing	Parachuting to the ground
Six by	Army truck
Sky Pilot	Army Chaplain
Small arms	Usually hand-held weapons firing
Smoke Pots at Kumhwa	Army Smoke Reg: geographic location CT 6539
Smoke round	Target-marking rocket or artillery
Smoked	Smoke grenade ignited inadvertently
Snake-pit	Hell of a fight in progress on ground
Snakes Head	CT 7755
Sniper's Ridge	Part of mountain 1062, CT 6740 and CT 6840
SOB Ridge	Son-of-a-bitch place, CT 6046
Spit-in-your-messkit	Point of proof
Split-out'er-here	Leave for a safer place
Square Lake	Geographic position CT 583478
Support fire	TACP, ordnance support in combat conditions
Syanora	Goodbye
TACP	Tactical Air Control Party
Tail-end Charlie	Last man in fighter-bomber flight
Talk to the Indian	Intelligence debriefing after a mission
Tango fighter	T-6 Mosquito
Tango six shooter	T-6 Mosquito
Tango Tango	On target; target or smoke round in sight
Tango-Oscar-Tango (TOT)	Time on target
Tare able	Target assessment damage
Timber	Something falling
Tin-can soldiers	Tank troops
Took-a-hit	Report of battle damage
Tracked vehicles	Tanks, artillery carriers ('Half Tracks')
Two point Seven Five	2.75in smoke rockets fired by T-6 (3 each per rack: total 12)
Uncle Nancy	UN personnel in Korea
Under cover	In bunker for protection
Victor Tango	Radar-fired artillery
Wachon Reservoir	Hwachon Reservoir Ct 9518
Walking out	Overrun by enemy, fighting way back to Allied lines
Water Boy	Controller; Radar control B-29 drops in MLR
Water boy	IX Corps/Division Fire Control Centre
Weapons carrier	Army pick-up
Web-Foot	Navy carrier pilot
Went in	Crashed
Wet Feet	TACP having to wade creek, flying – bailing out into water
Whiskey Flight	F-84s, K-2 TAEGU
White Horse Mountain	CT 3741 to CT 3839
WIA	Wounded in Action
Wilco	Understand and will do
WilliePete	White Phosphorus from artillery and air rockets
Wonsan	HK 2510

Preserved T-6/SNJ/Harvard/Wirraways

TYPE	C/N	USAAF SERIAL	EX-COUNTRY 1	EX-COUNTRY 2	EX-COUNTRY 3	CIVILIAN RGD	MUSEUM
Harvard IIB	14-201	42-664	Swiss AF	RCAF	n/a	n/a	Museum de Schweizerischen Fliergertruppe, Dubendorf AB, Switzerland
Harvard IIB	14-366	42-829	Flygvapnet	RCAF	n/a	n/a	Flygvapenmuseum, Malmslatt AB, Sweden
Harvard IIB	14-486	42-949	Flygvapnet	RCAF	n/a	n/a	Flygvapenmuseum, Malmslatt AB, Sweden
Harvard IIB	14-545	42-12298	Swiss AF	RCAF	n/a	n/a	Museum de Schweizerischen Flliergertruppe, Dubendfoft AB, Switzerland
Harvard IIB	14-555	42-12308	Netherlands AF	RCAF	n/a	n/a	Auto und Technik Museum, Sinsheim, Germany
Harvard IIB	14-565	42-12318	Flygvapnet	RCAF	n/a	n/a	Luftfartmuseet, Stockholm-Arlanda, Sweden
Harvard IIB	14-664	42-12417	Netherlands AF	RCAF	n/a	n/a	Thameside Aviation Museum, UK
Harvard IIB	14-719	42-12472	Dutch Navy	Netherlands AF	RCAF	PH-NID	Pioneer Hangaar Collection, Lelystad
Harvard IIB	14-725	42-12478	Flygvapnet	RCAF	n/a	n/a	Svedino's Bil Och Flygmuseum Sloinge, Sweden
Harvard IIB	14-733	42-12486	Netherlands AF	RCAF	n/a	n/a	MLM, Woensdrecht AB Gate Guard
Harvard IIB	14-739	42-124492	Netherlands AF	RCAF	n/a	n/a	Pole display Maasbracht, Netherlands
Harvard IIB	14-748	42-12501	Danish AF	RAF	n/a	n/a	Dansk Veteranflysamling, Stauning, Denmark
Harvard IIB	14-765	42-12518	Netherlands AF	RCAF	n/a	n/a	Militaire Luchtvaart Museum, Soesterberg
Harvard IIB	14-770	42-12523	Netherlands AF	RCAF	n/a	n/a	Westerschouwen, Scheise Estuary, Netherlands
Harvard IIB	14-772	42-12525	Flygvapnet	RCAF	n/a	n/a	Svedin's Bil Och Flygmuseum, Ugglarp, Sweden
Harvard IIB	14A-808	42-12509	Netherlands AF	RCAF	n/a	PH-TBR	Militair Luchtvaart Museum
Harvard IIB	14A-927	43-12626	Indian AF	RAF	n/a		Indian Air Force Museum, Palam AB
Harvard IIB	14A-966	43-12667	Danish AF	RAF	n/a	n/a	Danmarks Flyvemuseum, Billund
Harvard IIB	14A-1100	43-12801	Netherlands AF	RCAF	n/a	PH-TBR	Militaire Luchtvaart Museum, Soesterberg
Harvard IIB	14A-1184	43-12885	Dutch Navy	Netherlands AF	RAF	PH-KLU	Pionier Hangaar Collection, Lellystad
Harvard IIB	14A-1192	43-12893	Yugoslav AF	RAF	n/a	n/a	National Aviation Museum, Belgrade
Harvard IIB	14A-1263	43-12964	Netherlands AF	RAF	n/a	n/a	National War & Resistance Museum, Overloon, Netherlands
Harvard IIB	14A-1268	43-12969	Netherlands AF	RAF	n/a	n/a	Wings of Victory Museum, Veghel, Netherlands
Harvard IIB	14A-1269	43-12970	Netherlands AF	RAF	n/a	F-AZDS	Assoc. French Rech. Maint. En Vol Avions Historiques, Le Castellet, France

TYPE	C/N	USAAF SERIAL	EX-COUNTRY 1	EX-COUNTRY 2	EX-COUNTRY 3	CIVILIAN RGD	MUSEUM
Harvard IIB	14A-1420	43-13121	Danish AF	RAF	RCAF	n/a	Historiske Forening Museet, Karup, Denmark
Harvard IIB	14A-1459	43-13160	Netherlands AF	RAF	n/a	n/a	Militaire Luchtvaart Museum, Soesterber, Netherlands
Harvard IIB	14A-1462	43-13163	Netherlands AF	RAF	n/a	n/a	Musée Royal de L'Armée, Brussels, Belgium
Harvard IIB	14A-2110	KF410	RNAZ	n/a	n/a	n/a	RNAZ Museum, Wigram AB, New Zealand
SNJ-2	65-2009	BuNo2020	Skytypers Inc, Los Alamitos, CA	USN	n/a	N87613	Seminole Air Center, Seminole, Oklahoma, USA
Harvard II	66-2711	NZ918	RNAZ	n/a	n/a	n/a	Pole display, Pahiatua, New Zealand
Harvard II	66-2757	AH195	RNAZ	n/a	n/a	n/a	Museum of Transport & Technology, Auckland, New Zealand
Harvard II	75-3465	RCAF3191	RCN	RCAF	n/a	N3191G	Seminole Air Center, Seminole, Oklahoma, USA
Harvard II	76-3497	RCAF3223	Flygvapnet	RCAF	n/a	n/a	Jamatlands Flyghistoriska Museum, Ostersund, Sweden
AT-6A	77-4176	41-217	Portuguese AF	n/a	n/a	D-FOBY	Albatros Flugmuseum, Stuttgart Airport
AT-6A	76-6445	41-16107	FA Venezolana	n/a	n/a	n/a	Museo Aeronáutico, Maracay AB, Venezuela
AT-6A	78-7245	41-16867	IDAF	n/a	n/a	n/a	Ha-aretz Sciences et Technology Museum, Tel Aviv, Israel
Harvard II	81-4087	RCAF3820	Aéronavale	RCAF	n/a	n/a	Musée des Traditions de L'Aéronautique Navele, Rochefort AB, France
AT-6B	84-7640	41-17262	Royal Saudi AF	n/a	n/a	n/a	Saudi AF Museum Collection, Riyadh
Harvard II	0762	RCAF 3096	RCN	RCAF	n/a	C-FMGO	Reynolds Aviation Museum, Wetaskiwin, Alberta, Canada
Harvard IIA	88-9266	41-33160	RNZAF	RAF	n/a	n/a	RNZAF Historic Flight, Wigram AB, New Zealand
Harvard IIA	88-9269	41-33163	RNZAF	RAF	n/a	n/a	Ashburton Aviation Museum, New Zealand
Harvard IIA	88-9272	41-33166	RNZAF	RAF	n/a	n/a	RNZAF Historic Flight, Wigram AB, New Zealand
SNJ-4	88-11825	BuNo26966	Argentina Armada	US Navy	n/a	n/a	Museo de la Aviacion Naval Argentina, Espora NAS, Bahia Bianca, Argentina
Harvard IIA	88-12032	41-33561	RNZAF	RAF	n/a	ZK-SGQ	NZ Sport and Vintage Aviation Museum, Masterton, New Zealand
Harvard IIA	88-12033	41-33565	RNZAF	RAF	n/a	n/a	RAAF Museum, Port Cook, Victoria, Australia
SNJ-4	88-13081	BuNo27625	Argentina Armada	Flygvapnet	n/a	N1624M	Museo de la Aviacion Naval Argentina, Espora NAS, Bahia Bianca, Argentina
Harvard IIA	88-13907	41-33766	RNZAF	RAF	n/a	n/a	Pole display, RNZAF Wigram AB, Christchurch, New Zealand
Harvard III	88-14493	41-33840	RNZAF	RAF	n/a	n/a	Ferrymead Museum of Science & Technology, Christchurch, NZ
Harvard III	88-14493	41-33840	RNZAF	RAF	n/a	VH-SFY	RAAF Museum, Point Cook, Victoria, Australia
Harvard III	88-14555	41-33857	FA Portuguesa	SAAF	RAF	N15WS	Georgia Historical Aviation Museum, Stone Mountain, Georgia, USA

TYPE	C/N	USAAF SERIAL	EX-COUNTRY 1	EX-COUNTRY 2	EX-COUNTRY 3	CIVILIAN RGD	MUSEUM
Harvard III	88-14748	42-44554	FA Portuguesa	Royal Navy	n/a	H13HP	Breckenridge Aviation Museum, Breckenridge, Texas, USA
AT-6D	88-14780	42-44586	FA Brasileira	USAF	n/a	N205SB	Museo Aerospacial, Campo dos Afonsos, Rio de Janeiro, Brazil
Harvard III	88-15041	BuNo51938	FA Portuguesa	Royal Navy	n/a	n/a	Fleet Air Arm Museum, RNAS Yeovil-ton, Somerset, UK
Harvard III	88-15698	41-34067	FA Portuguesa	SAAF	RAF	ZS-WLP	SAA Museum Society, Johannesburg, RSA
Harvard III	88-15774	41-34083	Belgian AF	RAF	SAAF	n/a	SAAF Museum, Swartkop AB, RSA
Harvard III	88-15872	41-34118	RNZAF	RAF	n/a	n/a	Pedestal display Ashburton, New Zealand
Harvard III	88-15950	42-84169	Belgian AF	RAF	SAAF	n/a	Musée Royal de L'Armée, Brussels, Belgium
T-6D	88-15997	42-84216	Republic of Korea AF	USAFM	USAF	n/a	US Air Force Museum, Wright Patterson AFB, Dayton, Ohio, USA
XAT-6E	88-16022	42-84241	Rebuild	USAF	n/a	NX74108	Western Museum of Flight, Hawthorne, California, USA
SNJ-5	88-16056	BuNo43884	Spanish AF	USN	USAF	N29937	Kentucky Aviation Museum, Louisville, Kentucky, USA
Harvard III	88-16144	42-84363	RNZAF	RAF	n/a	n/a	RNZAF Historic Flight, Woodhouse AB, New Zealand
Harvard III	88-16326	42-84545	RNZAF	RAF	n/a	n/a	RNZAF Museum Wigram, Christchurch, New Zealand
Harvard III	88-16328	42-84547	RNZAF	RAF	n/a	n/a	Taranaki Transport & Technology Museum, New Plymouth, New Zealand
Harvard III	88-16712	42-84931	FA Portuguesa	Royal Navy	n/a	n/a	Fleet Air Arm Historic Flight, RNAS Yeovilton, Somerset, UK
AT-6D	88-17025	42-85244	IDFAF	USAF	n/a	4X-ARC	IDAF Museum, Hatzerim AB, Israel
AT-6D	88-17478	42-85697	Spanish AF	USAF	n/a	N29947	Cavanaugh Flight Museum, Dallas-Addison, Texas, USA
SNJ-5C	88-17660	BuNo90662	Argentina Armada	USN	USAF	n/a	Museo de la Aviacion Naval Argentina, Espora NAS, Bahia Blanca, Argentina
AT-6D	88-18266	42-86485	FA Brasileira	USAF	n/a	n/a	Museo Aerospacial, Compo dos Afoncos, Rio de Janeiro, Brazil
SNJ-5	121-4183	BuNo90982	Ejercito de Aire	USN	USAF	n/a	Museo del Aire, Cuata Vientos AB, Spain
SNJ-5	121-4207	BuNo91074	Spanish AF	USN	USAF	N39313	Air Combat Museum, Springfield, Illinois, USA
AT-6D	121-4228	44-81564	FA Brasileira	USAF	n/a	PT-TRB	Museo Aerospacial, Campo dos Afonsos, Rio de Janeiro, Brazil
AT-6F	121-4251	44-81796	Royal Thai AF	USAF	n/a	n/a	Royal Thai Air Force Museum, Don Muang AB, Bangkok, Thailand
T-6G	168-160	49-3056	Spanish AF	USAF	n/a	n/a	Museo del aire, Cuatro Vientos AB, Spain
T-6G	168-295	49-3191	Austrian AF	USAF	n/a	n/a	Heeresgeschichtliches Museum, Vienna, Austria
T-6G	168-415	49-3311	Spanish AF	USAF	n/a	N3931Y	Weeks Air Museum, Tamiami, Florida
T-6G	168-463	49-3349	Spanish AF	USAF	n/a	N6G	Combat Air Museum, Topeka, Kansas, USA

TYPE	C/N	USAAF SERIAL	EX-COUNTRY 1	EX-COUNTRY 2	EX-COUNTRY 3	CIVILIAN RGD	MUSEUM
T-6G	168-482	49-3368	Spanish AF	USAF	n/a	n/a	USAF Museum, Wright Patterson, AFB, Ohio, USA
T-6G	168-503	50-1289	L'Armée de l'Air	USAF	n/a	n/a	Yugoslavian National Aviation Museum as TF 152
T-6G	168-548	49-3424	Royal Hellenic AF	USAF	n/a	n/a	Royal Hellenic AF Museum, Tatoil AB, Greece
T-6G	168-556	49-3432	L'Armée de l'Air	USAF	n/a	F-AZGS	Assoc. des Amateurs d'Aeronefs de Collection, Les Ailes de France, Luneville, France
T-6G	168-644	49-3500	Royal Hellenic AF	USAF	n/a	n/a	Royal Hellenic AF Museum, Tatoi AB, Greece
T-6G	182-38	51-14351	L'Armée de L'Air	USAF	n/a	n/a	Musée de L'Air et Espace, Paris, France
T-6G	182-209	51-14522	L'Armée de L'Air	USAF	n/a	n/a	Musée de L'Air et Espace, Le Bourget, Paris, France
T-6G	182-241	51-14554	Royal Thai AF	USAF	n/a	n/a	Royal Thai Air Force Museum, Don Muang AB, Bangkok, Thailand
T-6G	182-244	51-14557	Royal Thai AF	USAF	n/a	n/a	Royal Thai Air Force Museum, Don Muang AB, Bangkok, Thailand
T-6G	182-334	51-14647	Royal Thai AF	USAF	n/a	n/a	Royal Thai Air Force Museum, Don Muang AB, Bangkok, Thailand
T-6G	182-349	51-14662	Royal Thai AF	USAF	n/a	n/a	RTAF 'Tango One' display team
T-6G	182-353	51-14666	Royal Thai AF	USAF	n/a	n/a	Royal Thai Air Force Museum, Don Muang AB, Bangkok, Thailand
T-6G	182-481	51-14794	Biafra AF	L'Armée de l'Air	USAF	n/a	Museo do Air, Sintra AB, Portugal
T-6G	182-720	51-15033	L'Armée de L'Air	USAF	n/a	n/a	Israeli Air Force Museum, Hazerim AB, Israel (as '10')
T-6G	195-1	51-17354	ROK AF	USAF	n/a	n/a	Korean War Museum, Seoul, South Korea
T-6J	CCF4-465	52-8544	Luftwaffe	USAF	n/a	D-FABU	Kyfwaffeb Nyseymn Yeterseb AB, Germany
T-6J	CCF4-486	52-8565	FA Portuguesa	Luftwaffe	USAF	n/a	Museo do Ar, Sintra AB, Portugal
T-6J	CCF4-491	52-8570	Luftwaffe	USAF	n/a	n/a	Norwegian AF Museum, Gardermoen, AB, Norway
T-6J	CCF4-499	52-8578	Luftwaffe	USAF	n/a	D-FABE	Fliegendes Museum Augsburg, Augsburg, Germany
T-6J	CCF4-517	52-8596	FA Portuguesa	Luftwaffe	USAF	n/a	Museo do Ar, Sintra AB, Portugal
AT-6D	88-		FA Brasileira	USAF	n/a	n/a	Museo Aerospacial, Compo dos Afoncos AB, Rio de Janeiro, Brazil
AT-6D	88-		FA Brasileira	USAF	n/a	n/a	Museo de Armas e Velculos Motor-izados Antigos, Bebeduoro, Brazil
AT-6F	119-		FA Brasileira	USAF	n/a	n/a	Museo Aeronáutico da Fundascau, Sao Paulo, Brazil
AT-6D	119-		FA Brasileira	USAF	n/a	n/a	Museo Aerospacial, Compo dos Afoncos AB, Rid de Janeiro, Brazil
AT-6D	119-		FA Brasileira	USAF	n/a	n/a	Museo de Armas e Velculos Motor-izados Antigos, Bebeduoro, Brazil
AT-6G			FA Chile	USAF	n/a	n/a	Gate Guard Los Condores AB, Chile

TYPE	C/N	USAAF SERIAL	EX-COUNTRY 1	EX-COUNTRY 2	EX-COUNTRY 3	CIVILIAN RGD	MUSEUM
AT-6G			FA Chile	USAF	n/a	n/a	Museo Aeronáutico, Los Cerilos AB, Chile
AT-6D			FA Chile	USAF	n/a	n/a	Museo Aeronáutico, Los Cerilos AB, Chile
AT-6			FA Colombiana	USAF	n/a	n/a	Gate Guard Madrid-Barroblanca AB, Colombia
AT-6			FA Colombiana	USAF	n/a	n/a	Museo Aeronautico, El Dorado, Bogota, Chile
AT-6			FA Colombiana	USAF	n/a	n/a	Gate Guard Luis F Pinto AB, Colombia
AT-6			FA Colombiana	USAF	n/a	n/a	Gate Guard Cali AB, Colombia
AT-6A			FA Ecuatoriana	USAF	n/a	n/a	Museo Aereo de FA Eduatoriana, Quito AB, Ecuador
AT-6			FA Ecuatoriana	USAF	n/a	n/a	Museo Aero de FAE, Quito, Chile
AT-6			FA Ecuatoriana	USAF	n/a	n/a	Museo Aero de FAE, Quito, Chile
Harvard IIB			Indonesian AF	Dutch AF	RAF	n/a	Armed Forces Museum, Djakarta, Indonesia
Harvard IIB			Indonesian AF	Dutch AF	RAF	n/a	Padang City Museum, Padang, Indonesia
Harvard IIB			Indonesian AF	Dutch AF	RAF	n/a	Indonesian AF Museum, Adisutjipto AB, Indonesia
Harvard IIB			Indonesian AF	Dutch AF	RAF	n/a	Indonesian Air Force Academy, Yogyakarta, Indonesia
Harvard IIB			Indonesian AF	Dutch AF	RAF	n/a	Indonesian Air Force Academy, Yogyakarta, Indonesia
Harvard IIB			Indonesian AF	Dutch AF	RAF	n/a	Indonesian Air Force Academy, Adisutjipto AB, Indonesia
AT-6D			IDFAF	USAF	n/a	n/a	Israeli Air Force Museum, Hazerim AB, Israel
AT-6D			IDFAF	USAF	n/a	n/a	Israeli Air Force Museum, Hazerim AB, Israel
AT-6D			IDFAF	USAF	n/a	n/a	Israeli Air Force Museum, Hazerim AB, Israel
AT-6D			IDFAF	USAF	n/a	n/a	Israeli Air Force Museum, Hazerim AB, Israel
AT-6D			IDFAF	USAF	n/a	n/a	Israeli Air Force Museum, Hazerim AB, Israel
AT-6D			IDFAF	USAF	n/a	n/a	Israeli Air Force Museum, Hazerim AB, Israel
AT-6D			IDFAF	USAF	n/a	n/a	Israeli Air Force Museum, Hazerim AB, Israel
AT-6D			IDFAF	USAF	n/a	n/a	Israeli Air Force Museum, Hazerim AB, Israel
T-6			Italian AF	USAF	n/a	n/a	Scuola Specialisti, Capua, Italy
T-6H			Italian AF	USAF	n/a	n/a	Gate Guard Viterbo AB, Italy
Harvard 4			Italian AF	n/a	n/a	n/a	Museo Dell'Aria, Castello di San Pelagio, Italy
T-6G			Italian AF	n/a	n/a	n/a	Museo Storica Dell Aeronautica Vigna de Valle AB, Rome
T-6G			Italian AF	n/a	n/a	n/a	Museo Nazionale Della Scienza e Della Technica, Milan, Italy

TYPE	C/N	USAAF SERIAL	EX-COUNTRY 1	EX-COUNTRY 2	EX-COUNTRY 3	CIVILIAN RGD	MUSEUM
T-6H			Italian AF	n/a	n/a	n/a	Assoc pour la Sauvegarde des Avions Anciens, Orion, France
T-6H			Italian AF	n/a	n/a	n/a	Museo Della Guerra, Italy
T-6G	182-		JMSDF	n/a	n/a	n/a	Tokorozawa Aviation Museum, Kokukoen Park, Tokyo, Japan
T-6G	182-		JMSDF	n/a	n/a	n/a	Display Gifu AB, Aichi, Japan
T-6G	182-		JMSDF	n/a	n/a	n/a	Kumagaya Air Force Technical School Collection, Kumagaya, Japan
T-6			Royal Air Maroc	Aéronavale	USN	n/a	Royal Air Maroc Engineering School, Casablanca-Anfa, Morocco
T-6			Royal Air Maroc	Aéronavale	USN	n/a	Royal Air Maroc Engineering School, Casablanca-Anifa, Morocco
T-6G			Pakistani AF	USAF	n/a	n/a	Pakistan Air Force Museum, Pershawa AB, Pakistan
AT-6G			Philippine AF	USAF	n/a	n/a	Philippine Af Museum, Villamor AB, Manila, Philippines
Harvard IIB			FA Portuguesa	SAAF	RAF	n/a	Museo do Ar, Sintra AB, Portugal
Harvard IIB			FA Portuguesa	SAAF	RAF	n/a	Museo do Ar, Alverca AB, Portugal
Harvard IIB			FA Portuguesa	SAAF	RAF	n/a	Museo do Ar, Sintra AB, Portugal
T-6J			FA Portuguesa	USAF	RAF	n/a	Museo do Ar, Alverca AB, Portugal
T-6G/J			FA Portuguesa	USAF	RAF	n/a	Museo do Ar, Montijo AB, Portugal
T-6G/J			FA Portuguesa	USAF	RAF	n/a	Museo do Ar, Montijo AB, Portugal
T-6G			Spanish AF	USAF	n/a	n/a	Museo del Aire, Cuatro Vientos AB, Spain
T-6G			Spanish AF	USAF	n/a	n/a	Patrimoine Aeronautique Nationale, Luxembourg-Findel, Luxembourg
T6-G			Spanish AF	USAF	n/a	n/a	Patrimoine Aeronautique Nationale, Luxembourg-Findel, Luxembourg
AT-6D			Spanish AF	USAF	n/a	n/a	Museo de Aire, Cuatro Vientos AB, Spain
T-6			Swiss AF	USAF	n/a	n/a	Swiss AF Museum, Dubendoft AB, Switzerland
T-6			Swiss AF	USAF	n/a	n/a	Swiss AF Museum, Dubendoft AB, Switzerland
AT-6D			Syrian AF	RAF	n/a	n/a	Syrian War Museum, Damascus
T-6G			Turkish AF	RAF	n/a	n/a	Tirk Hava Muzesi, Istanbul-Ataturk AB, Turkey
T-6			FA Venezolana	USAF	n/a	n/a	Maracay, Venezolana
T-6			FA Venezolana	USAF	n/a	n/a	Sucre AB, Venezuela

Notes

INTRODUCTION

1 This unforgettable rasping sound, so emotive of 'The Six' was brought about by her direct-drive propeller with high tip speeds.
2 *See* Don Monson, *Autobiography of a Tailhooker* (Palm Desert, Cal.,1995).
3 *See* John Hamlin, *The Harvard File* (Air Britain, Tonbridge, 1988).
4 David C. Fletcher & Doug MacPhail, *Harvard!; The North American Trainers in Canada* (San Josef, B.C., 1990).
5 *See* N. M. Parnell & C.A. Lynch, *Australian Air Force since 1911* (Sydney, NSW).

CHAPTER ONE

1 *See North American Aviation Inc. A Brief History of Operations Immediately Prior to and During World War II* (Southern California Aviation Foundation History).
2 *See* Joe Vella, 'The Genesis of the Wirraway', *Aviation Heritage*, Vol. 23, No. 1.
3 *See* Dan Hagerdorn, *North American NA-16/AT-6/SNJ, Warbird Tech Vol. II* (North Branch, 1997).
4 *Ibid.*
5 *See* Peter C. Smith, *Straight Down! The Story of the A-36 Dive-Bomber* (Manchester, 2000).
6 *See* Peter C. Smith, *Junkers Ju.87 Stuka* (Ramsbury, 1998).
7 *See* Peter C. Smith, *Aichi D3A1/2 Val* (Ramsbury, 1999).
8 *See* Colonel John A. DeVries, USAF, 'North American AT-6/SNJ Texan', *The Historical Aircraft Album, Volume XVI* (Temple City, California, 1980).
9 *See USAAC Engineering Section, Memorandum, Performance Test of North American Aviation Basic Training Airplane NA-16, Identity No X-2080*, Report, No. 4110, dated 27 May 1935.
10 Dan Hagerdorn suggests another reason for the NA-16s victory, that it 'was due more to the political clout of General Motors (NAAs corporate parent) than the qualities of the aircraft'. Hagerdorn, *North American NA-16/AT-6/SNJ, Warbird Tech Vol. II.*
11 Under Contract AE-43.
12 *See* Table NAA Charge Number List.
13 *See North American Aviation Inc. A Brief History of Operations Immediately Prior to and During World War II.*
14 *Ibid.*
15 *Ibid.*
16 David C. Fletcher and Doug MacPhail, *Harvard!*
17 *See* Smith, *Straight Down! The Story of the A-36 Dive-Bomber.*

CHAPTER TWO

1 The known BC-1-I conversions were 37-416, 37-432, 37-433, 37-437, 37-438, 37-444, 37-446, 37-447, 37-449, 37-637, 37-638, 37-639, 37-640, 37-642, 37-650, 37-657, 37-666, 38-366, 38-374, 38-381, 38-382, 38-387, 38-389, 38-390, 38-400, 38-403, 38-424, 38-440, 38-441 and 38-445.
2 *North American Aviation Inc. A Brief History of Operations Immediately Prior to and During World War II* (Southern California Aviation Foundation History).
3 However, Dan Hagerdorn contends that the K10W1 bore, 'little more than a passing resemblance to the NA-16' and that three view drawings of the Oak vary 'considerably' from the hitherto published ones and likewise the instrument panel bore 'little resemblance to any NAA panel I have found'.
4 *North American Aviation, Inc.*, op. cit.
5 *North American Aviation, Inc.*, op. cit.
6 *North American Aviation, Inc.*, op. cit.
7 *North American Aviation, Inc.*, op. cit.
8 *See* Dan Hagerdorn, *Alae Supra Canalem (Wings Over the Canal): The Sixth Air Force and Antilles Air Command* (Paducah, 1995).
9 For full details of the torturous negotiations by Monnet *see*: John McVickar Haight, Jr, *American Aid to France, 1938–1940* (Athenaeum, New York, 1970).
10 *See* Final Report, Hoppenot Mission to America, La Chambre Papers, Hoppenot Mission File. The French Air Ministry officially referred to the mission sent to the United States in December as the 'Hoppenot Mission', but Hoppenot himself preferred the title the 'Monnet Mission'.
11 *North American Aviation, Inc.*, op. cit.
12 *North American Aviation, Inc.*, op. cit.
13 *North American Aviation, Inc.*, op. cit.

CHAPTER THREE

1 *North American Aviation Inc. A Brief History of Operations Immediately Prior to and During World War II* (Southern California Aviation Foundation History).
2 Other sources state they had reached Hawaii, *see* David Mondey, *American Aircraft of World War II* (New York, 1982).
3 Accident losses were: 41-18890 collided with 41-18893 on 21 April, both lost; 41-18892 damaged in ground loop 10 September, not repaired; 41-18896 crashed on take-off, also on 10 September and written off; 41-18891 crashed and destroyed, 17 September.
4 *See* Walter D. Edmonds, *They Fought With What They Had* (Washington DC, 1996).
5 *North American Aviation, Inc.*, op. cit.
6 *North American Aviation, Inc.*, op. cit.

CHAPTER FOUR

1 *North American Aviation Inc. A Brief History of Operations Immediately Prior to and During World War II* (Southern California Aviation Foundation History) op. cit.
2 *See* Dan Hagerdorn, 'Lend-Lease to Latin America, Part I–Army Aircraft', *Journal American Aviation Historical Society*, Summer 1989.
3 *See North American Aviation, Inc., op. cit*
4 *See* Mark D. Clark, Editorial 'Warbirds History–North American T-6/SNJ Series', *Warbirds of America News*, Sport Aviation (Rockford, Illinois), p.17; and repeated by Ohlrich and Ethell; Larry Davis; Peter M. Bowers and others.
5 *See North American Aviation, Inc.* Other sources state only 61 were so sent.
6 *See* Kent A. Mitchell, 'Ranger-Powered XAT-6E', *American Aviation Historical Society Journal*, Vol 34, Number 2, Summer 1989.
7 *See* 'Progress in Power', *Ranger Aircraft Engines Division, Fairchild Engine and Airplane Construction Sales Brochure* (undated), p.9.
8 *See Fairchild Aviation News, Aviation Show Issue* (Fairchild Aviation, Incorporated, Woodside NY, December 1936 to January 1937), p.4.

CHAPTER FIVE

1 None of the so-called Harvard IVs, Canadian post-war conversions as the T-6G, and to be described later, served with the RAF.
2 By far the most comprehensive source of RAF Harvard deployment is John Hamlin's study for Air-Britain, *The Harvard File* (Tonbridge, 1988), which is highly recommended.
3 *See* Peter C. Smith, *Task Force 57* (Manchester, 2001) and *Curtiss SB2C Helldiver* (Ramsbury, 1998) for the full story of the British Pacific Fleet and problems with its American supplied aircraft.
4 These conversion factories were Martin Hearn, Hooton Park, Yorkshire and Rootes Securities at Blythe Bridge, Stoke-on-Trent, Staffs.
5 One aircraft (KF 2236) from this batch was selected at random from the production line, crashed while under test in the USA and was written off.

CHAPTER SIX

1 These details are taken from Air Ministry *Pilot's Notes for Harvard IIB*, prepared by Direction of Minister of Supply, promulgated by Order of the Air Council, 2nd Edition, London March, 1949. These notes were complementary to A.P. 2095 Pilot's Notes General.
2 Best sources for definitive notes on this are T. E. Doll, B. R. Jackson, and W. A. Riley, *Navy Air Colours Vols 1 and 2* (California, 1983).
3 *North American Aviation Inc. A Brief History of Operations Immediately Prior to and During World War II* (Southern California Aviation Foundation History).

CHAPTER SEVEN

1 One of the best descriptions was given by Colonel John A. DeVries, USAF, in his article 'North American AT-6/SNJ Texan', *The Historical Aviation Album, Volume XVI* (Temple City, 1980) (acknowledged here as DeVries). Another poignant account of learning to fly the T-6 was written by the late Jeff Ethell in his article 'T-6 Tyro', in *FlyPast* magazine (Stamford, July 1982) (acknowledged here as Ethell). There are many other such accounts I have drawn upon, including interviews and correspondence with former T-6 men.
2 Ethell, op. cit.
3 DeVries, op. cit.
4 Ethell, op. cit.
5 DeVries, op. cit.
6 DeVries, op. cit.
7 Arthur Murland Gill, personal communication, 26 February 2000. It all proved worthwhile for, in 1948, Arthur married Doris after her family had returned to England. The author and his wife are now proud to call them our friends.
8 Squadron Leader Norman E. Rose, op. cit.
9 Squadron Leader Norman E. Rose, op. cit.
10 Squadron Leader Norman E. Rose, personal communication, 30 January 2000.
11 DeVries, op. cit.
12 Squadron Leader Norman E. Rose, personal communication, op. cit.
13 DeVries, op. cit.
14 Squadron Leader Norman E. Rose to the author, op. cit.
15 Robert S. Mullaney, personal communication, 10 December 1999.
16 Norman E. Rose to the author, op. cit.
17 Arthur Murland Gill, personal communication, op. cit.

CHAPTER EIGHT

1 Named after Major-General Henry H. 'Hap' Arnold, Acting Deputy Chief of Staff for Aviation, USAAC, from October 1940. *See* Russell W. Ramsey, 'The Arnold Scheme: How the USAF (*sic*) Trained RAF Pilots 1941–1943', *Army Quarterly and Defence Journal*, Vol. 122, No. 1, (Tavistock, January 1992).
2 *See* William Wolf, DDS, 'USAAF Pilot Training in World War II', *The Historical Aviation Album* (Temple City, 1980).
3 *See* Masatake Okumiya and Jiro Horikoshi, *Zero! The Story of the Japanese Navy Air Force 1937–1945* (London, 1958); also W. D. Dickson, *The Battle of the Philippine Sea* (London and Annapolis, 1975), for further aspects of problems with training Navy pilots.
4 *See* Dr. Alfred Price, *The Luftwaffe Data Book* (London, 1997).
5 DeVries, op. cit.
6 Donald W. Monson, personal communication, 6 December 1999.
7 *See* Don Monson, *Autobiography of a Tailhooker, Part 1* (privately published, 1995); extracts reproduced here by courtesy of the author.
8 Arthur Gill, personal communication, 19 January 2000.
9 Squadron Leader Norman E. Rose, personal communication, 3 March 2000.
10 Flight Lieutenant Harry Knight, RAF, Rtd, personal communication, 13 April, 2000.
11 Figures from Richard C. Lukas, *Eagles East: The Army Air Force and the Soviet Union 1941–1945* (Tallahassee, 1970); also Department of State, Office of Foreign Liquidation, *Report on War Aid Furnished by the United States to the USSR* (Washington DC, 1945). Colonel DeVries' claims of 'several hundred' are unfounded. The route was Dallas–Great Falls–Calgary, Edmonton, Grande Prairie, Fort St John, Fort Nelson, Watson Lake, Whitehorse, Nortway, Tanacross, Big Delta-Fairbanks (Ladd).
12 *See* V. E. Farry, 'Texan Warriors–T-6 Aircraft in French Service', *Journal American Aviation Historical Society* (Winter, 1979).

CHAPTER NINE

1 The ultimate fate of these two aircraft is not clear. In June 1940, both were transferred to the Engineering School and A20-1 was employed during the war as an instructional airframe at the Melbourne Showgrounds; A20-2 may have been similarly employed.
2 All the information in this section is from Commonwealth Aircraft Corporation Pty. Ltd, Information Sheet 2.1, *Wirraway G.P./Trainer–General Structural and Technical information* (Port Melbourne, Australia, 1979).
3 According to data in *Wirraway Pilots Notes*, RAAF Publication No. 109, July 1945.
4 *See Letters from Flying Officer H. L. Colebrook, RAAF, RAAS Pacific, to The Secretary, Air Board, Air Force Headquarters, Melbourne, CI*, dated 4 August 1944 and 17 September 1944. These letters were kindly made available to the author by the RAAF Historical Section, Department of Defence, Canberra, and as far as the author is aware, are reproduced here for the first time in print.
5 This was the Australian version of the German 'Trombones of Jericho' wind-driven sirens which had been fitted to the Junkers Ju 87 *Stuka* dive bombers, with enormous effect on the morale of French, Dutch, Belgian and British troops in the spring of 1940. No doubt the Australians, in lieu of much else to frighten the Japanese infantrymen with, hoped their version might have the same impact on the Japanese! *See* Peter C. Smith, *Junkers Ju87 Stuka* (Ramsbury, 1998).
6 The top brass back in Melbourne, far from these terrible events, seemed incredulous at this account, and very sniffy about it, but Colebrook stuck to his guns. 'I can well understand that my account of the unit's activities and designation sound unorthodox. However, they are *fact*, and if necessary can be proven by many, including one decorated RAAF officer. The chaos in Malaya in the final stages caused many more amazing occurrences than this, many of which will never be known.'
7 Report, *Attempted Interception of Enemy T-97 Flying Boats at Vunakanua, 6-1-42, by Wirraway A20-437, F/Lt B.H. Anderson and P/O Butterworth;* Annex B. Air Historical Branch, Department of Defence, Air Force Office, A-LG-10, Russell Offices, Canberra, ACT, copy in author's collection.
8 The Kawanishi H6K5 Navy Type 97 had a defensive armament of one flexible 7.7mm Type 92 machine gun in an forward turret, and one 7.7mm Type 92 machine gun in an open dorsal position, plus two 7.7mm Type 92 machine guns, one in each blister on either beam, and one flexible 20mm Type 99 model cannon in a tail turret.
9 *See* Flight Lieutenant Tyrell, RAAF, account in *New Guinea Brief – Additional*, Annex C, pages 13-15. Made available to the author by the RAAF Historical Section, Department of Defence, Air Force Office, Canberra, ACT, dated 22 September 1989.
10 For the full story of the Vultee Vengeance in RAAF service *see* Peter C. Smith, *Vengeance! The Vultee Vengeance dive bomber* (Shrewsbury, 1986); and Peter C. Smith, *Jungle Dive bombers at War* (London, 1987).
11 *See* I. Laming, 'What Were They Like', *Aviation Heritage Magazine*, Vol 23, No. 2 (AOPA, April 1981).
12 For the most excellent and accurate background of the Imperial promises and political machinations, *see* Russell Grenfell, *Main Fleet to Singapore*, (London 1954); The 'main' fleet had turned out to be one brand-new battleship *Prince of Wales* and one ancient and unmodernized battle-cruiser, *Repulse*, and these were both sunk by Imperial Japanese Navy torpedo bombers on 10 December 1941. What remained of the allied navies were wiped out in the surface battles like the Battle of the Java Sea in February. As for air power, the British GOC I in Malaya, Lieutenant-General A. E. Percival, wrote that, 'There were in Malaya no transport aircraft, no long-range bombers, no dive bombers, no army co-operation aircraft and no special photographic reconnaissance aircraft. To sum up, there was in fact no really effective air striking force in Malaya, there were none of the aircraft which an army specially requires for close support.' He was also to write, 'Every day I ask London for two things, tanks and dive bombers!' He was to receive neither! *See* Lt General A. E. Percival, *The War in Malaya* (London, 1949). Thus Churchill's 'impregnable' fortress of Singapore had surrendered to a numerically smaller Japanese army within days and the Dutch East Indies, the Philippines, Hong Kong and Borneo had all been captured, leaving nothing at all between Australia and the enemy.
13 All the information in this section is from Commonwealth Aircraft Corporation Pty. Ltd, Information Sheet 5.1, *CAC Boomerang*, Port Melbourne, Australia, 1979.
14 The name was from the deadly Aboriginal hunting weapon which was lethal in skilled hands, and *not* the returnable practice- and toy- type with which the name has since become synonymous in Europe and the United States.
15 *See Australia in the War of 1939–1945, The Role of Science and Industry*, (Australian War Memorial, Canberra ACT).
16 Despite continued speculation by some American historians in popular aviation magazines of late, North American themselves quite categorically denied playing *any* part whatsoever in the design of the Boomerang.
17 All the information in this section is from Commonwealth Aircraft Corporation Pty. Ltd, Information Sheet 11.1, *The CA-28 Ceres Agricultural Aircraft* (Port Melbourne, Australia, 1979).
18 The Ceres was named after the Roman goddess of Agriculture. Ceres was the Roman name for Mother Earth, the protectress of agriculture and of all the fruits of the earth. She was the Corn Goddess and she had a daughter by Jupiter caller Proserpine. The Greeks called her Demeter.(*See Brewer's Dictionary of Phrase and Fable*, 14th Edition, Ivor H. Evans, London 1990)
19 Personal communication from Mr Neville, 23 November 1989.

CHAPTER TEN

1 According to *Sky Aviation* magazine.

2 *See* Paul A. Jackson, *Dutch Military Aviation 1945–1978* (Loughborough).

CHAPTER ELEVEN

1 Many sources give this designation, among them: James Fahey *USAF Aircraft 1947–1956* (Falls Church, Virginia, 1956); John F. Hamlin, *The Harvard File* (Tonbridge, 1988) and Peter M. Bowers, 'The Thundering Texan', *Wings Magazine*, Vol. 16, No. 6 (December, 1986). However, this is disputed by Dan Hagerdorn in 'North American NA-16/AT-6/SNJ', *Warbirdtech*, Vol. II (North Branch, Minnesota, 1997). He checked *every* Aircraft History Card for those MDAP Harvards assigned US serials and not one carried any reference to the T-6J. In 1953 the RCAF returned six of the 100 T-6Ds they borrowed between 1951 and 1954. They went back to the USAF after loan, and these *may* have received a T-6J listing at that time, but there is no confirmation of this. Some CCF Harvards also received the designation T-6H which further muddied the water.

2 While awaiting the building of the CCF4s, the RCAF took loan of 100 USAF T-6Ds for the period May 1951 to February 1954, and used them with their original US serial numbers. They were duly handed back and the six aircraft that had been written off during this period were replaced by CCF4s in 1952. *See* Appendix 5. For full details of RCAF aircraft Doug McPhail's excellent book, *Harvard! The North American Trainers in Canada, 1990,* is recommended.

3 *See* 'Il Texan in Italia', *Aerei* Vol VIII, (March 1980); also 'Il Velivolo da Addestramento', *ALI nuove*, No 3, 1968.

4 The author is indebted to the article by V. E. Ferry, 'Texan Warriors – T-6 Aircraft in French Service', Journal of the American Aviation Historical Society (Winter, 1979), for much of this information.

CHAPTER TWELVE

1 For this chapter the author wishes to acknowledge the unstinting help of The Mosquito Historical Foundation Association. Especially Sidney F. Johnston, President, and Jerry Allen, Historian. They have both supplied an enormous amount of eyewitness material and photographs, which have proved invaluable, and have also permitted me to quote from articles by Wayne S. Cole, B.G. Turner and also from letters from Lieutenant Colonel Randy Presley and John Payer, Lieutenant Colonel John E. Persons, Major Peter R. Tolputt and others. Also totally essential has been the *History of the 6147th Tactical Control Squadron* (Airborne) (Declassified AFSHRC, AF/IGSPB –R, Box No 398, Washington DC). For a full account *see* Cleveland, W.M., *Mosquitoes in Korea* (Peter Randall, Portsmouth, New Hampshire, 1991).

2 Edward R. Murrow, broadcast of Tuesday, 6 February, 1951, 7.45–8.00 EST, via the Columbia Broadcasting System, 'With the News'.

3 Lieutenant Colonel John E. Persons, USAF (Rtd), *A Mosquito Pilot: Korea, 6147 TAC, CON, GP, Some Recollections of Flying Combat May–August 1951 as a Mosquito*, letter to Sidney F. Johnston, 27 August 1983.

4 But *not*, as Larry Davis would have it, for the rest of the war, *see*: *T-6 Texan in Action* (Carrollton, Texas, 1989).

5 Lieutenant Colonel Randy Presley, USAF (Rtd) to Sidney F. Johnston Jr, 23 March 1984.

6 My thanks for this is due entirely to Jerry Allen, the Mosquitoes historian, who has patiently assembled many strands of the story and who generously allowed me to weave them all together here.

7 Intelligence Office, 6147th Tactical Control Group, APO 970; *Evasion and Escape Report, Interrogation of T-6, Mosquito, Observer.* Interrogated 28 May 1952. Interrogated by First Lieutenant William D. Harper, USAF, Assistant Intelligence Officer.

8 Peter Tolputt to his parents, dated 28 May 1952.

9 Captain John W. Payer, DFC, to Tom Crawford, 7 December 1992.

10 Tolputt to parents, op. cit.

11 *See* 'Easy Company Rescues Downed Observer', *Galahad Newsletter*, 224th Infantry Regiment, Vol. 3, Number 2, dated 27 May 1996.

12 Peter Tolputt to the author, 28 March 2000.

13 Peter Tolputt to the author, op. cit.

14 John Payer telephoned Peter in 1991; Al Gale visited Peter in England in 1993 and, 'finally shook the hand of the luckiest man I ever saw'. Peter visited Washington DC in May 1994 and on 27 May (42 years to the day) he met General Edward C. Meyer, whom as Second Lieutenant Meyer had helped in his rescue and who, between 1979 and 1983, had been Army Chief of Staff. General Meyer hosted a dinner at the Army-Navy Club for Peter, John Payer, Roger Lemire, and former Mosquito friends, Jack Appleby, and Curly Satterlee. Peter was the first to recognize his good fortune, as he told his parents the next day, 'Without doubt I'm the luckiest man in the Mosquitoes. Now its all over, and I can think back – it was a wonderful experience to have, but I'd rather not have it again!'.

CHAPTER THIRTEEN

1 Dr Gerald A. Swayze, personal communication, 6 December 1989.

2 Andrew Edie, personal communication, 8 April 2000.

3 Andrew Edie, personal communication, op. cit.

4 *See* '150 Free-Noise chicks', *Argus* (3 April, 1998).

5 Michael John Chapman, personal communication, 8 April 2000.

6 Andrew and Karen Edie, personal communication, op. cit.

7 Steven D. Eisner, personal communication, 4 September 1989.

8 Regrettably Gary has now sold his famous all-white 'Zero' Harvard, which has since been repainted black but which still flies.

9 The original team, and their aircraft, were: Anthony Hutton (G-BIWX a Noorduyn built Mark IVM ex Italian Air Force, carried RAF FT 239); Euan English, Tony Banfield (C-TEAC a Mark IIA built in Dallas in 1943, ex SAAF and Portuguese Air Force); Norman Lees (G-BDAM, a Mark IIB built by Noorduyn in 1943, ex RCAF and Swedish Air Force); Gary Numan (G-AZSC, a Mark IB built by Noorduyn in November, 1943, ex Dutch Air Force); Mike Brooke, Charles Everett, Pete John (N13631, Mark IV a CCF built in 1952 ex-Reno racer) and Pete Treadaway.

10 QFIs are Charlie Brown, Mike Chapman, David Cooke, Rod Dean, Mathew Hill, Patrick Jarvis, Anthony Jenner, Mark Johns, Stuart McKinnon, Bill Perrins, Victor Pierce, Ian Ramsay, Adrian Read, Jeff Rooney, Brian Salter, Andy Shuttleworth, Ken Snell, John Thurlow and Mark Waldren.

11 The outstanding gold paint scheme, with a red flash edged in white down the both sides of the fuselage, terminating in a white eagle head, of the original Golden Hawks was perpetuated by an SNJ flown by Bud Granley.

APPENDIX III

1 These valuable listings (ADM-98, 5 April 1950), were made available to the author by Dan Hagerdorn so that they could be placed on public record and not lost.

AUTHOR'S NOTE

Due to space and cost constraints, much material made available to the author, including all the colour photographs, black-and-white diagrams, and many tables, has not found a place in this book.

Index